ISLAMIC PEOPLES OF THE SOVIET UNION

ISLAMIC PEOPLES OF THE SOVIET UNION

(with an Appendix on the non-Muslim Turkic peoples of the Soviet Union)

Shirin Akiner

Kegan Paul International

London, Boston, Melbourne and Henley

First published in 1983
by Kegan Paul International Ltd
39 Store Street, London WC1E 7DD,
9 Park Street, Boston, Mass. 02108, USA,
296 Beaconsfield Parade, Middle Park,
Melbourne, 3206, Australia and
Broadway House, Newtown Road,
Henley-on-Thames, Oxon RG9 1EN

Set in Times by
Input Typesetting Ltd, London
and printed in Great Britain by
Hartnoll Print
Bodmin, Cornwall
© Shirin Akiner 1983

Library of Congress Cataloguing in Publication Data

Akiner, Shirin
Islamic peoples of the Soviet Union.
Bibliography: p.
Includes index.
1. Muslims—Soviet Union.   I. Title.
DK34.M8A35   947'.00882971   82–140
ISBN 0-7103-0025-5   AACR2

To my father
Abul Faiz Ziauddin Ahmad

Contents

4 Transcaucasia and Northern Caucasus 105

Preface

The aim of this book is to answer three basic questions about the Islamic peoples of the USSR: who they are, where they are and how many of them there are. It is convenient to speak of them as 'Soviet Muslims', grouping them all together under a single, collective heading, but they are in fact quite disparate. For this reason it was decided to treat each ethnic group individually here. This has the advantage of demonstrating the great diversity of these peoples, but it also entails a certain amount of unavoidable repetition. Cross-references indicate the main points of contact between the various groups, but since each section is intended to be complete in itself, this has been kept to a minimum. The historical introductions try to show how each ethnic group was formed, when it settled in its present location and how it came to be part of the Soviet Union. Apart from this, politics have been avoided, since the subject is far too complex to summarize without distortion and deserves a separate study of its own. For the same reason, projections for the future have not been included. The sections on language give a very brief summary of the extraordinarily rich linguistic heritage of these peoples. In order to show the effects of living in a multilingual society, material has been included on such questions as the maintenance of the mother tongue and the development of bilingualism; also, on the availability of educational facilities and printed matter in the national languages. There are some topics, such as economic status and religion, on which very little information exists, but it was felt better to give what is available, even if it is very general, rather than to avoid such subjects completely. For those who are familiar with Soviet studies, some of this will be self-evident, but for others it may be useful to have it actually stated.

Acknowledgments

I should like to take this opportunity to thank all the friends and colleagues who generously gave me their advice and, in particular, Dr M. Bainbridge, Lecturer in Turkish at the School of Oriental and African Studies, University of London, who suggested the format of the book. I am deeply grateful to my husband and son for patiently enduring the false optimism of my often repeated claim that I would 'be finished by next week'. Finally, I thank my publishers for their courtesy and help.

1

Introduction

Before speaking of the Muslim or Islamic peoples of the Soviet Union it is important to define the sense in which these terms are used. Any commentary on Islam will explain that being a Muslim means submission to the will of God; further, that there are certain articles of faith, the 'roots' of religion, which must be accepted, and certain actions, the 'branches' of religion, which must be performed. The former include belief in God, His Scriptures and His Apostles. The latter are: bearing witness to the oneness of God and the prophethood of Muhammed; performing the daily prayers; giving alms; keeping the fast of Ramadan; making the pilgrimage to Mecca. What such an explanation omits is the essential reasonableness of Islam. It is not, as the above might suggest, a straitjacket of rules, but rather a religion of the possible. It presents an ideal (*'azimah*), but accepts that it may not always be feasible to realize this; it recognizes, therefore, a doctrine of the 'permissible' (*rukhsah*), which in effect means that people should do the best they can under the prevailing circumstances. It is acknowledged that the reasons for not performing any or all of the prescribed duties may be inner weakness just as much as external pressures, but this is purely a matter for the individual's conscience.

The question of whether or not a person is a Muslim does not depend, ultimately, on the way he lives, but on the way he perceives himself in relation to the world. Consequently, a wide range of commitment is accommodated within Islam and this tolerance is one of the religion's great strengths, taking account as it does of the natural ebb and flow of piety in the lives of individuals and of societies. Non-Muslims frequently overlook this factor and, basing themselves on a single, strict interpretation of the term 'Muslim', find it incomprehensible that so many people who do not observe

1

the 'rules' should nevertheless vehemently refute the charge that they are not Muslims.

In fact, the only way in which a Muslim can sever himself from his community is by a conscious and voluntary rejection of Islam. Even then, the decision is not irreversible. Shi'i Muslims actually have a doctrine (*taqiyah* 'guarding oneself'), for which they claim the authority of the *shari'at*, which permits them to deny their faith in order to escape persecution. It may be true that 'generalizations are plateaux for tired minds', but if any useful general comparison could be made between Christianity and Islam, it would be that a definite decision is required to become a Christian, while a definite decision is required to cease being a Muslim. It is for this reason that in the Soviet Union today only those who are firmly committed to a Christian way of life will identify themselves as Christians, whereas virtually every member of a traditionally Muslim society will still claim to be a Muslim, no matter how loosely he adheres to Islamic precepts. Nationalism certainly plays a part in this, but it would be wrong to exaggerate its influence, for precisely the same phenomenon can be observed in parts of the world where nationalism is not an issue in the way that it is in the Soviet Union. In an effort to gauge the vitality of Islam, Soviet commentators sometimes resort to quantifying the numbers of 'firm believers', 'believers by tradition', 'hesitant believers' and so on. Such information is valuable, because it gives a profile of the situation at a particular moment, but its importance must not be overestimated: no religion, and least of all Islam, is an army whose strength can be judged by the number of men on active service. The present work eschews vain attempts to limit the definition of the term 'Muslim' to a specific formula and instead uses it in its widest sense to indicate a community's traditional perception of itself.

There are some forty-five and a half million Muslims in the USSR, one of the largest Muslim populations in the world, in size second only to those of such countries as Bangladesh, China, India, Indonesia and Pakistan. It is a population of quite exceptional ethnic, cultural and regional diversity. Soviet Muslims are found as far west as the borders of Poland, as far east as the borders of China; they are found in Siberia to the north and Central Asia and Transcaucasia to the south. In the ensuing pages it will be seen that they present a vast spectrum of ethnic groups: Turkic peoples, such as the Tatars, Azerbaidzhanis, Uzbeks and Uighurs; Iranians, such as the Tadzhiks, Ossetians, Kurds and Baluchis; Caucasians, such as the Avars, Lezghis and Tabasarans; and several other small groups, such as the Arabs, the Armenian Khemshils, the Chinese Dungans, the Central Asian Gypsies, the Mongol Sart Kalmyks and the Finno-Ugrian Mordvinians and Udmurts.

Their linguistic heritage is as varied, including some fifteen Turkic, ten Iranian and thirty Caucasian languages, not to mention Chinese, Mongol and an obscure form of Arabic. In the past they had no common medium of communication. Arabic was taught in all the *mektebs* and *medresses* (religious schools and colleges), but, as elsewhere in the Islamic world, the principal purpose of this was to make possible the reading and comprehension of the Qur'an. Only the best educated reached the stage of being able to write and converse in it. The situation was similar with Persian, the other great language of Muslim scholarship, and also with the Turkic literary languages Chagatai, Azeri (Azerbaidzhani), Tatar and Crimean Tatar, all of which were remote from the speech of the masses. The ordinary Muslims of the Russian Empire would have found it as difficult to communicate with their fellow-believers from other parts of the country as would, say, a Kashmiri with a Bengali. Russian is now beginning to provide them with a *lingua franca*, but even after a century or more of contact with this language, the incidence of bi-lingualism is surprisingly low (see p. 25), and it is still not easy for different groups of Soviet Muslims to communicate with one another.

The cultural and social origins of the Soviet Muslims are similarly disparate. The Tadzhiks, for example, represent an ancient urban tradition; the Kazakhs within living memory were still nomadic; the Pamiris even now lead an isolated existence in remote mountain valleys. The Tatars came to the Volga in the thirteenth century as conquerors, the Dungans moved to Russian territory as refugees scarcely a hundred years ago, while the Caucasians are descendants of the aboriginal population of the region in which they live. In the nineteenth century the Azerbaidzhanis became involved in the industrial developments centred on the Baku oil-fields; the Volga Tatars, much influenced by Western education and culture, had already produced a strong mercantile class. The Karakalpaks, meanwhile, were still primitive herders and farmers and the Turkmen were carrying on their traditional occupation of plundering their neighbours.

The differences between these peoples are legion. What binds them together can be summed up very briefly: they share a common citizenship and a common religion. For this reason, care must be taken in speaking of the Soviet Muslims as though they formed a distinct, homogeneous group: they do not. The Muslim population in the Soviet Union is certainly large, but unlike Muslim populations in most other countries, it cannot be said to have a corporate identity. It is formed of a great number of separate elements that have no direct links with one another.

Having said that religion is one of the only two things that the Muslim peoples of the Soviet Union have in common, it must be added that even here their experiences were not identical. The oasis-dwellers of Central Asia were amongst the earliest converts to Islam, adopting it within some fifty years of the Hijra (AD 622). The Arab conquest next carried the new religion to Transcaucasia and by the eighth century Daghestanis such as the Tabasarans and Kaitaks had started to become Muslims. Islam in the Caucasus was reinforced by the Ottoman campaigns of the sixteenth and seventeenth centuries, as well as by a strong Safavid influence throughout that period. Berke, the second Khan of the Golden Horde, was the first Tatar ruler to accept Islam (in 1262), but it was not until the reign of Uzbek (1312–42) that the general conversion of the Turkic peoples of the Horde was accomplished. (The Slav population remained Christian: there is no evidence that any efforts were made to force them to change their religion.) Most of the Kirghiz and Kazakh tribes remained Shamanists until the nineteenth century, when, already under Russian rule, Islam was spread amongst them by the Tatars.

This multiplicity of influences is reflected in the present situation. Most of the Soviet Muslims are Sunni, but about 10 per cent are Shi'i. Amongst the Sunnis, the majority are Hanafis, but there are several communities of Shafi'is in the Caucasus. Most of the Shi'is are *ithna'ashariyya* (followers of the Twelve Imams), but the Pamiris are Isma'ilis (followers of the Seven Imams); the latter belong to the Nizari sect, whose hereditary spiritual leader is the Aga Khan. Amongst the Kurds there are adherents of some of the small, less orthodox Shi'i groups. The diversity here, however, is more apparent than real. It is often difficult to find appropriate equivalents for Islamic concepts in a language such as English, which has evolved in response to Christian needs; consequently, it is easy for misunderstandings to arise. This is particularly true with reference to the 'sectarianism' of Islam, the basis for which is totally different from that of Christian sectarianism. There are no doctrinal rifts in Islam, nothing that can remotely be compared with, for example, the Catholic-Protestant controversy. The tenets of belief and obligatory duties are the same for all Muslims. The only differences are those concerned with interpretation of the law. Sunnis hold that Caliph Abu Bakr was the Prophet's rightful successor as leader of the community, the Shi'ah that it was Caliph 'Ali, the Prophet's son-in-law. The Sunnis accept 'Ali as a Caliph, but as the fourth, not the first. In general, the Shi'ah have a particular veneration for Caliph 'Ali and some of the smaller Shi'i groups carry this to great lengths. Both Sunnis and Shi'is accept the Traditions (*Hadith*) of the Prophet, but they follow different compilations. There are now four main Sunni schools of jurisprudence (including those of Abu Hanifah and Muhammad ash-Shafi'i) and one main Shi'i school (that of Ja'far as-Sadiq). All five are based on the same fundamentals, but by following different traditions or using a different process of reasoning (*qiyas*), they sometimes reach different, though equally valid, conclusions. So far as the performance of prayer is concerned, these divergences are very small, relating to such matters as the exact position of the hands at certain moments. The differences of opinion also extend to the laws of marriage, divorce and inheritance, but they amount to little more than legal niceties. A Muslim normally follows the school into which he is born, but there is nothing to prevent him from changing and he may even prefer to have a case tried by a judge following a school different from his own, if he feels that it would serve him better. In theory, a judge may also be asked to try a case according to the laws of a different school from the one in which he has been trained. In a country where the religious courts do have some competence, the question of which school is being followed obviously has some significance. In a secular state such as the Soviet Union where there are no religious courts at all, the question is irrelevant for all practical purposes. As regards the differences between Sunnis and Shi'is, there is no intrinsic reason why they should not live amicably together. The enmity which has often appeared to exist between the two communities can generally be traced to some other cause, such as the political rivalries of the Ottomans and Safavids. There is not and never has been any tension between the Muslims of the Russian Empire, or later the Soviet Union, because, quite simply, there is no reason why there should be.

An important aspect of Islamic experience is Sufism, the mystical discipline that guides the adept in his search for Divine Truth. Sufism has its origins in the very beginnings of Islam and represents its inspired, esoteric facet. There are different schools or 'paths' (*tariqa*) of mystic discipline, but though they may vary in method, their essential goal is the same. The sanction for a particular *tariqa* is always traced back through a chain of authorities (*silsilah*) to the Prophet himself.

The Sufi movement has played a vital part in the dissemination of Islam. By the eighth century AD it had made its appearance in Central Asia and before long, Merv and Bukhara emerged as leading centres of mysticism. Amongst the many illustrious Sufis associated with the region were Yusuf Hamadani (d. AD 1140), Ahmad Yasavi (mid-twelfth century), Najm ad-din al-Kubra (1145–1221) and Baha ad-din an-Naqshbandi (1318–89). Yasavi was the first Turkic mystic and it was due to him and his disciples, the countless itinerant *babas, atas* and *ishans* that followed in his wake, that Islam was firmly implanted amongst the Turkic peoples of Transoxiana, the Volga region, Anatolia and Azerbaidzhan. (The Turkic terms *baba* and *ata* literally mean 'father'; *ishan* is an honorific use of the Persian word for 'they'. The three terms are used synonymously; the first two are common terms of respect for Sufi teachers, but *ishan* in this context is a typically Central Asian usage.) All four men are of major importance in the history of Sufism, for they were crucial links in the transmission of the chief *tariqa* lines.

In its early stages, Sufism was only practised by the initiated. A holy man would attract disciples who in turn would devote their lives to the pursuit of mysticism. In the fifteenth century, however, it began to assume the character of a popular mass movement. A saint cult developed and there was a burgeoning of groups or orders. A hierarchy arose, consisting of a sheikh or 'guide' (*murshid*), deputies (*naibs, khalifas*), fully initiated disciples (*murids*) and lay or associate members. A sheikh might pass on the *tariqa* exactly as he had received it or he might reinterpret it, but the line of authority (*silsilah*) remained unbroken and in this way the movement was constantly able to renew itself, while at the same time preserving its continuity.

Some of the *tariqas* advocate a 'loud' *zikr* ('recitation of Divine Names'), others a 'silent'; some use the discipline of particular physical actions, such as dancing. The Naqshbandi is the most orthodox of all the Sufi ways and claims the *shari'at* (Islamic law) as its only rule. Its disciplines are silent and unobtrusive and can easily be incorporated into even the busiest of lives. The Naqsh-bandi is now the most influential Sufi school and has adherents all over the world. Amongst the regions in which it has traditionally had a strong following are Central Asia, the Volga, the Caucasus, India and Turkey.

In many communities Sufism became part of the very fabric of life. The local sheikh was doctor, teacher and general counsellor, while the group as a whole acted as a sort of mutual aid society, participating in communal celebrations and helping one another in times of trouble. Membership of a particular Sufi order was often determined by family tradition, since every event from the cradle to the grave would be punctuated by the help, advice and blessing of the local sheikh. Women were closely involved with the move-ment and able to take a more active part in it than was otherwise open to them. Craft guilds were closely associated with Sufi orders and this again nourished a sense of community. The intricate ram-ifications of Sufi influence thus permeated the whole of society, binding it together and preparing it to withstand external pressures when necessary. It is no coincidence that Sufi leaders have often been in the forefront of national struggles, for they more than any other organization are fanatically opposed to outside interference. This was seen in many parts of the colonial world and the Russian Empire was no exception. Notable examples of Sufi resistance were those of Sheikh Mansur (late eighteenth century) and Imam Shamyl (1834–59) in the Caucasus, Kurban-myrat (1881) at Gök-tepe in Turkmenia and Sheikh Madali (1898) at Andidzhan in Uzbekistan. In the Soviet period, too, Sufi leaders have been active in inspiring revolts, as, for example, Uzun Hadzhi and Imam Nadzhmuddin in Daghestan in 1920.

The relationship between Sufism and any form of external control has often been very delicate. Orthodox Islam has regarded some of its teachings with suspicion, since at times they verge on the panth-eistic. Also, by substituting loyalty to a group for loyalty to the community as a whole, Sufism can produce a divisive effect, which is contrary to the spirit of Islam. Secular governments have been even more uneasy about the movement. One of the first actions of the Republican government in Turkey was to close down all the dervish (Sufi) lodges and cells, and it is scarcely surprising that the Soviet government has tried equally hard to eliminate Sufism. The structure of Sufi orders, based on an oath of fealty, graduated stages of initiation and a tightly-knit hierarchy, is the ideal mould for a secret society, and secret societies, being uncontrollable, are by definition dangerous.

How Sufism has survived the undoubted persecution to which it has been subjected in the Soviet Union is hard to say, for the little information that emerges from time to time is patchy, inconclusive and sometimes contradictory. This is not surprising, for if the movement were to survive at all, secrecy would be its best protection. Considering the matter in its historical perspective, it would be most surprising if Sufism, so long an integral part of Muslim life in areas such as Central Asia and the Caucasus, should have been completely eradicated. However, a distinction must be made between two aspects of Sufism: the 'magical' and the intellectual. Soviet sources invariably mock the ignorance of the *ishans* and this, unfortunately, is probably all too justified. It is hardly the fault of the *ishans*, since it is not exactly easy for them to acquire a proper religious training; furthermore, ignorance in itself is not necessarily an obstacle to piety. On the other hand, when pious practice devolves to a sub-culture of magical charms and incantations, its spiritual value becomes questionable. Religion and superstition may be no strangers to each other, but that does not make them one and the same thing. The latter, no matter how comforting and attractive it sometimes seems, can never be a substitute for the former. Moreover, its power is bound to grow less as education becomes widespread. This is not, however, the essence of Sufism, but an accretion that has developed at the level of popular religion. On this level Sufism is certainly now in retreat in most countries, but on an intellectual level, shorn of the superstitious element, it is steadily expanding. This latter is the type of Sufism that is important in the religious life of the community and it would be interesting to know how it fares in the Soviet Union. Unfortunately, there is no information at all about this and it is impossible even to hazard a guess.

Muslims first came under Russian rule in the mid-sixteenth century, after the fall of Kazan (1552) and Astrakhan (1556) to Ivan IV. The Russians' immediate reaction to their new Muslim subjects was to do all they could to convert them to Christianity. They had some success amongst the Bashkirs and Chuvash, but the Tatars proved to be more obstinate. Despite discriminatory legislation and punitive measures such as the burning of mosques and confiscation of property, the great majority of Tatars refused to renounce Islam (those who did were known as *Krjasheny* and referred to separately in official documents). Towards the end of the eighteenth century, however, the attitude of the government towards Islam became less hostile. As the Empire expanded, it came into contact with more Muslim peoples and an over-harsh treatment of the Muslims within its boundaries could well have had an adverse effect on its foreign policy. In the Caucasus, Russia encountered the Scylla of Ottoman Turkey and the Charybdis of Safavid Persia: with consummate skill it out-manoeuvred both, to secure possession of Transcaucasia before the middle of the nineteenth century. This brought the second great influx of Muslim peoples into the Russian Empire. The third occurred in the second half of the nineteenth century, when the rapid advance of Russian rule in Central Asia added yet more subjects to the growing Muslim population of the Empire.

In 1788 Catherine the Great created a Muftiat, known as the 'Mohammedan Spiritual Assembly', at Orenburg. Three others were established during the nineteenth century, one in the Crimea in 1831 and two, a Sunni and a Shi'i, in Transcaucasia in 1872. These institutions were comparable to the *Ilmiye* ('Learned Institution') in the Ottoman Empire; they were also to provide the model for the later Soviet Spiritual Directorates. They had competence in certain areas of civil law and were able to organize the training of the *ulema* (Muslim scholars) on a formal basis, with regular examinations to ensure a uniform standard of education. The printing of Muslim books was allowed in 1800, and in 1806 alone nearly 26,000 were published, including 1,500 Qur'ans. Private Tatar printing presses were in operation by the middle of the century and the amount of printed Muslim literature rose with startling rapidity. The building and maintenance of religious buildings was usually allowed and at times even encouraged, so that by the early twentieth century there were over 26,000 mosques and 24,000 *medresses* (religious schools) in use in the Russian Empire (which did not, of course, include the Khanates of Khiva and Bukhara at this time). There was no longer any legal discrimination against Muslims, who enjoyed the same civil rights as the Slav population. The *ulema* were granted special privileges, including that of free mail and exemption from taxation; in the army, mullahs were provided for the Tatar units. In short, the situation of the Muslim population in the Russian Empire was such that visitors from abroad compared it favourably with that of the Muslim population in the British Empire in India.

The new-found tolerance of the Russian government was not to the liking of other Christian countries and was certainly not supported by the Orthodox Church. Russian missionaries tried as hard as their brothers in Africa and Asia to convert the great numbers of 'infidels' with whom they fortuitously found themselves united. Many of them were undoubtedly sincere and gifted men who did much to raise the educational level of the people amongst whom they worked; some were fine scholars who produced valuable ethnographical and linguistic studies. Nevertheless, they were constantly hampered by a lack of official support, which resulted in insufficient supplies of such basic necessities as money, trained clergy, books and schools. Not only did they often see their best endeavours producing no lasting results, but, to their amazement, that Islam itself was more successful than they were in making and keeping converts. In the second half of the nineteenth century and more especially after the Manifesto of 17 April 1905, granting freedom of conscience, many of those who had accepted Christianity in the preceding centuries, such as the Bashkirs, Chuvash and some of the Tatars, reverted to Islam; others, such as the Cheremiss (Maris) and Votiaks (Udmurts) and even some Slavs, also began to succumb to it. The Orthodox missionaries were so shaken by such trends that the anti-Muslim textbooks they produced at this time bear an uncanny resemblance to Soviet works on the same theme produced nearly a century later. However, they had little effect and at the time of the Revolution, Islam in the Russian Empire was stronger than it had ever been before, numbering some 20 million adherents.

After the Revolution the situation changed dramatically: the Soviet government's attitude is avowedly anti-religious and the inescapable corollary of that is that all religions must be eradicated. The formal institutions of a religion are the most obvious and most vulnerable targets and these were attacked first. In the case of Islam, this entailed the closing of thousands of mosques and *medresses*, the phasing out of *shari'at* courts (by 1927) and the abolition of the *waqf* (charitable endowment) system (by 1930). There were several other measures introduced that profoundly disturbed traditional Muslim values (see p. 31), but it is important to remember that the Soviet Union was not alone in acting in this way towards Islam. A comparable programme of secularization was being carried out at the same time in the Republic of Turkey: in 1924 the Caliphate was abolished, the *ulema* disbanded, the *mektebs* and *medresses* (Muslim schools and training colleges) incorporated into the state educational system, the *waqf* endowments replaced by a meagre state maintenance allowance; in 1925, the *shari'at* courts were abolished and the use of religious titles and the wearing of religious robes on the street forbidden; the Arabic script was replaced by the Latin in 1928. Iran, too, carried out a similar, though less radical, programme of secularization. The aims in these countries were quite different, however, for Turkey and Iran sought a division between the state and religion as part of the process of modernization and westernization, whereas in the Soviet Union, although the Constitution guarantees freedom of religion, the ultimate intention was and still is the total elimination of the 'opium of the people'. This goal remains a constant, though the means by which the government seeks to achieve it vary from open repression to granting a limited freedom, in the hope that it will atrophy of its own accord. At present the latter attitude prevails and the situation is certainly better than it has been at many times in the past. One of the main reasons for this is surely that now, as during the last century, the balance of power with the neighbouring Muslim countries is so delicate that the authorities prefer to pursue a more liberal policy towards the Muslims already within their state, than to provoke adverse reactions by too much oppression.

The administration of Islam in the Soviet Union is represented by four Spiritual Directorates. The most significant of these is the Spiritual Directorate of Central Asia and Kazakhstan (see p. 34). In pre-Revolutionary times there was no Muftiat here; the oldest and largest of the Muslim administrations of that period was based at Ufa, with responsibility for Central and Eastern Russia. In the nineteenth century the representatives of all the Muslim administrative bodies in Russia were noted for their support of the government. The Muslim administration in the Soviet Union continues this tradition by its unswerving loyalty to the present regime. It has been remarked, and not without reason, that the Directorates appear to be singularly useless in defending the position of Islam in the Soviet Union and that they are in effect little more than a propaganda exercise. It is certainly true that they are useful allies in the Soviet Union's dealings with the Muslim world, but the implication that they are not doing their duty towards their fellow-believers is less justified. The *ulema*, unlike the Christian clergy, have no sacerdotal function and bear no responsibility for the spiritual welfare of other Muslims. Their function is essentially to interpret religious law. Their *fetwas* (legal-religious opinions), which are no more than recommendations, are often concerned with such matters as whether or not certain parts of the ritual prayer should be recited aloud. Such preoccupations may seem trivial and pointless at a time when mosques are being closed down and Muslim peoples held in exile, but this is their preserve: intellectual deduction in accordance with acknowledged precepts. The intricacies of Islamic reasoning constitute a science of their own and, in the opinion of other Muslim scholars, the Soviet *ulema* are extremely proficient in it. As for 'representing' their fellow-believers, this is something for which they have no brief: it is assumed that as educated, responsible people they will do whatever is possible to help their community, but it is neither required nor expected that they do more.

Muslims have formed part of the Soviet Union for over sixty years now. Before that, they were under Russian rule for periods ranging between fifty and three hundred and fifty years. During this time official attitudes towards Islam have varied, but even when circumstances were most favourable, it was never as easy for Muslims to practise their religion as it would have been if they had lived in a Muslim state. Yet it is striking that they have not changed their religious allegiance. In the West recently there has been much talk of an 'Islamic revival' in the USSR. This is surely a misinterpretation of the situation: there is no evidence whatsoever to suggest that Soviet Muslims have ever been less (or more) devoted to their faith than they are now. It is true that they have not always been able to show it as openly, but that is a different matter. The survival of Islam is in fact a more interesting phenomenon than its 'revival' would have been, for in the nineteenth century it seemed to many that Islam was spiritually bankrupt. Travellers such as Schuyler and Vámbéry commented on the apparent absence of genuine religious conviction in Central Asia and it would have been hard for them then to foresee that a century later, under a very different regime, virtually all the indigenous population would still be identifying themselves as Muslims. Certainly many Soviet Muslims will explain that they do not practise their religion to any significant degree, but, as explained above, this is not as crucial as it might seem: the basis of belief is generally accepted to be the willingness to associate oneself with it, thus there is nothing hypocritical or fanciful in the

Soviet Muslims' claim that they belong to the Islamic community. Nationalism has undoubtedly been a factor in maintaining the influence of Islam, but in a wide rather than a narrow sense, with nationalism representing the sum of a people's culture, history and individuality, not simply a political perception. Islam has informed the consciousness of Uzbeks, Tatars, Avars and many others for so long that it is inconceivable that it should now cease to hold any meaning for them. To that extent Islam and nationalism are one and the same thing and on that level the future of Islam in the Soviet Union is assured. As regards its practice, the situation is less good, though even here matters are far from hopeless. Much inevitably depends on official attitudes, but a religion that has anything of value to offer does not die because of a faulty support system. Ultimately, Islam requires little more than individuals to ensure its survival: such things as a mosque where the community can gather and stand in line for the prayer, the services of a trained imam, the possibility of making the pilgrimage to Mecca, all these are desirable but not indispensable. Life could be easier for Soviet Muslims, but Islam in the Soviet Union is by no means moribund and there is every likelihood that it will survive the vicissitudes of the present as it has those of the past.

BRITISH ISLES

Arctic

North Sea

NORWAY

S W E D E N

GERMANY
W

E

F I N L A N D

Baltic Sea

Karelian ASSR

Nenets NR

Lithuanian SSR

Part of the
RSFSR

CZ

POLAND

Estonian SSR
Latvian SSR

Komi ASSR

Jamalo-Nenets

GARY

Byelorussian SSR

●Moscow

R U S S I A N

Komi Permjak NR

Khanty-Mansi NR

ROMANIA

Moldavian
SSR

Mari ASSR
Chuvash ASSR

Mordvinian ASSR

Udmurt ASSR

Ukrainian
SSR

Tatar ASSR

Bashkir
ASSR

SOVIET

Black Sea

*Azov
Sea*

Kalmyk
ASSR

Adygei AP

TURKEY

Adzhar ASSR
Georgian SSR
Armenian SSR

3
5
4

Checheno-Ingush
ASSR

Karakalpak ASSR

Kazakh SSR

Daghestan ASSR

*Aral
Sea*

Nakhichevan ASSR
Nagorno-Karabakh AP

Azerbaidzhan SSR

*Caspian
Sea*

I R A N

Turkmen SSR

Uzbek SSR

Kirghiz SSR

C H I N

Gorno-Badakhshan A

Persian Gulf

Tadzhik SSR

A F G H A N I S T A N

PAKISTAN

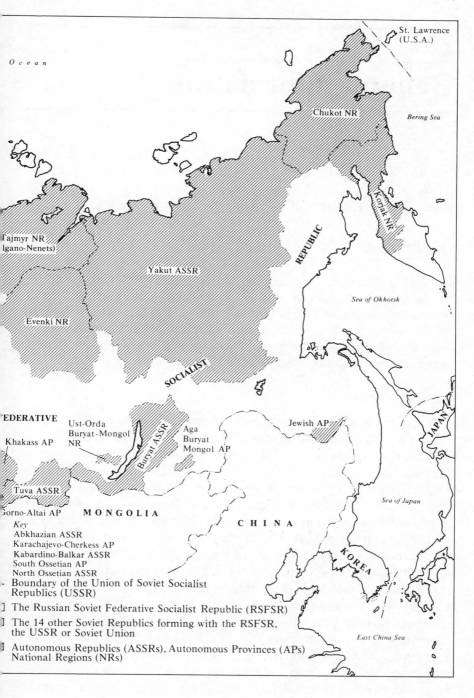

Ocean

St. Lawrence
(U.S.A.)

Chukot NR

Bering Sea

Koriak NR

REPUBLIC

Tajmyr NR
Igano-Nenets)

Yakut ASSR

Sea of Okhotsk

Evenki NR

SOCIALIST

JAPAN

FEDERATIVE

Ust-Orda
Buryat-Mongol
NR

Aga
Buryat
Mongol AP

Jewish AP

Khakass AP

Buryat ASSR

Tuva ASSR

Sea of Japan

Gorno-Altai AP   **MONGOLIA**

CHINA

KOREA

Key
Abkhazian ASSR
Karachajevo-Cherkess AP
Kabardino-Balkar ASSR
South Ossetian AP
North Ossetian ASSR
Boundary of the Union of Soviet Socialist
Republics (USSR)

] The Russian Soviet Federative Socialist Republic (RSFSR)

] The 14 other Soviet Republics forming with the RSFSR,
the USSR or Soviet Union

] Autonomous Republics (ASSRs), Autonomous Provinces (APs)
National Regions (NRs)

East China Sea

2
General information

The Soviet Union

STRUCTURE

The 1977 Constitution defines the Union of Soviet Socialist Republics as 'a unitary, federal and multinational state' (article 70). It
consists of fifteen equal Union republics, some of which contain
within their boundaries autonomous republics, autonomous provinces and autonomous regions. The supreme body of state power
in the Soviet Union is the USSR Supreme Soviet.

Union republics

A Union republic is a sovereign Soviet socialist state that has
united with other Soviet republics in the Union of Soviet
Socialist Republics. . . . The Union republic has its own
Constitution, which conforms to the USSR Constitution and
takes the republic's special features into account (article 76).
The jurisdiction of the USSR extends to such areas as the uniformity
of legislative regulation throughout the territory of the USSR (i.e.
all the Union republics), the implementation of a uniform social
and economic policy, questions of war and peace, the organization
of defence and the direction of the USSR Armed Forces, the representation of the USSR in international relations (article 73);
USSR laws have identical force on the territories of all the Union
republics (article 74). The rights of the Union republics include the
right of free secession from the USSR (article 72), 'the right to
enter into relations with foreign states, to conclude treaties and
exchange diplomatic and consular representatives with them, and
to participate in the activity of international organizations' (article

16

80). Most of these rights may be regarded as theoretical, since they have not yet been implemented in practice. The right of secession is given physical feasibility by the fact that each Union republic shares at least one border with a foreign power. The probability of such an event occurring in the foreseeable future does not, however, seem very strong.

The supreme body of state power in a Union republic is the Union-republic Supreme Soviet.

Autonomous republics

An autonomous republic is part of a Union republic. Outside the limits of the rights of the USSR and the Union republics, an autonomous republic independently resolves questions falling within its jurisdiction. An autonomous republic has its own Constitution, which conforms to the USSR Constitution and to the particular Union-republic Constitution and takes the autonomous republic's special features into account (article 82).

The supreme body of state power in the autonomous republic is the autonomous-republic Supreme Soviet.

There are twenty autonomous republics, sixteen in the Russian Soviet Federal Socialist Republic (RSFSR), one each in the Uzbek and Azerbaidzhan Soviet Socialist Republics and two in the Georgian Soviet Socialist Republic.

Autonomous provinces (*oblasti*)

An autonomous province is part of a Union republic or a territory. A law on an autonomous province is adopted by a Union-republic Supreme Soviet on the basis of a representation submitted by the autonomous province's Soviet of People's Deputies (article 86).

The body of state power in the autonomous province is the Soviet of People's Deputies.

There are eight autonomous provinces, five in the RSFSR, one each in the Georgian SSR, Azerbaidzhan SSR and Tadzhik SSR.

Autonomous regions (*okrugi*)

An autonomous region is part of a territory or province. Laws in autonomous regions are adopted by Union-republic Supreme Soviets (article 88).

The body of state power in the autonomous region is the Soviet of the People's Deputies.
There are ten autonomous regions, all in the RSFSR.

(Sharlet's translation of the 1977 Constitution has been used here and, for the sake of consistency, his terminology adhered to throughout the present work. It should be noted that other translations are possible, e.g. *oblast'* is often rendered by 'region' rather than by 'province' and *okrug* by 'area' rather than by 'region'. For a more detailed explanation of the constitutional structure of the USSR and the role of the Communist Party, see, for example, L. Schapiro, *The Government and Politics of the Soviet Union*.)

CITIZENSHIP AND NATIONALITY

Uniform Union citizenship is established in the USSR. Every citizen of a Union republic is a USSR citizen (article 33).
USSR citizens are equal before the law, regardless of origin, social or property status, race or nationality, sex, education, language, attitude to religion, nature or type of employment, place of residence or other circumstances. Equal rights for USSR citizens are ensured in all fields of economic, political, social and cultural life (article 34).
Women and men have equal rights in the USSR (article 35).
In Soviet parlance 'nationality' represents quite a different concept from 'citizenship'. The former is concerned with ethnic identity and does not have the political implications of the latter. Two terms are used to express nationality/ethnic identity: *narodnost'* (the term used in the 1926 Census) and *natsional'nost'*. *Natsional'nost'* is the quality of belonging to a *natsija*, which, according to the dictionary definition, is 'a stable community of people that has developed on the bases of common language, territory, economic life and psychological (spiritual) temperament'. *Narodnost'* represents an earlier and more primitive stage of social development; it, too, is founded on a common language and territory, but a unified economic and cultural life has yet to be achieved. Some of the ethnic groups that were listed separately (as *narodnosti*) in 1926 are now included in larger groupings, as they are not considered to constitute fully-fledged *natsional'nosti*. Every Soviet citizen has both citizenship and nationality; thus an Uzbek, for example, is by citizenship

Soviet and by nationality Uzbek; since Union republics also have citizenship (see article 33 above); every Soviet citizen is also a citizen of a Union republic.

ECONOMIC STATUS

No information is available on the incomes, standard of living or types of employment of the individual ethnic groups within the USSR. It is not possible, therefore, to compare the economic status of, for example, the Uzbeks with that of the Russians either as whole groups or as represented within each republic. Some comparison between the standards of living within the different republics is possible and from this it would appear that while standards have greatly improved during the last fifteen years in Azerbaidzhan, Kazakhstan and the Central Asian republics, they are still considerably lower than elsewhere in the USSR. (For a review of the available information see A. McAuley, *Economic Welfare in the Soviet Union*.)

There does not appear to be any discrimination against the non-Slav peoples in matters of housing policy. In most areas some traditional dwellings are still found, but new accommodation is almost invariably of the same type and standard throughout the Soviet Union. This very uniformity can be something of a mixed blessing, for the high-rise concrete boxes of two- and three-roomed flats that may be suitable in Moscow and Leningrad are far from appropriate in the climatic, social and cultural conditions of Central Asia. Truly adequate housing would require far greater sensitivity to local requirements. However, the Soviet Union is by no means alone in not, as yet, having developed regional styles of architecture that provide a satisfying solution to contemporary needs; even countries that have given much thought to this matter and have employed famous architects to attempt to solve the problem have not always been successful (cf. some of Le Corbusier's buildings in Chandighar).

Lack of information on the economic status of individual ethnic groups means that there is no specific information available on the occupations of women of different nationalities. In general, Soviet women do go out to work; they are found in all forms of employment and actively participate in politics at all levels. Factors that facilitate this are the provision of crèches and kindergartens (though these are not free) and equal educational and job opportunities for men and women. Muslim women in the Soviet Union now conform, of course, to the overall patterns prevalent in Soviet society. They themselves, however, represent two separate traditions. Those in rural areas have always undertaken an important share of the work of the community, employed as much outside the home, helping with the cultivation of crops and the tending of animals, as within the home, working at crafts such as carpet-weaving and knitting. This has changed little: though the majority now live on collective farms, their occupations have remained almost the same and they continue to be as active as before in supporting the economy of the community. In urban areas the situation was very different, since there the custom was for women to lead secluded lives within the home, fulfilling a primarily domestic role. In the Soviet Union, as indeed elsewhere, this has been changing during the last fifty years. Nevertheless, the establishment of new patterns is inevitably a slow process. It is not known what proportion of Muslim women in urban areas go out of the home to work, but it is unlikely to be as high as amongst the Slav population.

One obstacle that for long hindered women from developing their capabilities to the fullest extent was the fact that in some ethnic groups girls traditionally married early, which meant abandoning their education before reaching an advanced stage. This is no longer so common: amongst the Kirghiz, for example, in 1959 44 per cent of all the girls between the ages of 16 and 19 were married, but in 1970 only 20 per cent. Similar drops were noted in all the other Muslim groups. Large families of five and more children are still common, however, and in rural areas are even increasing. The level of educational achievement amongst women has improved considerably during the last twenty years, but it is still noticeably lower than amongst men. In rural areas the level of achievement is again lower. Factors such as these indicate that, while Muslim women in the Soviet Union today are undoubtedly better educated and have more opportunities open to them than was previously the case, not all sections of society have been equally affected by this.

EDUCATION

USSR citizens have the right to education. This right is ensured by the free nature of all types of education, the implementation of the universal compulsory secondary education of young people . . . by the opportunity for school instruction in one's native tongue (article 45).

Pre-school education, in the form of crèches for the age-group 0–3 years and kindergartens for that of 3–7 years, is not free, but neither is it compulsory. All other forms of education are, as stated in the Constitution, free, and full-time secondary education is compulsory for children between the ages of 7 and 15 years. As a ten-year school programme is in the process of being introduced to replace the previous eight-year programme, most children now remain at school until 17–18 years of age. All schools are co-educational. State boarding schools (in which the tuition is free, but parents contribute towards the board and lodging of the children) provide an important service for isolated communities.

The school system falls into three sections:
(a) primary (grades 1–3);
(b) incomplete secondary (grades 1–8, i.e. 3 primary + 5 secondary grades);
(c) complete secondary (grades 1–10/11, i.e. 3 primary + 5 compulsory secondary + 2/3 'higher' secondary grades).

The eight-year programme ('incomplete secondary') requires full-time study, but the additional years required for the ten-year programme ('complete secondary') can be achieved by either part-time or full-time study. Most schools provide the full range of education, but in some rural areas primary schools exist as separate units; in such cases the children transfer to the nearest secondary school to complete their education.

There is a unified curriculum for the whole of the USSR, but each Union republic, autonomous republic, province or region may vary it in order to take account of local requirements (the teaching of the national literature, history, etc.). In the national (i.e. non-Russian) schools, the period of instruction may be increased by two to three hours per week per grade, or the whole of the school programme extended from ten to eleven years, in order to cope with the extra load of teaching the language and literature of both Russian and the national language. Higher education is provided by universities and institutes; some of the latter are 'polytechnic', consisting of several faculties, others are 'monotechnic', specializing in a single field. Institutes tend to have a narrower and more practical orientation, but there is no difference in the standard of training. All higher education is directed towards a profession: there are no 'general' courses. Study can be full-time (day), part-time (evening) or part-time extension-correspondence. Most establishments cater for all three forms. The majority of students receive state stipends; financial help is also provided by such bodies as collective farms and factories. The qualification for higher education is by competitive examination. This includes compulsory papers in Russian language and literature.

Very little information is available on the subject of language as the medium of instruction. In the mid-1950s an indication was given of the number of Russian-medium schools as opposed to non-Russian-medium schools in the Union republics, percentages of pupils attending them and numbers of languages used as media of tuition per republic. Since then no such information has been released. At that time the situation in Azerbaidzhan, Kazakhstan and the Central Asian republics was as shown in Table 2.1.

Table 2.1 Russian-medium and non-Russian-medium tuition

	Russian schools %	*Non-Russian schools (incl. national lang.) %*	*Pupils in Russian schools %*	*No. of languages used*
UzSSR	5.5	94.5	20	7
KazSSR	43.0	57.0	66	6
AzSSR	4.8	95.2	23	4
KirSSR	19.0	81.0	49	5
TadzhSSR	1.7	98.3	16	6
TurkSSR	7.2	92.8	49	5

(Source: *Kul'turnoje stroitel'stvo*, 1956, pp. 186–7.)

The situation is likely to have altered considerably by now, but the majority of schools almost certainly still use the national language. The ones that have probably suffered are the minority language schools, such as the Kazakh, Kirghiz, Tadzhik and Turkmen schools which used to exist in the UzSSR. The Russian-medium schools are likely to have increased greatly.

In the autonomous republics the proportion of Russian-medium schools was always higher than in the Union republics and in the autonomous provinces and regions higher still. Now there are some autonomous republics in which there is no tuition at all in the national language, e.g. the Kabardino-Balkar, where neither Kabardian nor Balkar schools exist. In others, tuition in the national language is provided only at pre-school level, e.g. in the Checheno-Ingush ASSR, or in the primary grades, e.g. in the Daghestan ASSR, where Darghin, Kumyk, Lak, Lezghi, Nogai and Tabasaran are used in pre-school education and grades 1–2; and Avar, the main language of the republic, only in pre-school and grade 1. The only autonomous republics to provide a complete secondary education (grades 1–10) in the national languages are the Bashkir and the Tatar. In the autonomous provinces and regions there appears to be no tuition whatsoever in the national languages. No information is available on schools providing instruction in the vernacular for the ethnic groups that have no titular area (e.g. the Dungans and Uighurs), or the groups, often quite sizeable, that live away from their titular or traditional area (e.g. the Kazakhs in the RSFSR). It is probable that some level of instruction in the national language is available to them, though it may not be very much. The Crimean Tatars, still in exile in Central Asia, have no schools of their own.

Most higher education is in Russian. Universities in the Union republics often provide tuition in the national language and in Russian, but the natural sciences and specialized technical subjects are almost invariably taught in Russian only. In the autonomous republics tuition in universities is generally only in Russian, but there are sometimes facilities for studying the national language and literature as individual subjects. In institutes, where the education is usually more technical than in universities, tuition is almost invariably in Russian, though in pedagogical institutes there is likely to be some training in the relevant national languages. No specific information is available on this point, however. (For a review of the use of national languages in Soviet education, see B. Silver in *Soviet Studies*, vol. 26, 1974.)

The Constitution guarantees every Soviet citizen the opportunity to education in the native language (see article 45 cited above). Parents also have the right to choose the language in which they wish their children to be taught. Where a choice of schools exists, some parents may well prefer to send their children to Russian-language schools, but there are many cases, as already mentioned, where no such choice exists, since there are no native language schools to

Table 2.2 Level of education of the Islamic peoples in 1970 per 1,000 of the population living in their titular republic or province of 10 years of age and above

	Higher and Secondary complete and incomplete	Higher only
Uzbeks	420	26
Kazakhs	403	31
Tatars	447	24
Azerbaidzhanis	437	39
Tadzhiks	387	21
Turkmen	433	25
Kirghiz	407	28
Chuvash	453	19
Avars	308	18
Lezghis	358	30
Darghins	270	17
Kumyks	348	23
Bashkirs	376	17
Chechens	219	7
Ossetians* (North Ossetian ASSR)	509	52
Ossetians* (South Ossetian Aut. Province)	445	62
Kabardians	417	26
Karakalpaks	383	31
Ingush	252	15
Karachais	346	32
Adygeis	435	37
Abkhazians*	427	45
Balkars	356	29
Cherkess	421	30

*The majority of these peoples are not Muslims.

give it substance. It is true that the lack of proper educational facilities in some languages is balanced by two considerations: firstly, that in the area where the majority live, their national language may be taught as an individual subject in the local Russian-language schools, hence the children need not be totally illiterate in their mother tongue; secondly, that in many cases no form of education was available in these languages before the Soviet period. Nevertheless, it is regrettable that the Constitution lays down a right that cannot be realized by all sections of the Soviet population. In the 1920s and 1930s considerable efforts were made to ensure that it was made feasible, but since then the role of Russian in Soviet education has been greatly strengthened. This does facilitate the creation of a common medium of communication, which must be an important consideration in any multi-national, multi-lingual state, yet it is unfortunate that it should be done at the expense of satisfying people's legitimate need for education in their mother tongue in what is, after all, their native country.

Despite these obstacles, the level of national language maintenance amongst the Muslim peoples of the Soviet Union is still remarkably high. In most cases the percentage of people claiming their 'own' (i.e. national) language as mother tongue has only dropped by a few decimal points since 1926; in some (e.g. amongst the Bashkirs and Kurds), it has even risen. Yet without proper educational facilities there is a danger that all these languages will be relegated to a position of secondary importance, which will jeopardize their function as fully valid literary languages, as well as threatening cultural continuity within a community. Furthermore, excessive emphasis on Russian as the sole medium of instruction at all levels (as is now the situation in many areas) must mean that great numbers of people are unable to profit from the facilities that are provided, since the proportion of non-Russians who have a good command of Russian is still extremely low (only 23.4 per cent in 1979). The unavoidable conclusion is that the lack of adequate tuition in the indigenous languages must be the occasion of very real education deprivation to some.

LANGUAGE

Official Language

There is no *de jure* 'official' language in the USSR, since all the languages of the indigenous peoples of the Soviet Union are considered to be equal before the law and in theory may be used by citizens in all administrative, judicial and other official proceedings (article 159). However, in practice the situation is somewhat different. Russian has, undeniably, a special status: apart from the fact that it is the mother tongue of by far the largest ethnic group

Table 2.3 Percentage of Islamic peoples claiming their own (i.e. national) language as mother tongue

	1926	1979
Uzbeks	99.1	98.5
Kazakhs	99.6	97.5
Tatars	98.9	85.9
Azerbaidzhanis	93.8	97.9
Tadzhiks	98.3	97.8
Turkmen	97.3	98.7
Kirghiz	99.0	97.9
Chuvash	98.7	81.7
Avars	99.3	97.7
Lezghis	97.4	90.9
Darghins	98.3	98.3
Kumyks	99.2	98.2
Laks	99.4	95.0
Tabasarans	92.9	97.4
Nogais	97.2	90.3
Rutuls	98.6	99.1
Tsakhurs	57.3	95.2
Aguls	100.0	98.3
Bashkirs	53.8	67.0
Chechens	99.7	98.6
Ossetians*	97.9	88.2
Kabardians	99.3	97.9
Karakalpaks	87.5	95.9
Uighurs	52.7	86.1
Ingush	99.5	97.4
Karachais	99.5	97.7
Kurds	34.4	83.6
Adygeis	(see Cherkess)	95.7
Turks	n.a.	84.7
Abkhazians*	83.9	94.3
Balkars	99.6	96.9
Dungans	99.2	94.8

Table 2.3—*continued*

	1926	1979
Cherkess	98.4	91.4
Persians	67.8	30.7
Abazins	94.4	95.3
Tats*	86.6	67.4
Baluchis	99.9	98.1

*The majority of these peoples are not Muslims.

in the USSR, it was introduced as a compulsory school subject in 1938 (and possibly still is today, though information on this point is not clear), is the only medium of instruction in schools in many areas, is the medium of instruction in most fields of higher education (see section on Education), is the common language of administration and inter-republic communication, of the armed forces, scientific research and high technology. In other words, the lack of a good command of Russian would be a serious handicap in any field which required higher education and/or inter-republic contacts. All the other languages suffer to a greater or lesser degree because of the pre-eminence accorded to Russian. The need for a common state language is obvious, but the need to encroach on the other national languages to the extent that Russian is now doing is not so obvious. It would be understandable if the internal administration of a Union republic were carried out in both Russian and the republic's own language, but far from this being the case, in some republics even the street signs and public notices are in Russian only. In the autonomous republics and provinces and the national regions Russian is usually the only language of administration. In theory a citizen can ask for any official proceedings in which he is involved to be conducted in his own language, but in practice the necessary translation facilities are often simply not available for this to be a valid option.

What is extraordinary is that despite all the pressures to learn Russian, the efforts made to promote the study of it and the indisputable advantages which accrue from this, by 1970 the number of people who could claim to have a 'fluent command' of the language was still very low. Amongst the Uzbeks it was only 14.5 per cent, amongst the Tadzhiks and Turkmen, 15.4 per cent, amongst the Azerbaidzhanis, 16.6 per cent. Within these groups it was the urban males who had most knowledge of Russian; in rural areas of Azer-

Table 2.4 Percentage of Islamic peoples with good knowledge of Russian (as second language)

	1970	1979
Uzbeks	14.5	49.3
Kazakhs	41.8	52.3
Tatars	62.5	68.9
Azerbaidzhanis	16.6	29.5
Tadzhiks	15.4	29.6
Turkmen	15.4	25.4
Kirghiz	19.1	29.4
Chuvash	58.4	64.8
Daghestani peoples	41.7	60.3
including Avars	37.8	59.3
Lezghis	31.6	47.6
Darghins	43.0	64.1
Kumyks	57.4	72.6
Laks	56.0	73.0
Tabasarans	31.9	59.0
Nogais	68.5	75.6
Rutuls	30.7	52.0
Tsakhurs	12.2	22.4
Aguls	39.8	62.9
Bashkirs	53.3	64.9
Chechens	66.7	76.0
Ossetians*	58.6	64.9
Kabardians	71.4	76.7
Karakalpaks	10.4	45.1
Uighurs	35.6	52.1
Ingush	71.2	79.6
Karachais	67.6	75.5
Kurds	19.9	25.4
Adygeis	67.9	76.7
Turks	22.4	46.4
Abkhazians*	59.2	73.3
Balkars	71.5	77.4

Table 2.4—*continued*

	1970	1979
Dungans	48.0	62.8
Cherkess	70.0	69.6
Persians	33.9	57.1
Abazins	69.5	75.4
Tats*	57.7	61.3
Baluchis	2.9	4.9

*The majority of these peoples are not Muslims.

baidzhan, only 1.6 per cent of the women knew the language. By 1979 the situation appeared to have improved so dramatically as to be somewhat unconvincing: amongst the Uzbeks the percentage of those with a good knowledge of Russian had leapt to just under 50 per cent, amongst the Azerbaidzhanis to just under 30 per cent. It will be interesting to see if this trend continues and whether over the next few decades Russian does succeed in penetrating all layers of Soviet society.

National Language

The term is used to indicate the language traditionally spoken by an ethnic group. It is usually eponymous – the Uzbeks' national language is Uzbek – but not invariably so: the Afghans' national languages are Dari and Pushtu.

In the 1926 Soviet Census, 150 separate national languages were listed. Only some twenty of these had a developed literary form at the time. During the following years great efforts were made to provide the 'underdeveloped' languages with alphabets and standardized literary norms of grammar, vocabulary and orthography. It was a fascinating and extremely complicated linguistic exercise, since many of the languages consist of groups of dialects that differ so widely as to be virtually mutually incomprehensible. There are often marked divergences in the speech of neighbouring villages or of different clans within the same village; even a language as tiny as Yagnobi, consisting of some 2,500 words and spoken by less than 2,000 people, can boast two distinct dialect groups. Some of the literary languages developed during the 1930s were abandoned after the war and nothing has been published in them since. Books, newspapers and periodicals are still published in most of the indigenous languages of the Soviet Union, however, even though the scope and volume of printed material is very small in some cases.

There is a strong political bias in Soviet publishing and a high proportion of all the material that is produced is devoted to this subject in one way or another. Thus, even a language in which very little is published will be liberally provided with the works of Marx, Engels, Lenin and Brezhnev. There is also a great reliance on translated literature in all fields, including, of course, the Russian classics. There is nothing intrinsically wrong with translated litera-ture, for it does utilize the resources of the recipient language and can assist in its development, but it becomes pernicious when it is used to such an extent that it swamps the original literature. A review of the book-lists of several of the national languages indi-cates that this is precisely what is happening at present. Another serious shortcoming in Soviet publishing in the national languages is the inadequacy of the technical and specialized professional lit-erature. It is true that at the very highest level of research it is sensible to publish material in an international language such as Russian, but there are many levels below that at which it would be helpful to have more available in the other national languages. The great majority of people find it easier to read, whether for work or for pleasure, in their own language. There is no linguistic reason why this could not be provided in the languages that already have a well-developed literary tradition, and in the others, if they are truly to develop, efforts must be made to expand them in all direc-tions, including that of specialized concepts.

Scripts

With very minor exceptions, all the languages of the Muslim peoples of the Russian Empire that had a written form used the Arabic script. Most of them adopted a modified form of that script *c*. 1923. The Latin script was introduced *c*. 1930 and for many, a second form of the Latin script was introduced *c*. 1935. The Cyrillic script was adopted for all the languages of the Muslim peoples in the USSR *c*. 1940 and remains in use today. The only use of the Arabic script, apart from in works intended for export and in specialist editions of Arabic and Persian classics, etc., is in the Uzbek edition of the religious journal *Muslims of the Soviet East* and in a Kazakh and two Uighur newspapers; it is not clear whether these news-papers are available in the USSR or whether they are only for export to China (where the Arabic script is still used alongside the Latin for these languages).

RELIGION: ISLAM IN THE USSR

USSR citizens are guaranteed freedom of conscience, that is, the right to profess any religion or to profess none, to perform religious worship or to conduct atheistic propaganda. . . . In the USSR the church is separate from the state, and the school is separate from the church (article 52).

Under Soviet rule, the practice of Islam has been greatly changed. During the first decade, polygamy and the wearing of the veil were abolished; *shari'at* (Qur'anic) courts, *medresses* (religious schools) and many of the mosques were closed; the institution of *waqf* (charitable endowments) was terminated and the *hajj* (pilgrimage to Mecca) prohibited, the giving of the *zakat* (prescribed tithe) and *sadaqah* (voluntary alms) and the keeping of the fast were strongly discouraged. The printing of Qur'ans and other religious material ceased, to be replaced by a torrent of virulently anti-Islamic polemic. Since religious 'propaganda' was not permitted, there was no way of combating this. It became difficult to attend the few mosques that remained open and virtually impossible to attend Sufi *zikr* (litany recitation) sessions. No *ulema* (Muslim scholars) were trained at this time and, most serious of all perhaps, it was forbidden to teach children under the age of eighteen the precepts of their religion. The traditional Islamic way of life was totally disrupted by measures that ranged from the introduction of pig farming in Muslim areas to the abolition of the Arabic script, which, because it is the script in which the Qur'an is written, has a very special significance for Muslims.

The Second World War marked a turning-point for Islam in the Soviet Union. The situation in general began to improve, though, paradoxically, individual Muslim groups (e.g. the Crimean Tatars, Chechen, Ingush, Karachais, Balkars, etc.) suffered more than ever and many died as a result. The major advance was the official sanctioning of four Spiritual Directorates. Before the Revolution four similar institutions had existed (one each in Ufa and the Crimea and two in Transcaucasia), with competence in such matters as the training and appointing of *ulema*, the maintenance of mosques and the publication of religious material; but when, in the Soviet period, these Muftiats ceased to function, there was no administrative framework to take responsibility in these areas. The recognition of the Spiritual Directorates was a token of, if not tolerance, at least acknowledgment of the existence of Islam. The number of mosques open for worship gradually increased (though there was a devastating wave of closures in the early 1960s), the *hajj* was re-allowed for selected groups of pilgrims, a small amount of religious publishing was permitted and, eventually, two *medresses* were re-opened. A trickle of students even began to be sent to Islamic universities abroad to continue their education. International conferences and seminars on Muslim themes have been held in such cities as Samarkand, Tashkent and Dushanbe in recent years. Representatives of the Soviet *ulema* also participate in Muslim conferences abroad. Even if such activities as these have a distinct political motive (and this is clearly perceived by all concerned), it is nevertheless important that they are taking place.

Anti-Islamic literature continues to appear and official attitudes vary from outright oppression to indifferent tolerance, but most Soviet Muslims who wish to attend a mosque today will probably find that the only real obstacle is one of distance, since some areas are extremely badly provided for in this respect. It is hard to know how many people go to the mosque regularly, but in private conversations Soviet imams give the impression that quite a large number do. Certainly the mosques are packed on such occasions as *'Idu'l-Azha* (the Festival of the Sacrifice) and *'Idu'l-Fitr* (the Festival of the Breaking of the Fast of Ramadan) and hundreds of people join in communal celebrations (Demidov, *Sufizm* . . ., p. 146, notes that in 1972 the two *'Ids* were marked by hundreds of 'believers' and 'unbelievers', including many young people, making a pilgrimage to the tomb of Ismamut-ata; he comments that this was in no way exceptional; Vakhabov, *Muslims in the USSR*, pp. 36–40, waxes lyrical on the same theme and, indeed, eye-witness accounts bear out his testimony). No special dispensations are given by the Soviet authorities to those keeping the fast and no provision is made for taking time off on the festivals, but clearly a large number of Muslims do persist in fasting and in celebrating on the appropriate occasions. Burials are often performed in accordance with Muslim requirements. Circumcision is widespread and it is likely that such customs as the *'aqiqah* (ceremony performed after birth) are still practised.

About 90 per cent of the Soviet Muslims are Sunnis. Nearly all of them follow the Hanafi school. The exceptions are some 1,600,000 Daghestanis and several thousand Kurds, who follow the Shafi'i school. Amongst the Daghestanis, the Nogais are exceptional in following the Hanafi school. The majority of the Kurds in the Soviet Union are Shi'i.

Amongst the 10 per cent of Soviet Muslims who are Shi'i, the great majority are *ithna'ashariyya* ('Twelvers', those who believe in the Twelve Imams; this is the largest of the Shi'i groups). They include 70 per cent of the Azerbaidzhanis (approximately 3,800,000; the remainder of the Azerbaidzhanis are Sunnis) and the Persian/Iranian colonies in Central Asia and Transcaucasia; there are also a few small communities of Shi'ah belonging to other ethnic groups (e.g. the Tats and some of the Lezghis). Most of the Pamiri peoples are Isma'ilis (followers of the Seven Imams) of the Nizari sect, whose spiritual leader is the Aga Khan. There are some 50–60,000 Pamiris today; a few thousand are Sunnis (Hanafi school). Amongst the Kurds there are adherents of the *'Ali ilahi* (Deifiers of 'Ali) sects, including that of the *Ahl-i Haqq* (People of God).

In the Soviet Union there are also representatives of two other religious groups that most Muslims do not accept as part of Islam. These are the Baha'is and the Yazidis. The former are followers of Baha'Allah (b. 1817), a Persian who propagated a new religion, combining Christian and Islamic elements. There are a few thousand of them, found amongst the Persian/Iranian communities of Transcaucasia and Central Asia. The Yazidis are a Kurdish tribal group. Theirs is also a synthetic religion, combining Nestorian Christian, Jewish, Manichaean, Zoroastrian and Islamic elements. In the 1926 Census they were listed separately from the other Kurds, but this is no longer the case. They constitute about 20 per cent of the total Kurdish population, i.e. today there are probably some 23,000 Yazidis in the Soviet Union. There are also Yazidis in Iran and Iraq, giving a total Yazidi population of approximately 100,000.

Spiritual Directorates

The Spiritual Directorates are concerned with every aspect of the administration of Islam in the Soviet Union. They come under the Council for Religious Affairs of the Council of Ministers of the USSR. There are four Directorates and each is responsible for a specific region.

1 Spiritual Directorate of Central Asia and Kazakhstan (Sunni)

Its headquarters are in Tashkent (Uzbek SSR); its working language is Uzbek. It follows the Hanafi school. Its Chairman of more than twenty years' standing is Mufti Ziauddinkhan ibn Ishan Babakhan(ov). He was preceded in this office by his father, Mufti Ishan Babakhan ibn Abdul Majidkhan. Mufti Babakhanov's deputies are Sheikhs Abdulgani Abdullayev and Yusufkhan Shakirov. The latter has been Vice-chairman since 1979. There are five Kazis, who represent the Directorate in the five republics that fall within its jurisdiction (the Kazakh, Kirghiz, Tadzhik, Turkmen and Uzbek SSRs). The present Kazi for the Kazakh SSR is Sheikh Yahya Baisenbayev, for the Tadzhik SSR Abdullajan Kalonov. There is also a Council of *Ulema*, composed of Muslim scholars, that debates questions concerning the practice of Islam in the Soviet Union and is responsible for producing *fetwas* (legal-religious opinions). The Managing Secretary of this Directorate is Gulamjan Mirzayakubov. The Directorate has an International Department that makes arrangements for pilgrims who are going on the *hajj*; the deputy chief of this department is a graduate of the El-Beida University in Libya, Atakul Mavlyankulov.

The Directorate of Central Asia and Kazakhstan was officially founded in 1946; the occasion of its thirtieth anniversary was marked by a special Muslim conference held in Tashkent in 1976. In many respects this is the most important of the four Directorates. It is the biggest, since it is responsible for the largest geographical area (the Kazakh, Kirghiz, Tadzhik, Turkmen and Uzbek SSRs) and for more than half of the Muslim population of the Soviet Union. It produces nearly all the very limited number of Islamic publications that appear there and it administers the only two Soviet *medresses* (see below). It also has the only major Islamic library in the Soviet Union; the basis of this fine collection of Islamic works was the personal library of Mufti Babakhanov's father. The Directorate has regular contact with Muslims abroad, since it has organized a number of international conferences on its own territory in recent years and frequently sends delegates to similar events in other countries. Furthermore, Muslims from all parts of the world visit Central Asia to see the many monuments that are so closely associated with the history of Islam. The proximity of the region to such countries as Iran and Pakistan gives it special relevance as a showpiece of Soviet achievements in a uniquely Muslim context.

These factors have contributed to elevate the Directorate's Chairman, Mufti Babakhanov, to what is widely regarded as the position of unofficial Muslim ambassador of the Soviet government. It is he who usually makes pronouncements for foreign consumption on the state of Islam in the USSR and who comments on international affairs that concern Muslims, e.g. the conflict in the Middle East. He is a member of the World Peace Council and is a familiar figure at conferences abroad.

2 Spiritual Directorate of the European USSR and Siberia (Sunni)

Its headquarters are in Ufa (Bashkir ASSR); its working language is Tatar. It follows the Hanafi school. Its Chairman is Mufti Talgat Tazeyev (elected in 1980 at the age of 32); he succeeded the elderly Abdulbari Isayev, who only held office for a few years. It was the Mufti of Ufa, Abdurrahman Rasulayev, who during the last war was instrumental in convincing Stalin of the necessity for making some concessions towards the Soviet Muslims, including the creation of the four Directorates. The present Vice-chairman of this Directorate is Faiz ur-Rahman Sattar and its Managing Secretary is Abbas Bibarsov. This Directorate has spiritual jurisdiction over all the Muslims of the RSFSR except those of Northern Caucasus and Daghestan; it also has jurisdiction over the Byelorussian and Lithuanian SSRs.

3 Spiritual Directorate of Northern Caucasus and Daghestan (Sunni)

Its headquarters are in Makhachkala (Daghestan ASSR); its working language is Arabic. It follows the Shafi'i school. Its Chairman is Mufti Mahmud Gekkiev (elected in 1978) and its Vice-chairman is Sheikh Ahmad Dakayev. Mufti Gekkiev's other deputy is Sheikh Izuddin Muhammedov, formerly Managing Secretary of this Directorate. This Directorate has had its own International Department since 1978.

4 Spiritual Directorate of Transcaucasia (Sunni-Shi'i)

Its headquarters are in Baku (Azerbaidzhan SSR); its working language is Azerbaidzhani. It follows the Jafari and Hanafi schools. Its Chairman is Sheikh ul-Islam Allahshukur Pashayev (elected in 1980 at the age of 31); its Vice-chairman is Mufti Ismail Ahmedov.

The former is a Shi'i, the latter a Sunni (for the use of the term 'Sheikh ul-Islam' for the Shi'i Chairman in place of 'Mufti' for the Sunni, cf. usage in Iran). This Directorate has also had its own International Department since 1978; its Director is Sabir Hasanov. The Directorate has spiritual jurisdiction over the Muslims of the Armenian, Azerbaidzhan and Georgian SSRs.

Mosques

The mosques are wholly dependent on the local community for financial support. They are administered by the *mutawalliyat*, an executive committee consisting of three members elected from amongst the believers. This committee is responsible for the maintenance of the mosque and is empowered to represent the community of believers in matters involving dealings with state organizations or other groups of Muslims. The *mutawalliyat* present regular reports to their community; a three-man auditing committee is also elected to supervise their activities. Each mosque that is open for worship has an imam, called in the Soviet Union *imam-khatib*, since there is only one person to fulfil the functions of both imam and khatib. It is not known how many mosques actually have muezzins and, if they do, how often their muezzins publicly proclaim the call to prayer. All the Soviet *ulema* must be registered with the Spiritual Directorates: they are appointed and paid by the Directorates and no 'unauthorized', i.e. unregistered, person is allowed to perform any religious function whatsoever.

It is impossible to know how many mosques are now open for worship, since Soviet sources are curiously evasive on this point. Estimates vary widely; one of the most recent suggests that there are as few as 450, of which 143 are in Central Asia and Kazakhstan, about 200 in European USSR and Siberia, 45 in Northern Caucasus and 16 in Azerbaidzhan (*Religion in Communist Lands*, vol. 7, no. 3, 1979, pp. 151–2). In the last few years some new mosques have been built (e.g. in Gorkij in 1978) and some existing ones repaired.

Medresses

There are two *medresses* in the Soviet Union: one in Bukhara and one in Tashkent. Both were originally foundations of the sixteenth century, but were closed, like all the other *medresses*, after the Revolution. Dates given for the reopening of the first, the Mir-i Arab in Bukhara, vary somewhat: Bennigsen and Lemercier-

Quelquejay give 1945 in one work (*Religion in Communist Lands*, vol. 7, no. 3, p. 153) and 1952 in another (*Islam in the Soviet Union*, p. 178). Other writers suggest yet other dates and this confusion is indicative of the extreme difficulty of obtaining precise information of this sort. All that is certain is that the Mir-i Arab *medresse* is still open and has about seventy students. The course lasts seven years; boys are admitted only after they have completed their military service. Entrance is by competitive examination, including a stiff test in Arabic. Learning enough Arabic to qualify can be a major problem for would-be applicants, since it is extremely difficult in the normal course of events to find anybody who can read the Arabic script, let alone teach candidates the grammar. Not surprisingly, there are some years when nobody qualifies for entry. Vakhabov (*Muslims in the USSR*, p. 28) comments with charming cynicism that the 'directors of the Bukhara Madrasah can pick the best applicants'; he does not say that there is nowhere for the 'less good' applicants to go, since the Mir-i Arab provides only the elementary stage of training. The next level is provided by the Tashkent *medresse*. It is generally agreed that the Barak Khan *medresse* here was opened in 1958. However, it appears to have been closed down at some point (in the early 1960s?) and was reopened in 1971. It was renamed in honour of Ismail al-Bukhari (who is buried near Samarkand) in 1974, on the occasion of the 1,200th anniversary (Muslim calendar) of his birth. The course in this *medresse* lasts four years. Some of its graduates already hold important posts, e.g. Allahshukur Pashayev, Chairman of the Spiritual Directorate of Transcaucasia, Jafar Ponchayev, imam-khatib of the Leningrad Friday mosque and Gulamjan Mirzayakubov, Managing Secretary of the Directorate of Central Asia and Kazakhstan. Selected students are sent abroad to complete their studies at such Muslim universities as Al-Azhar in Cairo, Al-Quarawiyin in Morocco and El-Beida in Libya. Most of these students are appointed to eminent positions in the Islamic administration in the Soviet Union. At present, for example, the two deputy muftis in the Directorate of Central Asia and Kazakhstan (Abdullayev and Shakirov) and the mufti of the Directorate of the European USSR and Siberia (Tazeyev) are all graduates of Al-Azhar.

At the end of October 1982 the 45-year old Mufti Shamsuddinkhan Babakhan, formerly rector of the Tashkent medresse, was elected Chairman of the Spiritual Directorate of Central Asia and Kazakhstan.

Publications

The number of religious publications produced by the Spiritual Directorates is minute, particularly when compared with the volume of defamatory propaganda. In the period 1948–75 nearly 1,000 anti-Islamic works were published in the languages of the Muslim peoples of the USSR alone, not counting all those published in Russian (*Religion in Communist Lands*, vol. 7, no. 3, p. 157). The Directorate of Central Asia and Kazakhstan, meanwhile, has only produced six editions of the Qur'an (the last in conjunction with the other Directorates), a complete edition of the *Sahih* of al-Bukhari (1973), a collection of his Hadith on personal good conduct (*al-Adab al-Mufrad*, 1970), the three-item Hadith (*as-Sulasiyat*), a collection of Mufti Babakhanov's *fetwas* (1945), an album of Muslim architectural monuments (1956), a religious calendar and a book on the Caliph Othman Qur'an in Tashkent, written by Ismail Mahdum Sattiyev, former Deputy chairman of the Central Asian Directorate. (The Hadith of at-Tirmizi are about to appear shortly, apparently.) It also produces a quarterly journal, *Muslims of the Soviet East* (first appeared in 1968, originally in Uzbek and Arabic editions, then, since 1974, in French and English as well). There is no question of ordinary Soviet Uzbek Muslims being able to read the journal, assuming that they could obtain it in the first place, since the Uzbek edition is printed in the Arabic script, which has not been used to write Uzbek for the last fifty years. The Soviet *ulema*, on the other hand, can and do read it (Vakhabov, p. 54), since most of them know Uzbek and their knowledge of Arabic is, in any case, excellent. A Persian edition has recently appeared.

The Directorate of the European USSR and Siberia has co-operated with the other Directorates to publish one of the six Soviet editions of the Qur'an; it has also produced one book on Islamic practices, *Islam ve Islam dini* ('Islam and the Faith of Islam'), Ufa, 1957, by Mufti Shakir ibn Sheikh ul-Islam Akhabalidin; it is in Tatar, but again printed in the Arabic script and therefore incomprehensible to ordinary Soviet Tatar Muslims who are now ignorant of this script. The other Directorates do not appear to have published anything at all, apart from co-operating in the one joint edition of the Qur'an.

The following tables show the size and regional distribution of the Islamic 'nationalities' of the Soviet Union as listed in the relevant censuses. Here, as in the other tables listing all the Islamic peoples,

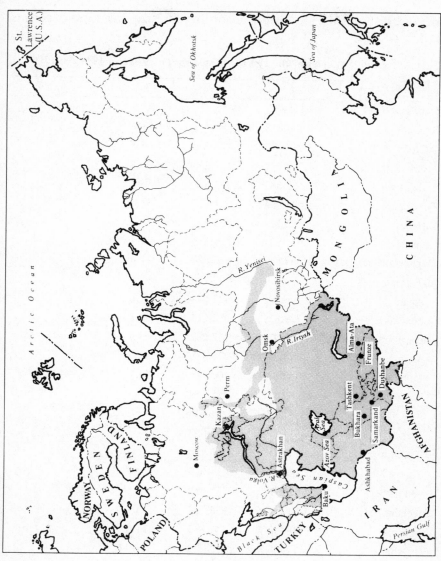

Regional Distribution of the Islamic Peoples of the Soviet Union

the ethnic groups are listed according to size (as in the census reports).

Table 2.5 Islamic peoples of the USSR as listed in the 1970 and 1979 censuses

	1970	*1979*	*% growth*
Uzbeks	9,195,093	12,455,978	35.5
Kazakhs	5,298,818	6,556,442	23.7
Tatars	5,930,670	6,317,468	6.5
Azerbaidzhanis	4,379,937	5,477,330	25.1
Tadzhiks	2,135,883	2,897,697	35.7
Turkmen	1,525,284	2,027,913	33.0
Kirghiz	1,452,222	1,906,271	31.3
Chuvash	1,694,351	1,751,366	3.4
Daghestani peoples	1,364,649	1,656,676	21.4
including			
Avars	396,297	482,844	21.8
Lezghis	323,829	382,611	18.2
Darghins	230,932	287,282	24.4
Kumyks	188,792	228,418	21.0
Laks	85,822	100,148	16.7
Tabasarans	55,188	75,239	36.3
Nogais	51,784	59,546	15.0
Rutuls	12,071	15,032	24.5
Tsakhurs	11,103	13,478	21.4
Aguls	8,831	12,078	36.8
Bashkirs	1,239,681	1,371,452	10.6
Chechens	612,674	755,782	23.4
Ossetians*	488,039	541,893	11.0
Kabardians	279,928	321,719	14.9
Karakalpaks	236,009	303,324	28.5
Uighurs	173,276	210,612	21.6
Ingush	157,605	186,198	18.1
Karachais	112,741	131,074	16.3
Kurds	88,930	115,858	30.3
Adygeis	99,855	108,711	8.9
Turks	(79,000)†	92,689	17.3

Table 2.5—*continued*

	1970	*1979*	*% growth*
Abkhazians*	83,240	90,915	9.2
Balkars	59,501	66,334	11.5
Dungans	38,644	51,694	33.8
Cherkess	39,785	46,470	16.8
Persians	27,501	31,313	13.9
Abazins	25,448	29,497	15.9
Tats*	17,109	22,441	31.2
Baluchis	12,582	18,997	51.0
Total	36,848,455	45,544,114	23.6
% of total Soviet population:	15.2	17.4	

*The majority of these peoples are not Muslims; however, Muslim minorities within other ethnic groups are also not listed separately (e.g. the Adzhars).
†Approximate estimate; not listed separately in the census in 1970.
Note: In addition to the above, there are small groups of Muslims belonging to other Soviet 'nationalities', e.g. the Georgian and Armenian, and others, e.g. the Afghans, who are not listed separately in the latest census.

Table 2.6 Approximate percentage ethnic composition of the Islamic peoples of the USSR in 1979

Turkic (Uzbeks, Kazakhs, Tatars, Azerbaidzhanis, Turkmen, Kirghiz, Chuvash, Bashkirs, Karakalpaks, Kumyks, Uighurs, Karachais, Turks, Balkars, Nogais)	85.0
Iranian (Tadzhiks, Ossetians, Kurds, Persians, Tats, Baluchis)	8.0
Caucasian (Chechens, Kabardians, Ingush, Adygeis, Abkhazians, Cherkess, Abazins and all the Daghestanis except the Nogais)	6.9
Others (including Dungans)	0.1

Table 2.7 Republics and Autonomous Provinces in which the titular (or main indigenous) population is Muslim

	Titular people
Union Republics	
Uzbek SSR	Uzbeks
Kazakh SSR	Kazakhs
Azerbaidzhan SSR	Azerbaidzhanis
Kirghiz SSR	Kirghiz
Tadzhik SSR	Tadzhiks
Turkmen SSR	Turkmen
Autonomous Republics	
Bashkir ASSR (RSFSR)	Bashkirs
Checheno-Ingush ASSR (RSFSR)	Chechen
	Ingush
Chuvash ASSR (RSFSR)	Chuvash
Daghestan ASSR (RSFSR)	Daghestanis
	(incl. Avars, etc.)
Kabardino-Balkar ASSR (RSFSR)	Kabardians
	Balkars
North Ossetian ASSR	Ossetians*
Tatar ASSR (RSFSR)	Tatars
Abkhazian ASSR (Georgian SSR)	Abkhazians*
Karakalpak ASSR (Uzbek SSR)	Karakalpaks
Nakhichevan ASSR (Azerbaidzhan SSR)	Azerbaidzhanis
Autonomous Provinces	
Adygei Aut. Prov. (RSFSR)	Adygeis
Karachai-Cherkess Aut. Prov. (RSFSR)	Karachais
	Cherkess
Gorno-Badakhshan Aut. Prov. (Tadzhik SSR)	Pamiri Tadzhiks
South Ossetian Aut. Prov. (Georgian SSR)	Ossetians*

*Not all of these peoples are Muslims

Titular people as % of total population of area			Russians as % of total population of area		
1959	*1970*	*1979*	*1959*	*1970*	*1979*
62.1	65.5	68.7	13.5	12.5	10.8
30.0	32.6	36.0	42.7	42.4	40.8
67.5	73.8	78.1	13.6	10.0	7.9
40.5	43.8	47.9	30.2	29.2	25.9
53.1	56.2	58.8	13.3	11.9	10.4
60.9	65.6	68.4	17.3	14.5	12.6
22.1	23.4	24.3	42.4	40.5	40.3
34.3	47.8	52.9	49.0	34.5	29.1
6.8	10.7	11.7			
70.2	70.0	68.4	24.0	24.5	26.0
69.3	74.3	77.8	20.1	14.7	11.6
45.3	45.0	45.5	38.7	37.2	35.1
8.1	8.7	9.0			
47.8	48.7	50.5	39.6	36.6	33.9
47.2	49.1	47.6	43.9	42.4	44.0
15.1	15.9	17.1	21.4	19.1	16.4
30.6	31.0	31.1	4.5	3.6	2.4
90.2	93.8	95.6	2.2	1.9	1.4
23.2	21.1	21.4	70.4	71.7	70.6
24.4	28.2	29.7	51.0	47.1	45.1
8.7	9.0	9.4			
89.7	91.3	90.4	1.9	0.9	1.4
65.8	66.5	66.4	2.5	1.6	2.1

Table 2.8 Approximate percentage regional distribution of the Islamic peoples of the USSR in 1979

Central Asia and Kazakhstan	58.0
(Uzbeks, Kazakhs, Tadzhiks, Turkmen,	
Kirghiz, Karakalpaks, Uighurs, Turks, Dungans,	
Persians, Baluchis)	
Transcaucasia and Northern Caucasus	21.0
(Azerbaidzhanis, Daghestanis, Chechens,	
Ossetians, Kabardians, Ingush, Karachais,	
Kurds, Adygeis, Abkhazians, Balkars, Cherkess,	
Abazins, Tats)	
European USSR and Siberia	21.0
(Tatars, Chuvash, Bashkirs)	

Note: These percentages are based on the location of the majority of a given group; the overall picture is fairly accurate, but some of the groups are of course quite dispersed, e.g. the Tatars, and the whereabouts of others is not certain, e.g. the Kurds and Persians

Table 2.9 Slav peoples of the USSR as listed in the 1970 and 1979 censuses

	1970	*1979*	*% growth*
Russians	129,015,140	137,397,089	6.5
Ukrainians	40,753,246	42,347,387	3.9
Byelorussians	9,051,755	9,462,715	4.5
Poles	1,167,523	1,150,991	− 1.4
Bulgarians	351,168	361,082	2.8
Czechs	20,981	17,812	−15.1
Slovaks	11,658	9,409	−19.3
Total	180,371,471	190,746,485	5.8
% of total Soviet population	74.6	72.8	

For a list of the Turkic peoples, the next largest ethnic group in the Soviet Union, see p. 388.

GENERAL STATISTICS

Area

USSR	22,402,200 sq. km
RSFSR	17,075,400 sq. km

Population

	1970	1979
USSR	241,720,134	262,084,654
RSFSR	130,079,210	137,409,921

Average density of population per sq. km

	1970	1979
USSR	10.9	11.8
RSFSR	7.6	8.1

Urban/rural distribution of the population

	1970		1979	
	Urban	Rural	Urban	Rural
USSR	56.3	43.7	62.3	37.7
RSFSR	62.3	37.7	69.3	30.7

Growth rate per 1,000 of the population

	1940	1965	1970	1979
USSR	13.2	11.1	9.2	8.1
RSFSR	12.4	8.1	5.9	5.0

Age structure of the Soviet population in 1970

Age-group	Numbers	% of total
0–9	44,985,596	18.6
10–14	24,988,366	10.3
15–19	21,999,236	9.1
20–29	30,875,621	12.8
30–39	37,738,539	15.6

Age structure of the Soviet population in 1970—*continued*

Age-group	Numbers	% of total
40–49	31,258,643	12.9
50–59	21,090,916	8.7
60 and over	28,514,429	11.8
age unknown	268,788	0.1

Age structure of the Russian population in 1970

Age-group	Numbers	% of total
0–10	23,429,675	18.2
11–15	12,962,024	10.0
16–19	9,659,595	7.5
20–29	17,079,960	13.2
30–39	20,892,773	16.2
40–49	17,827,807	13.8
50–59	12,086,310	9.4
60 and over	14,964,898	11.6

Percentage of males/females in relation to total Russian population

	1926	1970
Men	47.2	45.2
Women	52.8	54.8

Percentage of married Russians in specified age-groups

	16–19	20–29	30–39	40–49	50–59	60 and over
Men						
In 1959	2.3	52.3	93.2	96.5	95.4	83.7
In 1970	2.3	50.3	89.7	94.3	94.9	87.3
Women						
In 1959	9.3	61.5	75.4	57.0	42.7	25.6
In 1970	9.1	66.0	84.5	75.7	53.0	27.8

Size of family units (living together) in the USSR

	1970	1979
Average size of families	3.7	3.5
Average size of families in urban areas	3.5	3.3
Average size of families in rural areas	4.0	3.8

Size of family units (living together) in the RSFSR

	1970	1979
Average size of families	3.5	3.3
Average size of families in urban areas	3.4	3.2
Average size of families in rural areas	3.8	3.4

Percentage of family units of different sizes in relation to total number of families in the USSR

No. in family	2	3	4	5	6	7	8	9	10 and over
1970	25.4	26.2	24.1	12.6	5.9	2.8	1.5	0.8	0.7
1979	29.7	28.9	23.0	9.5	4.1	2.0	1.2	0.7	0.9

Percentage of family units of different sizes in relation to total number of families in the RSFSR

No. in family	2	3	4	5	6	7	8	9	10 and over
1970	26.5	27.9	24.9	12.1	5.0	2.0	0.9	0.4	0.3
1979	31.6	31.5	23.4	8.6	3.0	1.1	0.5	0.2	0.1

Ethnic composition of the Soviet population

	1926	1970	1979
Russians	77,791,124 (52.9%)	129,015,140 (53.4%)	137,397,089 (52.4%)
Ukrainians	31,194,976 (21.2%)	40,753,246 (16.9%)	42,347,387 (16.2%)
Uzbeks	3,904,622 (2.7%)	9,195,093 (3.8%)	12,455,978 (4.8%)
Byelorussians	4,738,923 (3.2%)	9,051,755 (3.7%)	9,462,715 (3.6%)
Tatars	2,916,536 (2.0%)	5,930,670 (2.5%)	6,317,468 (2.4%)

Ethnic composition of the Soviet population—*continued*

	1926	1970	1979
Kazakhs	3,968,289	5,298,818	6,556,442
	(2.7%)	(2.2%)	(2.5%)
Azerbaidzhanis	1,706,605	4,379,937	5,477,330
	(1.2%)	(1.8%)	(2.1%)
Others*	20,806,840	38,095,475	42,070,245
	(14.2%)	(15.8%)	(16.1%)

*Including nearly 100 other listed ethnic groups

Ethnic composition of the RSFSR

	1926	1970	1979
Russians	74,072,096	107,747,630	113,521,881
	(73.6%)	(82.8%)	(82.6%)
Tatars	2,846,734	4,757,913	5,010,922
	(2.8%)	(3.7%)	(3.6%)
Ukrainians	7,873,331	3,345,885	3,657,647
	(7.8%)	(2.6%)	(2.7%)
Chuvash	1,114,813	1,637,028	1,689,847
	(1.1%)	(1.3%)	(1.2%)
Bashkirs	712,366	1,180,913	1,290,994
	(0.7%)	(0.9%)	(0.9%)
Others	14,004,134	11,409,841	12,238,630
	(13.9%)	(8.8%)	(8.9%)

Percentage of mixed nationality marriages in the USSR

	1959	1970
Total	10.2	13.5
In urban areas	15.1	17.5
In rural areas	5.8	7.9

Percentage of mixed nationality marriages in the RSFSR

	1959	1970
Total	8.3	10.7
In urban areas	10.8	12.5
In rural areas	5.6	7.7

Percentage of literacy in the Russian Empire/USSR for the age-group 9–49 years

1897	1926	1939	1959	1979
28.4	56.6	87.4	98.5	99.8

The Soviet definition of literacy does not insist upon the ability to read and write fluently, only the ability to read; nevertheless, though a more stringent test might alter the percentages slightly, the present level of literacy is undoubtedly high by any standards.

Level of education per 1,000 of the Soviet population of 10 years of age and above

	1959	1970
Primary		
Total	310	293
Men	377	328
Women	258	265
Higher and secondary (complete and incomplete)		
Total	361	483
Men	392	522
Women	338	452
Higher only		
Total	23	42
Men	27	48
Women	20	37

Level of education per 1,000 Russians living in the RSFSR of 10 years of age and above

	1959	1970
Primary		
Total	327	296
Men	418	349
Women	261	255
Higher and secondary (complete and incomplete)		
Total	364	494
Men	382	520
Women	352	472
Higher only		
Total	23	43
Men	27	47
Women	21	39

Percentage of Soviet population claiming their own language as mother tongue

1970	1979
93.9	93.1

Percentage of Soviet population with good knowledge of Russian (as second language)

1970	1979
17.3	23.4

Numbers of newspapers, journals and other periodicals, published in Russian in selected years in the RSFSR, with annual circulation

	1965	1979
Newspapers	3,728 (17,550,000,000)	4,066 (27,995,000,000)
Journals and periodicals	2,463 (1,279,900,000)	3,782 (2,410,900,000)

Number of books and pamphlets published in Russian in selected years

	1913	1940	1965	1979
No. of titles	23,805	34,404	57,521	61,958
Print run	80,218,000	345,728,000	1,038,412,000	1,452,210,000

Explanatory notes

Within each section the ethnic groups that constitute separate Soviet 'nationalities' are listed according to size; the others are listed alphabetically.

The names of the peoples discussed in this book are given in the plural form in Russian, as this is the form in which they are usually encountered in reference works, but in the singular form in their own languages wherever possible. Where more than one form of a name is found in English, this is indicated in the section heading.

'Town' (*gorod*): each Union republic has its own definition of this term. In the RSFSR it entails a minimum of 12,000 inhabitants, of whom a minimum of 85 per cent must be engaged in urban-type employment.

'Settlement' (*poselok gorodskogo tipa*): there are various types of 'settlements', but in general they have a minimum of 3,000 inhabitants, of whom 85 per cent are engaged in urban-type employment.

'Mother tongue' (*rodnoj jazyk*): as defined in the 1926 Census, it is the language which a person speaks best or habitually speaks. Parents are empowered to decide what is their children's 'mother tongue'. In the 1926 Census the question relating to literacy in a person's 'mother tongue' referred specifically to literacy in that person's national language and not to literacy in the 'mother tongue' (in cases where the two were not one and the same).

'Second language': in the census this is defined as a language of which the speaker has a 'fluent command' (*svobodno vladejet*), in addition to his mother tongue.

'Pamphlet' (*broshjura*): the term is used for a paper-bound booklet consisting of 5–48 pages; it can be on any subject; the slightness of the format does not necessarily mean that the work itself will be lightweight.

Classification of the Turkic languages

There is no one, standard classification of the Turkic languages. In order to give some idea of the possible alignments, two schools of thought have been represented here: that of the eminent Soviet Turkologist, N. A. Baskakov, and that used in the Table of Contents of *Philogiae Turcicae Fundamenta*, vol. 1 (based on J. Benzing; the *Fundamenta* also includes an exposition of the quite different approach of K. Menges).

When giving the Ethnic Composition of a republic, etc., the various nationalities are here listed according to ethnic groups and not, as in the census reports, in order of size. When percentages are given for numbers of people with 'good knowledge of a language other than their own or Russian', the intention is, as indicated, to show the incidence of tri-lingualism. In the census reports, when the information is quantified in this way in what is apparently the same category, the percentages are in fact based on a combination of the figures for a good knowledge of the national language and of any other language apart from Russian as 'second languages'. They are thus slightly higher than the percentages given here.

Level of education

The level of formal education achieved is indicated, i.e. primary (3 grades of school), incomplete secondary (8 grades), complete secondary (10–11 grades), higher (all forms of further education). See further pp. 21–5.

Sources

All the statistical information is drawn from the relevant census returns and *Narodnoje khozjajstvo SSSR v 1979 g.* Where there are discrepancies the most recent source has been used (e.g. the data concerning the Uzbek SSR in 1959 as given in the 1970 Census does not tally with that given in the 1959 Census; here the 1970 data have been used). Full information concerning the 1979 Census is not yet available. In the tables given in this book, a lack of data at present has been indicated by n.a. (not available). To date, more information has been released concerning the RSFSR than the other republics. This has resulted in some apparent discrepancies in the following tables, where, for example, population estimates regarding the RSFSR are very accurate, but for the other republics they are only now becoming available. Detailed breakdowns of the ethnic composition of the republics are also not yet available; in the following tables, if data concerning a particular ethnic group are at present unavailable, that group has been subsumed under the heading 'Others'.

Material concerning the publication of books, pamphlets, newspapers and periodicals has been taken from *Narodnoje khozjajstvo SSSR v 1979 g., Jezhegodnik knigi* and *Letopis' periodicheskikh izdanij SSSR* (various years); where there are discrepancies (e.g. in the *Letopis'*), the latest data have been used.

The estimates for sections of ethnic groups living outside the Soviet Union have been taken from Soviet sources (e.g. the *Bol'shaja sovetskaja entsiklopedija*, 3rd edn.); where other sources are used, this is indicated in the text.

Full details of works referred to in the text are given in the Selected bibliography.

Transliteration

Although the languages of the Muslim peoples of the USSR are now written in the Cyrillic script, the alphabets used for them are all different: the symbols often have different values and within the alphabets they are arranged in a different order. To avoid excessive confusion, a standard transliteration of the Russian Cyrillic alphabet has been used here, but it should be noted that this does not always faithfully convey the pronunciation in a particular language. Furthermore, it has not always been possible to be strictly consistent, or rather, it was felt that in some cases consistency would be more misleading than inconsistency. This was particularly the case where a name was already well known in another form of transliteration, e.g. *Majidkhan* is used in some contexts instead of *Madzhidkhan*, *Yusuf* instead of *Jusuf*. Where a place-name has an established English form, that is used instead of a transliterated form, e.g. *Kazan* instead of *Kazan'*.

Most of the equivalents are self-evident, but the following may need some explanation:

ch   as *ch* in *ch*urch
dzh   as *j* in *j*oke
kh   as *ch* in lo*ch*
zh   as *s* in plea*s*ure
j   as *y* in *y*acht or, in Arabic words, *j* as in *j*oke
y   similar to undotted *i* in Turkish
'   soft sign in Russian; it is also used for *'ain* and *hamza* in Arabic and the stops in the Caucasian languages.

Abbreviations

ASSR	Autonomous Soviet Socialist Republic
ArmSSR	Armenian Soviet Socialist Republic
AzSSR	Azerbaidzhan Soviet Socialist Republic
DaghASSR	Daghestan Autonomous Soviet Socialist Republic
GeorgSSR	Georgian Soviet Socialist Republic
KazSSR	Kazakh Soviet Socialist Republic
KirSSR	Kirghiz Soviet Socialist Republic
RSFSR	Russian Soviet Federal (Federative) Socialist Republic
SSR	Soviet Socialist Republic
TadzhSSR	Tadzhik Soviet Socialist Republic

TurkSSR	Turkmen Soviet Socialist Republic
USSR	Union of Soviet Socialist Republics
UzSSR	Uzbek Soviet Socialist Republic

Glossary

fetwa	opinion on a point of Islamic law pronounced by a mufti
hadith	traditions of the Prophet
imam	one who leads the prayers; chief functionary of a mosque
khatib	preacher
medresse	religious training college
mekteb	elementary religious school
mufti	authority on Islamic law who is authorized to pronounce legal opinions; in the Soviet Union, the title given to the head of the Sunni Spiritual Directorates
tariqa	Sufi 'way' or school
ulema	Muslim scholars
ulus	land, state, people
waqf	endowment in perpetuity of property for religious or charitable purposes

3
European USSR and Siberia

TATARS

Own name: *Tatar*; Russian name: *Tatary*.

Over half of them live in the Volga region, but large colonies of Tatars are to be found in virtually every republic of the Soviet Union.

1 HISTORICAL BACKGROUND

The term 'Tatar' is confusing, since it has been used with different meanings at different periods. Russians have for centuries used it for any Muslim of Turkic origin living in European Russia. In a strictly historical sense, however, it is most frequently used for the Turkic (mainly Kipchak) tribes who constituted the bulk of the Mongol army that invaded Russia in the early thirteenth century. Present-day Russia formed the core of the western wing of the Mongol Empire, known as the Ulus of Dzhuchi or the Golden Horde. The rulers here, as elsewhere in the Mongol Empire, were direct descendants of Genghiz Khan, but the Turkic element was so powerful that by the early fourteenth century the Golden Horde had succumbed to its influence and become in effect a Turkic state. Despite its size, it retained a structure based on tribal alliances and from the beginning groups split off from the main body to form separate hordes or colonies (e.g. the Nogais, Crimeans, Uzbeks and Grand Duchy Tatars: see pp. 159, 87, 266 and 85). The Turkic/ Kipchak element was thus disseminated over a wide area, stretching from the borders of modern Poland to the foothills of the Pamirs, from the Black Sea to Siberia. The history of each of these groups followed its own course and in time some of them acquired new

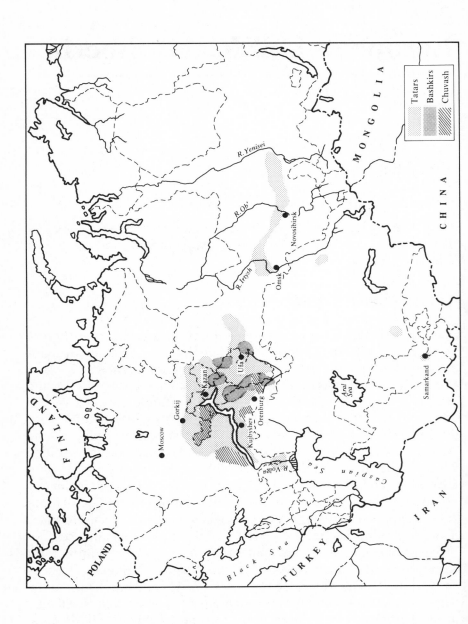

ethnic designations. The word 'Tatar' continued to be used for the Turkic tribes of the Volga region, however, and they continued to represent the basis of the Golden Horde. When it disintegrated into still smaller units, new Tatar states emerged, the Astrakhan and Kazan Khanates. Both were formed during the mid-fifteenth century, Kazan the larger of the two, slightly later than Astrakhan. A century later they fell to Ivan the Terrible, Kazan in 1552, Astrakhan in 1556.

The relationship between the Tatars and the Russians was complex. Ostensibly the fall of Kazan and Astrakhan brought about a reversal of roles, since the Tatars, having been the 'oppressors' for some 300 years, suddenly became the 'oppressed'. However, it is clear that at certain levels there was a tendency towards integration from the earliest period. The Tatars were too disunited to hold their vast state together without the support of the indigenous population: they intermarried with the Russian princely families and gave as well as received help in the inter-factional manoeuvrings that characterized the politics of both communities. The fact that the Tatars had been converted to Islam (Khan Uzbek, ruler of the Golden Horde from 1312 to 1342, is credited with the final conversion of his state) does not appear to have presented any obstacles to this mutual co-operation. By the sixteenth century some of the Tatar nobility had gained a position of power and influence amongst the Russians which they held not so much as representatives of a foreign master, but which they had won for themselves in Russian society. This situation continued after the Tatar Khanates had been taken and the only remaining Tatar stronghold was in the Crimea.

The Russian attitude to the mass of the Tatar population of the Khanates, however, was very different from that shown to the Tatar aristocracy that had been more or less assimilated into Russian circles. In Kazan and Astrakhan the Russians adopted a harsh, illiberal policy that aroused bitter resentment, easily fanned into open revolt. Many rebel leaders found support there, including Bolotnikov (1606–7), Stenka Razin (1667–71) and Pugachev (1773–5). Efforts were made to forcibly convert the Tatars to Christianity, but they met with little success, despite such measures as the wholesale destruction of mosques, confiscation of Tatar property and curtailment of civil rights. The Tatar merchant class, which by this time was very active, was crippled by restrictions imposed upon its trading activities. At the same time thousands of Tatars were deported to the north, to work in the shipyards of Kronstadt and Riga and on the Ladoga Canal.

The situation improved under Catherine the Great (1762–96), who revoked some of the most repressive anti-Tatar legislation. 'The Orenburg Mohammedan Spiritual Assembly' was created in Ufa in 1788; under the direction of a Mufti, it had jurisdiction over religious and some civil matters. Mosques and medresses were rebuilt and many of the trading restrictions lifted; the privileges of the Tatar nobility were restored and they were set on a par with the Russian nobility. The first high school (*gimnazija*) was opened in Kazan in 1758, a university in 1804. The first grammar of Tatar was published in Moscow in the second half of the eighteenth century, and in 1800 a printing press was set up for the printing of Tatar books (later books in other Turkic languages, such as Uzbek and Kazakh, were also printed here). The Tatars rapidly took advantage of the new opportunities offered to them and great advances were made in both intellectual and commercial spheres. However, the improvements in the Tatar condition were only temporary: in the second half of the nineteenth century the Russian government once more adopted a repressive policy towards them and introduced another campaign of Russification and Christianization. Conditions for the Tatar peasantry had remained extremely bad even during the relatively favourable period of the late eighteenth to early nineteenth centuries, and the Emancipation of Serfs (1861), far from improving matters, did little more than aggravate their grievances. There was again much unrest in the area, punctuated by outbursts of violence that in turn provoked harsh retaliatory measures. Anti-Russian feeling (Muslim-inspired and often led by members of the Naqshbandi order) was rife and over the next few years a number of Tatars chose to emigrate to Turkey.

Despite the difficulty of the circumstances, however, the intellectual life of the Tatars continued to flourish. They were much influenced by European ideas and far from being a conservative, backward-looking society they were probably the most progressive Turkic people of their day. They were deeply conscious of the need for educational reform, the need to keep abreast of contemporary scientific achievements. At the same time they were firmly committed to Islam and to their concept of themselves as an integral part of the Turkic-speaking world. Furthermore, they felt the need for unity amongst the Turkic peoples of the Russian Empire and their cultural and ideological (eventually political) work was directed towards this goal, rather than towards a more narrowly nationalistic one. It was they who provided the main inspiration for the *Dzhadid* ('new') movement in education which played such an important part in developing the self-awareness of the Turkic/Muslim peoples of Central Asia. The literacy rate of the Tatars themselves was exceptionally high (only slightly lower than that of the Russians) and it was accompanied by an impressive number of printed publications. By the early twentieth century the Tatars dominated the political life of the Russian Muslims with ease, virtually acting as their leaders. When the *Ittifaq al-Muslimin* 'Muslim Union' (also known as *Rusija Müsülmanlarynyng Ittifaqy* – 'Union of Russian Muslims') was founded in St Petersburg in 1906 at the Second All-Russian Muslim Congress, eleven of the fifteen members of the Central Committee were Volga Tatars. They were active, too, in many other organizations, reflecting all shades of political affiliation.

In the First World War the Volga Tatars, like the Crimeans, were conscripted into the Russian Army. Many of them deserted and the existing tension in the region was heightened by the efforts of émigré Tatar leaders in Turkey. It crystallized into a separatist movement, but total autonomy proved to be an impossible dream: there was an attempt to set up an independent federation of Ural-Volga states in 1917, but it was overthrown in 1918 and Soviet power established in its place. Czech Interventionists and the White Army under Kolchak briefly gained control of the region in the summer of 1918, but were driven out by the Red Army in mid-1919. On 27 May 1920 the Tatar ASSR was created with the RSFSR.

The creation of the Tatar ASSR added a new and specific connotation to the term 'Tatar' by making it the official designation of the titular population of that republic. At the same time it continues to be used in a much wider sense, referring to people who are not in any way connected with the Tatar ASSR or indeed the Volga region, e.g. the Crimean, Siberian, Byelorussian and Lithuanian Tatars. The histories of these peoples have been quite different from those of the Volga Tatars since the fourteenth century. Their languages are different and so, too, are their education, cultural and occupational backgrounds. Thus the profile of the 'Tatars' presented by Soviet statistics is inevitably somewhat distorted, since it includes under one heading these diverse elements. The Siberian Tatars in particular are the antithesis of the Volga Tatars, the one group being highly urbanized and possessing a long intellectual tradition, the other (the Siberians) being mainly rural dwellers with, at the beginning of this century, a very low level of literacy. The picture presented of the dispersal of the Tatars is also misleading, since the use of the single term 'Tatar' implies a stronger ethnic and territorial link than in fact exists. While it is true that the Volga Tatars have shown great mobility and are now found in all parts of the Soviet Union, it must not be forgotten that some of the other Tatar peoples were settled in their present habitat as early as the thirteenth century and never had a particular connection with the Volga region. Furthermore, the territory of the former Tatar Khanates was larger than that covered by the Bashkir, Chuvash and Tatar ASSRs of today: thus the presence of Tatars in the peripheral regions has a historic basis and is not due to out-migration. Finally, when there has been migration, it has not always been voluntary, as is evidenced by the deportation of the Crimean Tatars in 1944.

Tatar ASSR (Tatarstan Avtonomijale Sovet Sotsialistik Respublikasy), also known as *Tataria* or *Tatarstan*

Situated on the Middle Volga in the forest and forest-steppe zone; it is bordered to the north by the Mari and Udmurt ASSRs, to the east by the Bashkir ASSR, to the west by the Chuvash ASSR (all within the RSFSR). *Area*: 68,000 sq. km. *Capital*: Kazan (population in 1979: 993,000). The Republic has 18 towns and 22 settlements. *Population* (1979): 3,445,412. Average density of population per sq. km (1979): 50.5.

Chief resources: major reserves of oil and natural gas.

Industries include: oil and gas extraction (one of the most important in the USSR), machine-building, power, chemical and petro-chemical industries; food (edible oils, flour, meat, cheese, alcoholic drinks etc.), timber, fur-processing and other light industries; a motor industry is being developed.

Agriculture: grain farming (rye and wheat) and, to a lesser extent, the cultivation of crops such as sunflowers, hemp, sugar beet, potatoes, fruit and vegetables; stockbreeding of animals for meat, milk and wool; pigs are also raised.

2 NUMBER AND DISTRIBUTION

Number of Tatars

	1926	1959	1970	1979
	2,916,536	4,967,701	5,930,670	6,317,468

Regional distribution of Tatars

	1926	1959	1970	1979
Tatar ASSR	1,164,342 (40.0%)	1,345,195 (27.1%)	1,536,431 (25.9%)	1,641,607 (26.0%)
Bashkir ASSR	461,871 (15.8%)	768,566 (15.5%)	944,507 (15.9%)	940,446 (14.9%)
Crimean ASSR*	179,094 (6.1%)	—	—	—
Chuvash ASSR	22,635 (0.8%)	31,357 (0.6%)	36,217 (0.6%)	37,573 (0.6%)
RSFSR†	933,248 (32.0%)	1,929,570 (38.8%)	2,240,758 (37.8%)	2,391,296 (37.9%)
Kazakh ASSR/SSR	80,642 (2.8%)	191,680 (3.9%)	287,712 (4.9%)	313,460 (5.0%)
Kirghiz ASSR/SSR	4,902 (0.2%)	56,266 (1.1%)	69,373 (1.2%)	72,018 (1.1%)
UzSSR	28,401 (1.0%)	445,036 (9.0%)	573,733 (9.7%)	648,764 (10.3%)
TurkSSR	4,769 (0.2%)	29,946 (0.6%)	36,457 (0.6%)	40,432 (0.6%)
Elsewhere in USSR	36,632 (1.2%)	170,085 (3.4%)	205,482 (3.4%)	231,872 (3.6%)

*Disbanded in 1944.
† Not including the Tatar, Bashkir, Chuvash, Crimean, Kazakh or Kirghiz ASSRs.

Percentage of Tatars in relation to total population of individual republics

	1926	1959	1970	1979
Tatar ASSR	44.9	47.2	49.1	47.6
Bashkir ASSR	17.3	23.0	24.7	24.5
Chuvash ASSR	2.5	2.9	3.0	2.9
Crimean ASSR	25.1	—	—	—
Kazakh ASSR/SSR	1.2	2.1	2.2	2.1
Kirghiz ASSR/SSR	0.5	2.7	2.4	2.0
UzSSR	0.5	5.5	4.9	4.2
TurkSSR	0.5	2.0	1.7	1.5

Urban/rural distribution of Tatars (in main areas of habitation)

	1926		1970	
	Urban	Rural	Urban	Rural
RSFSR	394,782 (13.9%)	2,451,952 (86.1%)	2,364,191 (49.7%)	2,393,722 (50.3%)
UzSSR	22,878 (80.6%)	5,523 (19.4%)	421,022 (73.4%)	152,711 (26.6%)
TurkSSR	3,686 (77.3%)	1,083 (22.7%)	33,464 (91.8%)	2,993 (8.2%)

Ethnic composition of the Tatar ASSR

	1926	1959	1970	1979
Total population	2,593,779	2,850,417	3,131,238	3,445,412
Tatars	1,164,342 (44.9%)	1,345,195 (47.2%)	1,536,431 (49.1%)	1,641,607 (47.6%)
Chuvash	127,330 (4.9%)	143,552 (5.0%)	153,496 (4.9%)	147,088 (4.3%)
Krjasheny*	99,041 (3.8%)	—	—	—
Russians	1,118,834 (43.1%)	1,252,413 (43.9%)	1,328,738 (42.4%)	1,516,023 (44.0%)
Others	84,232 (3.2%)	109,257 (3.8%)	112,573 (3.6%)	140,694 (4.1%)

*Included with the Tatars in 1959, 1970 and 1979.

Urban/rural distribution in the Tatar ASSR in 1970

	Urban	*Rural*
Total population	1,613,955	1,517,283
Tatars	593,665 (36.8%)	942,766 (62.1%)
Chuvash	27,191 (1.7%)	126,305 (8.3%)
Russians	934,387 (57.9%)	394,351 (26.0%)
Others	58,712 (3.6%)	53,861 (3.5%)

3 STATUS

The Tatars enjoy full Soviet citizenship. They are found in all occupations and in all income brackets. Their standard of housing is comparable to that of other national groups in the Soviet Union. The women go out to work, as elsewhere in the Soviet Union.

Literacy

In 1926	In 1970
33.6%	Over 99%

In 1926, 906,306 Tatars were literate in their own language (92.5% of the total literate Tatar population).

Level of education per 1,000 Tatars living in the RSFSR of 10 years of age and above

	1959	*1970*
Primary		
Total	321	318
Men	387	358
Women	270	284
Higher and secondary (complete and incomplete)		
Total	329	442
Men	355	475
Women	308	417
Higher only		
Total	10	22
Men	11	26
Women	9	20

Level of education per 1,000 Tatars living in the UzSSR of 10 years of age and above

	1959	1970
Primary		
Total	277	274
Men	323	305
Women	245	253
Higher and secondary (complete and incomplete)		
Total	436	535
Men	455	552
Women	423	522
Higher only		
Total	26	49
Men	28	47
Women	24	51

In general in the Soviet Union the level of education of an ethnic group is higher within its main or titular area than it is outside. With the Tatars, on the contrary, the level of education is markedly higher in Central Asia than in the RSFSR. This is probably due in large part to the presence of the Crimean Tatars, who traditionally had a high level of education.

4 LANGUAGE

The national language is Tatar (not to be confused with Crimean Tatar). It belongs to the West Turkic group (*Fundamenta* classification); it can also be classed as belonging to the Kipchak group, Kipchak-Bolgar sub-group (Baskakov). The language to which it is most closely related is Bashkir.

Tatar contains three main dialectal divisions: the central dialects, spoken by the Volga Tatars; the western or Mishar dialects, spoken mostly by Tatars outside the Tatar ASSR (the Mishars were formerly listed as a separate people, but they are now grouped with the Tatars; the majority live in the Bashkir and Mordvinian ASSRs); the eastern or Siberian dialects, spoken by the Baraba, Tomsk, Tobol, Tara, Omsk, etc. Tatars. There are also some 'mixed' dialects: that of the Astrakhan Tatars, spoken by Tatars such as the Kundurs from the Caucasus, which has been heavily influenced by the speech of the Volga Tatars but still preserves some features that are typical of Nogai; that of the Kasimov Tatars, settled in the former Rjazan' Province (*gubernija*), present-day Kasimov District (*rajon*), which is midway between the central and western group; that of the Teptjars, which is mid-way between Tatar and Bashkir; that of the Nagaibaks and other Tatars of the Urals. The differences between these dialects are lexical, phonetic and morphological. They are all still very much alive (e.g. there are about 45,000 speakers of the Astrakhan dialect, 110,000 of the Nagaibak, about 300,000 of the Teptjar), but the existence of a single literary language, based on the Kazan dialect (belonging to the central group), is gradually eroding the differences by creating standardized norms of syntax, orthography (indirectly pronunciation) and vocabulary. The language still shows a very strong Arabic and Persian influence, and, to a lesser extent, Turkish, but the Russian element is steadily gaining ground, particularly in such fields as administration and technology. The new loans are adopted in their original form, but the earlier loans (some of which entered Tatar several centuries ago) have been considerably modified. The formation of calques, based on Russian models, has become one of the chief ways of enlarging the modern vocabulary. Russian is generally used for administrative, judicial and other official proceedings, but in theory Tatar can also be used if necessary.

Percentage of Tatars claiming Tatar as their mother tongue

	1926	1959	1970	1979
Total	98.9	92.1	89.2	85.9
In urban areas	96.2	87.5	83.4	n.a.
In rural areas	99.4	96.1	96.3	n.a.

Percentage of Tatars with good knowledge of Russian

	1926	1959	1970	1979
As mother tongue	0.7	7.0	10.2	13.2
As second language	n.a.	n.a.	62.5	68.9

In 1958 Tatar was the medium of instruction in grades 1–10 (complete secondary) in the national schools in the RSFSR; in 1972 this was still the case and, in addition, it was used in pre-school education; in 1972 it was taught, too, as an individual, optional subject in Russian-medium schools in grades 1–10 (Silver, p. 33).

More recent information is not available. There is a university at Kazan (founded in 1804), but it does not appear to provide any tuition in Tatar; it does, however, possess a Department of Tatar Language and Literature. There are also a number of specialized institutes (e.g. of Aviation, Chemical Technology and Medicine) in the Tatar ASSR.

In the Tatar ASSR there are radio and television broadcasts in Tatar, as well as in Russian. There are also transmissions in Tatar in the Bashkir ASSR.

Newspapers are published in Tatar in the Tatar and Bashkir ASSRs; some regional (*rajonnyje*) papers in Tatar are also published in the Chuvash ASSR. The Tatar press appeared slightly later than the Uzbek, Azerbaidzhani, Kazakh and Crimean Tatar, but it developed rapidly in volume and variety and by 1917 was second only to the Azerbaidzhani; in the next three years there was an even greater proliferation of Tatar periodicals, outstripping by far the total number of publications in all the other languages of the Muslim peoples of the Russian Empire. The chief centre of the Tatar press was Kazan, but Astrakhan, Orenburg, Ufa, St Petersburg and Moscow also produced a significant number of publications and even such towns as Tomsk in Siberia and Troick and Ural'sk in the Kazakh lands produced one or two of their own. The very first Tatar periodical publication was *Mirat* ('The Mirror'), published 1902–9 in St Petersburg. It was soon followed by others, reflecting all shades of current political and religious affiliations. Amongst the most influential were *Vaqt* ('Time' – Orenburg, 1906–18), which circulated in Central Asia and Siberia, as well as in Eastern Russia, *Shura* ('Council' – Orenburg, 1908–18, a supplement to *Vaqt*), *Din ve Ma'ishat* ('Faith and Life' – Orenburg, 1906–17) and *Bayan ul-Haqq* ('Explanation of the Truth' – Kazan, 1906–14).

The main Tatar-language papers of today published in the Tatar ASSR include *Sotsialistik Tatarstan* ('Socialist Tatarstan' – first appeared in 1918) and *Tatarstan jashlere* ('Tatar Youth' – first appeared in 1920); in the Bashkir ASSR, *Kyzyl Tang* ('Red Dawn' – first appeared in 1918). In the Tatar ASSR newspapers are also published in Russian and there are regional (*rajonnyje*) papers in Chuvash and Udmurt. Amongst the main journals and other periodicals published in Tatar are *Tatarstan kommunisty* ('Communist of Tataria' – first appeared in 1920), *Jalkyn* ('Flame', a paper for Young Pioneers – first appeared in 1924, originally under a different title) and *Azat khatyn* ('Free Woman' – first appeared in 1926).

Books and pamphlets are published in Tatar (e.g. 131 titles in 1976; of these, 11 were specialized textbooks on technical and scientific subjects).

Number of books and pamphlets published in Tatar in selected years

	1913	1940	1965	1979
No. of titles	340	329	230	200
Print run	1,671,000	4,922,000	3,365,000	2,664,000

In 1913 more than twice as many titles were published in Tatar as in Uzbek, Kazakh and Azerbaidzhani together (37, 40 and 91 titles respectively). The print runs of the Tatar books were also much greater. In 1979 the number of titles published in Tatar was considerably less than in 1913; it stood in seventh place amongst the languages of the Muslims of the USSR, coming after Uzbek (1,058 titles), Azerbaidzhani (843), Kazakh (720), Kirghiz (467), Tadzhik (306) and Turkmen (282).

Scripts and alphabets

Until 1905	Arabic script, Arabic alphabet
1906–20	Arabic script, modified alphabet
1921–9	Arabic script, further minor modifications
1927	Latin script, first alphabet
1927–39	Latin script, second alphabet
1939	Cyrillic script

Further improvements are considered necessary, particularly in order to make possible the differentiation between guttural *k* and *g* and velar *k* and *g*.

5 RELIGION

The great majority of Tatars are Sunni Muslims (Hanafi school); a comparatively small number were converted to Christianity during the sixteenth to eighteenth centuries, but many of these returned to Islam in the late nineteenth and early twentieth centuries (see Krjashens: p. 431).

The Volga Tatars, along with the Bashkirs and Chuvash, were the first Muslims to come under Russian rule and have thus been exposed to European culture for a much longer period than the other Muslim peoples of the Empire. In many ways they assimilated this influence very thoroughly and were able to integrate into the social fabric of the state. Nevertheless, despite a trend to 'rationalize' and reinterpret Islam in a more liberal way, particularly strong at the turn of this century, the Tatars remained as firmly Muslim as ever. Indeed, they propagated their faith with such vigour in European Russia and Siberia (e.g. amongst the Votiaks, Mordvins and Cheremiss) that the Christian missionaries were seriously perturbed. The Tatars were also extremely active in Central Asia and here the Russians encouraged (for a time at least) their efforts to convert the Kirghiz and Kazakhs. Inspired partly by pan-Islamic and partly by pan-Turkic ideals, they played a crucial part in establishing Islam amongst these nomad peoples.

One of the main reasons why the Tatars were so influential was their high level of education. They were well provided with teachers and schools (their own as well as Russian) and their espousal of the 'new method' syllabus, with its emphasis on such subjects as mathematics, natural sciences and modern languages, was a natural outcome of their progressive ideas. The Tatar medresses enjoyed an excellent reputation and were considered by many to be far superior to those of Samarkand and Bukhara. Amongst the scholars they produced were some highly original thinkers, such as Mardzhani Shihabeddin (1818–89), who had a profound impact on the intellectual climate of Islam in Russia. Furthermore, the Muftiat of Orenburg (seated at Ufa, founded in 1788) was the oldest and most important of the four Muslim Spiritual Assemblies in the Russian Empire; it had jurisdiction over all of Central and Eastern Russia and was thus able to maintain close links with the *ulema* in these areas.

Today the Tatars have lost much of their former pre-eminence. Their medresses were closed after the Revolution and have not been reopened: their *ulema* must now go to the Mir-i Arab and the Ismail al-Bukhari medresses in the Uzbek SSR for training. There is a Spiritual Directorate at Ufa, the language of which is Tatar; it has charge of the Muslims of the European USSR and Siberia (some 8 million Muslims in all), but it is much less conspicuously active than its counterpart in Central Asia and Kazakhstan (e.g. in the forty odd years of its existence it appears to have produced only one publication in Tatar, a 69-page booklet on Muslim worship entitled *Islam ve Islam dini: Islam i musul'manskoje bogosluzhenije*, published in Ufa 1957). The Chairman of the Directorate is Mufti Talgat Tazejev, until recently Imam of the Friday Mosque in Kazan; Tazejev, who received some of his education at the Al-Azhar university in Cairo, was elected to his present post in 1980, at the early age of 32, a marked contrast to his predecessor Mufti Abdulbari Isajev, who was already in his seventies at the time of his election in 1976.

The Tatars are better served with mosques than some of the other Muslim peoples of the Soviet Union. Apart from one in Kazan, there are mosques in most cities that have a large population of Tatars. Some, such as those in Moscow and Leningrad, are old, but others are new (e.g. one was built in Gorkij in 1978).

The Sufi movement used to be very strong in the Volga region (a Sufi sheikh, al-Bakhrazi of Bukhara, is credited with receiving the submission to Islam of Berke, second Khan of the Golden Horde). It was particularly strong in the nineteenth century, when the Tatars' proselytizing activities were at their height. The main Sufi school in the region was the Naqshbandi. A curious offshoot of this was the order known as 'God's Regiment of Vaisov', founded in 1862 by Bahauddin Vaisov (1804–93). The 'Regiment' espoused an amalgam of ideals drawn from various sources, including Tolstoy and the Old Believers (Tolstoy was interested in the order, but utterly perplexed by its aims). The hallmark of the Vaisites was their extreme intolerance of other beliefs and even of other Muslims. The order became quite powerful and in 1917–18 its members proved to be useful allies of the Bolsheviks, on whose side they fought. Their leader, Bahauddin's son, was killed in 1918 and after that the group soon disintegrated.

There is no information available on whether or not the Sufi movement still survives amongst the Tatars today.

6 OUTSIDE THE SOVIET UNION

There are approximately the following numbers of Tatars in:

Bulgaria	6,000
China	8,000
Poland	1,000
Romania	22,000
Turkey	10,000

(*Source*: Baskakov, *Vvedenije v izuchenije tjurkskikh jazykov*, p. 8.)

These figures are only rough estimations; furthermore, they do not distinguish between Tatars of different origins, e.g. Byelorussian/Lithuanian, Crimean and Volga. Those in Poland are mostly of Byelorussian/Lithuanian origin (see p. 86), while those in Turkey are Crimean and Volga Tatars. The figure given for Turkey is surprisingly low: in the second half of the nineteenth century over a million Tatars emigrated there from the Nogai and Kuban' steppes; at the same time there was a great movement of Crimean Tatars to Turkey. From both groups there have been many later migrations, thus the present number of Tatars in Turkey must be several million.

CHUVASH

Own name: *Chuvash*; Russian name: *Chuvashi*.

The majority live in the Chuvash ASSR, but considerable numbers are found in the Bashkir and Tatar ASSRs and in the Kujbyshev and Ul'janovsk districts (*oblasti*) of the RSFSR,

1 HISTORICAL BACKGROUND

The forebears of the Chuvash were Finno-Ugric tribes of the Middle Volga and the Turkic-speaking Bolgars, who established a state on the Rivers Kama and Volga in the sixth to eighth centuries. By the tenth century the Chuvash were apparently already identifiable as a separate people (the Arab traveller Ahmad ibn Faldan mentions the *Suvas* or *Savas*, whom he encountered on the Volga in 922). In the early thirteenth century they were conquered by the Golden Horde. Later, when the Horde began to break up into smaller divisions (during the fifteenth century), they formed part of the Kazan Khanate. After Kazan fell to Ivan the Terrible (1552), the Chuvash passed under Russian rule. They were required to pay *jasak* (tribute). Gradually they found themselves dispossessed of nearly all their land. The poverty-stricken peasants were forced to abandon their traditional occupation of farming and to seek work as bonded labourers in the timber industry or hauling barges up and down the Volga. Some left the region altogether in search of employment, a few of them migrating to Turkey.

Islam began to establish itself in the Volga Bolgar state towards the end of the ninth century. Some of the Chuvash may have become Muslims at this period, but the majority probably adopted Islam while under the sway of the Golden Horde. Under Russian rule intensive efforts were made to Christianize them and, unlike the Tatars, many of the Chuvash were baptized, particularly during the eighteenth and nineteenth centuries. However, here, as elsewhere in the former Kazan Khanate, there was little love for the Russians and the threat of open revolt was never far from the surface. Rebels of any nationality found ready sympathy, including Stenka Razin (1667–71) and Pugachev (1773–5). The unrest continued throughout the nineteenth century. The Emancipation of Serfs (1861) did nothing to improve the lot of the Chuvash peasantry, who had been registered as 'state peasants' since the early eighteenth century. The drive towards the conversion of the Chuvash to Christianity proceeded hand in hand with a policy of Russification. Nevertheless, there was some interest in the Chuvash language. The first grammar of the language (in the Cyrillic script, as Chuvash had no written form at this stage) appeared in 1769 and it was soon followed by translations of the scriptures and other religious texts into Chuvash. The Faculty of Oriental Languages at Kazan University (founded in 1804) pioneered research in the language and a number of works on the subject appeared in the nineteenth and early twentieth centuries, including V. P. Vishnevskij's grammar and dictionary (published in 1836). There was some instruction in Chuvash in the local schools towards the end of the nineteenth century and in 1868 the first Chuvash secondary school was opened in Simbirsk (today known as Ul'janovsk). This was converted into a seminary in 1875, but continued to be of influence in the cultural and intellectual life of the Chuvash, providing as it did a degree of higher education in the vernacular.

There were a number of anti-government uprisings in the early twentieth century, the most serious being that of the summer of 1913 in the Jadrin district. Soviet power was established in Cheboksary in March 1917 and by May 1918 it had spread throughout Chuvashia. During the Civil War there was fighting here between the various opposing factions (Red and White armies, Interventionists and nationalists), but the Bolsheviks finally gained control in 1920.

On 24 June 1920 the Chuvash Autonomous Province was created within the RSFSR; in 1925 it was transformed into the Chuvash ASSR (still within the RSFSR).

Chuvash ASSR (Chavash Avtonomilljo Sovetla Sotsializmla Respubliki), also known as *Chuvashia*

Situated on the Middle Volga, mainly on the right bank; it is bordered to the north and north-west by the Mari ASSR, to the east by the Tatar ASSR, to the south-west by the Mordvinian ASSR (all of which are part of the RSFSR). *Area*: 18,300 sq. km. *Capital*: Cheboksary (population in 1979: 308,000). The Republic has 9 towns and 6 settlements. *Population* (1979): 1,298,611. Average density of population per sq. km (1979): 70.7.

Chief resources: forests covering one-third of its territory; deposits of limestone, oil shale and peat.

Industries include: metal-working (engineering), timber and chemical industries; wood-working (e.g. furniture making), food (alcoholic drinks, confectionery, meat, etc.) and other light industries.

Agriculture: grain farming (rye and wheat) and the cultivation of fodder crops, potatoes, hemp and hops; stockbreeding, particularly of cattle for meat and dairy produce; pigs are also raised.

2 NUMBER AND DISTRIBUTION

Number of Chuvash

1926	1959	1970	1979
1,117,419	1,469,766	1,694,351	1,751,366

Regional distribution of Chuvash

	1926	1959	1970	1979
Chuvash ASSR	667,695 (59.8%)	770,351 (52.4%)	856,246 (50.5%)	887,738 (50.7%)
Tatar ASSR	127,330 (11.4%)	143,552 (9.8%)	153,496 (9.1%)	147,088 (8.4%)
Bashkir ASSR	84,886 (7.6%)	109,970 (7.5%)	126,638 (7.5%)	122,344 (7.0%)
RSFSR*	234,902 (21.0%)	412,345 (28.1%)	500,648 (29.5%)	532,677 (30.4%)
Elsewhere in USSR	2,606 (0.2%)	33,548 (2.3%)	57,323 (3.4%)	61,519 (3.5%)

*Not including the Chuvash, Tatar and Bashkir ASSRs, which are listed separately above.

Percentage of Chuvash in relation to total population of individual republics

	1926	*1959*	*1970*	*1979*
Chuvash ASSR	74.7	70.2	70.0	68.4
Tatar ASSR	4.9	5.0	4.9	4.3
Bashkir ASSR	3.2	3.3	3.3	3.2

Urban/rural distribution of Chuvash in the RSFSR

	1926	*1970*
Urban	15,941 (1.4%)	452,604 (27.6%)
Rural	1,098,872 (98.6%)	1,184,424 (72.4%)

Ethnic composition of the Chuvash ASSR

	1926	*1959*	*1970*	*1979*
Total population	894,390	1,097,859	1,223,675	1,298,611
Chuvash	667,695 (74.7%)	770,351 (70.2%)	856,246 (70.0%)	887,738 (68.4%)
Tatars	22,635 (2.5%)	31,357 (2.9%)	36,217 (3.0%)	37,573 (2.9%)
Russians	178,890 (20.0%)	263,692 (24.0%)	299,241 (24.5%)	338,150 (26.0%)
Others	25,170 (2.8%)	32,459 (2.9%)	31,971 (2.6%)	35,150 (2.7%)

Urban/rural distribution in the Chuvash ASSR in 1970

	Urban	*Rural*
Total population	436,494	787,181
Chuvash	193,636 (44.4%)	662,610 (84.2%)
Tatars	9,697 (2.2%)	26,520 (3.4%)
Russians	217,502 (49.8%)	81,739 (10.4%)
Others	15,659 (3.6%)	16,312 (2.1%)

3 STATUS

The Chuvash enjoy full Soviet citizenship. They are found in all occupations and in all income brackets, but the majority are engaged in such work as farming, hop-growing and apiculture. Their standard of housing is comparable to that of other national groups in the Soviet Union. The women go out to work, as elsewhere in the Soviet Union.

Literacy

In 1926	In 1970
32.2%	Over 99%

In 1926, 322,274 Chuvash were literate in their own language (89.6% of the total literate Chuvash population).

Level of education per 1,000 Chuvash living in the RSFSR of 10 years of age and above

	1959	1970
Primary		
Total	316	323
Men	373	360
Women	277	296
Higher and secondary (complete and incomplete)		
Total	332	424
Men	414	494
Women	278	374
Higher only		
Total	8	17
Men	14	25
Women	5	11

4 LANGUAGE

The national language is Chuvash. It belongs to the Bolgar group (*Fundamenta* and Baskakov classification).

Chuvash possesses a number of dialects, which fall into two main divisions: the lower (*anatri*) and the higher (*virjal*). The former are found in the area to the south of the confluence of the Kama and Volga Rivers, the latter to the north, in the more mountainous regions along the Volga. One of the main differences between them is the use of *u* in the lower (*anatri*) group in place of *o* in the upper (*virjal*) group (cf. lower: *pus*; upper: *pos* – head).

Chuvash, being unlike any other modern Turkic language, occupies a very isolated position amongst them. It shows affinities with the language of the Volga Bolgars (from whom the Chuvash are thought to be partly descended), but it also has a large fund of loan-words (Slav and Finno-Ugric, amongst others) and features that seem to link it with the Mongol and Tungusic languages. Some scholars have doubted whether it should in fact be classed as a Turkic language, but it is now generally accepted as such, though it still remains something of an enigma.

Russian is generally used for administrative, judicial and other official proceedings, but in theory Chuvash can be used if necessary.

Percentage of Chuvash claiming Chuvash as their mother tongue

	1926	1959	1970	1979
Total	98.7	90.8	86.9	81.7
In urban areas	82.2	71.2	68.0	n.a.
In rural areas	99.0	95.6	94.7	n.a.

Percentage of Chuvash with good knowledge of Russian

	1926	1959	1970	1979
As mother tongue	1.1	9.0	13.0	18.1
As second language	n.a.	n.a.	58.4	64.8

In 1958 Chuvash was the medium of instruction in grades 1–7 (incomplete secondary) in the national schools in the RSFSR (probably only in the Chuvash ASSR); in 1972, only in pre-school and in grades 1–4 (primary +1); in 1972 it was taught as an individual, optional subject in Russian-medium schools in grades 1–10 (Silver, p. 33). More recent information is not available. There is a Chuvash State University (founded in 1967) in Cheboksary, but tuition there is apparently entirely in Russian. There are also specialized Institutes of Agriculture and Pedagogy.

In the Chuvash ASSR there are radio and television broadcasts in Chuvash, as well as in Russian.

Newspapers are published in Chuvash, Russian and Tatar; newspapers in Chuvash are also published in the Bashkir and Tatar ASSRs. The main Chuvash-language publications in the Chuvash ASSR include the paper *Kommunizm jalave* ('The Banner of Communism' – first appeared in 1918) and *Pioner sassi* ('Young Pioneer's Call' – first appeared in 1931). There was no Chuvash press before the 1917 Revolution.

Books and pamphlets are published in Chuvash (e.g. 67 titles in 1976; of these, 7 were specialized textbooks on technical and scientific subjects).

Number of books and pamphlets published in Chuvash in selected years

	1913	1940	1965	1979
No. of titles	56	125	132	86
Print run	93,000	1,024,000	862,000	821,000

Scripts and alphabets

Chuvash is the only Turkic language of the Soviet Union for which the Cyrillic script has always been used. Before the advent of the Russians there were no written works in Chuvash. In the second half of the eighteenth century, Russian missionaries began trying to devise an alphabet that was suitable for representing Chuvash. The quest was continued under Soviet rule, but the task is not an easy one and there is as yet no satisfactory solution. The most complete of the alphabets was the one created by I. Ja. Jakovlev (himself a Chuvash, educated in the famous Faculty of Oriental Languages at Kazan University), but it was only the first of his three attempts and was only used for a very short period (1871–2).

1769–1820	Cyrillic script, first alphabet
1820–66	Cyrillic script, second alphabet
1866–71	Cyrillic script, third alphabet
1871–2	Cyrillic script, fourth alphabet
1872–3	Cyrillic script, fifth alphabet
1873–1933	Cyrillic script, sixth alphabet
1933–8	Cyrillic script, seventh alphabet
1938	Cyrillic script, eighth alphabet

5 RELIGION

Some of the Chuvash are Orthodox Christians, others are Sunni Muslims. No information is available on the ratio of the one group to the other. Many of the Chuvash who were converted to Christianity when they came under Russian rule, reverted to Islam during the nineteenth century; after the Manifesto of 17 April 1905, allowing freedom of worship, yet more began openly to practise Islam. The Chuvash Muslims come under the spiritual jurisdiction of the Directorate of the European USSR and Siberia (Ufa).

BASHKIRS

Own name: *Bashkurt*; Russian name: *Bashkiry*.

The majority live in the Bashkir ASSR, but increasing numbers are to be found in the Tatar ASSR and neighbouring regions of the RSFSR.

1 HISTORICAL BACKGROUND

The Bashkirs represent an intermingling of Finno-Ugric tribes of the South Urals and Turkic tribes such as the Kipchak, Kazakhs, Volga Bolgars, Kara-Katais, Bala-Katais, Kilairs, etc. By the ninth to tenth centuries they were already settled in the area they occupy today, between the Volga, Kama, Tobol and Ural Rivers. They were mostly nomadic cattlebreeders and hunters. They were also skilled in collecting honey from wild bees (honey and wax were important trade commodities) and in the mining and working of iron ore and copper. In the early thirteenth century they were conquered by the Golden Horde. They were under the immediate rule of Dzhuchi's son Sheiban (Batu, another of Dzhuchi's sons, had inherited the overall command of the Golden Horde on the death of their father; Dzhuchi had in turn received this western part of the Mongol Empire as patrimony from his father, Genghiz Khan). After the dissolution of the Golden Horde during the fifteenth century, the Bashkirs found themselves divided between its various legatees: those in the north came under the Kazan Khanate, in the north-east under the White (Siberian) Horde, in the south (the majority) under the Nogai Horde. Ivan the Terrible conquered the Tatar states of the Volga in the mid-sixteenth century, after which the Bashkirs, too, came under Russian rule. A garrison was established at Ufa (the present capital of the Bashkir ASSR) in 1574; it became a town in 1586 and developed into an important administrative centre. Several other towns and forts were soon built in the region, such as Samara (now Kujbyshev) and Orenburg.

The Bashkirs were required to pay *jasak* (tribute) to the Russians, as well as many other taxes. As in Chuvashia, their lands were expropriated and the population was soon disastrously impoverished. There were several uprisings in the seventeenth century, but none achieved any lasting success. As the mining industry developed in the eighteenth century, conditions continued to deteriorate for the Bashkirs. The great mineral wealth of the country attracted Russian speculators, who united with the State to cheat the Bashkirs of their remaining possessions. Dispossessed of their lands, many of the peasants were forced to work in the mines and factories virtually as slave labour. The unrest of the previous century continued, with many major outbreaks of violence occurring. The Pugachev rebellion (1773) also received strong support from the Bashkirs, who fought for him under their own leader, Salavat Yulai (Yulajev). He was defeated in 1774 and this Bashkir uprising, as the others, was ruthlessly crushed.

The Bashkirs began to adopt Islam as early as the tenth century, long before the advent of the Golden Horde. Under Russian rule, they were subjected to enforced conversion to Christianity. However, many of them retained their allegiance to Islam and in 1788 Catherine the Great permitted the establishment of the Orenburg Mohammedan Spiritual Assembly in Ufa, which had jurisdiction over both religious matters and such peripheral religious-civil matters as the registration of births and deaths, etc. The Assembly was under the direction of a mufti. Another eighteenth-century development was the lifting of *jasak* in 1754, but in its stead the Bashkirs became liable for military service.

The nineteenth century was markedly more peaceful than the preceding centuries, though the influx of Russian settlers into Bashkiria after the Emancipation of Serfs (1861) further undermined the position of the indigenous population. The industrial development of the region was also of little benefit to them, since their chief involvement in it was to provide a cheap source of labour. Educational facilities in Bashkir were non-existent, intellectual activity almost equally so. Exceptional was the work of Muhammed Salim

Umitbaj (Umitbajev), who translated Pushkin's 'Fountain of Bakh-chisaray' into Bashkir and wrote a little in Bashkir himself. A couple of primers appeared in the early twentieth century, but these meagre works only emphasize the underdeveloped state of literary Bashkir then, particularly in comparison with Chuvash and, even more strikingly, Tatar.

At the time of the 1917 Revolution there was a strong Muslim-dominated nationalist movement in Bashkiria. During the Civil War there were attempts to create an autonomous state. In their efforts to achieve this, some of the Bashkir leaders supported the Soviet side, some the White. The region constantly changed hands: Soviets gained control of Ufa in October 1917, Bashkir autonomy was proclaimed in Orenburg in December, Czech Interventionists and the White Army (Dutov and Kolchak) took Ufa in July 1918, the Red Army briefly regained Ufa and Orenburg at the beginning of 1919, Kolchak again took the region in March 1919 and remained in control till June, when the Red Army (led by Frunze) finally recaptured Ufa. Meanwhile the Bashkir troops had already gone over to the Soviet side in February 1919 and on 23 March, the Bashkir ASSR was created, the first autonomous republic within the RSFSR.

Bashkir ASSR (Bashkort Avtonomijaly Sovet Sotsialistik Respublikasy), also known as Bashkiria or Bashkortostan

Situated in the south Ural mountains; it is bordered to the west by the Tatar and Udmurt ASSRs (all three ASSRs within the RSFSR). *Area*: 143,600 sq. km. *Capital*: Ufa (population in 1979: 969,000). The Republic has 17 towns and 39 settlements. *Population* (1979): 3,844,280. Average density of population per sq. km (1979): 26.8.

Chief resources: major reserves of oil and natural gas; deposits of brown coal, salt, iron ore and non-ferrous ores, including copper; rich agricultural land and forests covering nearly one half of its territory.

Industries include: oil extraction and refining (one of the most important in the USSR), production of natural gas, machine-building, iron and steel, copper, power, chemical and petrochemical industries; food, wood-working, production of building materials and other light industries.

Agriculture: grain farming (wheat, rye and oats) and the culti-vation of fruit, vegetables, potatoes and other industrial crops;

stockbreeding of cattle (for meat and dairy produce), sheep (meat and wool), horses (for which Bashkiria has traditionally been famous) and pigs; apiculture (another traditional occupation); forestry.

2 NUMBER AND DISTRIBUTION

Number of Bashkir

	1926	1959	1970	1979
	713,693	989,040	1,239,681	1,371,452

Regional distribution of Bashkir

	1926	1959	1970	1979
Bashkir ASSR	625,845	737,711	892,248	935,880
	(87.7%)	(74.6%)	(72.0%)	(68.2%)
RSFSR (not incl. Bash. ASSR)	86,521	216,090	288,665	355,114
	(12.1%)	(21.8%)	(23.3%)	(25.9%)
Elsewhere in USSR	1,327	35,239	58,768	80,458
	(0.2%)	(3.6%)	(4.7%)	(5.9%)

Urban/rural distribution of Bashkirs in the RSFSR

	1926	1970
Urban	14,127	288,017
	(2.0%)	(24.4%)
Rural	698,239	892,896
	(98.0%)	(75.6%)

Ethnic composition of the Bashkir ASSR

	1926	1959	1970	1979
Total population	2,665,346	3,340,267	3,818,075	3,844,280
Bashkirs	625,845	737,711	892,248	935,880
	(23.5%)	(22.1%)	(23.4%)	(24.3%)
Tatars	461,871	768,566	944,507	940,446
	(17.3%)	(23.0%)	(24.7%)	(24.5%)
Mishars*	135,960	—	—	—
	(5.1%)			

	1926	*1959*	*1970*	*1979*
Teptjars*	23,290 (0.9%)	—	—	—
Chuvash	84,886 (3.2%)	109,970 (3.3%)	126,638 (3.3%)	122,344 (3.2%)
Russians	1,064,707 (39.9%)	1,416,805 (42.4%)	1,546,304 (40.5%)	1,547,893 (40.3%)
Ukrainians	76,710 (2.9%)	83,594 (2.5%)	76,005 (2.0%)	75,571 (2.0%)
Others	192,077 (7.2%)	223,621 (6.7%)	232,373 (6.1%)	222,146 (5.7%)

*No longer listed separately; grouped with the Tatars now.

Urban/rural distribution in the Bashkir ASSR in 1970

	Urban	*Rural*
Total population	1,839,163	1,978,912
Bashkirs	175,950 (9.6%)	716,298 (36.2%)
Tatars	408,769 (22.2%)	535,738 (27.1%)
Chuvash	31,043 (1.7%)	95,595 (4.8%)
Russians	1,100,003 (59.8%)	446,301 (22.6%)
Ukrainians	49,680 (2.7%)	26,325 (1.3%)
Others	73,718 (4.0%)	158,655 (8.0%)

3 STATUS

The Bashkirs enjoy full Soviet citizenship. They are found in all occupations and in all income brackets; many are engaged in farming and stockbreeding; in the forest regions the main occupations are hunting, apiculture and working in the timber industry; a large number of Bashkirs are also employed in the republic's other industries (oil, mining, etc.). Their standard of housing is comparable to that of other national groups in the Soviet Union. The women go out to work, as elsewhere in the Soviet Union.

Literacy

In 1926	In 1970
24.3%	Over 99%

In 1926, 69,269 Bashkir were literate in their own language (40.0%
of the total literate Bashkir population).

**Level of education per 1,000 Bashkirs living in the RSFSR of 10 years of age and
above**

	1959	*1970*
Primary		
Total	329	357
Men	388	395
Women	287	326
Higher and secondary (complete and incomplete)		
Total	273	369
Men	324	410
Women	237	335
Higher only		
Total	6	15
Men	9	20
Women	4	11

4 LANGUAGE

The national language is Bashkir. It belongs to the West Turkic
group (*Fundamenta* classification); it can also be classed as belonging to the Kipchak group, Kipchak-Bolgar sub-group (Baskakov).

Bashkir possesses a number of dialects, which fall into two main
divisions: the 'mountain' group, consisting of the north-east and
south-east dialects, and the 'steppe' group, consisting of the
south-west and some of the central dialects. The differences between the two groups are lexical, phonetic and morphological. The
literary language is based on the eastern and southern dialects. The
vocabulary of Bashkir differs considerably from that of Tatar,
though in other respects the two languages are close. Especially
noteworthy is its fund of archaic Turkic roots, many of which are
no longer found in other modern Turkic languages. It has a number
of Mongol loan-words, but comparatively few Arabic and Persian.
Almost all the Russian borrowings are in the form of calques.

Russian is generally used for administration, judicial and other official proceedings, but in theory Bashkir can be used if necessary.

Percentage of Bashkirs claiming Bashkir as their mother tongue

	1926	1959	1970	1979
Total	53.8	61.9	66.2	67.0
In urban areas	72.8	73.3	73.2	n.a.
In rural areas	53.4	59.1	63.6	n.a.

Bashkir is one of the very few languages in the Soviet Union which is better preserved in urban areas than in rural.

Percentage of Bashkirs with good knowledge of Russian

	1926	1959	1970	1979
As mother tongue	0.1	2.7	4.5	7.1
As second language	n.a.	n.a.	53.3	64.9

Percentage of Bashkirs with good knowledge of a language other than Bashkir or Russian (in most cases Tatar)

	1926	1970	1979
As mother tongue	52.4	29.3	25.9
As second language	n.a.	1.3	1.3

In 1958 Bashkir was the medium of instruction in grades 1–10 (complete secondary) in the Bashkir ASSR; this was still the case in 1972; in 1972 it was also taught as an individual, optional subject in Russian-medium schools in grades 1–10 (Silver, p. 33). More recent information is not available. In the Bashkir State University (founded in 1957) there are departments of Bashkir and Tatar philology, but tuition in the university appears to be in Russian. There are some specialized institutes, e.g. of Agriculture, Medicine, Oil and Pedagogy, in the Bashkir ASSR.

In the Bashkir ASSR there are radio and television broadcasts in Bashkir, as well as in Russian.

Newspapers are published in Bashkir, as well as in Russian, Chuvash, Mari, Tatar and Udmurt. Amongst the major Bashkir-language newspapers is *Sovet Bashkortostany* ('Soviet Bashkiria' – first appeared in 1918); the main Tatar paper in the Bashkir ASSR is *Kyzyl tang* ('Red Dawn' – first appeared in 1918). Periodicals and journals are also published in Bashkir, e.g. *Bashkortostan uky-tyusyhy* ('Teacher of Bashkiria' – first appeared in 1920) and *Bash-kortostan kyzy* ('Daughter of Bashkiria' – first appeared in 1968). There was no Bashkir-language press before 1917.

Books and pamphlets are published in Bashkir (e.g. 81 titles in 1976; of these, 3 were specialized textbooks on technical and scientific subjects).

Number of books and pamphlets published in Bashkir in selected years

	1913	1940	1965	1979
No. of titles	—	187	131	120
Print run	—	914,000	1,082,000	946,000

Scripts and alphabets

Bashkir cannot really be said to have become a literary language until the Soviet period. Up till the nineteenth century the so-called 'Turki' language was used; it was replaced by Tatar towards the end of that century. Both these languages were written in the Arabic script. There were some efforts by Russian scholars to devise a Slavonic or Latin-based alphabet for Bashkir, but they met with little success.

1923–30   Arabic script, modified alphabet
1930–9   Latin script, first alphabet
1939–40   Latin script, second alphabet
1940   Cyrillic script

The present alphabet is considered to contain some fundamental shortcomings, particularly in the reconciling of the norms of Russian orthography (in loan-words) with those of Bashkir. Further changes are not excluded.

5 RELIGION

The majority of Bashkirs are Sunni Muslims (Hanafi school). Some were converted to Christianity during the sixteenth to eighteenth centuries, but many of these reverted to Islam in the nineteenth century. In 1788 Catherine the Great founded the 'Orenburg Mohammedan Spiritual Assembly', the first administrative organ of the Muslims in the Russian Empire; originally based in Orenburg, it was soon moved to Ufa. A Muslim administration is still centred in Ufa, the Spiritual Directorate of the European USSR and Siberia. Its present Chairman is Mufti Talgat Tazejev, who was elected in 1980 at the age of 32. He was formerly Imam of the Friday Mosque in Kazan. His Deputy Chairman is Faiz ur-Rahman Sattar. There is a Friday Mosque open for worship in Ufa.

Byelorussian and Lithuanian Tatars

The Tatars of Byelorussia and Lithuania (and Poland) are descendants of settlers from the Golden Horde who came to the Grand Duchy of Lithuania between the early fourteenth and early sixteenth centuries. When the community was at its height in the sixteenth century, it numbered some 200,000. The Grand Duke Vitaut/Witold (1392–1430), during whose reign the main influx of Tatars occurred, granted them the right to intermarry with the indigenous Slav population and to have the children of such unions brought up in the faith of the father. Many of the Tatars had by this time accepted Islam and this measure enabled them to preserve their religion in their new environment. Close contacts with the Slavs, however, soon led to the loss of their language: by the mid-sixteenth century the majority no longer knew any language except Byelorussian or Polish. They integrated well into the Slav community and for centuries it was only their religion that set them apart from the rest of society.

The first Tatar settlements were in the Byelorussian cities of Hrodno, Minsk, Troki (today Trakai: the birthplace of Haji Girey, first Khan of the Crimean Horde; see p. 87) and Vilna. Until the beginning of the sixteenth century, the Tatars of the Grand Duchy were very closely involved with the internal politics of the Golden Horde and there was considerable movement between the Volga and the lands of the Grand Duke. Toktamysh, a prince of the White Horde who gained the throne of the Golden Horde towards the end of the fourteenth century, was one of several Tatar leaders to appeal to the Grand Duchy for assistance. The Tatars in their turn were valuable allies in the Grand Duchy's struggle against the Teutonic Knights and other enemies. During this period the Tatars who had settled in the Grand Duchy were able to receive religious literature and teachers from the Islamic world. Trade and diplo-

matic contacts were also well developed: thus, though part of a
Christian, mainly Slav state, this north-western colony of Tatars
was by no means isolated from the main body of their ethnic group.
Later, as the Grand Duchy's interests became more circumscribed
and particularly after its union with Poland (in 1569), the position
changed; the Tatars' links with the outside world were drastically
reduced and they were forced to find the means of ensuring the
continuity of their religious life within their own community. They
began to translate the Qur'an and other religious texts into Byelorussian and Polish, writing these languages, however, in the Arabic
script, since this represented for them an indispensable symbol of
Islam.

   In the seventeenth century the Tatars were subjected to a certain
amount of persecution on the part of the Catholic Polish authorities
(the same treatment was meted out to the Orthodox Christian
community, for it was not so much an anti-Islamic as an anti-non-
conformist movement). The situation improved in the eighteenth
century, but by this time some of the Tatars had emigrated to
Ottoman lands. At the end of the eighteenth century much of
Poland came under Russian rule (a result of the three Partitions of
Poland: 1772, 1793, 1795), including the territory of the former
Grand Duchy, where the Tatars had originally settled. The change
of government did not particularly affect the Tatars, but the emigrations which had started under Polish rule continued and the
Tatar community steadily diminished. In the mid-nineteenth century the Tatars began to attract the interest of a number of eminent
orientalists (e.g. A. Muchlinskij, Professor of Turkish at St Petersburg University) and this in turn stimulated the Tatars' own curios-
ity about their culture and history.

   In the aftermath of the First World War and the Russian Revolution, Western Byelorussia (incorporating such cities as Vilna and
Hrodno) became Polish, whilst Eastern Byelorussia (incorporating
Minsk) became part of the Soviet Union, forming the Byelorussian
SSR. The Tatars, like the Byelorussians, were thus split between
two states. Nothing more has been heard of those who remained
under Soviet rule, but those who found themselves as part of the
Polish state were extremely active in their efforts to arouse the
self-awareness of their people and to make known their history to
others. Mainly due to their work, these descendants of the Tatars
of the Grand Duchy became known as 'Polish Tatars'. With the
encouragement of the Polish government, Tatar students went to

study in the Al-Azhar university in Cairo and contacts were developed with several Muslim states; when the Tatars of Poland appealed for financial aid to build a mosque in Warsaw, King Abdulaziz of Saudi Arabia was one of the first to respond. By this time, however, Europe was on the brink of war: Poland was invaded by German and Soviet troops and when the war was over, all the Tatar intellectuals had disappeared, dead or deported. The international border had been re-drawn and most of Western Byelorussia united with the Eastern, Soviet half, to become part of the Lithuanian SSR (e.g. the city of Vilna/Vilnius) and the Byelorussian SSR (e.g. the city of Hrodno). The majority of the Grand Duchy Tatars were now divided between two Soviet republics. Nothing is known of their present position, but since their religion was the only thing that set them apart from the local Slav population and it is unlikely that this has survived in a sufficiently strong form to continue to distinguish them, this ancient community of Grand Duchy Tatars may now be said to be dead. In Poland, on the other hand, a few mosques are still found in Bialystok, the province contiguous with the Byelorussian SSR, and in Warsaw there is a revival of scholarly interest in the Tatar community. The size of the community is not known, but it does not appear to amount to more than a few scattered villages.

Crimean Tatars

Own names: *Krym-tatar, Krym-türk*; Russian name: *Krymskije tatary*; formerly also *Tavricheskije ('Tauride') tatary*.

The Crimean Tatars are at present still in exile in Central Asia, Kazakhstan and the Urals, though small groups have already succeeded in returning to the Crimea and re-settling in their former homeland.

1 HISTORICAL BACKGROUND

The Crimean Tatars are the descendants of the Crimean Horde, an offshoot of the Golden Horde, and Anatolian Turks who began to settle in the Crimea in the thirteenth century. An independent Crimean state was created by Haji Girey, a prince from the Tatars of the Grand Duchy of Lithuania (see p. 85), in the early fifteenth century. In 1475 it was conquered by Sultan Mehmet II and it remained under Ottoman domination until 1774 (the Treaty of Küchük Kainarji), when it had a brief period of independence before being incorporated into the Russian Empire in 1783. Russian rule in the Crimea began with generous promises and assurances, but the reality soon turned out to be very different. Repressive policies, Russification measures and heavy Slav immigration into the area caused many Tatars to emigrate to Turkey. There were a number of attempts to move the Tatars who remained away from the coastal region, culminating in the major deportation and resettlement drive of 1855, prompted by the outbreak of the Crimean War. This was accompanied by a policy of encouraging yet more Tatars to emigrate, with the result that after a century of Russian rule the Tatar population of the Crimea had fallen from some 500,000 to 200,000 or less.

Despite the unfavourable circumstances, there was an awakening of Crimean Tatar national awareness towards the end of the nineteenth century. The principal inspiration for this was the energetic educational reformer and ardent Pan-Turkist Ismail Gaspirali (also known as Gasprinsky). Much of his work was done outside the Crimea, mostly amongst the Volga Tatars, but he had considerable influence amongst his own people and was responsible for the modernization of the curriculum in many of their schools. There were also strong links with Ottoman Turkey during this period, for there was a large Crimean Tatar colony in Istanbul formed partly of émigrés and partly of students who had gone there for higher education. Strong nationalist and separatist trends began to emerge and in 1917 there were attempts to set up an independent state. Turkey recognized the Crimea's independence in 1918, soon followed by Germany. The Bolsheviks almost immediately overthrew the nationalist government, but were themselves then dislodged by the German troops who occupied the area in April 1918. After the evacuation of the Germans, the Soviets briefly regained control, only to be ousted by the White Army in June 1919 (first under General Denikin, then Baron Wrangel). Towards the end of 1920 the Red Army yet again took the Crimea and this time was able to hold it. The Crimean ASSR was created within the RSFSR in October 1921. Consequently many Crimean Tatar leaders were forced to take refuge abroad, e.g. in Turkey and Romania.

During the Second World War the Crimea was occupied by German troops from 1941–4. Throughout the war Crimean Tatar men fought in the Red Army and in the Soviet resistance movement, many of them receiving awards for outstanding valour. The civilian population bore the brunt of savage German reprisals for this, yet the overwhelming majority certainly remained loyal to the Soviet government (Nekrich, pp. 13–35, amongst others, documents this period very thoroughly). Nevertheless, on 18 May 1944, a few weeks after the liberation of the Crimea, its entire Tatar population, not excluding soldiers still serving in the Red Army, was deported for alleged treason. Without warning, they were crowded into cattle trucks and sent to Central Asia and Kazakhstan, Siberia and the Urals. The penal conditions they had to endure during and in the early years after deportation caused many of them to die, particularly amongst the women, the children and the old. The exact extent of the losses is not known, but it is estimated that some 46 per cent of the 194,111 Tatars dispatched in 1944 perished.

   In 1967 the Crimean Tatars were officially 'rehabilitated' and in theory free to return home (cf. the Chechens, Ingush, Karachais, Balkars). In practice, however, those who attempted to return were deported, some many times over, as they persisted in their efforts to be allowed to settle again in their native land. Typical of the tenacity with which they are fighting for this right of return is the case of Musa Mahmut, who burned himself to death in 1975 in protest at the threat of renewed exile. Soviet sources now no longer refer to the Crimean Tatars as traitors, but say instead that they 'migrated' to Central Asia: the myth that they moved of their own volition and have happily 'taken root' (*ukorenilis'*) in their new settlements is constantly reiterated, yet the Tatars remain singularly unimpressed by it and continue to agitate openly, but peacefully and using only legal channels, to be allowed to live where their forebears lived for over 500 years. The situation in the Crimea, though, is not promising. The Crimean ASSR was disbanded in 1946 and incorporated into the Ukrainian SSR; a large influx of Ukrainians and Russians and the determined eradication of all trace of the Tatar past (e.g. place-names have been changed, mosques destroyed, cemeteries ploughed up) have served to Slavonicize the region and an early return of the Crimean Tatars to the Crimea is at present hard to envisage.

2 NUMBER AND DISTRIBUTION

Today there are probably some 500,000 Crimean Tatars, the majority of them living in Tashkent and Samarkand.

Ethnic composition of the Crimean ASSR in 1926

Total population	713,823
Tatars*	179,094 (25.1%)
Germans	43,631 (6.1%)
Jews	39,921 (5.6%)
Greeks	16,036 (2.2%)
Crimean Jews (Krymchaks)	6,000 (0.8%)
Karaims	4,213 (0.6%)
Russians	301,398 (42.2%)
Ukrainians	77,405 (10.8%)
Others (including non-Soviet citizens)	46,125 (6.5%)

*The Crimean Tatars have never been listed separately in Soviet censuses, but nearly all the Tatars listed here would probably have been Crimean Tatars.

Urban/rural distribution of Tatars in the Crimean ASSR in 1926

Urban	38,738	(21.6%)
Rural	140,356	(78.4%)

3 STATUS

In theory, now that they have been 'rehabilitated' they enjoy the same rights and responsibilities as other Soviet citizens, but as their desire to return to the Crimea brings them into constant conflict with the authorities they are in fact often subject to harassment, intimidation and even outright persecution. Official policy towards them in this matter is extraordinary, since there is nothing that can in any way be construed as illegal (i.e. contrary to Soviet law) or unreasonable in the Crimean Tatars' wish to return to the region in which they have been settled for over 500 years.

The majority are employed as labourers and factory workers; in the early period of their exile it was extremely difficult for them to find suitable employment, hence their concentration in areas of unskilled labour. Their standard of housing is now comparable to that of other national groups in the Soviet Union, though in the first years of exile it was very much sub-standard. The women go out to work, as elsewhere in the Soviet Union.

Literacy

In the early twentieth century the Crimean Tatars had a remarkably high standard of literacy, as did the Volga Tatars (in 1926 the Tatars as a group had a literacy rate of 33.6 per cent compared with the 45.1 per cent of the Russians). During the 1930s and 1940s they lost virtually all their intellectuals; furthermore, the education of the young was seriously disrupted due to a chronic lack of facilities and also to the language barrier, for though Crimean Tatar is a Turkic language, it is by no means identical with Uzbek, Kazakh or Kirghiz and the children in particular had great problems of comprehension. In recent years the younger generation has made a determined effort to improve their position and many of them now have higher education (see p. 64).

4 LANGUAGE

The national language is Crimean Tatar (not to be confused with Volga Tatar; see p. 64). It belongs to the West Turkic group (*Fundamenta* classification); it can also be classed as belonging to the Kipchak group, Kipchak-Polovtsian sub-group (Baskakov).

It contains a number of dialects, including a southern group which is close to Turkish (in the *Fundamenta* this group is called *Krimosmanisch* and is classified, separately from the other dialects, as South Turkic). The modern literary language is based on the central dialects. The vocabulary is basically Kipchak, but shows a strong Turkish influence. It also contains a large number of Arabic and Persian loan-words. New terms are formed by juxtaposing existing words to form new combinations, adding derivational suffixes to loan-words (e.g. *planlashtyrmak*, 'to plan') and by direct borrowings from Russian. In recent years Uzbek and Kazakh have caused some linguistic interference in the language of the generation that has grown up in exile, but for the most part the literary language seems to have been well preserved.

Russian and to a lesser extent Uzbek, Kazakh, etc. (depending on the place of exile) are used for all administrative, judicial and other official proceedings.

There are no schools in which Crimean Tatar is the medium of instruction, but there are some national (Uzbek-medium) schools in the Uzbek SSR in which Crimean Tatar is taught as an individual, optional subject in the first few grades. There is a Department of Crimean Tatar at the Nizami Pedagogical Institute, Samarkand. Most Crimean Tatars in the Uzbek SSR attend Uzbek-medium schools and a number have enrolled at the State Universities in Tashkent and Samarkand in the Uzbek section. There are a few broadcasts in Crimean Tatar in the Uzbek SSR; they are mostly devoted to folk music.

The Crimean Tatar press came into being in 1883 with the appearance of Gaspirali (Gasprinsky)'s *Terdzhuman-Perevodchik* ('Interpreter'). This was the first major Turkic-language paper of the Russian Empire (and at times the only one). Published in Bahchisaray, it achieved an impressive circulation, penetrating as far afield as Siberia, Central Asia and Transcaucasia. Its language was a synthesis of Ottoman Turkish and Crimean Tatar and was more or less comprehensible in all parts of the Turkic world. Through its pages, Gaspirali propagated his ideals of reform, co-operation with the West and pan-Turkic unity. The influence of this paper, which survived until 1918, was enormous, but it was not the only pre-Revolutionary Crimean Tatar periodical: after 1905 a number of others appeared, though none survived for long. In the first decades of the Soviet period there were several Crimean Tatar publications, but these all ceased after the deportation of the Crimean Tatars in 1944. The Crimean Tatar press was revived in 1957 when *Lenin bajragy* ('Lenin's Banner') began to appear. It was followed by the journal *Jildiz* ('Star') in 1976.

No books or pamphlets were published in Crimean Tatar between 1944 and 1965 (it is probable that none were published after 1938, when the Cyrillic script was introduced, but it has not been possible to obtain information relating to this period). A single title was published in 1965, but since then the number of publications has been steadily growing (e.g. 15 titles were published in 1976; none of these were specialized textbooks on technical and scientific subjects).

Scripts and alphabets

Until mid-nineteenth century	Arabic script, Arabic alphabet
1883–1917	Arabic script, minor reforms
1918–28	Arabic script, reformed alphabet
1929–38	Latin script
1938	Cyrillic script

5 RELIGION

The Crimean Tatars are Sunni Muslims (Hanafi school). If they were back in the Crimea, they would come under the spiritual jurisdiction of the Directorate of the European USSR and Siberia (Ufa). At present, in so far as they are under any spiritual jurisdiction, it is that of the Directorate of Central Asia and Kazakhstan (Tashkent).

6 OUTSIDE THE SOVIET UNION

There are approximately 5,000,000 Crimean Tatars in Turkey (*Soviet Asian Ethnic Frontiers*, p. 14). The largest single community is centred round Eskishehir. There are also Crimean Tatar colonies in Poland and Romania (numbers not available).

Siberian Tatars

As previously explained (see p. 55), the term 'Tatar' has been applied to people of various origins. In Siberia it was used for two groups: (a) for Turkic-speaking tribes who at an early date (sixth to eighth centuries AD?) assimilated the indigenous Kettic and Samoyedic tribes of southern Siberia; (b) for descendants of the White Horde, a branch of the Mongol army that invaded the territory of present-day Russia in the early thirteenth century and established the state known as the Golden Horde. Formerly 'Tatars' of both groups were identified by their location. Now those of the first group are considered to form separate nationalities:

Abakan Tatars
Chulym Tatars
Meletski Tatars   }   now known as Khakass; see p. 405
Minusinsk Tatars
Yenisei Tatars

Kuznetski Tatars
Kondoma Tatars   }   now known as Shors; see p. 417
Mrass Tatars

Chernevyje Tatars   now known as Altais; see p. 411

This group are for the most part Shamanists with a thin veneer of Christianity.

The second group are now listed simply as 'Tatars'; they include:

Baraba Tatars

Irtysh Tatars

Tara Tatars

Tobol Tatars

Tomsk Tatars

Tura Tatars

Tjumen' Tatars

Jalutorovski Tatars

This group are mostly Sunni Muslims (Hanafi school).

    The Mongol invasion of Russia in the early thirteenth century was led by sons of Dzhuchi, the eldest son of Genghiz Khan. The overall commander of the campaign and first khan of the conquered territory in the west was Batu. His state came to be known as the Golden Horde. His brother Orda was given charge of the lands to the north, known as the White Horde (*Ak Orda*). The two dynastic lines were subsequently often rivals for supreme mastery of the whole of the western state. Amongst the most famous of the khans of the White Horde were Toktamysh and Sheiban, forebears of the first Uzbek dynasty (see p. 270). The bulk of the population in the White Horde, as in the Golden Horde, was composed of Turkic Kipchak tribes. They were a mobile, volatile force, ever ready to change allegiances and to migrate vast distances. As the core of the Golden-White Horde began to weaken during the fifteenth century, Siberia first came under the sway of Abul Khayr, founder of the

Uzbek Khanate, then of the Nogai Horde and finally achieved independence towards the end of the fifteenth century under Ibak Khan. His territory, the Siberian Khanate, extended from the Baraba Steppe (just north of present-day Kazakhstan) virtually to the Arctic Ocean, and had its capital at Chingi-Tura (today Tjumen'). The Siberian khans exacted tribute from the local tribes of the Taiga and whenever possible attempted to encroach on the lands of the Volga Khanates. In 1555, however, three years after the fall of Kazan to Ivan the Terrible, the Siberian Khanate itself was forced to pay tribute to Muscovy. Khan Kuchum, who assumed control of the Khanate in the 1560s, abrogated this agreement and instead took the offensive against the Russians. He was finally defeated in 1581, when his capital Sibir' (later to give its name to the whole region) was taken by Yermak's Cossack troops. Russian strongholds were established in Tjumen' in 1586, Tobol'sk in 1587, Tara in 1594, Tomsk in 1604.

The Siberian Tatars were originally known by their tribal names (e.g. Shibani, the clan of Sheiban). During the sixteenth century, when they started paying tribute to the Russians, they were called *jasakly*, 'tribute-people'. As newcomers from Bukhara, the Volga region and other parts of European Russia began to settle in the area, the earlier wave of arrivals became known as *top jerli khalk* 'local people'. Their chief occupations were hunting and trapping (e.g. of sable, fox, marten, squirrel, ermine, bears and wolves), horse-breeding and porterage. The last was of particular importance, for the rivers of Siberia were major trade routes, leading east via the Irtysh and Ishim to Bukhara and west across the Urals and along the Volga to Muscovy. During the nineteenth century many of the Tatars sought work in the cities, in the saw-mills and tanneries, but the traditional occupations of hunting and trapping were still maintained and even today are quite widespread, though now most Tatars live on collective farms, often in mixed Russian-Tatar communities.

By religion the Siberian Tatars are Sunni Muslims (Hanafi school). The first contacts with Islam were provided by traders from the east. The Golden Horde was converted to Islam in the early fourteenth century and the leaders of the White Horde (e.g. Toktamysh) also accepted Islam at about this period. The conversion of the broad mass of the Tatars in Siberia probably took much longer, however, and was not complete until the beginning of the nineteenth century (cf. the Kazakhs and Kirghiz). After the Russian conquest of Siberia, Christian missionaries were active in the region, but the descendants of the White Horde, unlike the other Turkic peoples of Siberia (e.g. the Yakuts, Khakass and Shors) were relatively unresponsive to Christianity. Their ultimate acceptance of Islam was no doubt helped by prolonged contacts with Muslim peoples such as the Bukharans who settled amongst them in the late fifteenth to early sixteenth centuries and the Volga Tatars who moved to Siberia from the late eighteenth century onwards; there was a particularly strong influx of Kazan Tatars into the Tobol'sk region in the nineteenth century. The religious centre of the Siberian Muslims was at Jembajevo in the Tjumen' region, but each village had its own mosque and cemetery. The chief religious authority was the *akhun*. Today Siberia comes under the jurisdiction of the Spiritual Directorate based in Ufa (see p. 35). It is known that there is a Friday Mosque in Omsk, but it is not known how many other mosques are open for worship in this region.

The languages of the Siberian Tatars are dialects of Kipchak and are thus related to Volga Tatar. The steady influx of Volga Tatars into the area has had some influence on the indigenous forms of Tatar. None of these forms are written and Volga Tatar is used as the literary language and the medium of instruction in schools. Research on the Siberian Tatar dialects was begun by the eminent Turkologist V. V. Radlov in the second half of the nineteenth century (though as early as the eighteenth century, visiting scholars had noted down words and made comments upon the structure of these languages, e.g. G. F. Miller, 1733–4, D. G. Messerschmidt, 1719, and I. G. Georgi, 1776–80). In the Soviet period this work has been continued, but the number of native speakers with a fluent knowledge of these languages is diminishing as Volga Tatar and Russian gain ever greater currency.

As mentioned above, the Tatars were formerly identified by their location, and their names are of purely geographic significance. Nevertheless, isolated from one another as they were, individual groups developed particular customs and linguistic features. The two that have received most attention from ethnographers and philologists are the Baraba and the Chulym Tatars.

Baraba Tatars

Own name: *Paraba*; Russian names: *Barabintsy, Barabinskije tatary*.

Their traditional territory is the Baraba Steppe; they were pushed out of their most fertile lands by Russian settlers and now live mostly between the Om' and the Tara, tributaries of the River Irtysh, in the Novosibirsk District (*oblast'*) of the RSFSR. They believe their name to be derived from the word *parma* 'don't go', referring to an incident in the reign of Khan Kuchum (see above), but this is most probably a folk etymology; their name and the name of the Baraba Steppe are almost certainly of non-Turkic origin. Their language shows affinities with, on the one hand, Tatar and Bashkir (Volga-Ural group) and on the other, Kazakh and Altai. In 1926 there were 7,528 Barabas. In the 1960s (*Jazyki narodov SSSR II)* there were thought to be about 8,000.

Chulym Tatars/Kiueriks/Ketsiks

Own name: *Kjuerik* ('Squirrel': cf. the tendency of Turkic peoples to assume animal names, e.g. *It*, 'dog', *Bars*, 'leopard'); Russian name: *Chulymskije tatary*.

The Chulym Tatars live on the banks of the River Chulym, in the vicinity of the town Achinsk. When the Russians conquered western Siberia in the sixteenth century, some of the Baraba Tatars moved eastwards and amalgamated with other Turkic-speaking peoples already settled in the region of the Chulym. Their legends and songs still commemorate their separate origin. As a group, the Chulym Tatars were heavily Russified at an early date. By the end of the last century few spoke their own language. The group now includes a small community of Ketsiks, another Turkic-speaking tribe who in the late nineteenth century were settled to the south of Mariinsk.

The Chulym Tatars now form part of the Khakass national group (see p. 405).

Tara Tatars

Own name: *Tarlyk*; Russian name: *Tarskije tatary*.

The Tara Tatars live on the banks of the River Irtysh near the mouth of the Tara. There are four main tribal groupings. They appear to have been settled here since the seventeenth century. In 1926 there were 11,517 of them (*Narody Sibiri*); it is not known how many there are today. Included amongst them are a group of Bukharans.

Tobol Tatars

The Tobol Tatars live on the River Tobol and on the Irtysh between Tara and Tobol'sk. There are amongst them a number of Bukharans and Volga Tatars, particularly in the vicinity of Tobol'sk and further west. In 1926 there were 32,102 Tobol Tatars (*Narody Sibiri*).

Tjumen' Tatars

The Tjumen' Tatars live near the towns of Tjumen' and Jaluto-rovsk. They include a number of Bukharans and Volga Tatars. In 1926 there were 22,636 of them (*Narody Sibiri*).

There are still large numbers of Tatars in Siberia (over half a million) but it is not possible to tell from the census what percentage of these are 'indigenous' Tatars and what percentage more recent settlers. In all probability the local groups are being rapidly assimilated by the incoming Russians and Volga Tatars.

Bukharans of Siberia

Own names: *Bukharlyk, Pukharlyk*; Russian name: *Bukhartsy (sibirskije)*.

The Siberian Bukharans live in the Tjumen' and northern Omsk Districts (*oblasti*) of the RSFSR. They settled in this region during the fifteenth to sixteenth centuries. At this period there was an active trade link between Siberia and Bukhara: products of the north such as furs, skins and fish were sent via the Ishim and the Irtysh to Central Asia in return for such commodities as tea, paper, dried fruits, ironmongery and luxury goods (e.g. mirrors and ornaments). The Bukharans controlled most of this trade and a number of them moved to the Tjumen'–Tobol'sk–Omsk area, where

they settled along the Rivers Tobol, Tara and Irtysh. They intermingled with the local Tatar population, who, like themselves, were
Sunni Muslims (Hanafi school). Eventually they adopted the Tatar
language and became virtually indistinguishable from them. As a
result of this, the relevant estimates in the 1926 Soviet Census, in
which the Siberian Bukharans are listed separately, are highly in-
accurate. They are now listed with the Tatars.

1926 Census figures

Population: 12,012
Urban dwellers: 6.2 per cent
Percentage claiming own language (presumably Tatar) as their
    mother tongue: 97.9.
Percentage claiming Russian as their mother tongue: 0.4.
Literacy: 3,139 (26.1 per cent); of these, 1,719 (54.8 per cent of the
    total literate population) were literate in their own language.

Kundurs

Own names: *Kara-Agach, Karagach*; Russian name: *Kundurskije
tatary*.

The Kundurs are a branch of the Nogais, descendants of the Karagach tribe who split off from the main body of the Nogais in the
thirteenth century and eventually settled on the Lower Volga. Their
chief occupations were agriculture and market gardening. They
have now been largely assimilated by the neighbouring Astrakhan
Tatars, but in their language they still preserve some typically Nogai
features (phonetic, morphological and lexical), which set it apart
from that of the surrounding peoples.

By religion they are Shi'i Muslims.

The Kundurs have never been separately listed in the census and
there is no information available on the present size of the
community.

Mishars/Meshcherjaks

Own name: *Mishar*; Russian names: *Mishari, Meshcherjaki*.

The Mishars are a group of Volga Tatars, descendants of settlers from the Golden Horde who set up minor states to the west of the Volga during the period of the Horde's disintegration (fourteenth to fifteenth centuries). They intermingled with Finno-Ugric tribes, such as the Mordvinians and Meshchers, and their language now incorporates many Finno-Ugric loans. Russian has also had an important influence on their vocabulary. They tend to live in small groups of villages or settlements in the Tatar, Chuvash and Mordvinian ASSRs, as well as in the neighbouring regions of the RSFSR. Some live in the Bashkir ASSR; these are called *Meshcherjaki*. The Mishars were listed separately in the 1926 Census, but thereafter grouped with the Tatars. The Meshcherjaks were listed first with the Mishars, then they, too, were combined with the Tatars.

Both Mishars and Meshcherjaks are Sunni Muslims.

1926 Census figures

Population: 242,640; of these, 135,960 (56.0 per cent) lived in the Bashkir ASSR.
Urban dwellers: 1.5 per cent.
Percentage claiming own language as their mother tongue: 81.2.
Percentage claiming Russian as their mother tongue: 15.8.
Literacy: 62,164 (25.6 per cent); of these, 52,171 (83.9 per cent of the total literate population) were literate in their own language.

Nagaibaks

Own name: *Nogaibak*; Russian name: *Nagaibaki*.

The Nagaibaks are descendants of the Nogais who were converted to Christianity in the eighteenth century. Many of them eventually reverted to Islam and intermarried with the local Tatars and Bashkirs. The majority now live in the Bashkir ASSR. They speak a dialect of Tatar. In the early Soviet period an attempt was made to develop this into a separate literary language: an alphabet, based on the Cyrillic script, was created for it in 1923 and some publications appeared, including a periodical in 1934. Since the war, however, nothing has been published in Nagaibak and it seems unlikely that it will be revived as a literary medium. It still survives as a spoken language, though; Baskakov estimates the numbers of 'Ural Tatars and Nagaibaks' at about 110,000 (*Vvedenije* . . ., p. 287).

No more accurate information on the size of the community is available, since the Nagaibaks are no longer listed separately in the census but are instead grouped with the Tatars or Bashkirs.

1926 Census figures

Population: 11,219.
Urban dwellers: 0.7 per cent.
Percentage claiming own language as their mother tongue: 95.2.
Percentage claiming Russian as their mother tongue: 0.3.
Literacy: 4,715 (42.0 per cent); of these, 1,360 (28.8 per cent of the
   total literate population) were literate in their own language.

Teptjars

Own name: *Tipter*; Russian name: *Teptjari*.

The name 'Teptjar' is derived from Persian/Turkish *defter* 'register, account book' and refers to the records kept by the Bashkirs of the quit-rent paid to them for the use of their lands by a variety of immigrants who arrived from the central Volga region after the fall of the Kazan Khanate (1552). Thus it is not an ethnic designation, but one of purely administrative significance. Amongst the Teptjars there were a number of Turkic peoples, mainly Tatars, but also some Chuvash, along with other groups such as Maris, Mordvinians and Udmurts. The Teptjars were considerably influenced by the Bashkirs and some of those who were not already Muslims were converted to Islam after settling in Bashkiria. When the 1926 census was taken, great efforts were made to distinguish between the different types of Teptjars (i.e. Teptjars of Tatar origin, Teptjars of Chuvash origin etc.) and only those who identified themselves simply as 'Teptjars', not as 'Teptjar-Chuvash', for example, were listed in this way. In subsequent censuses this distinction was not made and all the Teptjars were classed as either Tatars or Bashkirs (apart from those who had already been listed in 1926 as Chuvash, Mari, etc.).

1926 Census figures

Population: 27,387; of these, 23,290 (85.0 per cent) lived in the
   Bashkir ASSR.

Urban dwellers: 0.8 per cent.
Percentage claiming own language as their mother tongue: 2.3.
Number claiming Russian as their mother tongue: 15 people.
Literacy: 6,659 (24.3 per cent).

Miscellaneous

Finno-Ugric Peoples

In the first half of the nineteenth century 'thousands of baptized
Tatars, Tshuvashes, and other aborigines became followers of Mohammed' (Bobrovnikoff in *The Moslem World*, vol. I, p. 6). The
'aborigines' included the Cheremiss (now known as Maris), the
Mordvinians and the Votiaks (now known as Udmurts). These
three peoples today have titular ASSRs in the Volga region. It is
not known how many of them are Muslims, for even the
nineteenth-century estimates vary widely. The following approximate figures are given by Bobrovnikoff for 1897: of the 500,000
Votiaks (Udmurts), 10 per cent were heathen or under the influence
of Islam; the influence of Islam was still growing; in addition, there
were Votiaks who had become Muslim in the eighteenth and early
nineteenth centuries and these called themselves 'Tatar', having
completely adopted Tatar customs; of the 450,000 Cheremiss
(Maris), about a quarter were heathen and greatly inclined towards
Islam; the influence of Islam was growing and many were already
converted and Tatarized; amongst the Mordvinians there was as yet
little Islamic influence.

It is not known what proportion of the Maris, Mordvinians and
Udmurts are now Muslim, but as there are large numbers of Tatars
in all three republics and many Maris, Mordvinians and Udmurts
also live in the Bashkir, Chuvash and Tatar ASSRs, it is probable
that the Muslim element has remained strong amongst them.
According to the 1979 Census, their numbers and regional distribution was as follows:

	Maris	Mordvinians	Udmurts
Total population	621,961	1,191,765	713,696
Number in titular republic	306,627	338,898	479,702
Number in Bashkir ASSR	106,793	—	—
Number in Chuvash ASSR	—	20,276	—
Number in Tatar ASSR	16,842	29,905	29,330
Number of Tatars in Mari ASSR	40,917		
in Mordvinian ASSR	45,765		
in Udmurt ASSR	99,141		

Besermen

Own name: *Besermen*; Russian name: *Besermjane*.

The Besermen live in the Udmurt ASSR, in the Glazovskij and Balezinskij Regions (*rajony*). They speak Udmurt with an admixture of Tatar. They are now regarded as a sub-group of the Udmurts (and included with them in the census returns), but it is thought that they are probably of Turkic origin, possibly descendants of the Volga Bolgars. Plano Carpini, the papal envoy who travelled through this region on his way to Mongolia in 1246, speaks of 'Besermen' as being subjects of the Tatars. The Russian Chronicles also refer to 'Besermen', but it is not certain that the term always indicates the group who are today known by this name, since it is a common derivation from *Musulman*. The modern Besermen are indeed Muslims (Sunni), but it is quite possible that the term had a much wider application before it became a specific ethnonym.

According to the 1926 Census, there were 10,035 Besermen, 9,962 (99.3 per cent) of whom claimed their own language as mother tongue; 16.6 per cent were literate, over half of them in their own language. It is not known how many Besermen there are today.

Altais

Some of the peoples now known as Altais are Muslims, in particular the Teleut group, of whom there were just under 2,000 in 1926. See p. 435. The other Altais are Christians or Shamanists.

Slavs

During the nineteenth century there was a significant expansion of
Islam amongst peoples who had previously been converted to
Christianity (e.g. the Chuvash). Some Slavs were also affected by
this movement; no figures are available, but the number was almost
certainly very small and probably restricted to isolated communities
where there was a strong Tatar presence. Bartol'd is amongst those
who mentions the conversion of Slavs to Islam (*Mir islama, I*:
p. 594).

Tatars Re-converted

The Tatars in general did not accept Christianity, but small numbers
were baptized at various periods. They were known as *Krjasheny*
(see p. 431). During the nineteenth century many of these reverted
to Islam.

4
Transcaucasia and Northern Caucasus

AZERBAIDZHANIS

Own names: *Azerbaidzhanly*, *Azeri* (the latter is now considered archaic); Russian names: *Azerbajdzhantsy*, *Aderbidzhantsy*.

The Azerbaidzhanis were formerly also known as (Azerbaidzhani) Turks or Tatars. They were listed simply as 'Turks' in the first Soviet census. The majority live in the Azerbaidzhan SSR and the Nakhichevan ASSR within the Azerbaidzhan SSR (though not in the Nagorno-Karabakh Autonomous Province, where the population is predominantly Armenian); there are also substantial communities in the neighbouring Armenian and Georgian SSRs and in the Daghestan ASSR, and smaller groups in Central Asia and Kazakhstan.

I HISTORICAL BACKGROUND

The territory of present-day Azerbaidzhan has been inhabited since paleolithic times. It was ruled by the Medes (from the late eighth century BC) and the Persians of the Achaemenian dynasty (from the mid-sixth century BC). When Alexander overthrew the Persian Empire in the early fourth century BC (*c.* 328), a vassal of his, Atropates ('Protected by Fire'), founded an independent state in this region. The term *Azerbaidzhan* is ultimately derived from 'Atropates' (via Arabic and Turkish). The Sasanids gained control of much of the area in the early third century AD and it remained part of their empire until the Arab conquest of Transcaucasia in the mid-seventh century. Azerbaidzhan was predominantly Iranian-speaking at this period and the Arabs who settled there were gradually assimilated by the indigenous population. The next wave of immigrants, however, imposed themselves on the area to such an extent that they radically changed its character. These were Turkic tribes from Mongolia. They began to appear in the eastern regions of Azerbaidzhan as early as the seventh century, but the main influx took place during the eleventh century with the Seljuk-Oghuz invasions. Under their influence the whole region became Turkish-speaking.

The early thirteenth century brought the Mongols. Two wings of the Mongol Empire, the Golden Horde (Ulus of Dzhuchi) to the north and the Il-Khans (Ulus of Hulagu) to the south, laid claim to Azerbaidzhan, but neither was able to establish lasting supremacy over it. In 1386 Timur, ruler of Transoxiana (Ulus of Chagatai), conquered southern Azerbaidzhan, while in the north power passed into the hands of the Shirvanshahs of Derbent. After Timur's death in 1405, the Shirvanshah Ibrahim briefly managed to unite the two halves, but they were soon divided again, the north remaining under the Shirvanshahs and the south falling to Oghuz-Turkmen tribes, first the Kara-koyunlu, then the Ak-koyunlu. In 1502 Shah Ismail, founder of the Safavid dynasty, took Tabriz, the Ak-koyunlu capital. He established Azerbaidzhan as the nucleus of his future empire, despite the fact that the Safavids were Persian speakers from Ardebil, and by religion Shi'i Muslims, whilst the Azerbaidzhanis were by this time Turkish speakers and Sunni. The Ottomans frequently invaded and occupied Tabriz between 1514 and 1603, but Shah Abbas restored Persian domination of the area.

Trade contacts between Azerbaidzhan and Muscovy had begun in the late fifteenth century, with Baku providing an important outlet on the Volga-Caspian route. For Peter the Great, Azerbaidzhan represented the gateway to the Near East and he was eager to establish a firm hold on the Caspian coast. In 1722–3 Russian troops occupied Derbent and Baku; the Ottomans retaliated by immediately taking possession of the rest of Transcaucasia (including Tbilisi, Yerevan, Nakhichevan and Gandzha). Persia, meanwhile, was in a state of collapse, ravaged by an invasion of Afghan tribes. The Treaty of Constantinople (1724) confirmed the Ottoman control of Georgia, Shirvan and Azerbaidzhan and the Russian control of the Caspian region. In 1735, however, Russia relinquished this to Nadir Shah, who had succeeded in re-establishing order in Persia. Nadir Shah also drove the Ottomans out of Azerbaidzhan and brought the area back under Persian rule. After Nadir Shah's death in 1747, central control weakened and the dominant powers were local khanates such as those of Baku, Gandzha, Karabakh, Kuba, Nakhichevan, Shemakha and Talysh. Towards the end of the eighteenth century Persia (under Agha Mohammed) tried to reassert its hold over Azerbaidzhan and in response Russia (under Catherine II) again occupied Baku and Derbent, as well as Gandzha, Kuba and Shemakha. The struggle continued for a few years longer, during which period Russia steadily strengthened its position in Transcaucasia. By 1805 several of the khanates had become Russian protectorates, amongst them Karabagh and Shirvan. The ensuing war between Persia and Russia ended in 1813, confirming the territorial gains of the latter. They were ratified by the Treaty of Turkmanchai (1828) which also gave Russia possession of the khanates of Nakhichevan and Yerevan and finally established the River Araks as the boundary between the two states, thereby dividing Azerbaidzhan (as it had been under the Mongols, over 600 years previously) between the northern and the southern empires. Once under Russian rule, the khanates were abolished and direct military control established.

During the second half of the nineteenth century there was a ferment of intellectual activity in Russian Azerbaidzhan. Educational reformers, scholars and writers were eager to develop Azeri Turkish culture by absorbing the best of the European tradition and producing something of their own, unique but relevant to the modern world. Questions such as the Latinization of the alphabet were discussed; new schools were opened and a vernacular theatre and opera were created (the first opera written in Azerbaidzhani was *Leila and Madzhnun* in 1908). The first proper Azerbaidzhani newspaper, *Ekinchi* ('Sower'), was published by Hasan Melikzade Zerdabi (Melikov) in 1875. Mirza Fath Ali Ahunzade (Akhundov) laid the foundations for modern Azerbaidzhani literature. Literary circles (*medzhlis*) appeared in a number of cities, fostering interest in new genres and encouraging new talents.

At the same time industry was being developed in Azerbaidzhan, particularly the oil-fields of Baku. By the end of the nineteenth century, Baku had become one of the largest industrial centres of the Russian Empire and it was for a while the chief producer of oil in the world. The building of the Transcaucasian railway (1883), linking Baku with the Black Sea coast and central Russia, was an essential part of this process. It also aided the development of a multi-national urban proletariat, which was to prove fertile ground for revolutionary ideas. The first general strike in Transcaucasia

Key

1 Georgians

2 Chechens

3 Ingush

4 Avars (including: **A** Andis, **B** Botlikhs, **C** Godoberins, **D** Chamals,
     E Bagulals, **F** Tindis, **G** Karatais, **H** Akhvakhs, **I** Didois,
     J Khvarshins, **K** Khunzals, **L** Archins)

5 Laks

6 Darghins	16 Abazins	25 Azerbaidzhanis
7 Tabasarans	17 Russians	26 Kumyks
8 Lezghis	18 Ukrainians	27 Nogais
9 Aguls	19 Ossetians	28 Karachais
10 Rutuls	20 Kurds	29 Balkars
11 Tsakhurs	21 Tats and	30 Kalmyks
12 Adygeis	Mountain Jews	31 Uninhabited
13 Kabardians	22 Talysh	territory
14 Cherkess	23 Armenians	
15 Abkhazians	24 Greeks	

Scale

0   50   100

km

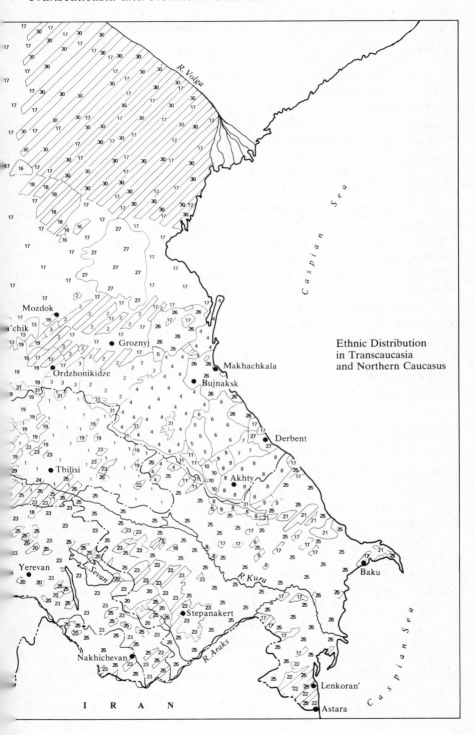

Ethnic Distribution
in Transcaucasia
and Northern Caucasus

started in Baku in July 1903. One of those in charge of revolutionary activities in Baku during this period was Stalin, who referred to the city as the revolutionary centre of the Caucasus. Meanwhile the nationalists were also organizing themselves. The Musavat ('Equality') party was founded in 1911. In 1918, after the Bolsheviks had seized power in Baku and other regions of eastern Azerbaidzhan, the nationalist, for the most part under the leadership of the Musavatists, set up an independent state with Yelizavetpol' (formerly Gandzha, today Kirovabad) in western Azerbaidzhan as its capital. Baku was taken by the British (under General Dunsterville) in August 1918; almost immediately they were forced to withdraw by Ottoman-German forces (under Nuri Pasha), who occupied the city in September; after the Armistice in November, however, they evacuated the area and Baku was reoccupied by the British (under General Thomson) and other Allied troops (French and American). They recognized the Musavatist government as the official representatives of Azerbaidzhan, but in November 1919 they, too, evacuated Baku and the Bolsheviks (under Kirov, Mikojan and Ordzhonikidze) took the city on 28 April 1920; the Azerbaidzhan SSR was proclaimed that same day. Two years later the Azerbaidzhan, Armenian and Georgian SSRs were united to form the Transcaucasian Soviet Federal Socialist Republic. On 5 December 1936 the three again became separate Union republics.

Azerbaidzhan SSR (Azerbajdzhan Sovet Sosialist Respublikasy), also known as *Azerbaidzhan*

Situated in the Eastern Caucasus, on the shores of the Caspian Sea; it is bordered to the south by Iran, to the north by the Daghestan ASSR (within the RSFSR), to the north-west by the Georgian SSR, to the south-west by the Armenian SSR and Turkey. *Area*: 86,600 sq. km. *Capital*: Baku (population in 1979: 1,022,000). The Republic has 60 towns and 125 settlements. *Population* (1979): 6,026,515. Average density of population per sq. km (1979): 69.6.

Chief resources: major reserves of oil and natural gas; deposits of alunite, pyrites, iron ores, lead, zinc, copper, molybdenum, cobalt, mercury, gold, silver, several rare metals, common salt, and building materials (e.g. marl, marble and limestone).

Industries include: oil extraction and refining, production of natural gas, machine-building (mainly connected with the oil industry), mining, power, chemical and petrochemical, aluminium, iron and steel industries; manufacturing (e.g. textile, knitwear, footwear), production of building materials, silk, tobacco, wine-making, food (based on the processing of local produce, e.g. canning of fish) and other light industries; carpet-making (hand and factory), for which the region has long been famous.

Agriculture: irrigation is needed in most areas; the most important crops are cotton (one of the major cotton-producing areas of the USSR), tobacco and grapes; tea, hard and soft fruits, nuts, olives and saffron are also cultivated; stockbreeding is extremely important, particularly of sheep; cattle, riding horses and pigs are also raised (167,000 head of pigs in 1979); fishing (including the production of caviar) and sericulture are other major branches of the economy.

The Azerbaidzhan SSR contains one Autonomous Republic, the Nakhichevan, and one Autonomous Province, the Nagorno-Karabakh. Statistics for the Azerbaidzhan SSR automatically include these two areas unless otherwise stated.

Nakhichevan ASSR

Created on 9 February 1924; although administratively part of the AzSSR, it is situated in the Armenian SSR; to the south and west it is bordered by the River Araks, the international frontier between the USSR and Turkey and Iran. Over 90 per cent of the population of the Nakhichevan ASSR are Azerbaidzhanis. *Area*: 5,500 sq. km. *Capital*: Nakhichevan (population in 1970: 33,000). The Republic has 3 towns and 3 settlements. *Population* (1979): 240,459. Average density of population per sq. km (1979): 43.4.

Chief resources: deposits of salt and various building materials (e.g. marble, gypsum); mineral springs.

Industries include: mining (particularly of salt), cotton-ginning, silk, food (canning, jam-making, alcoholic drinks etc.) and other light industries.

Agriculture: cultivation of cotton, tobacco, grapes and other fruits, wheat; stockbreeding; sericulture.

Nagorno-Karabakh Autonomous Province

Created on 7 July 1923; it is situated in the south-eastern region of the Caucasus. Over 80 per cent of the population are Armenians, 18 per cent are Azerbaidzhanis. *Area*: 4,400 sq. km. *Capital:* Stepanakert (population in 1973: 32,000). The Province has 2 towns

and 7 settlements. *Population* (1979): 162,181. Average density of
population per sq. km (1979): 36.6.

Chief resources: deposits of polymetallic ores and building materials (marble and lime). Industries are connected with the processing of local resources, e.g. silk, wine-making and food
industries.

Agriculture: cultivation of grapes, cotton and grain; stockbreeding of sheep, cattle, horses (for which the region is famous) and
pigs; sericulture; apiculture.

2 NUMBER AND DISTRIBUTION

Number of Azerbaidzhanis

	1926*	1959	1970	1979
	1,706,605	2,939,728	4,379,937	5,477,330

*Listed as Turks.

Age structure of the Azerbaidzhani population in 1970

Age-group	Number	% of total
0–10	1,614,294	36.9
11–15	580,751	13.3
16–19	295,277	6.7
20–29	418,593	9.6
30–39	601,031	13.7
40–49	322,288	7.4
50–59	174,170	4.0
60 and over	292,354	6.7
age unknown	81,179	1.9

Percentage of males/females in relation to total Azerbaidzhani population

	1926*	1970
Men	52.7	50.0
Women	47.3	50.0

*Listed as Turks.

Percentage of married Azerbaidzhanis in specified age-groups

Age-group	16–19	20–29	30–39	40–49	50–59	60 and over
Men						
In 1959	4.3	54.8	94.2	97.3	96.6	89.8
In 1970	1.6	40.8	92.4	96.8	96.3	89.8
Women						
In 1959	27.8	75.5	83.8	67.4	52.1	27.0
In 1970	18.3	73.2	88.8	80.7	57.0	28.8

Regional Distribution of Azerbaidzhanis

	1926	1959	1970	1979
AzSSR	1,437,977 (84.3%)	2,494,381 (84.9%)	3,776,778 (86.2%)	4,708,832 (86.0%)
GeorgSSR	137,921 (8.1%)	153,600 (5.2%)	217,758 (5.0%)	255,678 (4.7%)
ArmSSR	76,870 (4.5%)	107,748 (3.7%)	148,189 (3.4%)	160,841 (2.9%)
DaghASSR	23,428 (1.4%)	38,224 (1.3%)	54,403 (1.2%)	64,514 (1.2%)
Kaz.ASSR/SSR	20 (0.0%)	31,854 (1.1%)	57,699 (1.3%)	73,345 (1.3%)
UzSSR	21,565 (1.3%)	40,511 (1.4%)	38,898 (0.9%)	59,779 (1.1%)
RSFSR (not incl. the Dagh. and Kaz. ASSRs listed separately above)	4,539 (0.3%)	32,720 (1.1%)	41,286 (0.9%)	87,907 (1.6%)
Elsewhere in USSR	4,285 (0.3%)	40,690 (1.4%)	44,926 (1.0%)	66,434 (1.2%)

Percentage of Azerbaidzhanis in relation to total population of individual republics

	1926	1959	1970	1979
AzSSR	63.3	67.5	73.8	78.1
GeorgSSR	5.2	3.8	4.6	5.1
ArmSSR	8.7	6.1	5.9	5.3
DaghASSR	3.0	3.6	3.8	4.0
Kaz.ASSR/SSR	0.0	0.4	0.4	0.5
UzSSR	0.4	0.5	0.3	0.4

Migration of Azerbaidzhanis in 1968–9

Total number of migrants: 55,800.
Percentage who migrated within the AzSSR: 94.5 per cent
Percentage who migrated to the Armenian SSR: 3.0 per cent
Percentage who migrated to the Georgian SSR: 2.5 per cent

Urban/rural distribution of Azerbaidzhanis (in main areas of habitation)

	1926		1970	
	Urban	Rural	Urban	Rural
AzSSR	244,143 (17.0%)	1,193,834 (83.0%)	1,558,788 (41.3%)	2,217,990 (58.7%)
GeorgSSR	6,588 (4.8%)	131,333 (95.2%)	39,669 (18.2%)	178,089 (81.8%)
ArmSSR	5,753 (7.5%)	71,117 (92.5%)	14,590 (9.8%)	133,599 (90.2%)
DaghASSR	8,129 (34.7%)	15,299 (65.3%)	22,318 (41.0%)	32,085 (59.0%)

Ethnic composition of the AzSSR

	1926	1959	1970	1979
Total population	2,270,060	3,697,717	5,117,081	6,026,515
Azerbaidzhanis	1,437,977* (63.3%)	2,494,381 (67.5%)	3,776,778 (73.8%)	4,708,832 (78.1%)
Talysh	77,323 (3.4%)	——†	——†	——†
Kurds	41,193 (1.8%)	1,487 (0.0%)	5,488 (0.1%)	n.a.

	1926	1959	1970	1979
Lezghis	37,263 (1.6%)	98,211 (2.7%)	137,250 (2.7%)	158,057 (2.6%)
Avars	19,104 (0.8%)	17,254 (0.5%)	30,735 (0.6%)	35,991 (0.6%)
Tsakhurs	15,552 (0.7%)	2,876 (0.1%)	6,208 (0.1%)	8,546 (0.1%)
Tatars	9,948 (0.4%)	29,552 (0.8%)	31,787 (0.6%)	31,350 (0.5%)
Armenians	282,004 (12.4%)	442,089 (12.0%)	483,520 (9.4%)	475,486 (7.9%)
Tats	28,443 (1.3%)	5,887 (0.2%)	7,769 (0.2%)	8,848 (0.1%)
Jews	31,325‡ (1.4%)	40,204 (1.1%)	41,288 (0.8%)	35,497 (0.6%)
Russians	220,545 (9.7%)	501,282 (13.6%)	510,059 (10.0%)	475,255 (7.9%)
Ukrainians	18,241 (0.8%)	25,778 (0.7%)	29,160 (0.6%)	26,402 (0.4%)
Others	51,142 (2.3%)	38,716 (1.0%)	57,039 (1.1%)	62,251 (1.0%)

* Listed as Turks.
† No longer listed separately, grouped with the Azerbaidzhanis, though in 1959 it was noted that there were 10,514 Talysh speakers in the AzSSR.
‡ This figure includes 20,578 'Jews', 10,270 'Mountain Jews', 427 'Georgian Jews', 48 'Central Asian Jews' and 2 'Crimean Jews' ; these groups were listed separately in 1926.

Percentage of mixed nationality marriages in the AzSSR

	1959	1970
Total	7.1	7.8
In urban areas	11.8	12.8
In rural areas	2.0	2.0

Growth rate of the AzSSR per 1,000 of the population

1940	1965	1970	1979
14.7	30.2	22.5	18.1

Size of family units (living together) in the AzSSR

	1970	1979
Average size of families	5.1	5.1
Average size of families in urban areas	4.5	4.5
Average size of families in rural areas	5.7	5.8

Percentage of family units of different sizes in relation to total number of families in the AzSSR

No. in family	2	3	4	5	6	7	8	9	10 and over
1970	14.9	15.1	16.0	14.3	13.4	10.2	7.6	4.6	3.9
1979	15.0	14.6	17.3	15.3	12.8	9.2	6.7	4.2	4.9

Urban/rural distribution in the AzSSR in 1970

	Urban	Rural
Total population	2,564,551	2,552,530
Azerbaidzhanis	1,558,788 (60.8%)	2,217,990 (86.9%)
Tatars	31,043 (1.2%)	744 (0.0%)
Armenians	344,577 (13.4%)	138,943 (5.4%)
Jews	40,812 (1.6%)	476 (0.0%)
Russians	470,191 (18.3%)	39,868 (1.6%)
Others	119,140 (4.6%)	154,509 (6.1%)

3 STATUS

The Azerbaidzhanis enjoy full Soviet citizenship. They are found in all occupations and in all income brackets. Their standard of housing is comparable to that of other national groups in the Soviet Union. The women go out to work, as elsewhere in the Soviet Union.

Literacy

In 1926	In 1970
8.1%	Over 99%

In 1926, 133,031 Azerbaidzhanis were literate in their own language (96.2 per cent of the total literate Azerbaidzhani population).

Level of education per 1,000 Azerbaidzhanis living in the AzSSR of 10 years of age and above

	1959	*1970*
Primary		
Total	206	283
Men	214	273
Women	198	292
Higher and secondary (complete and incomplete)		
Total	365	437
Men	467	521
Women	275	357
Higher only		
Total	24	39
Men	36	55
Women	14	23

Number of schools in the AzSSR in 1979/80 (not including special schools, e.g. for the deaf): 4,300
Number of pupils: 1,600,000*
Number of higher educational establishments in the AzSSR in 1979/80: 17
Number of students: 105,200*

*These figures refer to the total number of pupils/students in the AzSSR and therefore include Azerbaidzhanis and non-Azerbaidzhanis alike.

4 LANGUAGE

The national language is Azerbaidzhani. It belongs to the South Turkic group (*Fundamenta* classification); it can also be classed as belonging to the Oghuz group, Oghuz-Seljuk sub-group (Baskakov). The languages it is most closely related to are the Turkish of Turkey and Turkmen; it also shares some features in common with Gagauz, Uzbek, Nogai and Kumyk.

There are four main dialect groups: the eastern branch, including the dialects of Kuba, Baku, Shemakha and Lenkoran'; the western branch, including those of the Kazakh, Gandzha and Karabakh districts and the Airums (see p. 245); the southern branch, including those of Nakhichevan and Yerevan; the northern branch, including that of Nukha. There are also a number of sub-dialects. The Baku and Shemakha dialects provide the basis for the modern literary language. The vocabulary has retained a strong Arabic and Persian influence. The Russian loan-words, which have been entering Azerbaidzhani in increasing numbers in recent years, are often subjected to some phonetic modification, e.g. *revolusija* for *revolutsija* ('revolution').

Azerbaidzhani is used along with Russian for administrative, judicial and other official proceedings.

Percentage of Azerbaidzhanis claiming Azerbaidzhani as their mother tongue

	1926	*1959*	*1970*	*1979*
Total	93.8	97.6	98.2	97.9
In urban areas	98.4	96.4	96.7	n.a.
In rural areas	93.0	98.2	99.2	n.a.

Percentage of Azerbaidzhanis with good knowledge of Russian

	1926	*1959*	*1970*	*1979*
As mother tongue	0.1	1.2	1.3	1.8
As second language	n.a.	n.a.	16.6	29.5

Percentage of speakers claiming Azerbaidzhani as their mother tongue in the AzSSR

1926	*1970*
63.1	73.3 (of these, 99.5% are Azerbaidzhanis)

The majority of schools in the Azerbaidzhan SSR are Azerbaidzhani-medium schools; they provide the full range of schooling (primary, secondary complete and incomplete). In 1958 the following languages were also used as media of instruction in the AzSSR: Russian and probably also Armenian and Lezghi; outside the AzSSR, in 1958 Azerbaidzhani was used as a medium of instruction in the RSFSR (DaghASSR) and possibly also in the Armenian SSR (Lipsett, pp. 185–6). More recent information is not available, other than that both Azerbaidzhani and Russian-medium schools are still known to exist in the AzSSR; also, in the RSFSR there was in 1972 tuition in Azerbaidzhani in grades 1–2 and pre-school, and it was taught as an individual, optional subject in Russian-medium schools in grades 1–8 (Silver, pp. 33–4). The Kirov Azerbaidzhan State University (founded in 1919) in Baku provides instruction in both Azerbaidzhani and Russian. There are also a number of specialized institutes (e.g. of Agriculture, Medicine, Oil and Chemicals, Pedagogy) and a State Conservatoire (founded in 1921). No information is available on the medium of instruction used in these institutes, but in the technical and scientific fields it is almost certainly only Russian, whereas in pedagogy, for example, considerable use is likely to be made of Azerbaidzhani.

In the AzSSR there are radio and television broadcasts in Azerbaidzhani, as well as in Russian and Armenian.

Newspapers and periodicals are published in Azerbaidzhani, as well as in Russian and Armenian. The very first Azerbaidzhani periodical (also the first in any of the languages of the Muslim peoples of the Russian Empire) was *Tiflis Ekhbary* ('Tiflis News'), an Azerbaidzhani (Azeri) edition of *Tiflis vedomosti*, a journal published in Tbilisi in Russian, Georgian and, from 1830–2, Persian. The Azerbaidzhani edition replaced the Persian and ran for one year (1832–3). The first independent Azerbaidzhani publication was Zerdabi's *Ekinchi* ('The Sower'), which was published in Baku from 1875 to 1877. Other publications soon followed, particularly after 1905. Amongst the most notable were *Sharg-i Rus* ('The Russian East' – published in Tbilisi, 1903–5), *Hayat* ('Life' – Baku, 1905–6), *Irshad* ('The Guide' – Baku, 1905–7), *Iqbal* ('Prosperity' – Baku, 1913–15) and the Bolshevik organs *Tekammul* ('The Achievement of Perfection' – Baku, 1906–7) and *Yoldash* ('The Comrade' – Baku, 1907). The main Azerbaidzhani-language newspapers of today include *Kommunist* ('Communist' – first appeared in 1919), *Azerbaidzhan gjandzhlari* ('Azerbaidzhani Youth' – first appeared in 1919), *Azerbaidzhan muallimi* ('Azerbaidzhani Teacher' – first appeared in 1934), *Edebijjat ve inchesenet* ('Literature and Art' – first appeared in 1934), *Azerbaidzhan pioneri* ('Azerbaidzhani Pioneer' – first appeared in 1938) and *Sovet kendi* ('Azerbaidzhani Village' – first appeared in 1953); amongst the main periodicals are *Azerbaidzhan gadyny* ('Azerbaidzhani Woman' – first appeared in 1923), *Azerbaidzhan kommunisti* ('Azerbaidzhani Communist' – first appeared in 1939) and *Ulduz* ('Star' – first appeared in 1967). There are also some technical journals, e.g. *Azerbaidzhan neft teserrufaty* ('The Azerbaidzhan Oil Industry' – first appeared in 1920).

Regional papers in Azerbaidzhani are published in the Armenian and Georgian SSRs and the Daghestan ASSR (in the Derbent region, where there is a high concentration of Azerbaidzhanis).

Books in Azerbaidzhani (Azeri) were first printed in Tabriz in the 1820s. By the second half of the nineteenth century there were printing presses in Baku, Shemakha and Gandzha. In 1913, more books were published in Azerbaidzhani than in any other language of the Muslim peoples of the Russian Empire except Tatar. In 1979 Azerbaidzhani was still in second place, now coming after Uzbek (1,058 titles).

Books and pamphlets are published in Azerbaidzhani in the AzSSR and in other republics in the Soviet Union (e.g. a total of 387 titles in 1976; of these, 107 were specialized textbooks on technical and scientific subjects).

Number of newspapers, journals and other periodicals published in the AzSSR in selected years, with annual circulation

	1965	1979
No. of newspapers	82 (218,000,000)	123 (524,000,000)
In Azerbaidzhani only	56 (141,000,000)	98 (399,000,000)
No. of journals and periodicals	102 (7,600,000)	110 (26,800,000)
In Azerbaidzhani only	67 (6,200,000)	58 (26,100,000)

Number of books and pamphlets published in Azerbaidzhani in selected years throughout the Russian Empire/USSR

	1913	1940	1965	1979
No. of titles	91	622	1,023	843
Print run	112,000	3,968,000	8,524,000	11,183,000

Number of books and pamphlets published in the AzSSR in 1979, with total print run

Total no. of titles	1,301	(13,900,000)
No. of titles in Azerbaidzhani	834	(11,100,000)

Scripts and alphabets

The question of adopting the Latin script in place of the Arabic was first discussed in the nineteenth century by educational reformers such as Ahunzade, but the change was not made until the Soviet period.

Until 1929	Arabic script
1922–33	Latin script, first alphabet
1933–8	Latin script, second alphabet
1938–9	Latin script, third alphabet
1939 (May)	Cyrillic script, first alphabet
1939 (August)	Cyrillic script, second alphabet
1940–51	Cyrillic script, third alphabet
1951–58	Cyrillic script, fourth alphabet
1958	Cyrillic script, fifth alphabet

The great number of alphabets used for Azerbaidzhani during the last fifty years is not quite as confusing as would at first appear, since in most cases the differences between them are very small (usually concerning no more than a single letter). The present alphabet is considered to be reasonably satisfactory, but further improvements are not excluded.

5 RELIGION

Approximately 70 per cent of the Azerbaidzhanis are Shi'i Muslims and 30 per cent are Sunni (Hanafi school). The Spiritual Directorate of Transcaucasia is based in Baku. There have been several changes of leadership recently: in 1978 the Chairman, Sheikh ul-Islam Ali Aga Suleiman, died at the age of 93; he was replaced by Sheikh ul-Islam Mirgazanfar Ibragimov, who also died shortly afterwards; in 1980 the present Chairman was elected, the 31-year-old Sheikh ul-Islam Haji Allashukur Pashajev, formerly Deputy Chairman of the Directorate of Transcaucasia. Pashajev was one of the first graduates of the Tashkent medresse. As is usual in this Directorate, he is a Shi'i Muslim, while the Deputy Chairman is a Sunni, Haji Ismail Ahmedov (elected in 1976). This Directorate has spiritual jurisdiction over the Muslims of Armenia, Azerbaidzhan and Georgia.

In Baku the Shi'is and Sunnis have separate Friday Mosques, the Taza-Pir for the former and the Azhdarbek for the latter. Many of the smaller mosques are used alternately by both communities. There are said to be only sixteen mosques open for worship in the whole of the Azerbaidzhan SSR (*Religion in Communist Lands*, vol. 7, no. 3, p. 152).

It is extremely rare to find Shi'i Muslims who are Sufis. There is, however, nothing to prevent a Shi'i from joining a Sunni order. The Naqshbandi was formerly the most popular *tariqa* in Azerbaidzhan. Nothing is known of its present strength.

6 OUTSIDE THE SOVIET UNION

According to Soviet estimates, there are approximately 4,000,000 Azerbaidzhanis in Iran (just over 40 per cent of the total population of Azerbaidzhanis) and a small number in Iraq (exact figure not known). In *Soviet Asian Ethnic Frontiers* (p. 74) it is estimated that there are 4,625,000 Azerbaidzhanis in Iran.

PEOPLES OF DAGHESTAN

Russian name: *Narody Dagestana*.

In Soviet census reports and other statistical analyses, the peoples of Daghestan are often listed together under this single collective heading. The term includes the following groups: Avars, Darghins, Kumyks, Laks, Lezghis, Nogais, Tabasarans, Tsakhurs, Rutuls and Aguls. When necessary these peoples are, of course, listed separately, but other, smaller groups who used to be listed separately (e.g. in the 1926 Census), are not usually distinguished now. These include: Akhvakhs, Andis, Archins, Bagulals, Botlikhs, Chamals, Didois, Godoberins, Kapuchins, Karatais, Khunzals, Khvarshins and Tindis, all of whom are now included with the Avars; also the Kaitaks and Kubachis, who are now included with the Darghins.

1 HISTORICAL BACKGROUND

Daghestan has been inhabited since prehistoric times. Its mountainous interior (Daghestan means 'Land of Mountains') afforded good protection against marauders, but little in the way of sustenance, since neither climate nor terrain were suited to farming.

Sheep provided the main source of livelihood (and are still an important branch of the economy today). In the summer they were driven up into the high mountain pastures, in winter kept in more sheltered valleys lower down. Until recent times these areas were almost totally inaccessible; even neighbouring valleys were usually only able to communicate with one another during the summer months. Since the 1930s road communications have been much improved, but the interior of Daghestan still remains extremely isolated.

Conditions were much more favourable on the coastal plain. Settled communities were formed at an early date and trade developed along the shores of the Caspian, providing an important link between Kievan Rus' and the Near East. The Gates of Derbent, the narrow pass which divides the coastal plain, served as a natural boundary between the north and the south. Despite the fact that it was also the road that linked the two and thereby repeatedly attracted invading armies, it symbolized a division between opposing spheres of influence that was not finally breached until the nineteenth century in a political or territorial sense, and not until the twentieth in a cultural and ideological sense.

One of the most significant events in the history of Daghestan was the Arab conquest. The region had been subjected to Arab incursions from AD 664 onwards, but it was only in the early part of the eighth century (during the Caliphate of Hisham) that they succeeded in establishing a base at Derbent. During the fourth and fifth centuries this area had belonged to the ancient state of Albania and Christianity had spread from there into the plains and mountains of Daghestan. When the Arabs introduced Islam, however, it spread rapidly, ousting Christianity and the still strong pagan cults. Nevertheless, though several of the mountain peoples (e.g. the Kaitaks, Laks and Tabasarans) began to accept Islam almost immediately, the full conversion of these peoples did not take place for several centuries, until the sixteenth century or later. This did not hinder local tradition from giving all the credit for the introduction of Islam to the Arabs; furthermore, many of the nobility liked to trace their descent from Arab commanders. These fancies may or may not have some historical basis, but what is certain is that for the next ten centuries Daghestan was firmly established as part of the Islamic world, as the northern limit of the cultural world of the Middle East.

The Arabs were succeeded by many other intruders: by the Seljuks in the eleventh century; by the Mongols in the early thirteenth century, who 'trampled on the nations which opposed their passage, penetrated through the gates of Derbend, traversed the Volga and the desert and accomplished the circuit of the Caspian Sea, by an expedition which had never been attempted and has never been repeated' (E. Gibbon, *The History of the Decline and Fall of the Roman Empire*, VII); Daghestan was fought over by Timur and Toktamysh of the Golden Horde in the late fourteenth century; occupied by the Ottomans in the second half of the sixteenth century; invaded by the Persians in the eighteenth century and finally annexed by Russia in the early nineteenth century. This marked the beginning of Daghestan's transition from an alignment with the south to an alignment with the north; henceforth it was to be a southern outpost of the Russian/Soviet state. However, the transition was not an easy one: the sense of belonging to the Islamic world was so great that religiously-inspired revolts continued into the twentieth century.

Even though nominally subject to foreign rulers such as the Khan of the Golden Horde or the Ottoman Sultan, the people of Daghestan always retained a virtually independent character. Their own local leaders were extremely powerful. Three states in particular emerged as major foci of power during the fifteenth and sixteenth centuries: the Utsmiyat of the Kaitaks, the Shamkhalat of the Kazikumukhs (Laks) and the Maasumat of the Tabasarans. Their support was of great importance for any campaign in the Caucasus and they not infrequently changed their allegiance from one side to another. In 1578, for example, they were all supporting the Ottomans, but by the early seventeenth century had become allies of Shah Abbas. Apart from these three large principalities, there were other, smaller groupings, such as the Sultanate of the Tsakhurs and the Rutul Mahal. There was also a system of tribal federations, called by Russian historians and ethnographers 'free societies', since they were not bound together by any formal structure of kinship or territorial claims, but by more or less voluntary alliances. Under the leadership of their chiefs (*beks*), they, like the larger states, would throw in their lot sometimes with one side, sometimes with another and in this way a strong but highly volatile force was built up, starting at the smallest unit and reaching to alliances on a multi-national level.

After Daghestan had been annexed by the Russians, many of the local princes retained a semblance of power, but as uprisings against the new order continued the principalities were gradually abolished (e.g. the Usmiyat in 1819, the Maasumat in 1828, the Shamkhalat in 1865) and their lands brought under direct Russian administration. The most significant uprising as well as the one which lasted longest was that led by the Avar Shamyl. It engulfed the whole of Daghestan for some thirty years and was directed against both the Russians and the indigenous chiefs and princes who had sided with them (or at least not opposed them). The movement sprang from a Sufi revival which took place in Shirvan towards the end of the eighteenth century. This revival stressed the importance of the *shari'at* (Qur'anic law) and gave as much attention to the outward observances of religion as to the inward. In the 1820s a Naqshbandi sheikh began to spread these teachings in Daghestan, where they proved to be the inspiration for a fiercely puritanical, anti-infidel upsurge of feeling. Disciples of the movement (*murids*) proclaimed a holy war against the invaders and sought to rid their land of all anti-Islamic elements, alien or indigenous. In 1830 Ghazi Muhammed became the leader or Imam of Daghestan; he was succeeded by Hamzat Bek from 1832 to 1834 and then by Shamyl, who ruled until 1859, when the Murid Uprising was finally crushed. There were more rebellions during the Russo-Turkish war of 1877–8, but the power of the princes, the traditional leaders, had been broken and their resistance to Russian rule at this late stage was ineffective.

As elsewhere in the Caucasus, the 1917 Revolution and subsequent Civil War brought immense confusion and bloodshed to the area. The Mensheviks and Social Revolutionaries established themselves in Daghestan towards the end of 1917, but were overthrown when the area was occupied by the White Army in September 1918. Meanwhile, Nadzhmuddin of Gotzo and Uzun Hadzhi (adherents of the Naqshbandi order) tried to revive the Imamate in the mountain regions. The Red Army defeated the White Army (under General Denikin) in 1920 and thereby re-established Soviet control of Daghestan. The Daghestan ASSR was proclaimed on 20 January 1921 (as part of the RSFSR). The uprising led by Imam Nadzhmuddin and Sheikh Uzun Hadzhi was finally quelled a few months later.

Daghestan ASSR

Situated in the RSFSR on the western shore of the Caspian Sea and the eastern region of the Northern Caucasus; it is bordered to the north by the Kalmyk ASSR, to the east by the Caspian, to the south by the Azerbaidzhan SSR, to the south-west by the Georgian SSR, the Kabardino-Balkar and the North Ossetian ASSRs. *Area:* 50,300 sq. km. *Capital:* Makhachkala, formerly known as Petrovsk-Port (population in 1979: 251,000). The Republic has 8 towns and 14 settlements. *Population* (1979): 1,628,159. Average density of population per sq. km (1979): 32.3.

Chief resources: oil, natural gas and coal.

Industries include: oil and natural gas extraction, machine building; food and other light industries; carpet-making and traditional handicrafts (e.g. silver inlay).

Agriculture: the cultivation of grain (mainly wheat, rice and maize), fruit and vegetables (irrigation is necessary in most areas); stockbreeding, particularly of sheep (mainly in the mountain regions).

2 NUMBER

Ethnic composition of the Daghestan ASSR

	1926	*1959*	*1970*	*1979*
Total	784,047	1,062,472	1,428,540	1,628,159
Avars	138,749 (17.7%)	239,373 (22.5%)	349,304 (24.5%)	418,634 (25.7%)
Akhvakhs	3,677 (0.5%)			
Andis	7,681 (1.0%)			
Archins	854 (0.1%)			
Bagulals	3,054 (0.4%)			
Botlikhs	3,354 (0.4%)	included with Avars		
Chamals	3,438 (0.4%)			
Didois	3,276 (0.4%)			
Godoberins	1,425 (0.2%)			

	1926	1959	1970	1979
Kapuchins	1,447 (0.2%)			
Karatais	5,305 (0.7%)			
Khunzals	98 (0.0%)	included with Avars		
Khvarshins	1,019 (0.1%)			
Tindis	3,812 (0.5%)			
Darghins	108,926 (13.9%)	148,194 (13.9%)	207,776 (14.5%)	246,854 (15.2%)
Kaitaks	14,424 (1.8%)	included with Darghins		
Kubachis	2,357 (0.3%)			
Lezghis	90,509 (11.5%)	108,615 (10.2%)	162,721 (11.4%)	188,804 (11.6%)
Laks	39,878 (5.1%)	53,451 (5.0%)	72,240 (5.1%)	83,457 (5.1%)
Tabasarans	31,915 (4.1%)	33,548 (3.2%)	53,253 (3.7%)	71,722 (4.4%)
Chechens	21,851 (2.8%)	12,798 (1.2%)	39,965 (2.8%)	49,227 (3.0%)
Rutuls	10,333 (1.3%)	6,566 (0.6%)	11,799 (0.8%)	14,288 (0.9%)
Aguls	7,653 (1.0%)	6,378 (0.6%)	8,644 (0.6%)	11,459 (0.7%)
Tsakhurs	3,531 (0.5%)	4,278 (0.4%)	4,309 (0.3%)	4,560 (0.3%)
Kumyks	87,960 (11.2%)	120,859 (11.4%)	169,019 (11.8%)	202,297 (12.4%)
Nogais	26,086 (3.3%)	14,939 (1.4%)	21,750 (1.5%)	24,977 (1.5%)
Turks/ Azerbaidzhanis*	23,428 (3.0%)	38,224 (3.6%)	54,403 (3.8%)	64,514 (4.0%)
Tatars	2,747 (0.4%)	4,564 (0.4%)	5,770 (0.4%)	n.a.¶
Tats	204 (0.0%)	2,813 (0.3%)	6,440 (0.5%)	7,437 (0.5%)

	1926	1959	1970	1979
Jews†	11,592 (1.5%)	21,427 (2.0%)	22,149 (1.6%)	18,733 (1.2%)
Russians	98,197 (12.5%)	213,754 (20.1%)	209,570 (14.7%)	189,474 (11.6%)
Ukrainians	4,126 (0.5%)	7,071 (0.7%)	8,996 (0.6%)	n.a.¶
Persians‡	3,448 (0.4%)	———	———	———
Others	17,693 (2.3%)	25,620 (2.4%)	20,432 (1.4%)	31,722 (1.9%)

*In 1926 the Azerbaidzhanis were listed as Turks.
†These are Mountain Jews; 9,490 of them claimed Tat as their mother tongue, 2,071 claimed Hebrew. In addition to the Mountain Jews, there were also 3,030 'ordinary' Jews, 1 Central Asian Jew and 1 Georgian Jew; in 1959 and later no distinction was made between the Jews of different origins and they were all listed together under a single heading.
‡In 1926 there were in addition 3,964 foreign (i.e. non-Soviet) Persians resident in the Daghestan ASSR.
¶ Specification not yet available, hence they are included under 'Others'.

In the Daghestan ASSR there are representatives of these ethnic groups:
1 *Caucasian*: Avars (including Akhvakhs, Andis, etc.), Darghins (including Kaitaks and Kubachis), Laks, Lezghis, Chechens, Rutuls, Tsakhurs, Aguls
2 *Turkic*: Kumyks, Nogais, Tatars, Azerbaidzhanis
3 *Iranian*: Tats, Persians
4 *Slav*: Russians, Ukrainians
5 *Semitic*: Jews

Percentages of the main ethnic groups in relation to the total population of the Daghestan ASSR

	1926	1979
Caucasian	65.1	66.9
Turkic	17.9	17.9
Slav	13.0	11.6

Urban/rural distribution of the main nationalities in the Daghestan ASSR

	1926		1970	
	Urban	*Rural*	*Urban*	*Rural*
Total population	81,360	702,687	504,854	923,686
Avars	2,013	136,736	63,839	285,465
	(2.5%)	(19.5%)	(12.6%)	(30.9%)
Darghins	891	108,035	44,278	163,498
	(1.1%)	(15.4%)	(8.8%)	(17.7%)
Lezghis	2,108	88,401	33,674	129,047
	(2.6%)	(12.6%)	(6.7%)	(14.0%)
Laks	1,127	38,751	30,395	41,845
	(1.4%)	(5.5%)	(6.0%)	(4.5%)
Tabasarans	34	31,881	7,535	45,718
	(0.0%)	(4.5%)	(1.5%)	(4.9%)
Rutuls	—	10,333	87	11,712
		(1.5%)	(0.0%)	(1.3%)
Aguls	—	7,653	192	8,452
		(1.1%)	(0.0%)	(0.9%)
Tsakhurs	—	3,531	65	4,244
		(0.5%)	(0.0%)	(0.5%)
Chechens	705	21,146	16,241	23,724
	(0.9%)	(3.0%)	(3.2%)	(2.6%)
Kumyks	6,544	81,416	69,867	99,152
	(8.0%)	(11.6%)	(13.8%)	(10.7%)
Nogais	36	26,050	2,406	19,344
	(0.0%)	(3.7%)	(0.5%)	(2.1%)
Tatars	1,139	1,608	4,832	938
	(1.4%)	(0.2%)	(1.0%)	(0.1%)
Turks/	8,129	15,299	22,318	32,085
Azerbaidzhanis	(10.0%)	(2.2%)	(4.4%)	(3.5%)
Tats	—	204	6,208	232
		(0.0%)	(1.2%)	(0.0%)
Russians	33,077	65,120	159,734	49,836
	(40.7%)	(9.3%)	(31.6%)	(5.4%)

3 STATUS

See individual sections.

4 LANGUAGE

Relative to its size, the Daghestan ASSR has one of the most
ethnically diverse populations in the world. This is reflected, too,
in its great linguistic variety. The main language groups represented
are the Caucasian, Turkic and Indo-European (Slav and Iranian).
Within each group, even languages that are in theory closely related
are often not mutually comprehensible (this is particularly true of
the Caucasian group). Furthermore, each language often contains
a number of dialects and sub-dialects and these, too, are frequently
mutually incomprehensible. This linguistic profusion made it extremely difficult for a standard literary language to evolve and, as
a result, relatively little was written in any of the Caucasian
languages prior to the Soviet period. Instead, Arabic was adopted
as the common literary medium. There was a long tradition of
Arabic scholarship in Daghestan, which reached its height in the
seventeenth and eighteenth centuries. Several students from Daghestan went to cities such as Damascus and Aleppo to complete their
education and all its poets and scholars used the language with
ease. When eventually some of them (for example, the Avars)
began to write in the vernacular, they continued to use Arabic as
well. At the time of the 1926 Soviet Census, the number of people
able to read and write was very low, but those who were literate
were often literate in Arabic rather than in their native language.
Even today, something of the Arabic heritage survives since it is
still the official language of the Spiritual Directorate of Northern
Caucasus and Daghestan (see p. 35).

During the last fifty years great efforts have been made to raise
the level of education throughout the Soviet Union. Part of this
campaign entailed providing scripts for languages that were hitherto
unwritten and creating literary norms for languages in which there
were many dialectal variants. These newly developed literary
languages then received some measure of official recognition by
being used as media of instruction, literature, administration, etc.
In Daghestan, however, the linguistic situation was so complex that
it was not possible to promote any one language to the status of
'official' medium: basic demands of comprehension necessitated the
use of the languages of all the main ethnic groups. Nevertheless, in
recent years there has been a tendency to limit the number of
languages used and to reduce their sphere of application. In 1958,
for example, primary education was available in Avar, Darghin,

Lak, Lezghi, Tabasaran, Kumyk, Nogai, Russian and probably also Azerbaidzhani and Chechen; by 1972 there was tuition in the first two grades of primary school in Darghin and Lezghi, in one grade in Avar and nothing at all in the other languages.

There is a university in Makhachkala and several specialized institutes, e.g. of Agriculture, Medicine, Polytechnic and Pedagogy. There does not appear to be any tuition in the languages of Daghestan at the university or the institutes, though in the Pedagogical Institute there is probably some training in at least the main languages that are still in use in the schools in this republic.

There are some radio and television broadcasts in the main languages (Avar, Darghin, Lak, Lezghi and Kumyk), as well as in Russian. Newspapers and periodicals are published in these languages and also in some of the other languages spoken in the Daghestan ASSR. The Daghestani press really dates from the Soviet period. Prior to this, one of the first papers to appear there (in 1915) was in Arabic. Books and pamphlets are published in some of the indigenous languages of Daghestan. See individual sections.

Number of books and pamphlets published in the languages of the Daghestan ASSR in selected years

	1913	1940	1965	1979
No. of titles	16	302	154	177
Print run	26,000	910,000	333,000	635,000

Scripts and alphabets

Until *c*. 1928 Arabic script (for those languages that were written, e.g. Avar)
1928–38 Latin script
1938 Cyrillic script

5 RELIGION

The great majority of Daghestanis are Sunni Muslims (Shafi'i school), but there are a few small pockets of Shi'is (e.g. amongst the Lezghis). Amongst the non-Muslims, there is an ancient community of Jews (the 'Mountain Jews') and small groups of Christians (e.g. amongst the Kabardians of Mozdok).

The Spiritual Directorate of the Northern Caucasus (which follows the Shafi'i school) is based in Makhachkala. The present Chairman is Mufti Mahmud Gekkiev, formerly Deputy Chairman of the Directorate. A graduate of the Mir-i Arab medresse, Mufti Gekkiev was elected Chairman in 1978, replacing Mufti al-Hafiz Omarov, who had held the post since 1976. Mufti Gekkiev's deputies are Ahmad Dakajev (formerly imam of the Makhachkala mosque) and Izuddin Muhammedov (formerly Secretary of the North Caucasian Directorate). Sheikh Dakajev holds the position of Deputy Chairman. The language of this Directorate is Arabic.

There are mosques in Makhachkala, Derbent, Tarki and other large towns in Daghestan. Recent data suggest that there are in all twenty-seven open for worship in this republic (*Religion in Communist Lands*, vol. 7, no. 3, p. 152). According to one Soviet author, a century ago there were 1,235 mosques here (Smirnov, *Mjuridizm . . .*, p. 87).

The Sufi movement has always been extremely strong in the Caucasus. There were no organized dervish 'monasteries' (*khanaka*, *tekke*), such as were common in Central Asia and Turkey, but the 'saint cult' was highly developed. A holy man (*sheikh*, *murshid*) would gather round him a group of disciples (*murids*), who would give him absolute loyalty and veneration. The sheikh usually had several assistants (*naibs*, *mazuns*) to help him keep in close touch with his followers. Thus, even though the community was physically very scattered, they were bound together in a tightly-knit organization. This gave the sheikh tremendous political potential: he did not need to be the active leader of a movement, for his influence was sufficient to command obedience without any overt display of power. It is typical of the situation in the Caucasus that the great national leaders such as the Imams Ghazi Muhammed and Shamyl were not sheikhs (*murshids*), but disciples (*murids*) and therefore subordinate to their spiritual teachers.

The main Sufi schools (*tariqas*) in the Caucasus were the Qadiri and the Naqshbandi. The latter was particularly strong and it still appears to be active today. Two of the Qadiri groups that are mentioned from time to time in Soviet sources are the Kunta Hadzhi (founded in 1862) and the Batal Hadzhi. Women have often played a prominent part in Sufi activities and this is particularly true of the Kunta Hadzhi group (Smirnov, op. cit.). There is no precise information available on the present state of Sufism in the Caucasus, but it has traditionally held such an important place in the life of the community that it would be most surprising if it had completely disappeared. The countryside is full of the tombs and shrines of holy men, whose *baraka* ('benevolence') has comforted generations of Daghestanis; even were there to be no more sheikhs, it is not likely that the aura of Sufism would be easy to eradicate in this region.

AVARS

Own name: *Maarulal* (literally 'mountain-dwellers'); Russian name: *Avartsy*.

The majority of Avars live in the mountains of the Daghestan ASSR, inhabiting a broad band that runs obliquely across the republic from the north-east to the west.

1 HISTORICAL BACKGROUND

Little is known about the origins of the Avars. Tribes who can be identified with them were mentioned by Pliny the Elder (first century AD). Ptolemy (second century AD) speaks of 'Savirs' and Arab writers of the ninth and tenth centuries of the 'Kingdom of Serir' and it is possible that they, too, were referring to the Avars. The Arabs had undoubtedly been in close contact with the Avars when they invaded the Caucasus in the first half of the eighth century. The Avars may not have been converted to Islam immediately, but their own traditions state that it was the Arabs, and in particular Abu Muslim, who brought the faith during this campaign. Certainly by the eleventh century Islam was well established and Tanus, later one of the capitals of the Avar Khanate, was known as a centre of Muslim learning. In the early thirteenth century Daghestan was invaded by the Mongols, becoming a nominal part of the Golden Horde; in the late fourteenth century it was fought over by Timur and Toktamysh. In the aftermath of this struggle, independent principalities began to form and to break away from the Golden Horde. Amongst them was the Avar Khanate. First centred round Tanus, it later established its main base at Khunzak. The Khanate was particularly powerful during the seventeenth and eighteenth centuries, when its rulers received tribute from neighbouring khans (e.g. of Shirvan and Derbent), as well as from the King of Georgia. The most famous Avar ruler of this period was Umma Khan (d. 1634), who codified the Avar customary law (*adat*). However, even at its height, the power of the Khanate was based on tribal federations who always retained a large degree of independence. The tribal divisions (known as *bo*) were so strong that traces of them still survive today.

The Avars were amongst the most culturally advanced of the Caucasian peoples. A tradition of Arabic scholarship was established at an early date, so though Avar itself (which was widely used as a *lingua franca* in Daghestan) was not written until relatively late, Arabic was able to provide the literary medium. Attempts were made to write Avar (using the Arabic script) from the mid-seventeenth century, but it was the poet Dibir, Kazi of Khunzak (1747–1827) who perfected the alphabet. Arabic still continued to be used, however, and many eighteenth- and nineteenth-century Avar poets and scholars used both languages with equal facility.

The Russian interest in the Caucasus had been growing throughout the eighteenth century. In 1803, one of the first of the Daghestani principalities to become a Russian protectorate was the Avar Khanate. At first the Khan retained some power, but after the 1821 uprising Russian rule became more overt. In 1830 a wave of popular reaction swept the country; deeply religious in character, it was led by sheikhs of the Naqshbandi order. The movement was dominated by Shamyl, the third Imam, who fought against the Russians for some thirty years, until finally defeated in 1859. After the Imamate had been vanquished, the Russians attempted to restore the Khanate, but it was short-lived: Ibrahim Khan was exiled in 1863 and the Khanate transformed into the Avar District (*okrug*) in 1864.

2 NUMBER AND DISTRIBUTION

Number of Avars

1926	1959	1970	1979
158,769	270,394*	396,297*	482,844*

*From 1959 the following peoples were included with the Avars: Akhvakhs, Andis, Archins, Bagulals, Botlikhs, Chamals, Didois (Tsezes), Kapuchins (Bezhetins), Karatais, Khunzals (Gunzibs), Khvarsins and Tindis; in 1926 the total sum of these peoples was 38,623. For statistics concerning these peoples, all of whom were listed separately in 1926, see pp. 246–57, 264.

Regional distribution of Avars

	1926	1959	1970	1979
RSFSR	139,664 (88.0%)	249,529 (92.3%)	361,613 (91.2%)	n.a.
DaghASSR only	138,749 (87.4%)	239,373 (88.5%)	349,304 (88.1%)	418,634 (86.7%)
AzSSR	19,104 (12.0%)	17,254 (6.4%)	30,735 (7.8%)	35,991 (7.5%)
Elsewhere in USSR	1 (0.0%)	3,611 (1.3%)	3,949 (1.0%)	

Urban/rural distribution of Avars in the Daghestan ASSR

	1926	1970
Urban	2,013 (1.5%)	63,839 (18.3%)
Rural	136,736 (98.5%)	285,465 (81.7%)

For *Ethnic composition of the Daghestan ASSR* and *Urban/rural distribution in the Daghestan ASSR* see pp. 126, 129.

3 STATUS

The Avars enjoy full Soviet citizenship. They are found in all occupations and in all income brackets, though the majority work on collective farms; some also work in the local industries (e.g. canning, brick-making) or in industrial enterprises in other parts of Daghestan. Amongst the traditional crafts which have been developed on a large scale are silver-inlay work and the making of the famous Caucasian cloaks (*burki*).

Their standard of housing is comparable to that of other national groups in the Soviet Union. The women go out to work, as elsewhere in the Soviet Union, but there is still a tendency for women to work separately from the men, e.g. the women usually care for the cattle, the men for the sheep.

Literacy

In 1926	In 1970
6.8%	Over 99%

In 1926, 9,206 Avars were literate in their own language (85.6 per cent of the total literate Avar population)

Level of education per 1,000 Avars living in the Daghestan ASSR of 10 years of age and above:

	1959	1970
Primary		
Total	295	323
Men	288	303
Women	301	339
Higher and secondary (complete and incomplete)		
Total	234	308
Men	354	419
Women	141	217
Higher only		
Total	5	18
Men	8	30
Women	1	8

4 LANGUAGE

The national language is Avar. It belongs to the Avaro-Andi-Didoi group of North-East Caucasian languages. There are two main dialect groups: a northern and a southern. The differences between them are phonetic, morphological and lexical. The northern group provides the basis for the literary language, though the southern group has also had some influence on its development. The dialects now appear to be losing ground to the literary or 'standard' language. The vocabulary still has a strong Arabic-Persian-Turkish element, but this is gradually giving way to Russian influence: e.g. *revolutsija* is now used for *inkilab* ('revolution'), *uchrezhdenije* for *idara* ('office').

Russian is generally used for administrative, judicial and other official proceedings, but in theory Avar can be used if necessary. Avar is one of the main literary languages of the Daghestan ASSR and is used by many of the peoples who have no written language of their own.

In 1958 Avar was the medium of instruction in grades 1–4 (primary +1) in some national schools; in 1972, only in grade 1 and pre-school; in 1972 it was also taught as an individual, optional

Percentage of Avars claiming Avar as their mother tongue

	1926	1959	1970	1979
Total	99.3	97.2	97.2	97.7
In urban areas	97.0	91.2	94.1	n.a.
In rural areas	99.3	97.9	97.9	n.a.

Percentage of Avars with good knowledge of Russian

	1926	1959	1970	1979
As mother tongue	0.0 (37 people)	0.8	1.0	1.3
As second language	n.a.	n.a.	37.8	59.3

Percentage of Avars with good knowledge of a language other than their own or Russian (mostly another Daghestani language)

	1970	1979
As mother tongue	1.9	1.0
As second language	5.1	5.7

subject in some Russian-medium schools in grades 1–10 (Silver, p. 33). More recent information is not available.

There is some radio and television broadcasting in Avar.

Newspapers are published in Avar; the main one is *Baarab bajrakh* ('The Red Banner' – first published in 1918). There is also an Avar edition of 'Woman of Daghestan', entitled *Maarulai* ('Mountain Woman'), which was started in 1957, and an Avar edition of the quarterly literary almanac of Daghestan, 'Friendship' (*Gjudulli*), which was started in 1952. There was no Avar press before the Soviet period.

Books and pamphlets are published in Avar (e.g. 11 titles in 1976; none of these were specialized textbooks on scientific or technical subjects).

Scripts and alphabets

Until 1928 Arabic script
1928–38   Latin script
1938   Cyrillic script

5 RELIGION

The Avars are Sunni Muslims (Shafi'i school).

LEZGHIS/LEZGHIANS

Own name: *Lezgi*; Russian name: *Lezginy*.

The majority of the Lezghis live in the south-east of the Daghestan ASSR, in such areas as the Kurakh, Kasumkent, Magaramkent, Akhty and Dokuzpara Regions (*rajony*); there are also Lezghi settlements in the Azerbaidzhan SSR, in the Kuba and Kusar Regions (*rajony*). Formerly all the mountain peoples of Daghestan were referred to as 'Lezghis'; now the term is used only for this specific group.

1 HISTORICAL BACKGROUND

The Lezghis are descended from indigenous tribes of the Caucasus. In many of their villages there are buildings with Kufic inscriptions (e.g. in Akhty), indicating that these settlements date from before the fourteenth century. The Lezghis, like many of the other peoples of Daghestan, were initially converted to Islam as a result of the Arab invasion of the Caucasus, though Islam did not fully penetrate the area for some centuries longer and it was the invasion of Timur, followed by the Ottoman occupation of Daghestan in the sixteenth century, that finally established its supremacy. Unlike many of the other Daghestanis, the Lezghis did not form a principality of their own, but retained the system of tribal federations or 'free societies', each of which made its own alliances, until the nineteenth century. The Lezghis who lived in what is now the Azerbaidzhan SSR formed part of the Kuba Khanate, while those in the Derbent region were nominally under the Derbent Khanate. When the Kazikumukh (Lak) Khanate expanded in the eighteenth century, they gained control of Lezghi lands for a period. In 1812 the Lezghis came under Russian rule, forming part of the Kiurin Khanate, later the Kiurin District (*okrug*).

The traditional occupations of the Lezghis are animal husbandry (mainly sheep-breeding) and some agriculture.

2 NUMBER AND DISTRIBUTION

Number of Lezghis

	1926	1959	1970	1979
	134,529	223,129	323,829	382,611

Regional distribution of Lezghis

	1926	1959	1970	1979
DaghASSR	90,509 (67.3%)	108,615 (48.7%)	162,721 (50.2%)	188,804 (49.3%)
AzSSR	37,263 (27.7%)	98,211 (44.0%)	137,250 (42.4%)	158,057 (41.3%)
Elsewhere in USSR	6,757 (5.0%)	16,303 (7.3%)	23,858 (7.4%)	

Urban/rural distribution of Lezghis in the Daghestan ASSR

	1926	1970
Urban	2,108 (2.3%)	33,674 (20.7%)
Rural	88,401 (97.7%)	129,047 (79.3%)

For *Ethnic composition of the Daghestan ASSR* and *Urban/rural distribution in the Daghestan ASSR*, see pp. 126, 129.

3 STATUS

The Lezghis enjoy full Soviet citizenship. They are found in all occupations and in all income brackets, though the majority work on collective farms; some work in the local industries (canning, mineral-water bottling, timber-processing, etc.) and many of the women work in carpet-weaving collectives. Their standard of housing is comparable to that of other national groups in the Soviet Union. The women go out to work, as elsewhere in the Soviet Union.

Literacy

In 1926	In 1970
7.1%	Over 99%

In 1926, none of the Lezghis were literate in their own language.

Level of education per 1,000 Lezghis living in the Daghestan ASSR of 10 years of age and above

	1959	1970
Primary		
Total	288	310
Men	262	283
Women	309	333
Higher and secondary (complete and incomplete)		
Total	286	358
Men	438	468
Women	163	259
Higher only		
Total	12	30
Men	23	49
Women	3	12

Level of education per 1,000 Lezghis living in the AzSSR of 10 years of age and above

	1959	1970
Primary		
Total	226	310
Men	230	301
Women	223	318
Higher and secondary (complete and incomplete)		
Total	340	381
Men	442	465
Women	241	300
Higher only		
Total	14	25
Men	22	41
Women	5	9

4 LANGUAGE

The national language is Lezghi. It belongs to the Lezghi group of Caucasian languages. It has three main groups of dialects: Kiurin, Samur and Kuba (the last group is spoken in the AzSSR). P. K. Uslar published the first grammar of Lezghi (which he called the 'Kiurin language') in the mid-nineteenth century, but most of the research into this language has been done in the last fifty years. The basis of the literary language was provided by the Gjunei dialect of the Kiurin group, a 'mixed' dialect which combines features of several of the other dialects. Lezghi contains a large number of loan-words from Arabic, Persian and Turkish (and/or Azerbaidzhani), as well as Russian; Russian influence on Lezghi dates back to the eighteenth century, but has become increasingly more noticeable in recent years, causing several long-established Arabic/Persian/Turkic loans to become obsolete: e.g. *ministerstvo* is now used for *maarif* ('ministry'), *sobranije* for *diwan* ('meeting'). All the loan-words, whatever their origin, undergo considerable phonetic modification in Lezghi.

Russian is generally used for administrative, judicial and other official proceedings, but in theory Lezghi can be used if necessary. Lezghi is one of the many literary languages of Daghestan and is used by many peoples whose own languages are not written (e.g. Aguls). Many Lezghis (especially of the younger generation) know Russian and (in the AzSSR) Azerbaidzhani.

Percentage of Lezghis claiming Lezghi as their mother tongue

	1926	1959	1970	1979
Total	97.4	92.7	93.9	90.9
In urban areas	87.5	83.0	84.1	n.a.
In rural areas	98.2	95.6	98.2	n.a.

Percentage of Lezghis with good knowledge of Russian

	1926	1959	1970	1979
As mother tongue	0.3	3.0	3.7	4.7
As second language	n.a.	n.a.	31.6	47.6

Percentage of Lezghis with good knowledge of a language other than their own or Russian (mostly another Daghestani language or Azerbaidzhani)

	1970	1979
As mother tongue	2.4	4.4
As second language	21.4	20.5

In 1958 Lezghi was the medium of instruction in grades 1–4 (primary +1) in some national schools; in 1972, only in grades 1–2 and pre-school; in 1972 it was taught as an individual, optional subject in some Russian-medium schools in grades 1–8 (Silver, p. 33). More recent information is not available.

There is some radio and television broadcasting in Lezghi.

Newspapers are published in Lezghi; the main one is *Kommunist* ('Communist' – first appeared in 1928). There are also Lezghi editions of the periodical 'Woman of Daghestan' (since 1957) and the quarterly literary almanac 'Friendship' (since 1952). There was no Lezghi press before the Soviet period.

Books and pamphlets are published in Lezghi (e.g. 18 titles in 1976; none of these were specialized textbooks on scientific or technical subjects).

Scripts and alphabets

There was very little writing in Lezghi before the Soviet period (Arabic was the main literary language); when it was used, it was written in the Arabic script or, briefly, in the Cyrillic script invented by P. K. Uslar in the mid-nineteenth century.

Until 1928 Arabic script
1928–38   Latin script
1938   Cyrillic script

5 RELIGION

The Lezghis are Sunni Muslims, except for the inhabitants of Miskindzha, Dokuzpara Region (*rajon*), who have been Shi'is for many centuries. Although religious practices are not as widespread as they used to be amongst the Lezghis, it is still not uncommon to find people who perform the ritual prayer (*namaz*) regularly and are devout observers of religious precepts (*Narody Kavkaza I*). There used to be many mosques (including big Friday Mosques) in the Lezghi lands; it is not known how many are still open for worship.

DARGHINS/DARGHIS

Own name: *Dargan*; Russian name: *Dargintsy*.

The Darghins inhabit the central part of the Daghestan ASSR, living in the Sergokala and Dakhadajev Regions (*rajony*). To the east lies the Caspian Sea; their neighbours to the south are the Tabasarans and the Aguls, to the west the Laks and the Avars, to the north the Kumyks. The Darghins are the third largest group of Daghestan peoples.

1 HISTORICAL BACKGROUND

The Darghins are an indigenous people of the Caucasus. Their conversion to Islam began at the time of the Arab conquest of the Caucasus in the first half of the eighth century. Towards the end of the fourteenth century, a principality known as the *Utsmiyat* (under a ruler entitled the *Utsmi*) was formed amongst the Kaitaks, whose territory lay to the south-west of the Darghins. Eventually, the power of the Utsmiyat was extended over most of the Darghins. (Now, however, the Kaitaks are considered to be a sub-group of the Darghins: see pp. 252–3). The region came under Russian rule in the early nineteenth century. The Utsmiyat was abolished in 1820 and direct Russian administration introduced. In 1860 the Darghin District (*okrug*) was created. The Darghins did not form part of Shamyl's Imamate.

The traditional occupations of the Darghins are animal husbandry (particularly sheep-breeding: the Darghins are famous for their special breed of black sheep) and small-scale farming. They were also extremely skilled as gold-workers. These are still the chief occupations of the Darghins today.

2 NUMBER AND DISTRIBUTION

Number of Darghins

1926	1959	1970	1979
108,963	158,149*	230,932*	287,282*

*From 1959 the Kaitaks and the Kubachis were included with the Darghins. See pp. 252, 259 for figures relating to the Kaitaks and Kubachis respectively.

Regional distribution of Darghins

	1926	1959	1970	1979
RSFSR	108,963 (100%)	152,563 (96.5%)	224,172 (97.1%)	n.a.
DaghASSR only	108,926 (100%)	148,194 (93.7%)	207,776 (90.0%)	246,854 (85.9%)
Kalmyk ASSR only	——	——	4,961 (2.1%)	8,590 (3.0%)
Elsewhere in USSR	——	5,586 (3.5%)	6,760 (3.0%)	

Urban/rural distribution of Darghins in the Daghestan ASSR

	1926	1970
Urban	891 (0.8%)	44,278 (21.3%)
Rural	108,035 (99.2%)	163,498 (78.7%)

For *Ethnic composition of the Daghestan ASSR* and *Urban/rural distribution in the Daghestan ASSR*, see pp. 126, 129.

3 STATUS

The Darghins enjoy full Soviet citizenship. They are found in all occupations and in all income brackets, though the majority work on collective farms. Their standard of housing is comparable to that of other national groups in the Soviet Union. The women go out to work, as elsewhere in the Soviet Union.

Literacy

In 1926	In 1970
4.9%	Over 99%

In 1926, 4,241 Darghins were literate in their own language (79.0 per cent of the total literate Darghin population).

Level of education per 1,000 Darghins living in the Daghestan ASSR of 10 years of age and above

	1959	1970
Primary		
Total	285	328
Men	299	324
Women	274	331
Higher and secondary (complete and incomplete)		
Total	208	270
Men	310	373
Women	132	191
Higher only		
Total	4	17
Men	8	29
Women	1	8

4 LANGUAGE

The national language is Darghin. It belongs to the North-East group of Caucasian languages, Darghin-Lak sub-group. It has seven main groups of dialects (including Kaitak and Kubachi). The vocabulary contains a number of Arabic, Persian and Turkish loanwords; they have undergone a certain amount of phonetic adaptation, e.g. Arabic *fikr* has become Darghin *pikru*, since Darghin does not possess the phoneme *f*. Russian has also had a strong influence on the Darghin vocabulary.

The Darghin dialects began to attract academic interest as early as the eighteenth century. Particularly significant was the work of the specialist in Caucasian languages P. K. Uslar in 1866–7; later, other eminent scholars such as A. Dirr, N. Trubetskoj and G. Dumesil devoted attention to the language.

Prior to the Soviet period Darghin was not written; the literary language here, as elsewhere in Daghestan, was Arabic. Today Darghin is one of the main literary languages of Daghestan.

Russian is generally used for administrative, judicial and other official proceedings, but in theory Darghin can be used if necessary.

Percentage of Darghins claiming Darghin as their mother tongue

	1926	1959	1970	1979
Total	98.3	98.6	98.4	98.3
In urban areas	96.7	94.3	94.6	n.a.
In rural areas	98.3	99.5	99.6	n.a.

Percentage of Darghins with good knowledge of Russian

	1926	1959	1970	1979
As mother tongue	0.0 (10 people)	0.9	1.3	1.4
As second language	n.a.	n.a.	43.0	64.1

Percentage of Darghins with good knowledge of a language other than their own or Russian (mostly another Daghestani language)

	1970	1979
As mother tongue	0.4	0.4
As second language	2.6	1.2

In 1958 Darghin was the medium of instruction in grades 1–4 (primary +1) in some national schools; in 1972, only in grades 1–2 and pre-school; in 1972 it was also taught as an individual, optional subject in Russian-medium schools in grades 1–8 (Silver, p. 33). More recent information is not available.

There are some radio and television broadcasts in Darghin.

Newspapers are published in Darghin; the main one is *Leninna bajrakh* ('Lenin's Banner' – first appeared in 1921). There are also Darghin editions of the periodical 'Woman of Daghestan' (since 1957) and the literary almanac 'Friendship' (since 1952). There was no Darghin press before the Soviet period.

Books and pamphlets are published in Darghin (e.g. 17 titles in 1976; none of these were textbooks on specialized scientific or technical subjects).

Scripts and alphabets

Until 1928 Arabic script (with additional symbols for specific sounds)
1928–38 Latin script
1938 Cyrillic script

5 RELIGION

The Darghins are Sunni Muslims (Shafi'i school), except for small communities in Kurush and Miskindzha, who are Shi'is. These Shi'i groups are certainly ancient, but nothing is known of their origin. (The Lezghis in these areas are also Shi'i: see p. 142.) They possibly adopted this form of Islam under the influence of the Safavids in the sixteenth and seventeenth centuries.

KUMYKS

Own name: *Kumuk*; Russian name: *Kumyki*.

The Kumyks live in the north-east of the Daghestan ASSR; their neighbours to the north are the Nogais, to the north-west and west the Chechens and Avars, to the south-west and south the Darghins, Tabasarans and Azerbaidzhanis of Derbent; to the east lies the Caspian Sea.

1 HISTORICAL BACKGROUND

The Kumyks are a Turkic-speaking people of the Caucasus. Their origins are not clear, but it seems probable that they represent an intermingling of indigenous Caucasian elements with Turkic-speaking tribes who migrated to Daghestan after the fall of the Khazar state in the tenth century. Linguistic evidence indicates that these Turkic tribes were mostly Kipchaks (Cumans/Polovtsians). By about the eleventh century the Kumyks, like the Darghins and Tabasarans to the south, had been converted to Islam.

There are three main groups of Kumyks: those of the so-called 'Kumyk Plain', in the vicinity of Khasav-jurt, those centred around Bujnaksk (formerly known as Temir-Khan-Shura) and those of the Khaidak (Kaitak) area. The second is by far the largest and historically-speaking most important group. During the fifteenth and sixteenth centuries these Kumyks formed a powerful state of their own, the *Shamkhalat* of Tarki. By the eighteenth century they had control over some of the Avars and Darghins. In the early nineteenth century, however, Russian expansion in the Caucasus put an end to the power of the native principalities and though the Shamkhalat survived in name at least for a while, it was finally abolished in 1867, when the area was incorporated into the Temir-Khan-Shura District (*okrug*) and came under direct Russian administration. The third group of Kumyks did not call themselves 'Kumyks' until recent times, identifying themselves instead only by the names of their villages (e.g.*Bashlyly*, 'from the village of Bashly'). They were formerly under the rule of the Utsmi of the Kaitaks (see p. 252).

2 NUMBER AND DISTRIBUTION

Number of Kumyks

	1926	1959	1970	1979
	94,549	134,967	188,792	228,418

Regional distribution of Kumyks

	1926	1959	1970	1979
RSFSR	94,510 (100%)	132,896 (98.5%)	186,690 (98.9%)	n.a.
DaghASSR only	87,960 (93.0%)	120,859 (89.5%)	169,019 (89.5%)	202,297 (88.6%)
Checheno-Ingush Aut. Prov./ASSR only	2,130 (2.3%)	5,556 (4.1%)	7,218 (3.8%)	8,087 (3.5%)
North Ossetian Aut. Prov./ASSR only	55 (0.1%)	3,921 (2.9%)	6,363 (3.4%)	7,610 (3.3%)
Elsewhere in USSR	39 (0.0%)	2,071 (1.5%)	2,102 (1.1%)	

Urban/rural distribution of Kumyks in the Daghestan ASSR

	1926	1970
Urban	6,544 (7.4%)	69,867 (41.3%)
Rural	81,416 (92.6%)	99,152 (58.7%)

For *Ethnic composition of the Daghestan ASSR* and *Urban/rural distribution in the Daghestan ASSR* see pp. 126, 129.

3 STATUS

The Kumyks enjoy full Soviet citizenship. They are found in all occupations and in all income brackets, but most are agricultural workers; about one third work in industry. Their standard of housing is comparable to that of other national groups in the Soviet Union. The women go out to work, as elsewhere in the Soviet Union.

Literacy

In 1926	In 1970
11.1%	Over 99%

In 1926, 8,567 Kumyks were literate in their own language (81.3 per cent of the total literate Kumyk population).

Level of education per 1,000 Kumyks living in the Daghestan ASSR of 10 years of age and above

	1959	1970
Primary		
Total	294	320
Men	319	321
Women	275	320
Higher and secondary (complete and incomplete)		
Total	236	348
Men	329	433
Women	159	274
Higher only		
Total	8	23
Men	13	33
Women	3	14

4 LANGUAGE

The national language is Kumyk. It belongs to the West Turkic group (*Fundamenta* classification); it can also be classed as belonging to the Kipchak group, Kipchak-Polovstian sub-group (Baskakov).

There are three dialect groupings in Kumyk, corresponding to the main areas in which the Kumyks are settled: Khaidak, Bujnaksk and Khasav-jurt. There are phonetic, morphological and lexical divergences between them. The Bujnaksk and Khasav-jurt groups serve as the basis for the literary language. Loan-words from Russian have been entering Kumyk for several centuries. The earliest borrowings underwent considerable phonetic modification, e.g. *pedire* from *vedro* ('bucket'); in modern times words have generally been adopted in their original form. There are now also many calques and derived words based on Russian roots. There used to be quite a strong Arabic-Persian element in Kumyk, but this appears to be losing ground to the growing Russian influence, e.g. *uchitel'* is replacing *mualim* ('teacher').

Russian is generally used for administrative, judicial and other official proceedings, but in theory Kumyk can be used if necessary.

Percentage of Kumyks claiming Kumyk as their mother tongue

	1926	1959	1970	1979
Total	99.2	98.0	98.4	98.2
In urban areas	97.7	96.0	96.9	n.a.
In rural areas	99.4	99.0	99.4	n.a.

Percentage of Kumyks with good knowledge of Russian

	1926	1959	1970	1979
As mother tongue	0.1	1.4	1.2	1.5
As second language	n.a.	n.a.	57.4	72.6

Percentage of Kumyks with good knowledge of a language other than their mother tongue or Russian (mostly another Daghestani language)

	1970	1979
As mother tongue	0.3	0.4
As second language	0.9	0.7

In 1958 Kumyk was the medium of instruction in grades 1–4 (primary +1) in national schools; in 1972, only in grades 1–2 and pre-school; in 1972 it was taught as an individual, optional subject in Russian-medium schools in grades 1–10 (Silver, p. 33).

There is some broadcasting in Kumyk.

The Kumyk press began in 1917 with the publication of two periodicals at Temir-Khan-Shura (now Bujnaksk). One of these, *Tang Cholpan* ('Morning Star'), survived for a year and was particularly interesting for the wide range of views it reflected. The main Kumyk paper today is *Lenin jolu* ('Lenin's Way' – first appeared in 1918). There are also Kumyk editions of 'Woman of Daghestan' (since 1957) and the literary almanac 'Friendship' (since 1952). Books and pamphlets are published in Kumyk (e.g. 18 titles in 1976; none of these were specialized textbooks on scientific or technical subjects).

Scripts and alphabets

Until 1921 Arabic script, Arabic alphabet
1921–8   Arabic script, modified alphabet
1928–38   Latin script
1938   Cyrillic script

5 RELIGION

The Kumyks are Sunni Muslims (Shafi'i school).

LAKS

Own name: *Lak*; Russian name: *Laktsy*; Avar name: *Tumal*; Darghin name: *Buluguni*; Lezghi name: *Jakhulvi*. The Laks were formerly known as *Kazikumukh* or *Kazikumyk*.

The majority live in the mountains of southern Daghestan, in the Lak, Kuli, and New Lak Regions (*rajony*) of the Daghestan ASSR. They are bordered to the north and north-east by the Darghins, to the south by the Rutuls, to the south-west by the Tsakhurs, to the west and north-west by the Avars.

1 HISTORICAL BACKGROUND

The Laks are an indigenous people of the Caucasus. Arab writers
of the ninth and tenth centuries, such as Masudi, refer to a people
called the 'Gumik' as the inhabitants of this area and these are
most probably the forebears of the present Laks. They were slower
to adopt Islam than some of their neighbours and at the time of the
Mongol invasion in the thirteenth century there were still some
non-Muslims amongst them. They began to emerge as a powerful
group during the fourteenth century, and by the fifteenth century
their principality or *Shamkhalat* (under the rule of a *Shamkhal*) was
one of the most important of the semi-independent states that
bordered the southern edge of the Golden Horde. The Laks (Kazikumukhs) gradually extended their territory to the north-east,
towards the coast, bringing much of the Kumyks' land under their
control. (The Kumyks, unlike the Kazikumukhs, are a Turkic
people; see p. 147.) Bujnaksk became their winter capital, Kumukh
their summer. From the sixteenth century onwards the Shamkhal,
like the rulers of the other Caucasian principalities, became embroiled in the struggles between Persia, Turkey and Russia for
mastery of Daghestan. By the late eighteenth century the Russians
were firmly entrenched in the northern Caucasus and in the early
nineteenth century several of the Daghestani principalities became
Russian protectorates. There were a number of uprisings during
the following years, as a result of which the Russians gradually
abolished all the native states and introduced direct administrative
control. The most significant rebellion was that led by the Avar
Shamyl. The Laks did not directly participate in this, but nevertheless their Shamkhalat was abolished in 1865.

2 NUMBER AND DISTRIBUTION

Number of Laks

	1926	*1959*	*1970*	*1979*
	40,380	63,529	85,822	100,148

Regional distribution of Laks

	1926	1959	1970	1979
RSFSR	40,246 (99.7%)	58,397 (91.9%)	78,625 (91.6%)	n.a.
DaghASSR only	39,878 (98.8%)	53,451 (84.1%)	72,240 (84.2%)	83,457 (83.3%)
Elsewhere in USSR	134 (0.3%)	5,132 (8.1%)	7,197 (8.4%)	

Urban/rural distribution of Laks in the Daghestan ASSR

	1926	1970
Urban	1,127 (2.8%)	30,395 (42.1%)
Rural	38,751 (97.2%)	41,845 (57.9%)

For *Ethnic composition of the Daghestan ASSR* and *Urban/rural distribution in the Daghestan ASSR* see pp. 126, 129.

3 STATUS

The Laks enjoy full Soviet citizenship. They are found in all occupations and in all income brackets, but the majority are engaged in agriculture and animal husbandry, particularly in sheep-rearing. There is an interesting traditional division of labour, of which some trace still survives, whereby the men are responsible for milking the sheep and the women the cows.

Their standard of housing is comparable to that of other national groups in the Soviet Union. The women go out to work, as elsewhere in the Soviet Union.

Literacy

In 1926	In 1970
8.4%	Over 99%

In 1926, 2,951 Laks were literate in their own language (87.1 per cent of the total literate Lak population).

4 LANGUAGE

The national language is Lak. It belongs to the North-East Caucasian group of languages, Darghin-Lak sub-group. It has five dialects: Kumukh, Vitskhin, Ashtikuli, Vikhli and Balkhar; the differences between them are mainly phonetic. The Kumukh dialect is the basis of the literary language. The vocabulary contains a number of loan-words from Arabic, Persian and Turkish, as well as from Russian. This last has had a particularly strong influence during recent years and been the medium through which Lak has acquired 'international' words (e.g. *revolutsija, sotsializm*).

There was some literature in Lak at least as early as the eighteenth century. The first known work is a translation of a Persian medical treatise, dated 1734. However, the chief literary language of Daghestan at this period was Arabic and relatively little was written in any other language. The first printed book was *Kazikumukhskaja azbuka*, a Lak (Kazikumukh) primer which appeared in 1865. It was the work of the great scholar of Caucasian languages, P. K. Uslar. Uslar invented an alphabet for Lak based on the Cyrillic script. It was intended for use in a Lak school and Uslar and his colleague A. Omarov wrote a number of textbooks using this script. The experiment was not a success, however, and the script was abandoned after the closing of the school. Later printed works used the Arabic script, including the Lak newspaper *Khkhjakhkhja barg* ('Dawn'), which was published in St Petersburg from 1912 to 1914.

Russian is generally used for administrative, judicial and other official proceedings, but in theory Lak can be used if necessary. Most Laks have some knowledge of the languages of neighbouring peoples, such as Avar, Kumyk and Darghin, as well as of Russian.

Percentage of Laks claiming Lak as their mother tongue

	1926	1959	1970	1979
Total	99.4	95.8	95.6	95.0
In urban areas	90.3	90.5	92.0	n.a.
In rural areas	99.7	98.4	98.8	n.a.

Percentage of Laks with good knowledge of Russian

	1926	1959	1970	1979
As mother tongue	0.0 (10 people)	3.2	3.7	4.1
As second language	n.a.	n.a.	56.0	73.0

Percentage of Laks with good knowledge of a language other than their mother tongue or Russian (mostly another Daghestani language)

	1970	1979
As mother tongue	0.8	0.9
As second language	2.8	2.0

In 1958 Lak was the medium of instruction in grades 1–4 (primary +1) in some national schools; in 1972, only in grades 1–2 and pre-school; in 1972 it was also taught as an individual, optional subject in Russian-medium schools in grades 1–8 (Silver, p. 33). More recent information is not available.

There is some broadcasting in Lak.

The Lak press really dates from the Soviet period: there was an attempt to publish a Lak paper in St Petersburg in 1912–14 and another Lak periodical made a brief appearance in 1917, but *Khkhjakhkhja barg* 'Dawn' (using the title of the original St Petersburg publication), which was started in 1922, was the first to become firmly established. Today there are three regional (*rajonnyje*) papers in Lak, serving the three main regions in which the Laks are concentrated; they are: *Khkhjakhkhja barg, Tsussalakral kolkhoznik* ('New-Lak Kolkhoznik' – since 1948) and *Channatsuku* ('Star' – since 1951). There is also a Lak edition of 'Woman of Daghestan' (entitled *Zunttal khami* 'Mountain Woman' – since 1957) and of the quarterly literary almanac of Daghestan, 'Friendship' (since 1952).

Books and pamphlets are published in Lak (e.g. 11 titles in 1976; none of these were specialized textbooks on scientific or technical subjects).

Scripts and alphabets

Until 1928 Arabic script (in 1860 also Cyrillic script)
1928–38   Latin script
1938   Cyrillic script

5 RELIGION

The Laks are Sunni Muslims (Shafi'i school). Formerly every village had at least one mosque; Kumukh, for example, had seven. There are no mosques open for worship in the Lak country today (*Narody Kavkaza I*).

TABASARANS

Own name: *Tabasaran*; Russian name: *Tabasarantsy*.

The Tabasarans live in the south-east of the Daghestan ASSR, in the Khiv and Tabasaran Regions (*rajony*). The majority are found in the valleys of such rivers as the Chirakh-chai and the Karachag-su. Their neighbours to the north are the Darghins, to the east the Azerbaidzhanis, to the south the Lezghis, to the west the Aguls.

1 HISTORICAL BACKGROUND

The earliest mention of the Tabasarans is in a seventh-century Armenian source, which speaks of them as one of the independent peoples of Daghestan. Arab historians also referred to them, calling their territory 'Tabarstan'. However, very little is known of their origins. It is now generally accepted that they are an indigenous Caucasian people, but earlier theories traced their descent from forebears as diverse as the Mongols, Jews, Persians and Armenians.

When the Arabs invaded the Caucasus in the eighth century, the Tabasaran lands were one of the areas that came under their direct control (the governor was a nephew of the Amir of Derbent). Due to Arab influence, the Tabasarans, like many of their neighbours, became Muslims. During the fifteenth century they formed a principality, known as the *Maasumat* or *Maisumat* of Tabasaran (under th; rule of the *Maasum/Maisum*). This became one of the three most powerful states in Daghestan (the others being the Shamkhalat of the Kazikumukhs and the Utsmiyat of the Kaitaks; see p. 124) and in the sixteenth and early seventeenth centuries played an important part in the Ottoman-Persian struggles for possession of the Caucasus. The state eventually split into two, the north ruled by a Kadi, the south remaining under the Maasum. Both parts came under Russian rule in the early nineteenth century. During the Murid Uprising (1834–59) the Tabasarans did not support Sha-myl, the Imam of Daghestan, but either sided with the Russians or remained neutral.

2 NUMBER AND DISTRIBUTION

Number of Tabasarans

	1926	1959	1970	1979
	31,983	34,700	55,188	75,239

Regional distribution of Tabasarans

	1926	1959	1970	1979
RSFSR	31,983 (100%)	34,228 (98.6%)	54,047 (97.9%)	n.a.
DaghASSR only	31,915 (99.8%)	33,548 (96.7%)	53,253 (96.5%)	71,722 (95.3%)
Elsewhere in USSR	——	472 (1.4%)	1,141 (2.1%)	

Urban/rural distribution of Tabasarans in the Daghestan ASSR

	1926	1970
Urban	34 (0.1%)	7,535 (14.1%)
Rural	31,881 (99.9%)	45,718 (85.9%)

For *Ethnic composition of the Daghestan ASSR* and *Urban/rural distribution in the Daghestan ASSR* see pp. 126, 129.

3 STATUS

The Tabasarans enjoy full Soviet citizenship. They are found in all occupations and in all income brackets, though the majority work on collective farms or in carpet-weaving co-operatives (women only). Their standard of housing is comparable to that of other national groups in the Soviet Union. The women go out to work, as elsewhere in the Soviet Union.

Literacy

In 1926	In 1970
1.6%	Over 99%

In 1926, none of the Tabasarans were literate in their own language.

4 LANGUAGE

The national language is Tabasaran. It belongs to the Lezghi group of Caucasian languages. It is closest to Agul and forms with it a sub-group of the Lezghi languages. There are two main dialect groups, a northern and a southern. The differences between them are phonetic and morphological. The dialect of Nitrik, one of the southern groups, was taken as the basis for the literary language. An alphabet was developed for Tabasaran in 1932 and since then a certain amount of literature has appeared in that language, both original works and translations.

Russian is generally used for administrative, judicial and other official proceedings, but in theory Tabasaran can be used if necessary.

Percentage of Tabasarans claiming Tabasaran as their mother tongue

	1926	1959	1970	1979
Total	92.9	99.2	98.9	97.4
In urban areas	100	93.3	94.3	n.a.
In rural areas	92.9	99.8	99.8	n.a.

Percentage of Tabasarans with good knowledge of Russian

	1926	1959	1970	1979
As mother tongue	0.0	0.5	0.9	1.5
As second language	n.a.	n.a.	31.9	59.0

Percentage of Tabasarans with good knowledge of a language other than their own or Russian (mostly another Daghestani language)

	1970	1979
As mother tongue	0.2	1.2
As second language	10.1	7.6

In 1958 Tabasaran was the medium of instruction in grades 1–4 (primary +1) in some national schools; in 1972, only in grades 1–2 and pre-school; in 1972 it was also taught as an individual, optional subject in Russian-medium schools in grades 1–8 (Silver, p. 33). More recent information is not available.

There is apparently no broadcasting in Tabasaran.

A newspaper is published in Tabasaran, *Tabasarandin nurar* ('Tabasaran Dawns' – since 1970: a continuation of a paper originally started in 1932) and there has been a Tabasaran edition of 'Woman of Daghestan' since 1962.

Books and pamphlets are intermittently published in Tabasaran (e.g. 8 titles in 1976, the first to be published in over ten years; none of these were specialized textbooks on scientific or technical subjects).

Scripts and alphabets

An alphabet based on the Latin script was created for Tabasaran in 1932; it was replaced by a new one, based on the Cyrillic script, in 1938.

5 RELIGION

The Tabasarans are Sunni Muslims (Shafi'i school). In every village there used to be a mosque; local saints (*pirs*) were also much revered and their graves treated as places of pilgrimage.

NOGAIS

Own name: *Nogai*; Russian name: *Nogajtsy*.

The majority of Nogais live in the 'Nogai Steppe' in the north of the Daghestan ASSR, between the Rivers Kuma and Terek. There

are also Nogais in the Achikulak Region (*rajon*) of the Stavropol'
Territory (*kraj*), the Chechen-Ingush ASSR and the Karachajevo-
Cherkess Autonomous Province. The Nogais are bordered to the
north-east by the Kalmyks, to the south by the Chechens; the
Caspian Sea lies to the east. There are three main tribal divisions:
the Nogais in the Achikulak Region, the Kara-Nogais in the
Kara-Nogai Region and the Ak-Nogais in the Karachajevo-Cher-
kess Autonomous Province.

1 HISTORICAL BACKGROUND

The Nogais are descendants of the Nogai Horde, which came into
being when the Golden Horde began to weaken towards the end
of the fourteenth century. It appears to have taken its name from
Nogai (d. 1300), one of the most powerful of the commanders of
the Golden Horde. The Nogai group of tribes represented a
stronger Mongol strain (Manghit in particular) than most of the other
components of the Golden Horde, but like the forebears of the
present-day Tatars (see p. 55), they were (or became) Turkic-
speakers. Until the sixteenth century they roamed the vast steppes
between northern Kazakhstan and southern Siberia; their chief
settlement was at Sarajchik at the mouth of the River Jaik. In the
mid-sixteenth century, after Astrakhan and Kazan had fallen to
Ivan IV (the Terrible), the Nogai Horde split into two main divisions: the Great Horde, which remained on the Lower Volga and
came under Russian rule (1555–7) and the Little Horde, whose
territory became the right bank of the River Kuban', the shores of
the Sea of Azov and southern Ukraine. In 1634 the predations of
the marauding Kalmyks of Siberia caused the Great Horde to move
to the south, where they were once more united with the Little
Horde. The whole of the Nogai Horde then became nominal subjects of the Crimean Tatars. Gradually, however, they were forced
out of this area by pressure from the Cossacks (Kazaks) and as a
result the Horde once more split up into smaller units, some of the
Nogais going further west to Budzhak (where they came under
Ottoman rule), some to the east, to Daghestan. The influence of
the Crimean Tatars remained strong, though, for the leaders of the
Nogais (*mirzas* and *sultans*) continued to be Crimean Tatars.
     The Nogais, like the rest of the Golden Horde, were converted
to Islam during the fourteenth century, when Uzbek Khan (1312–

42) made its acceptance compulsory for his people. Contacts with the Crimean Tatars in the seventeenth century, however, no doubt strengthened its hold upon the Nogais. When they moved to the Caucasus they in turn were instrumental in bringing about the conversion of peoples such as the Abazins. In the early nineteenth century Daghestan came under Russian rule: when the most serious of the uprisings prompted by this event had been crushed, that of the Murids under the Imam Shamyl (1834–59), several of the Nogais, like the Shkaraua Abazins and many of the other Caucasian peoples, chose to emigrate to Turkey.

The traditional occupation of the Nogais was nomadic herding. Under Russian rule they began to adopt a settled way of life and the majority now live on collective farms. In the past they were particularly famous for their skill as saddle-makers and this tradition to some extent still survives.

2 NUMBER AND DISTRIBUTION

Number of Nogais

	1926	1959	1970	1979
	36,274	38,583	51,784	59,546

Regional distribution of Nogais

	1926	1959	1970	1979
RSFSR	36,256 (100%)	37,656 (97.6%)	51,159 (98.8%)	n.a.
DaghASSR only	26,086 (71.9%)	14,939 (38.7%)	21,750 (42.0%)	24,977 (41.9%)
Cherkess/Karachaj -Cherkess Aut. Prov. only	6,206 (17.1%)	8,903 (23.1%)	11,062 (21.4%)	11,872 (19.9%)
Elsewhere in USSR	18 (0.0%)	927 (2.4%)	625 (1.2%)	

For *Ethnic composition of the Daghestan ASSR* see p. 126.
For *Ethnic composition of the Karachajevo-Cherkess Autonomous Province* see p. 204.

Urban/rural distribution of the Nogais in the RSFSR

	1926	1970
Urban	134	6,074
	(0.3%)	(11.9%)
Rural	36,122	45,085
	(99.7%)	(88.1%)

For *Urban/rural distribution of the main nationalities in the Daghestan ASSR* see p. 129.

For *Urban/rural distribution in the Karachajevo-Cherkess Autonomous Province* see p. 205.

3 STATUS

The Nogais enjoy full Soviet citizenship. They are found in all occupations and in all income brackets, but the majority work on collective farms and a smaller number in industry. Their standard of housing is comparable to that of other national groups in the Soviet Union. The women go out to work, as elsewhere in the Soviet Union.

Literacy

In 1926	In 1970
7.1%	Over 99%

In 1926, 639 Nogais were literate in their own language (24.7 per cent of the total literate Nogai population).

4 LANGUAGE

The national language is Nogai. It belongs to the Central Turkic group (*Fundamenta* classification); it can also be classed as belonging to the Kipchak group, Kipchak-Nogai sub-group (Baskakov). The languages it is most closely related to are Karakalpak and Kazakh.

There are three dialect groupings, corresponding to the main tribal divisions: Nogai, Ak-Nogai and Kara-Nogai. The literary language was developed during the Soviet period and the creation of standardized norms is gradually eroding dialectal differences. The divergences between the three groups are now mainly phonetic.

The vocabulary contains a large Arabic-Persian element, as well as Russian loans dating from before and after the Revolution.

Russian is generally used for administrative, judicial and other official proceedings, but in theory Nogai can be used if necessary.

Percentage of Nogais claiming Nogai as their mother tongue

	1926	1959	1970	1979
Total	97.2	90.0	89.8	90.3
In urban areas	76.5	85.4	88.2	n.a.
In rural areas	97.3	90.4	90.0	n.a.

Percentage of Nogais with good knowledge of Russian

	1926	1959	1970	1979
As mother tongue	0.3	1.9	1.8	2.4
As second language	n.a.	n.a.	68.5	75.6

Percentage of Nogais with good knowledge of a language other than their own or Russian (mostly another Daghestani language or Karachai)

	1970	1979
As mother tongue	8.5	7.3
As second language	0.7	0.7

In 1958 Nogai was the medium of instruction in grades 1–4 (primary +1) in national schools; in 1972, in pre-school only but it was taught as an individual, optional subject in Russian-medium schools in grades 1–8 (Silver, p. 33). More recent information is not available.

There is some broadcasting in Nogai in the Karachajevo-Cherkess Autonomous Province.

Two newspapers are published in Nogai: *Shollik majagy* ('Beacon of the Steppe' – since 1932) in the Daghestan ASSR and *Lenin joly* ('Lenin's Way' – since 1938) in the Karachajevo-Cherkess Autonomous Province.

Books and pamphlets are published in Nogai (e.g. 8 titles in 1976; none of these were specialized textbooks on scientific or technical subjects).

Scripts and alphabets

1928–31 Latin script, first alphabet
1931–5   Latin script, second alphabet
1935–6   Latin script, third alphabet
1936–8   Latin script, fourth alphabet
1938–44 Cyrillic script, first alphabet
1944–50 Cyrillic script, second alphabet
1950   Cyrillic script, third alphabet.

The differences between these alphabets are, apart from the change of script, very slight. However, the latest Nogai alphabet is still not considered to represent the language adequately and further changes are anticipated.

5 RELIGION

The Nogais are Sunni Muslims (Hanafi school; cf. the other Daghestani peoples, such as the Avars, Lezghis, etc., who follow the Shafi'i school).

RUTULS/RUTULIS

Own name: according to village; Russian name: *Rutul'tsy*.

The majority live on the upper reaches of the River Samur in the Rutul Region (*rajon*) of the Daghestan ASSR, but a few live across the border in the neighbouring Azerbaidzhan SSR. Their name in Russian is derived from that of their largest settlement, Rutul, which is also the administrative centre of the region. They have no collective term for themselves, identifying themselves only by village. They are bordered to the north by the Laks and the Darghins, to the north-east by the Aguls, to the east and south-east by the Lezghis, to the west by the Tsakhurs.

1 HISTORICAL BACKGROUND

The Rutuls are a numerically-small Caucasian people of southern Daghestan. They were settled in their present habitat on the River Samur at a very early date, possibly before AD 500. Their forebears may have been Christians (there is archaeological evidence to support this), but they adopted Islam at the time of the Arab conquest of Daghestan (eighth century) and have remained Muslims ever since. In several villages buildings are found bearing Kufic inscriptions; some date from the eleventh century, while others, particularly in Rutul itself, appear to be even older. Despite their rather isolated situation, the Rutuls played an active part in the ever-changing pattern of feuds and alliances of the Caucasian principalities. They were at their most powerful during the sixteenth to eighteenth centuries. Each village or tribal group had its own chieftain (*bek*); together they formed the 'Rutul Mahal', a loose federation or alliance that would follow a common policy. The beks were both the civil and military leaders of their people: by tradition, they were held to be descended from the Arabs who had first converted the Rutuls to Islam.

In the early nineteenth century the Russians advanced into Daghestan and the Rutuls, too, came under their rule. There were a number of uprisings against the Russians, but the most significant was that of 1838, as a result of which the Rutul Aga-Bek was defeated and the Rutul Mahal finally annexed by Russia. In 1844 it became part of the Samur District (*okrug*).

Apart from fighting, the traditional Rutul occupation was sheep-breeding. This remains important today, though agriculture is now also being developed, particularly the cultivation of cereals and potatoes. Amongst the traditional crafts practised by the Rutuls, carpet-weaving and the knitting of intricately patterned thick socks are still very much alive.

2 NUMBER AND DISTRIBUTION

Number of Rutuls

1926	1959	1970	1979
10,495	6,732	12,071	15,032

Regional distribution of Rutuls

	1926	1959	1970	1979
RSFSR	10,333	6,703	11,904	n.a.
	(98.5%)	(99.6%)	(98.6%)	
DaghASSR only	10,333	6,566	11,799	14,288
	(98.5%)	(97.5%)	(97.7%)	(95.1%)
Elsewhere in	162	29	167	
USSR	(1.5%)	(0.4%)	(1.4%)	

Urban/rural distribution of Rutuls in the Daghestan ASSR

	1926	1970
Urban	0	87
	(0.0%)	(0.7%)
Rural	10,333	11,712
	(100%)	(99.3%)

For *Ethnic composition of the Daghestan ASSR* and *Urban/rural distribution in the Daghestan ASSR* see pp. 126, 129.

3 STATUS

The Rutuls enjoy full Soviet citizenship. They are found in all occupations and income brackets, though the majority work on collective farms. Their standard of housing is comparable to that of other national groups in the Soviet Union. The women go out to work, as elsewhere in the Soviet Union.

Literacy

In 1926	In 1970
4.2%*	Over 99%

*The majority of these were literate in Arabic.

4 LANGUAGE

The national language is Rutul. It belongs to the Lezghi group of Caucasian languages. It has four dialects. It is not a written language. The most widely used literary language is Azerbaidzhani (a Turkic language); Russian stands in second place, Lezghi in third. The older generation knew some Arabic (mostly in order to read the Qur'an).

Russian is generally used for administrative, judicial and other official proceedings, but Azerbaidzhani is used along with Russian for other written transactions.

Percentage of Rutuls claiming Rutul as their mother tongue

	1926	1959	1970	1979
Total	98.6	99.9	98.9	99.1

Percentage of Rutuls with good knowledge of Russian

	1926	1959	1970	1979
As mother tongue	none	0.1	0.3	0.6
As second language	n.a.	n.a.	30.7	52.0

Percentage of Rutuls with good knowledge of a language other than their own or Russian (mostly Lezghi or Azerbaidzhani)

	1970	1979
As mother tongue	0.8	0.2
As second language	18.8	12.2

In 1958 Azerbaidzhani was the medium of instruction in grades 1–10 in some of the national schools in the RSFSR (including, presumably, the Daghestan ASSR); Lezghi was the medium of instruction in grades 1–4 (primary +1), at this time; in 1972 both Azerbaidzhani and Lezghi were used as media of instruction in some national schools in the RSFSR in grades 1–2 and pre-school; in 1972 both languages were also taught as individual, optional subjects in some Russian-medium schools in the RSFSR (Silver, pp. 33–4).

No information is available on the use of Rutul in broadcasting; it is almost certainly not used at all.

An Azerbaidzhani-language local paper has been published in the Rutul Region since 1932 (*Gyzyl Choban*, 'The Red Shepherd').

There are no publications in Rutul, since it is not a written language.

5 RELIGION

The Rutuls are Sunni Muslims (Shafi'i school).

TSAKHURS/TSAKHURIS

Own name: *Jykhi*; Russian name: *Tsakhury*.

The Tsakhurs live in the western part of the Rutul Region (*rajon*) of the Daghestan ASSR and across the border in the adjacent territory of the Azerbaidzhan SSR. The majority are settled on the upper reaches of the River Samur. Their neighbours to the north and north-east are the Laks, to the east the Rutuls, to the south the Azerbaidzhanis, to the north-west the Avars. Their name in Russian is derived from that of one of their main settlements, Tsakhur.

1 HISTORICAL BACKGROUND

The Tsakhurs are an indigenous Caucasian people of southern Daghestan. They live in extremely mountainous, difficult terrain and, as a result, their villages used to be virtually inaccessible for most of the year. Now they are linked by road to the outside world, but they still lead a very isolated existence. Nevertheless, Arab invaders in the seventh and eighth centuries succeeded in penetrating this area and the Tsakhurs, like their neighbours the Rutuls and other mountain peoples of the Caucasus, adopted Islam. By about the fifteenth century the Tsakhurs had formed themselves into a loose federation of tribes under the leadership of a *Sultan*. The seat of the Tsakhur sultanate was originally at Tsakhur, but in the seventeenth century it was moved to Elisu in Azerbaidzhan. In 1803 the Tsakhurs came under Russian rule, but the territorial integrity of the Elisu sultanate was specifically underlined. However, in 1844, when the Tsakhur Sultan Daniel-Bek supported Shamyl's uprising, the Russians abolished the sultanate and took direct control of the area. In 1852 the whole Tsakhur population was deported to Azerbaidzhan on the grounds that they might lend support to Shamyl; they were allowed to return to their own lands in 1860, after Shamyl had finally been defeated.

The chief traditional occupation of the Tsakhur was sheep-breeding and this is still the most important branch of the economy. Some farming is carried out, but the climate and the soil are not very favourable. Handicrafts are widely practised, particularly carpet-weaving and the knitting of thick, patterned socks. The Tsakhurs have long been known for their skill as stonemasons, carpenters, shoemakers and tailors and formerly the men would frequently leave their villages in search of work in one of these trades. They still tend to leave during the winter months, but the percentage has dropped from almost 100 per cent to 30–40 per cent.

2 NUMBER AND DISTRIBUTION

Number of Tsakhurs

	1926	1959	1970	1979
	19,085	7,321	11,103	13,478

Regional distribution of Tsakhurs

	1926	1959	1970	1979
RSFSR	3,533 (18.5%)	4,437 (60.6%)	4,730 (42.6%)	n.a.
DaghASSR only	3,531 (18.5%)	4,278 (58.4%)	4,309 (38.3%)	4,560 (33.8%)
AzSSR	15,552 (81.5%)	2,876 (39.3%)	6,208 (55.9%)	8,546 (63.4%)
Elsewhere in USSR	——	8 (0.1%)	165 (1.5%)	

Urban/rural distribution of Tsakhurs

	1926	1970
Urban	215 (1.1%)	1,304 (11.7%)
Rural	18,870 (98.9%)	9,799 (88.3%)

For *Ethnic composition of the Daghestan ASSR* and *Urban/rural distribution in the Daghestan ASSR* see pp. 126, 129.

The Tsakhurs who live in the Daghestan ASSR have maintained their language and their cultural identity, but those who live in the AzSSR are rapidly being assimilated. This may account for the enormous drop in the size of the Tsakhur population in the AzSSR between 1926–59.

3 STATUS

The Tsakhur enjoy full Soviet citizenship. They are found in all occupations and in all income brackets, though the majority work on collective farms. Their standard of housing is comparable to that of other national groups in the Soviet Union. The women go out to work, as elsewhere in the Soviet Union.

Literacy

In 1926	In 1970
4.7%	Over 99%

4 LANGUAGE

The national language is Tsakhur. It belongs to the Lezghi group of Caucasian languages. It is not a written language, though attempts were made to create an alphabet for it during the 1930s. The Tsakhur vocabulary contains many words of Arabic and Persian origin, as well as loan-words from Azerbaidzhani and Russian. The Tsakhurs of the Daghestan ASSR tend to use Russian as a literary language, those of the Azerbaidzhan SSR, Azerbaidzhani. The number of Tsakhurs claiming Tsakhur as their mother tongue, however, has almost doubled in recent years.

Russian is used for administrative, judicial and other official proceedings, but in the AzSSR Azerbaidzhani can also be used if necessary.

Percentage of Tsakhurs claiming Tsakhur as their mother tongue

	1926	1959	1970	1979
Total	57.3	99.2	96.5	95.2

No information is available on the medium of instruction in schools; it is most probably Russian in the Daghestan ASSR, Azerbaidzhani in the AzSSR.

Percentage of Tsakhurs with good knowledge of Russian

	1926	1959	1970	1979
As mother tongue	none	0.0 (1 person)	0.8	0.4
As second language	n.a.	n.a.	12.2	22.4

Percentage of Tsakhurs with good knowledge of a language other than their own or Russian (mostly Azerbaidzhani)

	1970	1979
As mother tongue	2.7	4.4
As second language	43.1	48.5

No information is available on the use of Tsakhur in broadcasting; it is probably not used at all.

There are no publications in Tsakhur, as it is not a written language.

5 RELIGION

The Tsakhur are Sunni Muslims (Shafi'i school).

AGULS/AGULIS

Own name: *Agul (shuj)*; also, according to village; Russian name: *Agultsy*.

The Aguls live in four ravines high in the mountains of southern Daghestan, the ravines of Aguldere, Khushandere, Kurakhdere and Khpjukdere. The majority are concentrated in Aguldere, in which sixteen of their twenty-one settlements are located. The administrative centre of the area, Tpig, is also situated in Aguldere. A road linking Tpig with the Lezghi settlement of Kaumkent was completed in 1936, the first metalled road to be constructed in this area. The Aguls are bordered to the north by the Darghins, to the north-east by the Kaitaks, to the south by the Lezghis, to the south-west by the Rutuls.

1 HISTORICAL BACKGROUND

The Aguls are a numerically-small Caucasian people of southern Daghestan. Until recent years they led an extremely isolated existence, their villages often scarcely accessible even from an adjacent valley. Like their neighbours the Kaitaks, the Aguls were converted to Islam at the time of the Arab conquest of Daghestan in the eighth century. They were under the nominal rule of various states, including, in the eighteenth century, the Kazikumukh (Lak) Khanate and the Tabasarans, but their main contacts were with the Lezghis, with whom they used to trade the products of their flocks (e.g. wool, fleeces and cheese). When Daghestan came under Russian rule in the early nineteenth century, so, too, did the Aguls, forming part of the Kiurin Khanate, which was later transformed into the Kiurin District (*okrug*).

The social structure of the Aguls was based on the extended family, which would sometimes consist of thirty to forty households, dominated by a single patriarch. Bonds between members of the extended family (known as *tokhum*) were strengthened by the practice of endogamy and the joint ownership of such economic assets as meadows and grazing grounds. Kinsmen were bound to help and defend one another. Collective farms have now taken the place of the tokhum and the patriarchal system has virtually disappeared.

Traditionally the chief occupation of the Aguls was sheep-rearing. This retains its importance today, with the flocks still being driven up to the rich mountain pastures during the summer. Agriculture is now being developed, and along with the cultivation of cereals such as wheat, barley and rye, orchards are also being introduced into the area.

2 NUMBER AND DISTRIBUTION

Number of Aguls

	1926	1959	1970	1979
	7,653	6,709	8,831	12,078

Regional distribution of Aguls

	1926	1959	1970	1979
RSFSR	7,653 (100%)	6,460 (96.3%)	8,751 (99.1%)	n.a.
DaghASSR only	7,653 (100%)	6,378 (95.1%)	8,644 (97.9%)	11,459 (94.9%)
Elsewhere in USSR	——	249 (3.7%)	80 (0.9%)	

Urban/rural distribution of Aguls in the Daghestan ASSR

	1926	1970
Urban	——	192 (2.2%)
Rural	7,653 (100%)	8,452 (97.8%)

For *Ethnic composition of the Daghestan ASSR* and *Urban/rural distribution in the Daghestan ASSR* see pp. 126, 129.

3 STATUS

The Aguls enjoy full Soviet citizenship. They are found in all occupations and income brackets, though the majority work on collective farms and are employed in sheep-rearing. Their standard of housing is comparable to that of other national groups in the Soviet Union. The women go out to work, as elsewhere in the Soviet Union.

Literacy

In 1926	In 1970
1.2%	over 99%

A number of Aguls now have higher education and have qualified as doctors, veterinary surgeons, agronomists, etc.

4 LANGUAGE

The national language is Agul. It belongs to the Lezghi group of Caucasian languages. It has four dialects. Lezghi serves as the literary language, since Agul is not a written language. However, though they belong to the same group, the two are not mutually comprehensible.

Russian is used for all administrative, judicial and other official proceedings, but Lezghi is used along with Russian for other written transactions. Agul remains strong as the spoken language, both at home and at work.

Percentage of Aguls claiming Agul as their mother tongue

	1926	1959	1970	1979
Total	100.0	99.4	99.4	98.3

Percentage of Aguls with good knowledge of Russian

	1926	1959	1970	1979
As mother tongue	0.0	0.4	0.2	1.2
As second language	n.a.	n.a.	39.8	62.9

Percentage of Aguls with good knowledge of a language other than their own or Russian (mostly Lezghi)

	1970	1979
As mother tongue	0.2	0.5
As second language	9.5	7.9

There may be some primary education available in Lezghi (though none, of course, in Agul, since it is not a written language). In 1958 Lezghi was the medium of instruction in grades 1–4 (primary +1) in national schools in the Daghestan ASSR; in 1972, only in grades 1–2 and pre-school; in 1972 it was also taught as an individual, optional subject in some Russian-medium schools (Silver, p. 33). The first schoolteachers in the Agul area were Lezghis and many of the trained personnel are still Lezghis. Thus, despite the fact that there may not be much education available in Lezghi at present, the influence of that language remains strong amongst the Aguls.

No information is available on the use of Agul in broadcasting; it is probably not used.

A regional newspaper for the Aguls was started in Lezghi in 1952.

There are no publications in Agul, since it is not a written language.

5 RELIGION

The Aguls are Sunni Muslims (Shafi'i school). There was formerly a mosque in every village. It is not known how many of these are still open for worship; probably very few, if any, since most of the mosques in Daghestan today are found in the larger towns.

CHECHEN

Own name: *Nokhcho*; Russian name: *Chechentsy*.

The majority live in the central and eastern parts of the Checheno-Ingush ASSR; some also live in the adjacent area of the Daghestan ASSR.

1 HISTORICAL BACKGROUND

The origins of the Chechen are unclear. They are probably an indigenous people of the Northern Caucasus. This theory is supported by their own legends and also by some archaeological evidence. They are mentioned in an Armenian source of the seventh century and also in early Georgian chronicles. Remains of churches indicate that at least some of the Chechen had been converted to Christianity by about the eighth century (probably through Georgia). They are known to their neighbours by widely differing names: the Turkic Kumyks call them *Michigish* ('People of the River Michik'), the Georgians *Kisty*, the Avars *Burtiel* and the Armenians *Nakhchatja* (from their own name *Nokhcho*). The Russian name is derived from that of the settlement *Bol'shoj Chechen* ('Big Chechen') on the River Argun. The Kabardians and Ossetians also began to use forms derived from this from the sixteenth century onwards.

The Chechen originally lived in the mountains but began to move down to the plains from the end of the fourteenth century. By the late sixteenth century many were settled on the River Sunzha, as was noted by Russian ambassadors in 1587. During the sixteenth century Islam was introduced amongst the Chechen by the Avars and Kumyks. Daghestan was an important centre of Islamic culture and learning at this period and a number of Chechen went there to receive their religious training. The Chechens actively supported the Murid Uprising led by Shamyl in the mid-nineteenth century (1834–59) and it was only after his defeat that their lands came under Russian rule. This caused many of the Chechen to emigrate to Turkey, while amongst those who remained insurrections and uprisings against the new order were frequent.

After the Russian Revolution there was a bitter struggle for power in the Caucasus. The Soviets assumed control in the Chechen territory at the end of 1917 and the Terek Soviet Republic was formed in March 1918 (as part of the RSFSR). The White Army occupied the area in 1919 and it was not until 1920 that Soviet rule was established once more. The Gorskaja ('Mountain') ASSR was formed on 20 January 1921, which incorporated Balkar, Chechen, Ingush, Kabardian, Karachai and Ossetian lands; Chechnia and several other areas were hived off in 1922 and when the Gorskaja ASSR was finally disbanded on 7 July 1924 Ingushetia also became an independent unit. The two remained as separate autonomous provinces until 15 January 1934, when they were again combined, this time to form a joint Checheno-Ingush Autonomous Province; it was transformed into an ASSR on 5 December 1936.

In the early Soviet period the clan system was still extremely strong amongst the Chechen. Land tenure was based upon joint clan ownership and when this was abandoned and collectivization introduced the Chechen opposed it fiercely. There were many acts of banditry and the situation was aggravated by massive political purges. When the war broke out, however, the majority of Chechen undoubtedly did oppose the Germans and fought bravely with the Red Army (many were decorated for valour). Nevertheless, in 1944 the entire Chechen and Ingush peoples were deported to Central Asia and Kazakhstan (including those from the Daghestan ASSR and other parts of the USSR). The Checheno-Ingush ASSR was retroactively disbanded in 1946, but by then Chechen and Ingush place-names had already been replaced by Russian and the land given to new settlers. In 1957 the Chechen and Ingush were officially 'rehabilitated', their republic reinstated and they themselves allowed to return home. Not surprisingly, they were not welcomed and there was great tension between the different national groups. This occasionally flared up into serious confrontations, as, for example, in August 1958. The situation has now improved, but still does not appear entirely happy.

Checheno-Ingush ASSR, also known as *Checheno-Ingushetia* (it combines the territories formerly known as Greater Chechnia, Little Chechnia and Ingushetia)

Situated in the RSFSR in the Northern Caucasus; it is bordered to the east and south-east by the Daghestan ASSR, to the south-west by the Georgian SSR, to the west by the North Ossetian ASSR. *Area*: 19,300 sq. km. *Capital*: Groznyj (population in 1979: 375,000). The Republic has 5 towns and 4 settlements. *Population* (1979): 1,155,805. Average density of population per sq. km (1979): 59.8.

Chief resources: oil and natural gas.

Industries include: oil extraction and refining (one of the most important in the USSR; crude oil is brought here from other areas), machine-building (mainly directed towards the oil industry), chemical and petrochemical industries; food and other light industries.

Agriculture: grain farming and the cultivation of sunflowers, sugar beet, vegetables, grapes and other fruit; stockbreeding, particularly of fine fleeced sheep.

2 NUMBER AND DISTRIBUTION

Number of Chechen

1926	1959	1970	1979
318,522	418,756	612,674	755,782

The net losses for the period 1939–59 are estimated to be a minimum of 22 per cent (Nekrich, p. 138).

Regional distribution of Chechen

	1926	1959	1970	1979
Chechen Aut. Prov./ Checheno-Ingush ASSR	291,259 (91.4%)	243,974 (58.3%)	508,898 (83.1%)	611,405 (80.9%)
Daghestan ASSR	21,851 (6.9%)	12,798 (3.1%)	39,965 (6.5%)	49,227 (6.5%)
Elsewhere in USSR	5,412 (1.7%)	161,984 (38.7%)	63,811 (10.4%)	95,150 (12.6%)

Urban/rural distribution of Chechen in Chechen Aut. Prov./Checheno-Ingush ASSR

	1926	*1970*
Urban	70 (0.0%)	90,805 (17.8%)
Rural	291,189 (100%)	418,093 (82.2%)

Ethnic composition of the Chechen Aut. Prov./Checheno-Ingush ASSR

	1926	*1959*	*1970*	*1979*
	(Chechen Aut. Prov.)	(Checheno-Ingush ASSR)		
Total population	309,787	710,424	1,064,471	1,155,805
Chechen	291,259 (94.0%)	243,974 (34.3%)	508,898 (47.8%)	611,405 (52.9%)
Ingush	130 (0.0%)	48,273 (6.8%)	113,675 (10.7%)	134,744 (11.7%)
Daghestani peoples	3,272 (1.1%)	17,019 (2.4%)	19,674 (1.8%)	22,023 (1.9%)
Russians	9,122 (2.9%)	348,343 (49.0%)	366,959 (34.5%)	336,044 (29.1%)
Others	6,004 (1.9%)	52,815 (7.4%)	55,265 (5.2%)	51,589 (4.4%)

For *Ethnic composition of the Ingush Aut. Prov. (1926)* see p. 199.

Urban/rural distribution in the Checheno-Ingush ASSR in 1970

	Urban	*Rural*
Total population	444,062	620,409
Chechen	90,805 (20.4%)	418,093 (67.4%)
Ingush	35,612 (8.0%)	78,063 (12.6%)
Daghestani peoples	3,741 (0.8%)	15,933 (2.6%)
Russians	269,947 (60.8%)	97,012 (15.6%)
Others	43,957 (9.9%)	11,308 (1.8%)

3 STATUS

Having been 'rehabilitated', the Chechen now enjoy full Soviet citizenship. They are found in all occupations and in all income brackets; most are engaged in agriculture and animal husbandry, but some work in the industrial enterprises in Groznyj (e.g. in the oil-refineries). Their standard of housing is now comparable to that of other national groups in the Soviet Union. The women go out to work, as elsewhere in the Soviet Union.

Literacy

In 1926	in 1970
2.9%	Over 99%

In 1926, 2,756 Chechen were literate in their own language (29.8 per cent of the total literate Chechen population).

Level of education per 1,000 Chechen living in the Checheno-Ingush ASSR of 10 years of age and above

	1959	*1970*
Primary		
Total	185	334
Men	286	369
Women	100	302
Higher and secondary (complete and incomplete)		
Total	110	219
Men	210	315
Women	26	133
Higher only		
Total	1	7
Men	3	13
Women	0.2	2

4 LANGUAGE

The national language is Chechen. It belongs to the North-East group of Caucasian languages, Nakhcho (i.e. Chechen) sub-group. It is very closely related to Ingush and the two were in fact considered to form one literary language until 1934; they are now considered to be separate. There are a number of dialect groups;

the dialect group of the plains formed the basis for the literary language. The vocabulary contains loan-words from Arabic, Persian, Turkish, Georgian and Russian (the last both pre- and post-revolutionary loans).

Russian is generally used for administrative, judicial and other official proceedings, but in theory Chechen can be used if necessary.

Percentage of Chechen claiming Chechen as their mother tongue

	1926	1959	1970	1979
Total	99.7	98.8	98.7	98.6
In urban areas	94.2	97.0	95.7	n.a.
In rural areas	99.8	99.4	99.5	n.a.

Percentage of Chechen with good knowledge of Russian

	1926	1959	1970	1979
As mother tongue	0.1	1.0	1.2	1.3
As second language	n.a.	n.a.	66.7	76.0

In 1958 Chechen was the medium of instruction in grades 1–4 (primary +1) in national schools; in 1972, pre-school only; in 1972 it was also taught as an individual, optional subject in Russian-medium schools in grades 1–10 (Silver, p. 33). More recent information is not available. There is a university and an Oil Institute at Groznyj. Tuition appears to be entirely in Russian at both establishments.

In the Checheno-Ingush ASSR there is some broadcasting in Chechen and Ingush, as well as Russian.

Newspapers and periodicals are published in Chechen and Ingush, as well as Russian. The first, and still the main, Chechen newspaper, *Leninan nek* ('Lenin's Way') appeared in 1923; there was a break in publication from 1945 to 1957.

Books and pamphlets are now published in Chechen (e.g. 25 titles in 1976; none of these were specialized textbooks on scientific or technical subjects).

Number of books and pamphlets published in Chechen and Ingush in selected years

	1913	*1940*	*1965*	*1979*
No. of titles	——	154	45	53
Print run	——	673,000	179,000	299,000

Scripts and alphabets

There were some attempts to write Chechen before the Soviet period (e.g. the Cyrillic alphabet invented by P. K. Uslar in the 1860s), but it was only after the Revolution that it was properly developed as a literary language, using the Arabic script for the first few years.

Until mid-1920s	Arabic script
1928–38	Latin script
1938	Cyrillic script

5 RELIGION

The Chechen are Sunni Muslims (Hanafi school). In 1837 there were 310 mosques in Chechnia (Smirnov, *Mjuridizm. . .*, p. 87). A much higher estimate is suggested for the 1930s: 2,675 mosques and houses of prayer; also 140 religious schools and 850 sheikhs and mullahs (Nekrich, p. 51). All the mosques and other religious buildings were closed when the Chechen and Ingush were deported in 1944. Two mosques were again opened for worship in 1978 (*Religion in Communist Lands*, vol. 7, no. 3, p. 152). The Chechen come under the spiritual jurisdiction of the Directorate of Northern Caucasus and Daghestan (Makhachkala).

The Sufi movement has traditionally been very strong in the Caucasus. The main orders were the Qadiri and the Naqshbandi. The latter in particular was extremely influential. The most active group today appears to be a Qadiri, the Kunta Hadzhi (founded in 1862).

OSSETIANS/OSSETES

Own names: *Ir, Digor* (tribal names); Russian names: *Osetiny*; also *Digory, Irony, Iry*.

The majority of Ossetians live in the central Caucasian region, on either side of the main mountain range. A ridge of mountains divides the area into two parts, which are administratively separate: the northern part forms the North Ossetian Autonomous Republic (within the RSFSR), the southern and smaller part, the South Ossetian Autonomous Province (within the Georgian SSR). There are also some Ossetians in the Kabardino-Balkar ASSR.

1 HISTORICAL BACKGROUND

The Ossetians are an Iranian people of the Caucasus. Several theories have been advanced as to their origins, but the most generally accepted view today is that they are the descendants of Scythian and Sarmatian tribes, in particular the Alans, who intermingled with indigenous Caucasian peoples. In 1888 a funeral stele was discovered, bearing an inscription written in Greek characters and dated 941. The language of this, the so-called 'Zelenchuk inscription' (named after the area in which it was found) is Alan and it is considered to represent the earliest recorded stage of the modern Ossetian language.

The original habitat of the Alans was somewhere between southern Russia and Central Asia, but by the sixth century they were settled in the central Caucasus. They adopted Christianity at about this period (probably under the influence of Byzantium, though they also had contact with the Georgians) and by the tenth century had their own bishop. Their state was at its most powerful during the tenth to twelfth centuries. Then, under the pressure of the Mongol invasions of the thirteenth century, the Alans were pushed back into the mountains and rapidly disintegrated, merging with local tribes and losing their distinctive identity, so that by the sixteenth century the name 'Alan' is no longer found in historical sources. Those who settled in Transcaucasia, in the area now divided between the North Ossetian ASSR and the South Ossetian Autonomous Province, came to be known as Ossetians. By the sixteenth century they were under the sway of the Kabardians, who in turn were subject to the Crimean Khans. When the Kabardians came under Russian protection in the mid-sixteenth century (see p. 191), so, too, did the Ossetians. Under the influence of the Kabardians, some of the Ossetian tribes began to adopt Islam, but during the eighteenth and nineteenth centuries Russian missionaries

were extremely active amongst them and the majority were re-
converted to Christianity.

The industrialization of Ossetia began when the mining industry
was developed during the mid-nineteenth century. The Social
Democrats established a base in Vladikavkaz (today known as Ordzhonikidze) in 1903. The Bolshevik organizations in the region were
under the direction of Kirov from 1909 to 1917. During the Civil
War (1918–20) Ossetia, like the rest of Transcaucasia, was the scene
of bitter fighting between the White Army (under Denikin), the
Bolsheviks (under Ordzhonikidze) and the Mensheviks. The Bolsheviks finally triumphed over their adversaries towards the end of
1920 in Northern Ossetia and slightly later in Southern Ossetia,
where the Mensheviks continued the struggle until February 1921.
In the former region the Ossetian District (*okrug*) was formed in
November 1920 and incorporated into the Gorskaja ('Mountain')
ASSR; it was transformed into an independent Autonomous Province on 7 July 1924 and into an Autonomous Republic (always
within the RSFSR) on 5 December 1936. Southern Ossetia was
incorporated into the Georgian SSR and was formed into an Autonomous Province (still within the Georgian SSR) on 20 April 1922.

*North Ossetian ASSR (Tsagat Iristony Avtonomon Soveton Sotsi-
aliston Respublika)*, also known as *Northern Ossetia*

Situated in the RSFSR in the central region of the Caucasus; it is
bordered to the east by the Daghestan ASSR, to the south by the
Georgian SSR (including the South Ossetian Autonomous Province), to the west by the Kabardino-Balkar ASSR. *Area*: 8,000 sq.
km. *Capital*: Ordzhonikidze, formerly known as Vladikavkaz
(population in 1979: 279,000). The Republic has 6 towns and 7
settlements. *Population* (1979): 592,002. Average density of population per sq. km (1979): 74.6.

    Chief resources: deposits of lead and zinc; good agricultural land.

    Industries include: processing of lead and zinc ores, machine-
building and mining; timber, knitwear, food and other light industries; carpet-making.

    Agriculture: mostly grain farming (maize, wheat and barley);
sugar beet, fruit and vegetables are also cultivated; stockbreeding
of livestock for milk and dairy produce.

South Ossetian Autonomous Province, also known as *Southern Ossetia*

Situated in the Georgian SSR on the southern slopes of the Great Caucasian range; it is bordered to the north by the North Ossetian ASSR (which forms part of the RSFSR). *Area*: 3,900 sq. km. *Capital*: Tskhinvali. The Province has 1 town and 4 settlements. *Population* (1979): 97,988. Average density of population per sq. km (1979): 25.1.

Industries include: mining, machine-building, timber; production of building materials, food and other light industries.

Agriculture: grain-farming (mainly winter wheat, barley and maize); stock-breeding (particularly of sheep).

2 NUMBER AND DISTRIBUTION

Number of Ossetians

	1926	1959	1970	1979
	272,272	412,592	488,039	541,893

Regional distribution of Ossetians

	1926	1959	1970	1979
North Osset. Aut. Prov./ASSR	128,321 (47.1%)	215,463 (52.2%)	269,326 (55.2%)	299,022 (55.2%)
South Osset. Aut. Prov.	60,351 (22.2%)	63,698 (15.4%)	66,073 (13.5%)	65,077 (12.0%)
Georgian SSR (not including the South Osset. Aut. Prov.)	52,947 (19.4%)	77,480 (18.8%)	84,112 (17.2%)	95,420 (17.6%)
Kabardino-Balkar Aut. Prov./ASSR	4,078 (1.5%)	6,442 (1.6%)	9,167 (1.9%)	9,710 (1.8%)
Tadzh.ASSR/SSR	150 (0.1%)	4,514 (1.1%)	5,755 (1.2%)	n.a.
Elsewhere in USSR	26,425 (9.7%)	44,995 (10.9%)	53,606 (11.0%)	

Urban/rural distribution of Ossetians in the North Ossetian Aut. Prov./ASSR

	1926	1970
Urban	387 (0.3%)	141,768 (52.6%)
Rural	127,934 (99.7%)	127,558 (47.4%)

Urban/rural distribution of Ossetians in the South Ossetian Autonomous Province

	1926	1970
Urban	1,152 (1.9%)	25,278 (38.3%)
Rural	59,199 (98.1%)	40,795 (61.7%)

Ethnic composition of the North Ossetian Aut. Prov./ASSR

	1926	1959	1970	1979
Total population	152,254	450,581	552,581	592,002
Ossetians	128,321 (84.3%)	215,463 (47.8%)	269,326 (48.7%)	299,022 (50.5%)
Ingush	23 (0.0%)	6,071 (1.3%)	18,387 (3.3%)	23,663 (4.0%)
Russians	10,063 (6.6%)	178,654 (39.6%)	202,367 (36.6%)	200,692 (33.9%)
Ukrainians	10,301 (6.8%)	9,362 (2.1%)	9,250 (1.7%)	10,574 (1.8%)
Others	3,546 (2.3%)	41,031 (9.1%)	53,251 (9.6%)	58,051 (9.8%)

Ethnic composition of the South Ossetian Autonomous Province

	1926	1959	1970	1979
Total population	87,375	96,807	99,421	97,988
Ossetians	60,351 (69.1%)	63,698 (65.8%)	66,073 (66.5%)	65,077 (66.4%)
Georgians	23,538 (26.9%)	26,584 (27.5%)	28,125 (28.3%)	28,187 (28.8%)
Others	3,486 (4.0%)	6,525 (6.7%)	5,223 (5.3%)	4,724 (4.8%)

Urban/rural distribution in the North Ossetian ASSR in 1970

	Urban	Rural
Total population	356,403	196,178
Ossetians	141,768 (39.8%)	127,558 (65.0%)
Ingush	6,541 (1.8%)	11,846 (6.0%)
Russians	161,169 (45.2%)	41,198 (21.0%)
Ukrainians	7,940 (2.2%)	1,310 (0.7%)
Others	38,985 (10.9%)	14,266 (7.3%)

Urban/rural distribution in the South Ossetian Autonomous Province in 1970

	Urban	Rural
Total population	36,441	62,980
Ossetians	25,278 (69.4%)	40,795 (64.8%)
Georgians	6,589 (18.1%)	21,536 (34.2%)
Others	4,574 (12.6%)	649 (1.0%)

3 STATUS

The Ossetians enjoy full Soviet citizenship. They are found in all occupations and in all income brackets; the majority are engaged either in agricultural work or, particularly in the North Ossetian ASSR, in industry. Their standard of housing is comparable to that of other national groups in the Soviet Union. The women go out to work, as elsewhere in the Soviet Union.

Literacy

In 1926	In 1970
21.2%	Over 99%

In 1926, 22,221 Ossetians were literate in their own language (38.5 per cent of the total literate Ossetian population).

Level of education per 1,000 Ossetians living in the North Ossetian ASSR of 10 years of age and above

	1959	*1970*
Primary		
Total	231	253
Men	286	293
Women	187	219
Higher and secondary (complete and incomplete)		
Total	431	509
Men	441	524
Women	423	497
Higher only		
Total	30	52
Men	36	60
Women	24	46

Level of education per 1,000 Ossetians living in the South Ossetian Autonomous Province of 10 years of age and above

	1959	*1970*
Primary		
Total	222	267
Men	248	295
Women	199	244
Higher and secondary (complete and incomplete)		
Total	362	445
Men	391	465
Women	339	427
Higher only		
Total	32	62
Men	38	69
Women	28	55

4 LANGUAGE

The national language is Ossetian. It belongs to the North-East group of Iranian languages and represents the development of Alan, one of the Scythian Sarmatian languages. Ossetian has two main dialect groups: Iron and Digor. The Digor dialect is the more archaic and is spoken only in a few areas in the north and west of the North Ossetian ASSR. The differences between the two dialects are phonetic as well as morphological. In the early Soviet period, both were used as literary languages, but gradually the Digor dialect was dropped in favour of the Iron. Digor is no longer a written language.

The first major work on the Ossetian language (covering both dialects) was the *Ossetian Grammar* of A. Shegren, published in St Petersburg in 1844. This was followed by a number of important studies by V. F. Miller, a Russian philologist of the late nineteenth and early twentieth centuries. During the Soviet period Ossetian has also been the subject of research, notably by V. I. Abaev.

Russian is generally used for administrative, judicial and other official proceedings, but in theory Ossetian can be used if necessary. In the South Ossetian Autonomous Province (which falls within the Georgian SSR) Georgian is also used.

Percentage of Ossetians claiming Ossetian as their mother tongue

	1926	1959	1970	1979
Total	97.9	89.1	88.6	88.2
In urban areas	87.2	82.1	84.9	n.a.
In rural areas	98.8	93.0	92.9	n.a.

Percentage of Ossetians with good knowledge of Russian

	1926	1959	1970	1979
As mother tongue	0.7	4.9	5.4	6.6
As second language	n.a.	n.a.	58.6	64.9

In 1958 Ossetian was the medium of instruction in grades 1–4 (primary +1) in national schools in the North Ossetian ASSR; in 1972 it was not used at all as a medium of instruction, but was taught as an individual, optional subject in grades 1–10. There is no specific information on the situation in the South Ossetian Autonomous Province, but there is probably tuition in the native language in grades 1–4, then further education in Russian, not Georgian (Silver, p. 33). There is a university and institutes of Mining and Metallurgy and Medicine in the North Ossetian ASSR and a Pedagogical Institute in the South Ossetian Autonomous Province. There is unlikely to be any tuition in Ossetian at any of these establishments except, probably, the Pedagogical Institute.

There are some radio and television broadcasts in Ossetian in the North Ossetian ASSR, along with Russian.

Newspapers and periodicals are published in Ossetian; the main Ossetian paper in the North Ossetian ASSR is *Rastdzinad* ('Truth'), which first appeared in 1923; in the South Ossetian Autonomous Province there is a regional paper, *Soveton Iryston* ('Soviet Ossetia'), which first appeared in 1924; amongst the periodicals published in Northern Ossetia is *Mach dug* ('Our Epoch'), which was started in 1934. The first Ossetian periodical publications appeared in 1906–12. They were all short-lived, though the very first, *Iron Gazet* 'Iron (i.e. Ossetian) Newspaper', was briefly revived in 1917. It was only after the Civil War that the Ossetian press (Iron and Digor) really emerged. The Digor press faded out in the 1930s.

Books and pamphlets are published in Ossetian (e.g. 58 titles in 1976; of these, one was a specialized textbook). Nothing has been published in the Digor dialect of Ossetian since the 1930s.

Number of books and pamphlets published in Ossetian in selected years

	1913	1940	1965	1979
No. of titles	5	108	82	80
Print run	3,000	414,000	176,000	150,000

Scripts and alphabets

The earliest monument in the Ossetian language is considered to be the Zelenchuk Inscription, a tenth-century inscription in the Alan language, written in Greek characters. The use of the Greek script for Alan/Ossetian does not appear to have survived after this, however, for no later examples of its use have yet been found. The next known attempts to write Ossetian were made in the eighteenth century by Russian and Georgian missionaries. In the mid-nineteenth century A. Shegren created a special alphabet (based on the Cyrillic script) for Ossetian and this, with some modifications introduced by V. F. Miller, was used until just after the Revolution.

Mid-nineteenth century–1923	Cyrillic scipt
1923–38	Latin script
1938	Cyrillic script for the Ossetians in Northern Ossetia
1938–54	Georgian script for the Ossetians in Southern Ossetia
1954	Cyrillic script for all the Ossetians

5 RELIGION

The majority of Ossetians are or were Orthodox Christians, but some (mainly the Digor) are Sunni Muslims. There is a Friday Mosque in Ordzhonikidze that is modelled on the Mohammed Ali Mosque in Cairo. The building was thoroughly restored in 1969, but it is not known whether or not it is open for worship; the indications are that it is treated simply as an architectural monument. The Ossetian Muslims come under the spiritual jurisdiction of the Directorate of Northern Caucasus and Daghestan (Makhachkala).

KABARDIANS/KABARDINIANS

Own name: *Keberdei*; Russian name: *Kabardintsy*.

The Kabardians live in the central region of the northern Caucasus. The majority are found in the Kabardino-Balkar ASSR, but there are also some settlements in the Adygei Autonomous Province.

1 HISTORICAL BACKGROUND

The Kabardians are descended from a group of Caucasian tribes who called themselves by the collective name *Adyge*. They eventually diverged to become what are today three separate national groups: the Kabardians, the Cherkess (Circassians) and the Adygei. They all retain the name *Adyge*, however, and the term *Keberdei*, for example, is used as an alternative only in the sense of being more specific.

The original homeland of the Adygei tribes was in the region of the Kuban' basin, but by the end of the fourteenth century a number of them were already settled on the left bank of the River Terek, in the area which came to be known as 'Greater Kabardia' (*Bol'shaja Kabarda*); by the beginning of the fifteenth century they were occupying the left bank or 'Little Kabardia' (*Malaja Kabarda*). During their eastward migration, this branch of the Adygei encountered the Alans who had been forced into the mountains by the Mongol invasions. A degree of assimilation took place and the Kabardians were the product of this intermingling. The power of the Kabardians grew throughout the fifteenth century, as they succeeded in subjugating several of the neighbouring peoples. During the sixteenth century they were harried by the incursions of the Crimean Tatars and to some extent came under their rule. Relations between the two were not entirely hostile for Crimean khans sometimes sent their sons to be brought up in the households of Kabardian princes; also, it was under Crimean influence that Islam was firmly established amongst the Kabardians at this period (though there had been Muslims in Kabardia for sometime already: remains of thirteenth- and fourteenth-century mosques have been found in the area). Nevertheless, in 1557 they sent ambassadors to Ivan IV (the Terrible) to ask for protection against the Tatars. This was granted and good relations were further cemented when in 1561, after the death of his first wife, Ivan married a Kabardian princess. In 1563 a Russian stronghold was established on the River Terek, followed by another in 1567. Before the end of the century the Russians were firmly entrenched in the area and ready to extend their influence deeper into the Caucasus in the seventeenth century. The Ottomans and Persians, however, were also trying to gain control of the Caucasus and the eighteenth century was marked by a succession of wars. The Treaty of Belgrade (1739) made Kabardia a neutral state, a 'buffer zone' between the Russians and the Ottomans; in 1774 (Treaty of Küchük Kainarji) it was finally united with Russia.

As the Russian expansion in the Caucasus continued, it was met with frequent uprisings and revolts on the part of the indigenous population. The most significant was that led by the Avar Shamyl (see p. 125), but it affected Kabardia less than other parts of the Caucasus, for though Shamyl tried to win the support of the Kabardian princes, they remained committed to the Russian side. The twentieth century brought new upheavals to the area: in the aftermath of the Revolution the Caucasus was plunged in turmoil as nationalist parties, foreign interventionists, Bolsheviks, Mensheviks and the White Army all struggled for supremacy. Soviet power was first established in Kabardia in 1918, but the Kabardino-Balkar Autonomous Province was not created until 16 January 1922; it was transformed into an Autonomous Republic on 5 December 1936. In August 1942 it was invaded by the Germans and occupied for some six months. A year later, in March 1944, the entire Balkar population was deported to Central Asia and Kazakhstan for alleged collaboration with the Nazis. The word 'Balkar' was dropped from the Republic's designation and not replaced until the official 'rehabilitation' of the Balkars in 1957 (see p. 227).

Kabardino-Balkar ASSR, also known as *Kabardino-Balkaria.* Situated in the RSFSR in the Northern Caucasus; it is bordered to the east and south-east by the North Ossetian ASSR, to the south-west by the Georgian SSR, to the west by the Karachajevo-Cherkess Autonomous Province. *Area*: 12,500 sq. km. *Capital*: Nal'chik (population in 1979: 207,000). The Republic has 7 towns and 8 settlements. *Population* (1979): 666,546. Average density of population per sq. km (1979): 54.0

Chief resources: deposits of molybdenum and tungsten.

Industries include: mining, processing of molybdenum and tungsten, machine-building and chemical industries; production of buildings materials, timber, food and other light industries.

Agriculture: grain farming (wheat and maize), fruit growing and viticulture; stockbreeding of sheep, pigs and horses; apiculture and sericulture.

2 NUMBER AND DISTRIBUTION

Number of Kabardians

	1926	1959	1970	1979
	139,925	203,620	279,928	321,719

Regional distribution of Kabardians

	1926	1959	1970	1979
Kabardino-Balkar	122,402	190,284	264,675	303,604
Aut. Prov./ASSR	(87.5%)	(93.5%)	(94.6%)	(94.4%)
Elsewhere in USSR	17,523	13,336	15,253	18,115
	(12.5%)	(6.5%)	(5.4%)	(5.6%)

Urban/rural distribution of the Kabardians in the Kabardino-Balkar Autonomous Province/ASSR

	1926	1970
Urban	866	58,211
	(0.7%)	(22.0%)
Rural	121,536	206,464
	(99.3%)	(78.0%)

Ethnic composition of the Kabardino-Balkar Autonomous Province/ASSR

	1926	1959	1970	1979
Total population	203,776	420,115	588,203	666,546
Kabardians	122,402 (60.1%)	190,284 (45.3%)	264,675 (45.0%)	303,604 (45.5%)
Balkars	33,197 (16.3%)	34,088 (8.1%)	51,356 (8.7%)	59,710 (9.0%)
Ossetians	4,078 (2.0%)	6,442 (1.5%)	9,167 (1.6%)	9,710 (1.5%)
Russians	15,344 (7.5%)	162,586 (38.7%)	218,595 (37.2%)	234,137 (35.1%)
Ukrainians	17,213 (8.4%)	8,400 (2.0%)	10,362 (1.8%)	12,139 (1.8%)
Others	11,542 (5.7%)	18,315 (4.4%)	34,048 (5.7%)	47,246 (7.1%)

Urban/rural distribution in the Kabardino-Balkar ASSR in 1970

	Urban	Rural
Total population	280,089	308,114
Kabardians	58,211 (20.8%)	206,464 (67.0%)
Balkars	13,816 (4.9%)	37,540 (12.2%)
Ossetians	5,352 (1.9%)	3,815 (1.2%)
Russians	168,374 (60.1%)	50,221 (16.3%)
Ukrainians	8,458 (3.0%)	1,904 (0.6%)
Others	25,878 (9.2%)	8,170 (2.7%)

3 STATUS

The Kabardians enjoy full Soviet citizenship. They are found in all occupations and in all income brackets; the majority are agricultural workers, but some are engaged in industry. Their standard of housing is comparable to that of other national groups in the Soviet Union. The women go out to work, as elsewhere in the Soviet Union.

Literacy

In 1926	In 1970
6.8%	Over 99%

In 1926, 2,261 Kabardians were literate in their own language (23.7 per cent of the total literate Kabardian population).

Level of education per 1,000 Kabardians living in the Kabardino-Balkar ASSR of 10 years of age and above

	1959	*1970*
Primary		
Total	265	294
Men	302	315
Women	235	276
Higher and secondary (complete and incomplete)		
Total	303	417
Men	357	468
Women	260	375
Higher only		
Total	9	26
Men	15	39
Women	4	15

4 LANGUAGE

The national language is Kabardian. It belongs to the North-West group of Caucasian languages, Abkhazian-Adygei sub-group. It is often referred to as 'Kabardino-Cherkess', since the two languages (Kabardian and Cherkess) are now considered to form a single literary language. Other closely related languages are Abkhazian, Abazin and Adygei. Adygei in particular is very close to Kabardian; both languages are called by their native speakers *Adyga-bza* ('Adygei language'), since the Kabardians also belong to the Adygei group (see Historical Background above). There are four main dialect groups in Kabardian: Greater Kabardian, Mozdok, Beslan and Kuban'. The Greater Kabardian group and in particular the Baksan dialect has been taken as the basis of the literary language. The differences between the dialect groups are fairly small, however, and relate mostly to phonetic and morphological phenomena. The vocabulary contains a considerable number of loan-words from

Arabic, Persian, Turkish and Russian. A striking characteristic of the native vocabulary is its high proportion of homonyms and polysemants.

The first Kabardian grammars were compiled by the Kabardian scholar and pedagogue Sh. B. Nogmov (1840, 1843); the first Russian-Kabardian dictionary appeared in 1889. During the Soviet period various aspects of the Kabardian language (historical development, dialectal variations, etc.) have been studied in some detail.

Russian is generally used for administrative, judicial and other official proceedings, but in theory Kabardian can be used if necessary.

Percentage of Kabardians claiming Kabardian as their mother tongue

	1926	*1959*	*1970*	*1979*
Total	99.3	97.9	98.0	97.9
In urban areas	91.4	90.8	93.7	n.a.
In rural areas	99.4	99.1	99.4	n.a.

Percentage of Kabardians with good knowledge of Russian

	1926	*1959*	*1970*	*1979*
As mother tongue	0.1	1.9	1.8	2.0
As second language	n.a.	n.a.	71.4	76.7

In 1958 Kabardian was the medium of instruction in grades 1–4 (primary +1) in national schools; in 1972 it was not used at all as a medium of instruction, but was taught as an individual, optional subject in Russian-medium schools in grades 1–10 (Silver, p. 33). More recent information is not available. There is a university at Nal'chik (founded in 1957), an Institute of Geophysics and a Research Institute of Economics, History, Language and Literature. There does not appear to be any tuition in Kabardian at these establishments.

In the Kabardino-Balkar ASSR there are some radio broadcasts in Kabardino-Cherkess, as well as in Russian and Karachai-Balkar. The same is true of the Karachajevo-Cherkess Autonomous Province.

The paper *Lenin guegu* ('Lenin's Way'–first appeared in 1920) is published in Kabardino-Cherkess in the Kabardino-Balkar ASSR and *Lenin nur* ('Lenin's Light'–first appeared in 1923) in the

Karachajevo-Cherkess Autonomous Province. In both areas papers are also published in Karachai-Balkar and Russian.

Books and pamphlets are published in Kabardian (e.g. 24 titles in 1976; none of these were specialized textbooks on scientific or technical subjects).

Number of books and pamphlets published in Kabardian and Balkar in selected years

	1913	1940*	1965	1979
No. of titles	——	41	54	62
Print run	——	172,000	109,000	172,000

*Figures for this year include publications in Cherkess.
Note: Kabardian and Balkar are two quite different languages: the former belongs to the Caucasian group, the latter to the Turkic.

Scripts and alphabets

1923–4 Latin script, first alphabet
1924–36 Latin script, second alphabet (N. F. Jakovlev's version)
1936 Cyrillic script (the Kabardians were the first of the non-Slav peoples to adopt the Cyrillic script in the Soviet period)

5 RELIGION

The Kabardians are Sunni Muslims, except for a small community in and around Mozdok in the North Ossetian ASSR who are Christians (Armenian-Gregorian rite).

In Kabardia, *c.* 1830, there were 113 mosques (Smirnov, *Mjuridizm. . .*, p. 87). Today there is probably a mosque open for worship in Nal'chik, the capital of the republic, but there are unlikely to be more than a handful of others elsewhere in the region, since there are estimated to be only forty-five mosques in the whole of the Northern Caucasus (*Religion in Communist Lands*, vol. 7, no,3, p. 152). Kabardia comes under the spiritual jurisdiction of the Directorate of Northern Caucasus and Daghestan (Makhachkala). The present Chairman of this Directorate, Mufti Mahmud Gekkiev, is a Kabardian.

INGUSH

Own name: *Galgai* (originally the name of the largest tribal group); Russian name: *Ingushi*.

The Ingush live mostly in the west of the Checheno-Ingush ASSR.

1 HISTORICAL BACKGROUND

The Ingush are closely related to the Chechen and, like them, are an indigenous Caucasian people. They have been settled in their present habitat for many centuries (an Armenian geographical work of the seventh century refers to them as one of the tribes of the Caucasus). They originally lived in the mountains, but from about the sixteenth century began to move to the plains. By the late eighteenth century a number of them had settled along the River Sunzha and in the nearby valley of the River Terek. One of their first settlements on the plains was called Angush (or Ingush) and the Kabardians took to using this as the name of the people. It was in turn adopted by the Russians. (The Ingush called themselves by their tribal names, e.g. Galgai.) The Ingush came under Russian rule in 1810, much earlier than the Chechen. In 1817 they were evacuated from the Sunzha area and concentrated around the military base of Nazran' (near the border of the present-day North Ossetian ASSR). Ingush from the mountains were also moved here and it became one of the main centres of the Ingush territory. The migrations continued throughout the nineteenth century (particularly between 1830 and 1860) and by the end of the century most of the Ingush were settled on the plains.

Like the Chechen, the Ingush were first converted to Christianity; later, under the influence of the Chechen, they adopted Islam, but the new religion did not take a firm hold amongst them until the early nineteenth century. They gave some support to Shamyl (see p. 125), but in general were little affected by the Murid Uprising.

Soviet rule was finally established in the Ingush territory in 1920. The Chechen and Ingush lands were incorporated into the Gorskaja ('Mountain') ASSR in January 1921. The Chechen region was hived off in 1922 and after the dissolution of the Gorskaja ASSR in 1924, the Ingush region became an independent Autonomous Province. The two regions were again united to form a single Autonomous Province in 1934 and this was transformed into an Autonomous

Republic in 1936. The pre-war period in the Checheno-Ingush ASSR was extremely tense, with much opposition to collectivization on the part of the local people. The Ingush, like the Chechen, fought in the Red Army against the Germans, but in 1944 they were denounced as traitors and the whole population (including those from outside the republic) was deported to Central Asia and Kazakhstan. The Checheno-Ingush ASSR was disbanded and the land given to new settlers (mainly Laks from the neighbouring region of the Daghestan ASSR). The Chechens and Ingush were rehabilitated in 1957, their republic reinstated (its territory actually increased) and they were allowed to return home. However, their return caused severe problems as tensions quickly developed between the recent settlers and the former inhabitants of the area. The Ingush demanded the repatriation of some 1,000 sq. km of their territory that had been given to the North Ossetian ASSR during their exile. Their request was not acceded to and in 1973 they were still demonstrating and petitioning for its return. It is not known whether they have yet achieved this.

For information on the Checheno-Ingush ASSR see p. 177.

2 NUMBER AND DISTRIBUTION

Number of Ingush

	1926	*1959*	*1970*	*1979*
	74,097	105,980	157,605	186,198

Net losses for the period 1939–59 are estimated to be a minimum of 9 per cent (Nekrich, p. 138).

Regional distribution of Ingush

	1926	*1959*	*1970*	*1979*
Ingush Aut. Prov./	69,930	48,273	113,675	134,744
Checheno-Ingush ASSR	(94.4%)	(45.5%)	(72.1%)	(72.4%)
North Ossetian Aut. Prov./ASSR	23	6,071*	18,387*	23,663*
	(0.0%)	(5.7%)	(11.7%)	(12.7%)
Elsewhere in USSR	4,144	51,636	25,543	27,791
	(5.6%)	(48.7%)	(16.2%)	(14.9%)

*After the Checheno-Ingush ASSR was disbanded some 1,000 sq. km of Ingush territory was transferred to the neighbouring North Ossetian ASSR; when the exiled Ingush were allowed to return to their homeland in 1957 some of them returned to this area, asking that it should be reunited with the reinstated Checheno-Ingush ASSR. From the regional distribution of the Ingush indicated in 1979 it would appear that quite a large number have not yet returned to the Caucasus and are presumably still in Central Asia.

Urban/rural distribution of Ingush in the Ingush Aut. Prov./Checheno-Ingush ASSR

	1926	1970
Urban	800 (1.1%)	35,612 (31.3%)
Rural	69,130 (98.9%)	78,063 (68.7%)

Ethnic composition of the Ingush Autonomous Province

	1926
Total population	75,082
Ingush	69,930 (93.1%)
Chechen	2,572 (3.4%)
Russians	922 (1.2%)
Others	1,658 (2.2%)

For *Ethnic composition of the Checheno-Ingush ASSR (1959–79)* and *Urban/rural distribution in the Checheno-Ingush ASSR (1970)* see p. 178.

3 STATUS

Having been 'rehabilitated', the Ingush now enjoy full Soviet citizenship. They are found in all occupations and in all income brackets, but the majority are agricultural workers. Their standard of housing is now comparable to that of other national groups in the Soviet Union. The women go out to work, as elsewhere in the Soviet Union.

Literacy

In 1926	in 1970
9.1%	Over 99%

In 1926, 937 Ingush were literate in their own language (13.9 per cent of the total literate Ingush population).

Level of education per 1,000 Ingush living in the Checheno-Ingush ASSR of 10 years of age and above

	1959	*1970*
Primary		
Total	197	311
Men	291	348
Women	118	277
Higher and secondary (complete and incomplete)		
Total	162	252
Men	291	353
Women	55	162
Higher only		
Total	5	15
Men	9	24
Women	2	7

4 LANGUAGE

The national language is Ingush. It belongs to the North-East group of Caucasian languages, Nakhcho (i.e. Chechen) sub-group. It is very closely related to Chechen and the two languages were in fact considered to form a single literary language until 1934; they are now considered to be separate languages. There are no dialects in Ingush. Its vocabulary contains loan-words from many sources, including Arabic, Persian, Georgian and Russian. Russian influence has been particularly strong in recent years. Ingush was not a written language until the Soviet period.

Russian is generally used for administrative, judicial and other official proceedings, but in theory Ingush can be used if necessary.

Percentage of Ingush claiming Ingush as their mother tongue

	1926	*1959*	*1970*	*1979*
Total	99.5	97.9	97.4	97.4
In urban areas	79.2	96.6	95.1	n.a.
In rural areas	99.6	98.6	98.8	n.a.

Percentage of Ingush with good knowledge of Russian

	1926	1959	1970	1979
As mother tongue	0.2	1.9	2.4	2.5
As second language	n.a.	n.a.	71.2	79.6

In 1958 Ingush was the medium of instruction in grades 1–4 (primary +1) in national schools; in 1972, pre-school only; in 1972 it was also taught as an individual, optional subject in Russian-medium schools in grades 1–10 (Silver, p. 33). More recent information is not available.

In the Checheno-Ingush ASSR there is some broadcasting in Chechen and Ingush, as well as Russian.

Newspapers and periodicals are published in Chechen and Ingush, as well as Russian; the first and still the main Ingush newspaper was *Serdalo* ('Light'), which began to appear in 1923. It was suspended from 1942 to 1957. A literary almanac, *Loaman Iujre* ('Morning of the Mountains'), was started in 1958.

Books and pamphlets are now published in Ingush (e.g. 13 titles in 1976; none of these were specialized textbooks on scientific or technical subjects). For numbers of books and pamphlets published in Chechen and Ingush in the years 1913, 1940, 1965 and 1979 see p. 181.

Scripts and alphabets

Ingush was not a written language until Z. K. Mal'sagov invented an alphabet for it in 1920, based on the Latin script.

1920–38 Latin script
1938   Cyrillic script

5 RELIGION

The Ingush are Sunni Muslims (Hanafi school). They come under the spiritual jurisdiction of the Directorate of Northern Caucasus and Daghestan (Makhachkala).

KARACHAIS

Own names: *Karachai, Karachaily:* Russian name; *Karachajevtsy.*

The majority of Karachais are now once more settled in the Karachajevo-Cherkess Autonomous Province in the RSFSR, Savropol' Territory (*kraj*).

1 HISTORICAL BACKGROUND

The Karachais are a Turkic-speaking people of the Northern Caucasus. Linguistic evidence suggests that they are descended from the Kipchak (Cuman/Polovtsian) group of tribes. Like the Balkars, to whom they are apparently closely related, they probably include a strong Alan element, since the area in which they have now been settled for several centuries was formerly occupied by the Alans. This theory is supported by the fact that the Megreli call them 'Alans'; also, their language and folklore show affinities with the Ossetians (descendants of the Alans) to the south.

An influx of Nogais into the area in the seventeenth century and contacts with the Crimean Tatars helped to introduce Islam to the Karachais, but local tradition ascribes their ultimate conversion to the influence of a Kabardian mullah, Ishak Efendi, in the eighteenth century. There had been a strong Russian presence on the River Terek since the mid-sixteenth century, particularly in neighbouring Kabardia, but the Karachais themselves did not come under direct Russian rule until 1828. The event provoked considerable opposition on the part of the indigenous population and by the 1870s the innumerable insurrections had led the Russian authorities to consider the deportation of the Karachais to Turkey (mass emigrations of other Muslim peoples, such as the Crimean Tatars and Circassians were taking place at this period). This policy was not implemented, however, and the Karachais remained in the Northern Caucasus.

In 1918 Soviet power was established in the Karachaj area for a brief period; it was overthrown almost immediately by the White Army, which remained in control until the spring of 1920, when it in turn was ousted by the Red Army. On 12 January 1922 the Karachaj-Cherkess Autonomous Province was formed; in 1926 it was divided into the Karachaj Autonomous Province and the Cherkess National District (which became an Autonomous Province in

1928: see p. 231). In August 1942 the German army entered the Karachaj Autonomous Province and held it for some five months. It was liberated in January 1943; on the 8th March 1944 the entire Karachaj population was deported to Central Asia and Kazakhstan, as punishment for alleged collaboration with the enemy forces (despite the fact that many thousands of Karachais had at that time been on active service in the Red Army). Great numbers of Karachai died during and as a result of the deportation and while in exile the education and cultural life of the community was disastrously disrupted. Thirteen years later, in 1957, they were 'rehabilitated', allowed to return to their homeland (much of which had become a wilderness during their absence, due to total neglect) and given back their civil rights. Their Autonomous Province, which had been dissolved after their deportation, was reinstated and united with the Cherkess Autonomous Province, as had been the case in the years 1922–6. By 1959 the return of the Karachais was well advanced.

Karachajevo-Cherkess Autonomous Province, also known as *Karachajevo-Cherkessia*

Situated in the Stavropol' Territory (*kraj*) of the RSFSR, on the northern slopes of the Great Caucasian range; it is a mountainous, heavily forested region, populated mostly in the north; it is bordered to the south-east by the Kabardino-Balkar ASSR, to the south by the Georgian SSR. *Area*: 14,100 sq. km. *Capital*: Cherkessk (population in 1979: 91,000). The Province has 4 towns and 9 settlements. *Population* (1979): 367,111. Average density of population per sq. km (1979): 26.2.

Chief resources: deposits of zinc and lead.

Industries include: mining, chemical and petrochemical industries; some machine-building; production of building materials, food and other light industries.

Agriculture: grain farming (wheat and maize) and the cultivation of sugar beet, sunflowers, fruit and vegetables; stockbreeding, particularly of sheep.

2 NUMBER AND DISTRIBUTION

Number of Karachais

1926	1959	1970	1979
55,123	81,403	112,741	131,074

The net losses for the period 1939–59 are estimated to be a minimum of 30 per cent (Nekrich, p. 138).

Regional distribution of Karachais

	1926	1959	1970	1979
RSFSR	55,116 (100%)	70,537 (86.7%)	106,831 (94.8%)	125,792 (96.0%)
Kara. (-Cherk.) Aut. Province only	52,503 (95.2%)	67,830 (83.3%)	97,104 (86.1%)	109,196 (83.3%)
Elsewhere in USSR	7 (0.0%)	10,866 (13.3%)	5,910 (5.2%)	5,282 (4.0%)

Urban/rural distribution of Karachais in the RSFSR

	1926	1970
Urban	1,756 (3.2%)	16,585 (15.5%)
Rural	53,360 (96.8%)	90,246 (84.5%)

Ethnic composition of the Karachaj/Karachajevo-Cherkess Autonomous Province

	1926	1959	1970	1979
Total population	64,579	277,959	344,651	367,111
Karachais	52,503 (81.3%)	67,830 (24.4%)	97,104 (28.2%)	109,196 (29.7%)
Abazins	2,738 (4.2%)	18,159 (6.5%)	22,896 (6.6%)	24,245 (6.6%)
Nogais	57 (0.1%)	8,903 (3.2%)	11,062 (3.2%)	11,872 (3.2%)
Cherkess	25 (0.0%)	24,145 (8.7%)	31,190 (9.0%)	34,430 (9.4%)
Russians	1,120 (1.7%)	141,843 (51.0%)	162,442 (47.1%)	165,451 (45.1%)

	1926	1959	1970	1979
Ukrainians	2,824 (4.4%)	4,011 (1.4%)	4,819 (1.4%)	n.a.*
Others	5,312 (8.2%)	13,068 (4.7%)	15,138 (4.4%)	21,917 (6.0%)

*Specific data not yet available, hence they are included under 'Others'.

Urban/rural distribution in the Karachajevo-Cherkess Autonomous Province in 1970

	Urban	Rural
Total population	112,454	232,197
Karachais	12,286 (10.9%)	84,818 (36.5%)
Abazins	2,781 (2.5%)	20,115 (8.7%)
Nogais	1,635 (1.5%)	9,427 (4.1%)
Cherkess	3,665 (3.3%)	27,525 (11.9%)
Russians	82,327 (73.2%)	80,115 (34.5%)
Ukrainians	3,279 (2.9%)	1,540 (0.7%)
Others	6,481 (5.8%)	8,657 (3.7%)

3 STATUS

Having been 'rehabilitated', the Karachais now enjoy full Soviet citizenship. They are found in all occupations and in all income brackets, but the majority work on collective farms. Their standard of housing is comparable to that of other national groups in the Soviet Union. The women go out to work, as elsewhere in the Soviet Union.

Literacy

In 1926	In 1970
9.2%	Over 99%

In 1926, none of the Karachais were literate in their own language.

Level of education per 1,000 Karachais living in the Karachajevo-Cherkess Autonomous Province of 10 years of age and above

	1959	1970
Primary		
Total	275	325
Men	306	342
Women	252	311
Higher and secondary (complete and incomplete)		
Total	246	346
Men	357	424
Women	160	278
Higher only		
Total	5	32
Men	9	45
Women	2	21

LANGUAGE

The national language is Karachai-Balkar (see the section on Balkars). It belongs to the West Turkic group (*Fundamenta* classification); it can also be classed as belonging to the Kipchak group, Kipchak-Polovtsian sub-group (Baskakov). The languages it is most closely related to are Kumyk and, to a lesser extent, Nogai.

Karachai-Balkar consists of two main dialects: the '*ch*-group' of the Karachais and the '*ts*-group' of the Balkars (cf. Karachai *küchük*, Balkar *kütsük* – 'small'). The modern literary language is based on a combination of the two dialects. The vocabulary differs from that of most other Turkic languages due to the influence of the neighbouring Caucasian and Iranian languages (e.g. Ossetian). It contains a number of Arabic and Persian loan-words and Russian words borrowed both before and after the Revolution. The early borrowings have undergone severe phonetic modification, e.g. *abychar* from *ofitser* ('officer'). Modern loans have usually been adopted in their original form.

Russian is generally used for administrative, judicial and other official proceedings, but in theory Karachai-Balkar can be used if necessary.

In 1958 Karachai-Balkar was the medium of instruction in grades 1–4 (primary +1) in the national schools; in 1972, it was taught only as

Percentage of Karachais claiming Karachai-Balkar as their mother tongue

	1926	1959	1970	1979
Total	99.5	96.8	98.1	97.7
In urban areas	94.7	86.3	93.1	n.a.
In rural areas	99.7	98.1	99.1	n.a.

Percentage of Karachais with good knowledge of Russian

	1926	1959	1970	1979
As mother tongue	0.0 (27 people)	1.5	1.6	2.0
As second language	n.a.	n.a.	67.6	75.5

an individual, optional subject in Russian-medium schools (Silver, p. 33). More recent information is not available. There is a Pedagogical Institute in Karachajevsk and a branch of the Stavropol' Polytechnic Institute in Cherkessk. Tuition at the latter is likely to be entirely in Russian.

In the Karachajevo-Cherkess Autonomous Province there are radio broadcasts in Karachai-Balkar, as well as in Kabardino-Cherkess, Abazin, Nogai and Russian.

Newspapers are also published in these languages, e.g. Kabardino-Cherkess *Lenin nur* ('Lenin's Light' – since 1923), Abazin *Kommunizm alashara* ('Light of Communism' – since 1938) and Nogai *Lenin joly* ('Lenin's Way' – since 1938). The Karachai-Balkar newspaper is *Leninni bajragy* ('Lenin's Banner' – first appeared in 1924, for a while under the title *Kyzyl Karachai*, 'Red Karachai'). Another Karachai-Balkar paper is published in the Kabardino-Balkar ASSR, *Kommunizmge dzhol* ('The Way to Communism' – first appeared in 1931). Both these Karachai-Balkar papers were suspended while the two peoples were in exile; publication was resumed in 1957. There is now also a literary almanac, *Shujokhluk* ('Friendship'), published quarterly in Nal'chik.

Books and pamphlets are published in Karachai-Balkar (e.g. 8 titles in 1976; none of these were specialized textbooks on scientific or technical subjects).

Scripts and alphabets

Until 1920 Arabic script, Arabic alphabet
1920–4   Arabic script, modified alphabet

1924–6	Latin script, first alphabet
1926–36	Latin script, second alphabet
1936–61	Cyrillic script, first alphabet
1961–4	Cyrillic script, second alphabet
1964	Cyrillic script, third alphabet (almost identical with the first)

This last alphabet is considered to be entirely satisfactory for the representation of Karachai-Balkar.

5 RELIGION

The Karachais are Sunni Muslims (Hanafi school). After the deportation of the Karachais all the mosques were closed in the Karachajevo-Cherkess Autonomous Province and none have apparently yet been reopened (*Religion in Communist Lands*, vol. 7, no. 3, p. 152). They come under the spiritual jurisdiction of the Directorate of Northern Caucasus and Daghestan (Makhachkala).

KURDS

Own collective name: *Kurmandzh*; a section call themselves *Soran*; they also use other tribal names; Russian name: *Kurdy*.

The majority live in Transcaucasia, particularly in the Armenian SSR, but there are also substantial groups of Kurds in Central Asia and Kazakhstan.

1 HISTORICAL BACKGROUND

The Kurds are an Iranian-speaking people of the Near East. Their ethnic origins are very complex, and little is known for certain of their early history. Their traditional homeland is the area known as Kurdistan, now divided between Iran, Iraq, Turkey and Syria. By the beginning of the tenth century a section of them had moved into Transcaucasia; a Kurdish dynasty, the Sheddadids of Dvin, ruled the territory between the Rivers Kura and Araks in the tenth to twelfth centuries. Also in the early tenth century another group of Kurdish tribes moved east into Transcaspia. The main influx of Kurds into this area occurred much later, however, during the reign of Shah Abbas in the seventeenth century. It came to be known as

'Khorasan Kurdistan'; from here, probably during the mid-nineteenth century, Kurdish tribes began migrating northwards into Turkmenia.

The Kurds never formed a united state of their own, but remained a federation of semi-independent tribes. During the fourteenth to eighteenth centuries they were under the nominal rule of the Persians and Ottomans. In the nineteenth century, as Russia expanded to the east and south, they began to come under Russian rule. The Treaty of Turkmanchai (1828) gave Russia control of Persian possessions in Transcaucasia, the Congress of Berlin (1878), of Ottoman possessions; the Russo-Persian frontier demarcation of 1893 was also favourable to Russia. All these territorial acquisitions included land on which Kurds were settled. More Kurds came under Russian/Soviet rule as they migrated in from other areas, principally from Turkey (e.g. during the periods 1853–6, 1877–8, 1914–18). There has also been some out-migration (e.g. in the 1920s to 1930s), to neighbouring countries such as Afghanistan.

Until the 1920s the Kurds in the Soviet Union were nomadic or semi-nomadic, each tribe having its own specific routes. After this period they were made to adopt a settled form of existence and to participate in the collectivization programme. The majority now live on collective farms and are engaged in farming and animal husbandry (they sometimes raise pigs, but still refuse to eat them). The Kurds in Georgia are an exception, for they are concentrated in the capital Tbilisi (Tiflis) and are industrial workers for the most part.

The most flourishing community of Kurds in the Soviet Union today is undoubtedly that in the Armenian SSR, where they have many of their own facilities, including publications in Kurdish, a section for Kurdish writers in the Armenian Union of Writers and a Kurdish section in the Armenian Academy of Sciences. The situation is less promising elsewhere. In Turkmenia the Kurds are rapidly being assimilated by the Turkmen, to the extent that some now identify themselves as Turkmen. In the Azerbaidzhan SSR, a Kurdistan District (*ujezd*) was created in 1923 (capital: Lachin), but later abolished. In 1941 a number of Kurds were deported from Transcaucasia on unspecified charges; they were exiled to Central Asia (Kirghiz SSR) and to the Kazakh SSR and have not yet been allowed to return, apparently.

From the point of view of religion, the Kurds fall into two main groups: the Muslims and the Yazidis. (The latter are sometimes called 'Devil-worshippers', but this is unjustified: their religion is a synthesis of elements from a variety of traditions, including Muslim, Nestorian Christian, Jewish and Zoroastrian.) In the 1926 Soviet Census the Yazidi and Muslim Kurds were listed separately, but thereafter no distinction was made. Another addition to the figures for the Kurds as given in 1959 (and presumably from then on) was that of a small group of Turks living in Turkmenia. These Turks apparently spoke only their own language and intermarried within their own community. No indication is given of the size of this group, but it is likely to have been no more than a few hundred at most.

2 NUMBER AND DISTRIBUTION

Number of Kurds (and Yazidis)

	1926	1959†	1970†	1979†
Kurds	54,661	*58,799	88,930	115,858
Yazidis	14,523	——	——	——

*The lack of growth in the joint Yazidi-Kurdish population in the period 1926–59 is attributable in some measure to migration out of the USSR, e.g. to Afghanistan.
†From 1959 the Yazidis are included with the Kurds.

Regional distribution of Kurds (and Yazidis)

	1926		1959	1970	1979
	Kurds	Yazidis			
Arm SSR	3,025 (5.5%)	12,237 (84.3%)	25,627 (43.6%)	37,486 (42.2%)	50,822 (44.0%)
AzSSR	41,193 (75.4%)	——	1,487 (2.5%)	5,488 (6.2%)	n.a.
GeorgSSR	7,955 (14.6%)	2,262 (15.6%)	16,212 (27.6%)	20,690 (23.3%)	25,688 (22.2%)
TurkSSR	2,308 (4.2%)	——	2,263 (3.8%)	2,933 (3.3%)	n.a.
KazSSR	——	——	5,836 (9.9%)	12,313 (13.8%)	n.a.
KirSSR	——	——	4,783 (8.1%)	7,974 (9.0%)	n.a.
Elsewhere in USSR	180 (0.3%)	24 (0.2%)	2,591 (4.4%)	2,046 (2.3%)	

The fact that the Yazidi-Kurdish population in the Armenian SSR more than doubled between 1926 and 1959 (in 1926 it accounted for 22.1 per cent of the joint total population, in 1959, 43.6 per cent) must be due in part at least to migrations (or deportations) from the Azerbaidzhan SSR, where the size of the Kurdish population was drastically reduced during this period (from 75.4 per cent of the total Soviet Kurdish population in 1926 to 2.5 per cent in 1959). In 1926, 90.1 per cent of the Azerbaidzhani Kurds lived in the Kurdistan District (*ujezd*) of the Azerbaidzhan SSR.

Urban/rural distribution of Kurds (and Yazidis)

	1926		1970
	Kurds	*Yazidis*	
Urban	1,875 (3.4%)	2,245 (15.5%)	34,317 (38.6%)
Rural	52,786 (96.6%)	12,278 (84.5%)	54,613 (61.4%)
(in the Georgian SSR only)			
Urban	1,093 (13.7%)	2,164 (95.7%)	20,031 (96.8%)
Rural	6,862 (86.3%)	98 (4.3%)	659 (3.2%)

Judging from the 1926 statistics, it would appear that the bulk of the present urban population of Kurds in the Georgian SSR is composed of Yazidis.

3 STATUS

The position is unclear. Certainly the Kurds in the Armenian SSR (the majority) enjoy full Soviet citizenship. Those (if any) who are still in exile clearly do not; even if they may be said to have 'taken root' (*ukorenilis'*) in Central Asia, freedom of movement and freedom to settle in all areas open for civilian settlement within one's own country are generally accepted human rights. It is hard to imagine that a vast number of Kurds would have voluntarily left the Kurdistan district, where they had been settled for several centuries, and moved to other areas. It is not, of course, impossible, but without further information, especially from the Kurds themselves, it must remain an open question.

They are found in all occupations and in all income brackets, particularly in the Armenian SSR; the majority, however, work on collective farms; the Kurds (Yazidis) in the Georgian SSR are for the most part found in industry. Their standard of housing is comparable to that of other national groups in the Soviet Union. The women go out to work, as elsewhere in the Soviet Union.

Literacy

	In 1926	In 1970
Kurds	3.7%	Over 99%
Yazidis	2.1%	——

In 1926, 47 Kurds (2.3 per cent of the total literate Kurdish population) and 32 Yazidis (10.4 per cent of the total literate Yazidi population) were literate in their own language.

Level of education per 1,000 Kurds living in the Armenian SSR of 10 years of age and above

	1959	1970
Primary		
Total	193	320
Men	245	346
Women	138	294
Higher and secondary (complete and incomplete)		
Total	111	176
Men	179	257
Women	43	98
Higher only		
Total	4	8
Men	6	13
Women	1	3

4 LANGUAGE

The national language is Kurdish. It belongs to the North-West group of Iranian languages. It has a number of dialect groups, each of which can be further subdivided into dialects and sub-dialects. The two main groups are *Kurmandzhi* (north-western) and *Sorani* (south-eastern). Other important groups are Gurani, Luri and

Zaza. The differences between them are mostly morphological. Apart from a common fund of Arabic and Turkish loan-words, the Kurdish of the Soviet Union also contains many Russian, Azerbaidzhani and Turkmen loans, while that spoken outside the Soviet Union contains English and French loans. Kurdish has a long literary tradition, dating back to the eleventh century and possibly earlier. It has produced writers of note throughout its history.

Russian is generally used for administrative, judicial and other official proceedings; in the Armenian SSR Armenian can also be used and in theory, Kurds everywhere can use Kurdish if necessary.

Percentage of Kurds (and Yazidis) claiming Kurdish as their mother tongue

	1926	1959	1970	1979
Kurds	34.4	89.9	87.6	83.6
Yazidis	96.4	—	—	—

Percentage of Kurds (and Yazidis) with good knowledge of Russian

	1926		1959	1970	1979
	Kurds	*Yazidis*			
As mother tongue	0.1 (37 people)	0.2 (36 people)	2.9	3.8	4.8
As second language	n.a.	n.a.	n.a.	19.9	25.4

Percentage of Kurds (and Yazidis) with good knowledge of a language other than their own or Russian (presumably Azerbaidzhani, Armenian or Turkmen)

	1926		1970	1979
	Kurds	*Yazidis*		
As mother tongue	65.2*	3.2	8.6	11.6
As second language	n.a.	n.a.	36.2	40.7

*42.9 per cent of the Kurds in the AzSSR alone claimed 'Turkish' (Azerbaidzhani) as their mother tongue.

In the 1960s (*Narody Kavkaza II*) there was some instruction in Kurdish in the Armenian SSR; it is not known to what level or whether, twenty years later, there is any tuition at all in Kurdish. There are important centres of Kurdish studies in Moscow, Leningrad and Yerevan. It is probable that there are some Kurds amongst the students there, but nothing is known of possible numbers.

No up-to-date information is available on the use of Kurdish in broadcasting.

A newspaper in Kurdish, *Ria taze* ('New Way') is published in Kurdish in the Armenian SSR. It first appeared in 1930, but was suspended from 1938 to 1955.

A few books and pamphlets are now published in Kurdish (e.g. 5 titles in 1976; none of these were specialized textbooks on scientific or technical subjects).

Scripts and alphabets

Until 1921	Arabic script
1921–9	Armenian script
1929–46	Latin script
1946	Cyrillic script

There is only one known publication in the Armenian script, a schoolbook which appeared in 1921. In the early 1930s there were a number of publications in the Latin script, but these petered out during the war years. Since 1946 there has been a small but fairly steady flow of material in the Cyrillic script. During the 1960s there was a certain revival of the Latin script, perhaps intended mainly for foreign consumption. Outside the Soviet Union, the Arabic and, to a lesser extent, the Latin script, are used for Kurdish.

5 RELIGION

There are two religious groups amongst the Kurds: the Muslims and the Yazidis. The majority of the Kurds in general are Sunni Muslims (Shafi'i school); the majority of the Muslim Kurds in the Soviet Union, however, are Shi'i; they include adherents of the extreme group of sects known as the *'Ali ilahi* ('Deifiers of Ali'), in particular of the *Ahl-i Haqq* ('People of God'). The main Shi'i areas used to be Azerbaidzhan, Georgia and Turkmenia, the Sunni Kurds being concentrated in Armenia. Now that most of the Kurds have left or been deported from Azerbaidzhan, there are probably Shi'i Kurds in Armenia as well. The Yazidis, who used to be listed separately in the census, were formerly found in Georgia and Armenia and it is probable that they are still there. In 1926 they constituted about 20 per cent of the total Soviet population of Kurds. The Muslim Kurds (Shi'i and Sunni) in Armenia, Azerbaidzhan and Georgia come under the spiritual jurisdiction of the Directorate of Transcaucasia (Baku).

6 WORLD DISTRIBUTION OF KURDS

There are no reliable figures for the total world population of Kurds. Soviet sources of the 1960s give the following approximate estimates:

Iraq	2,000,000	(20.0%)
Iran	3,500,000	(36.0%)
Syria	250,000	(2.5%)
Turkey	4,000,000	(41.0%)
USSR	59,000	(0.5%)

The recently published (1979) *Soviet Asian Ethnic Frontiers* (p. 84) gives these approximate estimates:

Iraq	1,500,000	(21.0%)
Iran	2,000,000	(28.0%)
Syria-Lebanon	350,000	(5.0%)
Turkey	3,200,000	(45.0%)
USSR	88,930*	(1.0%)

*1970 Soviet Census estimate

ADYGEIS

Own name: *Adyge*; Russian name: *Adygejtsy*.

The Adygeis live in the Adygei Autonomous Province; the majority are concentrated in the rich agricultural land along the lower reaches of the Laba and Kuban' Rivers, but some are settled in the foothills of the Caucasus range.

1 HISTORICAL BACKGROUND

The name 'Adyge' was used by a number of closely related, indigenous tribes of the north-west Caucasus. By the tenth century they are known to have been settled in the area bounded to the north by the River Kuban', to the east by the River Laba, to the south by the Abkhazian tribes and to the west by the Black Sea (i.e. the present-day Adygei Autonomous Province and the land between it and the Black Sea). The most powerful of the Adygei tribes at this time was the Zichi and this name was sometimes applied to the whole group. They were well known to foreign powers such as the Byzantines, due to their trading activities. They exported such commodities as honey, wax, caviar and furs and imported salt, textiles and weapons. During this period they began to adopt Christianity. In the early thirteenth century they came under the sway of the Golden Horde and several of the Adygei tribes moved eastwards towards the basin of the River Terek. These mingled with the Alans and eventually formed the Kabardian group (see p. 190). The Adygei who remained in the west came to be known as the 'Cherkess' ('Circassian'), a term which was later used as a general designation for the people of the Caucasus.

In the early sixteenth century, under the joint influence of the Ottomans and the Crimean Khans (the Crimean Khanate became a vassal state of the Ottomans in 1475), Islam began to penetrate the Adygei (i.e. Circassian) territory. It took time for the new religion to become firmly established, however, and the conversion of the Adygei was not complete until the early nineteenth century. At an inter-tribal assembly in 1822 it was decided to adopt judgment according to the *shari'at*, but local customary law (*adat*) continued to have a strong influence.

There were some 500,000–1,000,000 Adygei in the northern Caucasus at this period, but when the area came under Russian rule in the middle of the century, many emigrated to Turkey. By the end of the century the Adygei population in Adygeja (Circassia) had fallen to about one tenth of its former size.

In the early Soviet period two separate Adygei areas were created: the Adygei-Cherkess Autonomous Province (July 1922) and the Cherkess Autonomous Province (January 1922). In August 1928 'Cherkess' was dropped from the title of the former, so that it became simply the Adygei Autonomous Province; the latter was eventually combined with the Karachai Autonomous Province to form the Karachai-Cherkess Autonomous Province (see p. 202). The territory of the Adygei Autonomous Province was increased in August 1936 by the addition of the Maikop and Giagin regions. The term 'Adygei' was not used at all in the 1926 Census (though the Adygei-Cherkess Autonomous Province already existed); instead 'Cherkess' was used for all the Adygei groups (except, of course, the Kabardians, who had been separated from the main body of the Adygei for several centuries). The term 'Adygei' was later reinstated and the two words are now used with territorial rather than ethnic implications (i.e. 'Adygei' is used for the Adygei who live in the Adygei Autonomous Province, 'Cherkess' for the Adygei who live in the Karachai-Cherkess Autonomous Province).

Adygei Autonomous Province, also known as *Adygeja*

Situated in the north-west Caucasus, in the Krasnodar Territory (*kraj*) of the RSFSR. *Area*: 7,600 sq. km. *Capital*: Maikop (population in 1979: 128,000). The Province has 2 towns and 4 settlements. *Population* (1979): 404,390. Average density of population per sq. km (1979): 53.2.

Chief resources: major reserves of natural gas.

Industries include: machine-building, food (particularly canning), timber and other light industries.

Agriculture: cultivation of grain, tobacco, sugar beet, sunflowers, vegetables and fruit; stockbreeding, particularly of cattle; poultry-rearing; apiculture.

2 NUMBER AND DISTRIBUTION

Number of Adygei

	1926	1959	1970	1979
	(listed with Cherkess)	79,631	99,855	108,711

Regional distribution of Adygei

	1926	1959	1970	1979
Adygei-Cherkess/Adygei Autonomous Province	50,821*	65,908 (82.8%)	81,478 (81.6%)	86,388 (79.5%)
Elsewhere in USSR		13,723 (17.2%)	18,377 (18.4%)	22,323 (20.5%)

*Listed as Cherkess.

Urban/rural distribution of Adygei in 1970 in the Adygei Autonomous Province

Urban	10,397	(12.8%)
Rural	71,081	(87.2%)

Ethnic composition of the Adygei-Cherkess/Adygei Autonomous Province

	1926	1959	1970	1979
Total population	112,767	284,690	385,644	404,390
Adygei	50,821* (45.1%)	65,908 (23.2%)	81,478 (21.1%)	86,388 (21.4%)
Russians	29,102 (25.8%)	200,492 (70.4%)	276,537 (71.7%)	285,626 (70.6%)
Ukrainians	26,405 (23.4%)	7,988 (2.8%)	11,214 (2.9%)	12,078 (3.0%)
Others	6,439 (5.7%)	10,302 (3.6%)	16,415 (4.3%)	20,298 (5.0%)

*Listed as Cherkess

Urban/rural distribution in the Adygei Autonomous Province in 1970

	Urban	Rural
Total	152,651	232,993
Adygei	10,397 (6.8%)	71,081 (30.5%)
Russians	128,511 (84.2%)	148,026 (63.5%)
Ukrainians	6,180 (4.0%)	5,034 (2.2%)
Others	7,563 (5.0%)	8,852 (3.8%)

3 STATUS

The Adygei enjoy full Soviet citizenship. They are found in all occupations and in all income brackets, though the majority work on collective farms. Their standard of housing is comparable with that of other national groups in the Soviet Union. The women go out to work, as elsewhere in the Soviet Union.

Literacy

In 1926	In 1970
16.9%*	Over 99%

*Listed as Cherkess

Level of education per 1,000 Adygei living in the Adygei Autonomous Province of 10 years of age and above

	1959	1970
Primary		
Total	237	270
Men	283	297
Women	204	250
Higher and secondary (complete and incomplete)		
Total	329	435
Men	391	495
Women	285	386
Higher only		
Total	10	37
Men	17	48
Women	6	27

4 LANGUAGE

The national language is Adygei. It belongs to the North-West group of Caucasian languages, Abkhazian-Adygei sub-group. It is closely related to Kabardian, Cherkess, Abkhazian and Abazin. It has four dialect groupings: Abadzekh, Bzhedug, Temirgoj and Shapsug (originally these represented the main tribal divisions). The differences between them are chiefly phonetic. The Temirgoj now provides the norm for educated pronunciation. The Adygei vocabulary has many loans from Arabic (particularly in the religious sphere), Persian (trade) and Turkish (everyday life); there are also many Russian loans, both from the pre-revolutionary and the post-revolutionary periods. These loan-words have undergone considerable phonetic modification.

Russian is generally used for administrative, judicial and other official proceedings, but in theory Adygei can be used if necessary.

Percentage of Adygei claiming Adygei as their mother tongue

	1926	1959	1970	1979
Total	(see Cherkess, p. 235)	96.8	96.5	95.7
In urban areas		85.3	86.7	n.a.
In rural areas		98.8	99.2	n.a.

Percentage of Adygei with good knowledge of Russian

	1926	1959	1970	1979
As mother tongue	(see Cherkess, p. 235)	3.2	3.4	4.2
As second language		n.a.	67.9	76.7

In 1958 Adygei was the medium of instruction in grades 1–4 (primary +1) in national schools; in 1972 it was not used at all as a medium of instruction, but was taught as an individual, optional subject in Russian-medium schools in grades 1–10 (Silver, p. 33). There is a Pedagogical Institute at Maikop.

In the Adygei Autonomous Province there are some radio broadcasts in Adygei, as well as in Russian.

Newspapers are published in Adygei and Russian. The Adygei-language paper is *Sotsialisticheska Adygej* ('Socialist Adygeja' – first appeared in 1926). A quarterly literary almanac, *Zekoshnyg* ('Friendship'), was started in 1947. There was no Adygei press before the Soviet period.

Books and pamphlets are published in Adygei (e.g. 14 titles in 1976; none of these were specialized textbooks on scientific or technical subjects).

Scripts and alphabets

Adygei was not written until the Soviet period.

1918–27　Arabic script
1927–38　Latin script
1938　　　Cyrillic script

5 RELIGION

The Adygei are Sunni Muslims (Hanafi school). They come under the spiritual jurisdiction of the Directorate of Northern Caucasus and Daghestan (Makhachkala).

ABKHAZIANS

Own name: *Apsua*; Russian name: *Abkhazy*.

The Abkhazians live mainly in the Abkhazian ASSR; there are also settlements in the adjoining Adzhar ASSR.

1 HISTORICAL BACKGROUND

Present-day Abkhazia has been inhabited since ancient times. It was colonized by Greek settlers in the sixth and fifth centuries BC; towns such as Pitsunda and Sukhumi were originally founded during this period. The region formed part of the Kingdom of Colchis, land of the legendary Golden Fleece. Later, in the fourth to sixth centuries AD it was part of the Laz state, a vassal of the Byzantine Empire. In 523 Christianity was adopted as the state religion of Abkhazia. The Arabs invaded the Caucasus in the early eighth century and established bases in Derbent and Tbilisi (Tiflis); they also invaded Abkhazia but did not remain long, for by the early ninth century an independent kingdom had been formed there (though it paid tribute to the Arab court in Tbilisi). The Turkic Khazars were allies of the Abkhazians and one of the first Abkhazian kings, Leon II, married a Khazar princess. The power of the Abkhazian state was at its height during the ninth and tenth centuries. It was united with Georgia in 978, under a king, Bagrat III, who was of joint Abkhazian and Georgian descent. Abkhazia in theory retained its independent status after the union, but Georgian influence soon began to predominate. The Abkhazian nobility adopted the Georgian language and eventually this even came to replace Greek as the liturgical language.

The Ottomans invaded Abkhazia in the mid-fifteenth century; in the late sixteenth century it provided them with a springboard for their Caucasian campaign, with Sukhumi as one of their main bastions. Under Ottoman influence Islam began to spread amongst the Abkhazians, though Christianity remained strong for several centuries longer. Meanwhile, the Russians were steadily expanding their empire in the direction of the Caucasus and at the same time increasing their hold on the Black Sea. By the end of the eighteenth century they had annexed the Crimea; in 1810 Abkhazia became a protectorate. At first it retained a measure of independence and was able to govern its internal affairs, but in 1864 it came under direct Russian rule. There were a number of anti-Russian uprisings and in 1866 a large number of Abkhazians emigrated to Turkey. After the Russo-Turkish war of 1877–8 still more Abkhazians left for Turkey. As a result of this exodus the number of Abkhazians in Abkhazia dropped from some 128,000 to 20,000 by the end of the nineteenth century.

In the aftermath of the Russian Revolution there was fierce fighting throughout the Caucasus with many different groups striving for power. Soviet rule was finally established in Abkhazia on 4 March 1921. The Abkhazian Soviet Socialist Republic was formed in February 1922, in union with the Georgian Soviet Socialist Republic. In 1930 the Abkhazian SSR was transformed into an Autonomous Republic within the Georgian SSR.

Abkhazian ASSR (Apsnytei Avtonomte Sovette Sotsialistte Respublika) also known as *Abkhazia*

Situated in the Georgian SSR, in the north-west of Transcaucasia, bordered to the south-west by the Black Sea. *Area*: 8,600 sq. km. *Capital*: Sukhumi (population in 1979: 114,000). The Republic has 6 towns and 3 settlements. *Population* (1979): 486,082. Average density of population per sq. km (1979): 58.9.

Chief resources: fertile soil; a magnificent coastline.

Industries include: the cultivation of tobacco, tea and citrus fruits and related processing industries; Abkhazian grapes have been famous for centuries and viticulture and wine-making are now highly developed; other traditional products which have retained their importance are snuff and honey. Tourism is one of the major growth areas (centred on the Black Sea resorts).

2 NUMBER AND DISTRIBUTION

Number of Abkhazians

	1926	1959	1970	1979
	56,957	65,430	83,240	90,915

Regional distribution of Abkhazians

	1926	1959	1970	1979
Abkhazian SSR/ ASSR	55,918 (98.2%)	61,193 (93.5%)	77,276 (92.8%)	83,097 (91.4%)
Elsewhere in USSR	1,039 (1.8%)	4,237 (6.5%)	5,964 (7.2%)	7,818 (8.6%)

Urban/rural distribution of Abkhazians in the Abkhazian SSR/ASSR

	1926	1970
Urban	2,063 (3.7%)	24,446 (31.6%)
Rural	53,855 (96.3%)	52,830 (68.4%)

Ethnic composition of the Abkhazian SSR/ASSR

	1926	1959	1970	1979
Total population	186,004	404,738	486,959	486,082
Abkhazians	55,918 (30.1%)	61,193 (15.1%)	77,276 (15.9%)	83,097 (17.1%)
Georgians	67,494 (36.3%)	158,221 (39.1%)	199,595 (41.0%)	213,322 (43.9%)
Armenians	25,677 (13.8%)	64,425 (15.9%)	74,850 (15.4%)	73,350 (15.1%)
Russians	12,553 (6.7%)	86,715 (21.4%)	92,889 (19.1%)	79,730 (16.4%)
Ukrainians	4,647 (2.5%)	11,474 (2.8%)	11,955 (2.5%)	10,257 (2.1%)
Others	19,715 (10.6%)	22,710 (5.6%)	30,394 (6.2%)	26,326 (5.4%)

Urban/rural distribution in the Abkhazian ASSR in 1970

	Urban	Rural
Total population	215,108	271,851
Abkhazians	24,446 (11.4%)	52,830 (19.4%)
Georgians	73,687 (34.3%)	125,908 (46.3%)
Armenians	22,242 (10.3%)	52,608 (19.4%)
Russians	66,919 (31.1%)	25,970 (9.6%)
Ukrainians	8,594 (4.0%)	3,361 (1.2%)
Others	19,220 (8.9%)	11,174 (4.1%)

3 STATUS

The Abkhazians enjoy full Soviet citizenship. They are found in all occupations and in all income brackets, though the majority are involved in agricultural work. Their standard of housing is comparable to that of other national groups in the Soviet Union. The women go out to work, as elsewhere in the Soviet Union.

Literacy

In 1926	In 1970
11.3%	Over 99%

In 1926, 2,774 Abkhazians were literate in their own language (42.9 per cent of the total literate Abkhazian population).

Level of education per 1,000 Abkhazians living in the Abkhazian ASSR of 10 years of age and above

	1959	1970
Primary		
Total	226	292
Men	272	319
Women	188	268
Higher and secondary (complete and incomplete)		
Total	324	427
Men	356	458
Women	297	401
Higher only		
Total	16	45
Men	23	51
Women	10	40

4 LANGUAGE

The national language is Abkhazian. It belongs to the North-West group of Caucasian languages, Abkhazian-Adygei sub-group. Abkhazian and Abazin are so close that they could almost be said to represent two dialects of the same language. They each have their own sub-dialects, however, based on geographical areas. In Abkhazian there are the Abzhui and Bzyb dialects. The differences between them are phonetic. The literary language is based on the former. There are a number of Georgian and Turkish loan-words in Abkhazian, as well as later imports from Russian.

Russian is generally used for administrative, judicial and other official proceedings, but in theory Abkhazian can be used if necessary, as can Georgian.

Percentage of Abkhazians claiming Abkhazian as their mother tongue

	1926	1959	1970	1979
Total	83.9	95.0	95.9	94.3
In urban areas	85.3	88.8	90.4	n.a.
In rural areas	83.9	97.3	98.8	n.a.

Percentage of Abkhazians with good knowledge of Russian

	1926	1959	1970	1979
As mother tongue	0.2	3.1	3.1	4.1
As second language	n.a.	n.a.	59.2	73.3

In 1959 Abkhazian was used as a medium of instruction (Lewis, p. 184), but no information is available on the extent of its use. Today there is probably some instruction in Abkhazian in the primary grades and it is likely that it is taught as an individual, optional subject in some Russian and Georgian medium schools (judging by the situation in other ASSRs). There are some specialized institutes in Abkhazia, e.g. of Experimental Pathology and Therapy and of Pedagogy. There is probably some tuition in Abkhazian at the latter.

In the Abkhazian ASSR there are radio and television broadcasts in Abkhazian, as well as in Georgian and Russian.

Newspapers are also published in Abkhazian, Georgian and Russian. The first periodical publication in Abkhazian, *Abkhazija* ('Abkhazia'), appeared from 1918 to c.1920. However, the Abkhazian press is generally considered to have begun with *Apsny Kapsh* ('Red Abkhazia'), which appeared in 1922 and is still the main Abkhazian paper in the republic. The periodicals in Abkhazian are *Alashara* ('Light' – since 1955) and *Amtsabz* ('Flame' – for children: since 1957).

Books and pamphlets are published in Abkhazian (e.g. 49 titles in 1976; 3 of these were books on specialized technical subjects).

Scripts and alphabets

An alphabet based on the Cyrillic script was invented for Abkhazian by P. K. Uslar in 1862, but little was written in Abkhazian until the Soviet period. An alphabet of N. Marr's was used from 1926 to 1928, then abandoned.

1928–38 Latin script
1938–54 Georgian script
1954   Cyrillic script

5 RELIGION

Some Abkhazians are Sunni Muslims, some (particularly the Samurzakan tribe) are Orthodox Christians. No information is available on relative numbers. The Abkhazian Muslims come under the spiritual jurisdiction of the Directorate of Transcaucasia (Baku).

BALKARS

Own names: *Balkar, Malkar, Taulu* ('mountain-people'); also according to village; Russian names: *Balkary, Balkartsy*.

The majority of the Balkars are now once more settled in the Kabardino-Balkar ASSR (which forms part of the RSFSR). They live for the most part in the mountains.

1 HISTORICAL BACKGROUND

Like the Karachais, to whom they appear to be closely related, the Balkars are a Turkic-speaking people of the Northern Caucasus. They are known to have been settled in their present habitat by the fourteenth to fifteenth centuries (they are mentioned by name in a Georgian inscription on a cross of that date), but their ethnic origin is unclear. The main theories on this point are that they are (a) Khazars who retreated here after the break-up of the Khazar Khanate in the tenth to eleventh centuries; (b) Volga Bolgars forced back into the mountains by the Mongol invasion of the thirteenth century; (c) indigenous Caucasian tribes Turkicized through contact with immigrant Turkic peoples such as the two (Bolgars and Khazars) just mentioned. It is probable that the Balkars and the Karachais both contain an Alan element, since the Alans (an Indo-European people of the Black Sea coast) also retreated to this area under pressure of the Mongol onslaught.

Islam was introduced amongst the Balkars in the eighteenth century by the Crimean Tatars and by the Nogais of the Kuban' region. Prior to this some were animists, while others had already been converted to Christianity. Islam did not finally overcome either of these two traditions until the early twentieth century.

In the early nineteenth century Russia rapidly expanded its power in the Caucasus; by 1827 it had control of Balkaria, which at that time was a vassal of the Kabardians (see p. 190). In official sources of this period the Balkars were referred to as 'Mountain Tatars' in acknowledgment of the fact that they were a Turkic (or at least Turkic-speaking) people, as opposed to the Caucasian Kabardians. Soviet rule was first proclaimed in the area in December 1918, but here, as elsewhere in the Caucasus, there was fierce fighting between the rival factions and Soviet power was not finally established until 1920. In 1921 the Balkar District (*okrug*) was formed as part of the Gorskaja ASSR; on 16 January 1922 it was joined with Kabardia to create the Kabardino-Balkar Autonomous Province, which was transformed into an ASSR on 5 December 1936.

In October 1942 the German army occupied Nal'chik, the capital of the Kabardino-Balkar ASSR. Some collaboration did undoubtedly take place, but thousands of Balkars (and Kabardians) were at the time fighting with the Red Army and could in no way have been guilty of this. Nevertheless, on 8 March 1944, a year after the liberation of the republic, every single Balkar was rounded up and deported to Kazakhstan and Kirghizia; in April 1944 the name of their republic was changed from the 'Kabardino-Balkar ASSR' to the 'Kabardian ASSR'. Thirteen years later they were 'rehabilitated' and allowed to return home, though by this time much of their former lands had been reduced to a state of wilderness due to total neglect during the intervening period. In 1957 the Kabardino-Balkar ASSR was reinstated and efforts were made to acknowledge the existence of the Balkars, e.g. the main newspaper, *Kabardinskaja pravda* ('Kabardian Truth'), had its name changed to *Kabardino-Balkarsaja pravda* on 22 March 1957. By 1958 the return of the Balkars to Balkaria was well advanced.

For information on the Kabardino-Balkar ASSR see p. 192.

2 NUMBER AND DISTRIBUTION

Number of Balkars

	1926	1959	1970	1979
	33,307	42,408	59,501	66,334

The net losses for the period 1939–59 are estimated to be a minimum of 26.5 per cent (Nekrich, p. 138).

Regional distribution of Balkars

	1926	1959	1970	1979
Kabardino-Balkar	33,197	34,088	51,356	59,710
Aut. Prov./ASSR	(99.7%)	(80.4%)	(86.3%)	(90.0%)
Elsewhere in USSR	110	8,320	8,145	6,624
	(0.3%)	(19.6%)	(13.7%)	(10.0%)

In 1970, 4.6 per cent and 3.3 per cent of the Balkars were still in exile in the Kazakh and Kirghiz SSRs respectively. Even in 1979 they had still not all returned.

Urban/rural distribution of Balkars in the Kabardino-Balkar Autonomous Province/ASSR

	1926	1970
Urban	350	13,816
	(1.1%)	(26.9%)
Rural	32,847	37,540
	(98.9%)	(73.1%)

For *Ethnic composition of the Kabardino-Balkar Autonomous Province/ASSR* and *Urban/rural distribution in the Kabardino-Balkar ASSR* see p. 193.

3 STATUS

Having been 'rehabilitated', the Balkars now enjoy full Soviet citizenship. They are found in all occupations and in all income brackets, but the majority are agricultural workers on collective farms. Their standard of housing is comparable to that of other national groups in the Soviet Union. The women go out to work, as elsewhere in the Soviet Union.

Literacy

In 1926	In 1970
5.3%	Over 99%

In 1926, 278 Balkars were literate in their own language (15.9 per cent of the total literate Balkar population).

Level of education per 1,000 Balkars living in the Kabardino-Balkar ASSR of 10 years of age and above

	1959	1970
Primary		
Total	284	335
Men	310	345
Women	264	327
Higher and secondary (complete and incomplete)		
Total	239	356
Men	333	424
Women	165	297
Higher only		
Total	5	29
Men	9	44
Women	1	15

4 LANGUAGE

The national language is Karachai-Balkar. See under Karachai for classification.

Russian is generally used for administration, judicial and other official proceedings, but in theory Karachai-Balkar can be used if necessary.

Percentage of Balkars claiming Karachai-Balkar as their mother tongue

	1926	1959	1970	1979
Total	99.6	97.0	97.2	96.9
In urban areas	95.1	92.7	93.5	n.a.
In rural areas	99.7	98.0	98.6	n.a.

In 1958 Karachai-Balkar was the medium of instruction in grades 1–4 (primary +1) in national schools; after 1965–6 it was no longer

Percentage of Balkars with good knowledge of Russian

	1926	1959	1970	1979
As mother tongue	0.0 4 people	2.2	2.3	2.7
As second language	n.a.	n.a.	71.5	77.4

used as a medium of instruction; in 1972 it was taught as an individual, optional subject in Russian-medium schools in grades 1–10 (Silver, p. 33). More recent information is not available.

In the Kabardino-Balkar ASSR there are radio and television broadcasts in Karachai-Balkar, as well as in Kabardino-Cherkess and Russian.

Newspapers are also published in these languages.

For details of periodical publications and books and pamphlets in Karachai-Balkar, see p. 196. For publications in the Kabardino-Balkar ASSR, see p. 195.

Scripts and alphabets

See under Karachai.

5 RELIGION

The Balkars are Sunni Muslims (Hanafi school). They come under the spiritual jurisdiction of the Directorate of Northern Caucasus and Daghestan (Makhachkala).

CHERKESS/CIRCASSIANS

Own name: *Adyge*; also tribal names, e.g. *Abadzekh, Beslenej, Bzhedukh, Gatjukaj, Jererukoj, Kemgoj, Kheak, Nadkhokuadzh, Shapsug, Temirgoj*; Russian name: *Cherkesy*.

The majority of Cherkess live in the Karachajevo-Cherkess Autonomous Province.

1 HISTORICAL BACKGROUND

The term 'Cherkess' (or 'Circassian') is confusing, because, like

'Tatar', it has been used with different meanings in different periods. The Cherkess belong to the Adygei group (see p. 215) and their name appears to be derived from *Kerkety*, one of the Adygei tribal names. The whole group are referred to in the early Russian chronicles as *Kasogi/Kosagi*; at about the same period (*c.* tenth century AD) they were known to the Arabs, Persians and Georgians as *Kashak*. From the thirteenth century the name *Cherkas* began to be used (though not originally specifically for the Adygeis, rather more for the people of the southern Ukraine). This term, in the form *Cherkess*, came to be accepted as the general designation of all the north Caucasian peoples (e.g. Abkhazians, Abazins, Ossetians, etc.) and is still often used in this sense in Turkish and western European sources.

In the 1926 Soviet Census it was used for all the Adygei peoples except the Kabardians (see p. 190); later, it was restricted to Adygeis living in specific areas (principally the Karachajevo-Cherkess Autonomous Province) and this is the meaning it still has today. Meanwhile, 'Adygei' has become the general ethnic term for the group (as it always was in vernacular usage). The apparent drop in the Cherkess population between 1926 and 1959 is due to this redefinition of terms rather than to an actual drop in numbers.

For the history of the Cherkess, see the section on the Adygei, p. 215.

The Karachajevo-Cherkess Autonomous Province was created in January 1922 in the Stavropol' Territory (*kraj*) of the RSFSR; its administrative centre was Batalpashinsk (now known as Cherkessk). In April 1926 the two areas were divided (in the census in January of that year they were already listed separately), to form the Karachaj Autonomous Province and the Cherkess National District, which in turn became an Autonomous Province in 1928. The Karachaj Autonomous Province was abolished during the war (see p. 203); when it was reinstated in 1957, it was once more united with its former partner to become the Karachajevo-Cherkess Autonomous Province, with Cherkessk as its administrative centre again. For more information on the Karachajevo-Cherkess Autonomous Province see p. 203.

The Adygei-Cherkess Autonomous Province was formed on 27 July 1922; in August 1928 it became the Adygei Autonomous Province. The indigenous population, formerly known as 'Cherkess', are now known as 'Adygei'; see p. 216.

2 NUMBER AND DISTRIBUTION

Number of Cherkess

	1926 (Cherkess + Adygei)	1959	1970	1979
	65,270	30,453	39,785	46,470

Regional distribution of Cherkess

	1926 (Cherkess + Adygei)	1959	1970	1979
RSFSR	65,105 (99.7%)	28,986 (95.2%)	38,356 (96.4%)	44,572 (95.9%)
Cherkess/ Karachajevo-Cherkess Autonomous Province only	2,655 (4.1%)	24,145 (79.3%)	31,190 (78.4%)	34,430 (74.1%)
Adygei-Cherkess/ Adygei Autonomous Province only	50,821 (77.8%)	—*	—*	—*
Elsewhere in USSR	165 (0.3%)	1,467 (4.8%)	1,429 (3.6%)	1,898 (4.1%)

* Listed as Adygei; see above, also p. 217.

Urban/rural distribution of Cherkess in the RSFSR

	1926 (Cherkess + Adygei)	1970
Urban	1,744 (2.7%)	7,227 (18.8%)
Rural	63,361 (97.3%)	31,129 (81.2%)

Ethnic composition of the Cherkess Autonomous Province in 1926

Total population	36,951
Cherkess	2,655 (7.2%)
Kabardians	12,314 (33.3%)
Beskesek-Abaza (Abazins)	10,993 (29.8%)
Nogais	6,206 (16.8%)
Russians	1,473 (4.0%)
Others	3,310 (9.0%)

For *Ethnic composition of the Karachajevo-Cherkess Autonomous Province* and *Urban/rural distribution in the Karachajevo-Cherkess Autonomous Province* see pp. 204, 205.

3 STATUS

The Cherkess enjoy full Soviet citizenship. They are found in all occupations and in all income brackets, but the majority work on collective farms. Their standard of housing is comparable to that of other national groups in the Soviet Union. The women go out to work, as elsewhere in the Soviet Union.

Literacy

In 1926 (*including Adygeis*)	In 1970
16.9%	Over 99%

In 1926, 4,045 Cherkess (and Adygei) were literate in their own language (36.6 per cent of the total literate Cherkess population).

Level of education per 1,000 Cherkess living in the Karachajevo-Cherkess Autonomous Province of 10 years of age and above

	1959	1970
Primary		
Total	268	298
Men	306	311
Women	238	287
Higher and secondary (complete and incomplete)		
Total	307	421
Men	368	485
Women	260	370
Higher only		
Total	6	30
Men	11	40
Women	2	22

4 LANGUAGE

The national language is Cherkess. It is considered to form a single literary language with Kabardian, often referred to as 'Kabardino-Cherkess'. Kabardino-Cherkess belongs to the North-West group of Caucasian languages, Abkhazian-Adygei sub-group. It is most closely related to Adygei and both languages (Kabardino-Cherkess and Adygei) are in fact called by their respective native speakers *Adyga-bza*. Kabardino-Cherkess has four main dialect groupings: those of Greater Kabardia, the Mozdok area, the Beslanis (the group that now constitutes most of the 'Cherkess' people, i.e. those who live in the Karachajevo-Cherkess Autonomous Province) and the Kuban' region. The differences between them are mostly phonetic and morphological. The vocabulary contains a considerable number of Turkish, Persian and Arabic loan-words (particularly in the sphere of religious terminology), as well as a high proportion of Russian loan-words.

Russian is generally used for administrative, judicial and other official proceedings, but in theory Cherkess can be used if necessary.

In 1958 Cherkess was the medium of instruction in grades 1–4 (primary +1) in the national schools: in 1972, it was not used at all as a medium of instruction, but it was taught as an individual, optional subject in Russian-medium schools in grades 1–10 (Silver, p. 33).

Percentage of Cherkess claiming Cherkess as their mother tongue

	1926 *(Cherkess + Adygei)*	*1959*	*1970*	*1979*
Total	98.4	89.7	92.0	91.4
In urban areas	74.0	56.2	75.3	n.a.
In rural areas	99.1	96.3	96.5	n.a.

Percentage of Cherkess with good knowledge of Russian

	1926	*1959*	*1970*	*1979*
As mother tongue	1.1	6.7	5.4	5.9
As second language	n.a.	n.a.	70.0	69.6

There is some broadcasting in Kabardino-Cherkess in both the Kabardino-Balkar ASSR and the Karachajevo-Cherkess Autonomous Province; in addition, in both areas there are broadcasts in Karachai-Balkar and Russian and in the Karachajevo-Cherkess Autonomous Province there are also broadcasts in Nogai and Abazin.

Newspapers are published in Kabardino-Cherkess in both the Kabardino-Balkar ASSR and the Karachajevo-Cherkess Autonomous Province; in the former, the main Kabardino-Cherkess newspaper is *Lenin guegu* ('Lenin's Way'), which first appeared in 1920; in the latter, *Lenin nur* ('Lenin's Light'), which first appeared in 1923.

Books and pamphlets are published in Cherkess (e.g. 1 title in 1976) and also in Kabardian (e.g. 24 titles in 1976; none of these, nor the single one in Cherkess, were specialized textbooks on scientific or technical subjects).

Scripts and alphabets

Kabardino-Cherkess was not a written language until the Soviet period.

1923–4   Latin script, first alphabet
1924–36   Latin script, improved alphabet
1936   Cyrillic script

5 RELIGION

The Cherkess are Sunni Muslims (Hanafi school). They come under the spiritual jurisdiction of the Directorate of Northern Caucasus and Daghestan (Makhachkala).

6 OUTSIDE THE SOVIET UNION

There are some 150,000 Cherkess in the Near East, mostly in Turkey.

ABAZINS

Own name: *Abaza*; Russian name: *Abaziny*.

The Abazins live mainly in the Karachajevo-Cherkess Autonomous Province, on the upper reaches of the Great and Little Zelenchuk, Kuban' and Kuma Rivers; there are also some Abazins in the eastern part of the Adygei Autonomous Province.

1 HISTORICAL BACKGROUND

The Abazins are an indigenous people of the north-west Caucasus. They were originally settled along the Black Sea coast, a little to the north of the present-day Abkhazian ASSR, in the vicinity of Tuapse. They migrated inland to their present habitat between the fourteenth and sixteenth centuries, but some remained in the coastal region until as late as 1864. Like most of the other peoples along the eastern shores of the Black Sea, the Abazins adopted Christianity at an early date. Their conversation to Islam began after their move to the west, when they came under the influence of the Nogais and other Muslim peoples. The first converts date from the seventeenth century, but Christianity retained its hold for some time after this and the Abazins as a whole did not accept Islam until the mid-nineteenth century.

There are two main tribal groupings amongst the Abazins: the Tapanta ('Plains-dwellers') and the Shkaraua ('Mountain-dwellers'). During the Murid Uprising (led by the Avar Shamyl 1834–59), the Tapanta for the most part sided with the Russians, while the Shkaraua supported Shamyl. After the Murids had finally been defeated many thousands of the Shkaraua tribesmen emigrated to Turkey, the main exodus taking place in the years 1862–4.

In the 1926 Soviet Census the term 'Abazin' is not used at all; instead, these people are called 'Beskesek-Abaza' ('Five-division Abazins'; cf. the Nogai name for the Tapanta *Alty-kesek Abaza* 'Six-division Abazins').

2 NUMBER AND DISTRIBUTION

Number of Abazins

	1926 (Beskesek-Abaza)	1959	1970	1979
	13,825	19,591	25,448	29,497

Regional distribution of Abazins

	1926 (Beskesek-Abaza)	1959	1970	1979
RSFSR	13,825 (100%)	19,059 (97.3%)	24,892 (97.8%)	n.a.
Karachajevo-Cherkess Aut. Prov. only	13,731* (99.3%)	18,159 (92.7%)	22,896 (90.0%)	24,245 (82.2%)
Elsewhere in USSR	94 (0.7%)	532 (2.7%)	556 (2.2%)	

*10,993 Beskesek-Abaza were in the Cherkess Autonomous Province, 2,738 in the Karachaj Autonomous Province.

Urban/rural distribution of Abazins in the Karachajevo-Cherkess Autonomous Province

	1926	1970
Urban	——	2,781 (12.1%)
Rural	13,731 (100%)	20,115 (87.9%)

3 STATUS

The Abazins enjoy full Soviet citizenship. They are found in all occupations and in all income brackets, though the majority work on collective farms. Their standard of housing is comparable to that of other national groups in the Soviet Union. The women go out to work, as elsewhere in the Soviet Union.

Literacy

In 1926	In 1970
(*Beskesek-Abaza*)	
9.6%	Over 99%

In 1926, 216 of the Beskesek-Abaza were literate in their own language (16.3 per cent of the total literate Beskesek-Abaza population).

4 LANGUAGE

The national language is Abazin. It belongs to the North-West group of Caucasian languages, Abkhazian-Adygei sub-group. Abazin and Abkhazian are so closely related that they may almost be considered dialects of a single language. However, during the Soviet period they have been developed as separate literary languages. Abazin has two dialects, corresponding to the two main geographical locations of the Abazins: Tapanta ('plains-dwellers') and (A)shkaraua ('mountain-dwellers'). The majority of Abazins in the Soviet Union are Tapanta Abazins and a sub-dialect of theirs was taken as the basis for the literary language. The Abazin language has an extraordinarily complicated phonology with two vowels to over seventy consonants (it is considered to be the most phonetically complex of all the hundred or more languages spoken in the Soviet Union). It first attracted scholarly attention in the eighteenth century, but it is only in recent years that it has been studied in detail.

Russian is generally used for administrative, judicial and other official proceedings, but in theory Abazin can be used if necessary.

Percentage of Abazins claiming Abazin as their mother tongue

	1926	1959	1970	1979
Total	94.4	94.8	96.1	95.3
In urban areas	84.5	86.2	86.4	n.a.
In rural areas	94.5	95.8	98.1	n.a.

In 1958 Abazin was the medium of instruction in grades 1–4 (primary +1) in national schools; no other information is available.

There are some broadcasts in Abazin in the Karachajevo-Cherkess Autonomous Province.

Percentage of Abazins with good knowledge of Russian

	1926 (Beskesek-Abaza)	1959	1970	1979
As mother tongue	0.0 (3 people)	1.8	2.5	3.4
As second language	n.a.	n.a.	69.5	75.4

The newspaper *Kommunizm alashara* ('Light of Communism'), which first began to appear in 1938, is published in Abazin in the Karachajevo-Cherkess Autonomous Province.

Books and pamphlets are published in Abazin (e.g. 8 titles in 1976; none of these were specialized textbooks on scientific or technical subjects).

Scripts and alphabets

Abazin was not a written language until an alphabet was created for it in 1932–3; before that it had only been noted down in transcription.

1933–8   Latin script
1938   Cyrillic script

5 RELIGION

The Abazins are Sunni Muslims (Hanafi school). They come under the spiritual jurisdiction of the Directorate of Northern Caucasus and Daghestan (Makhachkala).

TATS

Own name: *Tat*; Russian name: *Taty*.

The Tats live in the Northern Caucasus, in the Apsheron region of the RSFSR, north-eastern Azerbaidzhan (in such areas as Konakhkent, Afrudzha, Chichi and Kuba) and the Daghestan ASSR (in such towns as Derbent, Makhachkala and Bujnaksk).

1 HISTORICAL BACKGROUND

The Tats are an Iranian people of Transcaucasia. Little is known of their origins, but they are thought to be descendants of settlers sent from Persia to defend the northern limits of the Sasanid empire during the fourth to fifth centuries A.D. They fall into three groups, distinguished by religion as well as by location: the Jewish Tats (called *Dzhukhur* by the other Tats; also known as 'Mountain Jews'), who live mostly in the Daghestan ASSR; the Muslim Tats, who live in the Apsheron region and northern Azerbaidzhan; and the Christian (Armenian-Gregorian rite) Tats, who live in certain settlements in northern Azerbaidzhan. The Tats who live in Azerbaidzhan are rapidly being assimilated and many now identify themselves as Azerbaidzhanis.

2 NUMBER AND DISTRIBUTION

Number of Tats

	1926	1959*	1970	1979
	28,705	11,463	17,109	22,441

*In 1959 and later the Jewish Tats were listed with the Jews; they are only identifiable by their language (if they still claim Tat as mother tongue). The Christian Tats may now be included with the Armenians. See also *Ethnic composition of the Daghestan ASSR*, p. 126.

Distribution of Tats

	1926	1959*	1970	1979
AzSSR	28,443 (99.1%)	5,887 (51.4%)	7,769 (45.4%)	8,848 (39.4%)
DaghASSR	204 (0.7%)	2,954 (25.8%)	6,440 (37.6%)	7,437 (33.1%)
Elsewhere in USSR	58 (0.2%)	2,622 (22.9%)	2,900 (17.0%)	6,156 (27.4%)

*It is not clear where some 20 per cent of the Tat population disappeared to in and after 1959; the drop in actual numbers in the Azerbaidzhan SSR is explained by the fact that many Tats began to identify themselves as Azerbaidzhanis after 1926, e.g. in 1959, 12,960 Tat-speakers were included with the Azerbaidzhanis (in addition to the 8,357 'Mountain Jews' who claimed Tat as their mother tongue and were listed with the Jews).

Urban/rural distribution of Tats

	1926	1970
Urban	7,173 (25.0%)	16,604 (97.0%)
Rural	21,532 (75.0%)	505 (3.0%)

3 STATUS

The Tats enjoy full Soviet citizenship. They are found in all occupations and in all income brackets, though the majority of Jewish Tats are engaged in agriculture, while the Muslim Tats who live in the area of Baku are predominantly employed in the oil industry.

Their standard of housing is comparable to that of other national groups in the Soviet Union. The women go out to work, as elsewhere in the Soviet Union.

Literacy

In 1926	In 1970
5.9%	Over 99%

In 1926, none of the Tats were literate in their own language.

4 LANGUAGE

The national language is Tat. It belongs to the South-West group of Iranian languages. In grammatical structure and vocabulary it is close to Persian and Tadzhik. There are many dialects, each village having its own particular features. They fall into two groups, which are based partly on regional differences, partly on religious: the dialects of the Jewish Tats, and the dialects of the Muslims and Christians. The two groups are scarcely mutually comprehensible. The Tat language first attracted scholarly attention in the middle of the nineteenth century in the work of I. N. Berezin. Since then it has been studied by several scholars, in particular by B. V. Miller, who invented an alphabet for it (based on the Latin script) in 1928. In the 1950s A. L. Grjunberg carried out detailed research on the dialects of the Muslim Tats. In the 1930s, attempts were made to introduce a special alphabet for the Kuba Tats and a few books were published in this in Baku, but it had no lasting success.

Russian is generally used for administrative, judicial and other official proceedings; in the AzSSR Azerbaidzhani is also used; in theory, Tat can be used if necessary.

Percentage of Tats claiming Tat as their mother tongue

	1926	1959	1970	1979
Total	86.6	70.9	72.6	67.4
In urban areas	78.8	70.7	72.2	n.a.
In rural areas	89.2	74.5	85.5	n.a.

Percentage of Tats with good knowledge of Russian

	1926	1959	1970	1979
As mother tongue	0.0 (12 people)	24.4	24.7	29.4
As second language	n.a.	n.a.	57.7	61.3

No information is available on the use of Tat as a medium of instruction; it is almost certainly not used.

No information is available either on the use of Tat in broadcasting; it is probably not used.

There is only one periodical in Tat, *Letopis' pechati Dagestana* ('Chronicle of the Daghestan Press'), which is also published in Avar, Darghin, Kumyk, Lak, Lezghi, Tabasaran and Russian.

Some books and pamphlets are published in Tat (e.g. 4 titles in 1976; none of these were specialized textbooks on scientific or technical subjects).

Scripts and alphabets

The Jewish Tats used the Hebrew script until *c.* 1929; the Muslim and Christian dialects do not appear to have been written until *c.* 1935.

1929–40 Latin script (invented by B. V. Miller)
c. 1935 Latin (?) script for the Muslim Tats
c. 1940 Cyrillic script

5 RELIGION

There are Jewish, Christian (Armenian-Gregorian rite) and Muslim Tats. The Muslims include Shi'is and Sunnis. No information is available on relative numbers. The Muslim Tats come under the spiritual jurisdiction of the Directorate of Transcaucasia (Baku).

ADZHARS

Own name: *Adzhareli*; Russian name: *Adzhartsy*.

1 HISTORICAL BACKGROUND

The Adzhars are a Georgian people who adopted Islam during the period when western Georgia was under Ottoman rule. (Cf. the Meskhetian Turks, who are Georgian Muslims of Turkish origin; see p. 261.) The Adzhars' homeland is on the south-east coast of the Black Sea, directly adjacent to Turkey. In the sixth to fourth centuries BC this area formed part of the Kingdom of Colchis. There were many Greek settlements along this coast, including that of Bathys, precursor of the modern Batumi (today capital of the Adzhar ASSR). Christianity reached the area early and by the time of the Council of Nicaea (325) there were bishops' sees at Trebizond to the south and Pitsunda to the north. The Arabs established a capital at Tbilisi (Tiflis) in the seventh century, but their direct rule was confined to eastern Georgia. It was not until the tenth century that Adzharia (like neighbouring Abkhazia: see p. 221) was incorporated into the Georgian kingdom. In the following centuries the country was ravaged by wave after wave of invading armies: the Seljuks in the eleventh century, the Mongols in the thirteenth, Timur in the fourteenth, the Ottomans in the fifteenth. From the mid-seventeenth century until the Russo-Turkish war of 1877–8, part of western Georgia (including the Adzhar region) was under Turkish rule; the rest of Georgia was united with Russia during the years 1801–29. The Congress of Berlin (1878) gave Russia possession of Batumi (as well as of Ardahan and Kars).

Under Russian rule industrial enterprises were developed in and around Batumi. It was linked by rail to Baku and Tbilisi (1883) and oil pipelines were constructed between it and Baku (1897–1907). It soon became the third largest city in Transcaucasia. In April 1918 it was taken by the Turks, then occupied by the British from December 1918 to 1920. Soviet rule was established in Tbilisi in February 1921; the Mensheviks were very strong in this area and Batumi remained their last outpost until they were finally ousted from there in July of that year. The Adzhar ASSR was created on 16 July 1922, as part of the Georgian SSR. The designation 'Adzhar ASSR' still remains, but the Adzhar population has been 're-classified': they are no longer listed as a 'nationality'.

Adzhar ASSR *(Acharis Avtonomiuri Sabchota Sotsialisturi Respublika)*, also known as *Adzharia* (or *Acharia)* and *Adzharistan* (in the 1926 Census it was referred to as the 'Adzharistan ASSR')

Situated in the Georgian SSR, bordered to the north and east by Georgia, to the south by Turkey, to the west by the Black Sea. *Area*: 3,000 sq. km. *Capital*: Batumi (population in 1979: 123,000). The Republic has 2 towns and 6 settlements. *Population* (1979): 354,224. Average density of population per sq. km (1979): 118.4.

    Industries include: oil-refining (crude oil from Baku), machine-building, food and tourism (centred on the Black Sea resorts).

    Agriculture: chiefly cultivation of citrus fruits and tea; also some tobacco.

2 NUMBER AND DISTRIBUTION

Only known for 1926: large numbers of Adzhars (possibly the whole population) were deported from the Adzhar ASSR in 1929, after an uprising of Adzhars in April of that year. As they are no longer listed separately in the census reports and no reference is made to them (or their language even) in Soviet sources, it is impossible to know how many are still left and what their present location is.

Number of Adzhars in 1926

71,426.

Distribution of Adzhars in 1926

70,828 (99.2 per cent of the total Adzhar population) in the Adzhar ASSR.

Urban/rural distribution of Adzhars in 1926

2,904 (4.1%) were urban dwellers, 68,522 (95.9%) rural dwellers.

3 STATUS

Unknown. Until they are 'rehabilitated' to the point where they are again mentioned in official sources, it is impossible to draw any conclusions, favourable or otherwise, about their present condition.

4 LANGUAGE

The national language is Adzhar, a western form of the Kartvelian group of Caucasian languages. Related languages are Georgian, Megreli and Laz. Georgian is the only member of this group to be a written language. Like Laz, Adzhar was much influenced by Turkish. It is not known how this language fares today, since it is not mentioned at all in such Soviet works as *Jazyki narodov SSSR: Iberijsko-kavkazskije jazyki* ('The Languages of the USSR: Ibero-Caucasian Languages').

5 RELIGION

The Adzhars are Sunni Muslims (Hanafi school). Theoretically, they should come under the spiritual jurisdiction of the Directorate of Transcaucasia (Baku), but in practice it would depend on their location, which at present is unknown.

Airums/Airyms

Own names: *Airum, Airym*; Russian names: *Airumy, Airymlary*.

The Airums (or Airyms) are a sub-group of the Azerbaidzhanis, who, according to local tradition, settled originally in the extreme north-west of Azerbaidzhan, in the Kazakh Region. From there they gradually migrated towards the south-east and today live in the western part of the Azerbaidzhan SSR, in such areas as the Dostafur and Kedabek Regions (*rajony*) and the mountains of the Tauz Region. They speak a dialect of Azerbaidzhani and closely resemble other Azerbaidzhanis, apart from a few local peculiarities of dress, etc. Their chief occupation is farming. They have never been separately listed in the census and there is no information available on the present size of the community.

Akhvakhs

Own name: *Ashvado*; Russian name: *Akhvakhtsy*; Avar name: *G'akhevalal.*

The Akhvakhs live in the Daghestan ASSR, the majority in the Akhvakh Region (*rajon*), but some also in the Sovietsky region. The Akhvakh language (*ashval'i mits'ts'i*) belongs to the Avaro-Andi-Didoi group (Andi sub-group) of the North-East Caucasian languages. It is close to Avar. It has two dialects, a northern and a southern; the differences between them are considerable, making it almost impossible for speakers of the one to comprehend speakers of the other. Avar is used both as the common literary language and the means of verbal communication between the two groups. However, there has been a local newspaper in Akhvakh (which dialect is not known) since 1932/3. It is entitled *Zaman* ('Time'). It appears to still exist, though its language is now sometimes identified as 'Avar'.

The Akhvakhs are Sunni Muslims.

1926 Census figures

Population: 3,683. Now listed with the Avars. It was estimated in 1960 (*Narody Kavkaza I*) that there were then about 4,000 Akhvakhs.
Urban dwellers: 0.9 per cent.
Percentage claiming Akhvakh as mother tongue: 100 per cent.
Number claiming Russian as their mother tongue: none.
Literacy: 4.4 per cent.

Andis/Andiis

Own name: *Kwannal*; Russian name: *Andijtsy*; Avar name: *Handisew.*

The Andis are found in the Botlikh Region of the Daghestan ASSR where the majority of them live in nine villages: Andi, Gunkha Gagatl', Rikvani, Ashali, Chankho, Zilo, Munib and Kvankhidatl' The Andi language belongs to the Avaro-Andi-Didoi group (Andi sub-group) of the North-East Caucasian languages. It is closel related to Avar; Avar serves as the literary language since Andi i not a written language. There are two main dialect groups: upper Andi (Andi proper) and lower Andi (Munib-Kvankhidatl' dialects). A curious feature of Andi is that there are differences between the speech of the sexes, i.e. the women in the village of Andi speak a sub-dialect of their own.

The Andis are Sunni Muslims.

1926 Census figures

Population: 7,840. It was estimated in 1960 (*Narody Kavkara I*) that there were then about 8,000 Andis. They are now listed with the Avars.

Urban dwellers: 1.2 per cent.

Percentage claiming Andi as their mother tongue: 98.1 per cent.

Number claiming Russian as their mother tongue: 1 person.

Literacy: 3.4 per cent.

Archins

Own name: *Arshishttib*; Russian name: *Archintsy*.

The Archins live in a number of small villages and settlements in the Charodin Region (*rajon*) of the Daghestan ASSR. The Archins are now listed with the Avars, but their language belongs to the Lezghi group of the North Caucasian languages. It contains a considerable number of Arabic, Persian and Turkish loan-words, but relatively few Russian. Archin is not a written language; primary education is given in Avar and most Archins have a good knowledge of Avar and Lak. There are no dialects in Archin.

The Archins are Sunni Muslims.

1926 Census figures

Population: 863. It was estimated in 1967 (*Jazyki narodov SSSR IV*) that there were then some 1,000 Archins. They are now listed with the Avars.

Urban dwellers: 3 people.

Percentage claiming Archin as their mother tongue: 99.5 per cent.

Number claiming Russian as their mother tongue: none.

Literacy: 4.4 per cent.

Bagulals

Own name: according to village; Russian names: *Bagulaly, Bagva-laly*; Avar name: *Bagvalal*.

The Bagulals live in villages in the Tsumadin and Akhvakh Regions (*rajony*) of the Daghestan ASSR. They have no collective name of their own but call themselves after the name of their village. Their language belongs to the Avaro-Andi-Didoi group (Andi sub-group) of the North-East Caucasian languages. It is very close to Tindi. Each village has its own dialect. Most Bagulals have a good knowledge of Avar and this language serves as the literary language. Avar has had a considerable influence on the vocabulary of Bagulal; it was also the medium through which many Arabic, Persian and Turkish words were introduced into that language. In recent years a number of Russian loan-words have been assimilated into Bagulal.

The Bagulals are Sunni Muslims.

1926 Census figures

Population: 3,054. It was estimated in 1960 (*Narody Kavkaza I*) that there were then about 4,500 Bagulals. They are now listed with the Avars.
Urban dwellers: none.
Percentage claiming Bagulal as their mother tongue: 99.9 per cent.
Number claiming Russian as their mother tongue: none.
Literacy: 7.3 per cent.

Botlikhs

Own name: according to village; Russian name: *Botlikhtsy*.

The Botlikhs live in the villages Botlikh (*Buikh-e*) and Miarsu (*Kil-u*) in the Botlikh Region (*rajon*) of the Daghestan ASSR. Their language (which they call *buikhali* or *buikhadali mts'ts'i*) belongs to the Avaro-Andi-Didoi group (Andi sub-group) of the North-East Caucasian languages. It contains a number of Arabic, Persian and Turkish loan-words, as well as several Russian. The dialectal differences between the two villages are slight. Most Botlikhs have a good knowledge of Avar and this is used as the literary language, since Botlikh is not a written language.

The Botlikhs are Sunni Muslims.

1926 Census figures

Population: 3,354. It was estimated in 1960 (*Narody Kavkaza I*) that there were then some 2,000 Botlikhs. They are now listed with the Avars.
Urban dwellers: none.
Percentage claiming Botlikh as their mother tongue: 83.2 per cent.
Number claiming Russian as their mother tongue: none.
Literacy: 12.2 per cent.

Budukhs

Own name: no collective name; Russian names: *Budukhtsy*, *Budugtsy*.

The majority of Budukhs live in the village of Budukh (*Budad*), Konakhkend Region (*rajon*) of the Azerbaidzhan SSR. Their language (which they call *budad mez*) belongs to the Lezghi group (Shahdag sub-group) of the North Caucasian languages. It is closely related to Kryz and Khinalug. Budukh contains a large number of Arabic, Persian and Turkish loan-words, as well as a growing number of Azerbaidzhani and Russian loan-words. Budukh is not a written language; most Budukhs know Azerbaidzhani and this language serves as the literary language.
The Budukhs are Sunni Muslims.

Population: approximately 1,000 in the 1960s (*Jazyki narodov SSSR IV*), but in the 1926 Soviet Census only one single Budukh was listed.

Chamals

Own name: according to village; Russian name: *Chamalintsy*; Avar name: *Ch'amalal*.

The Chamals live in the Tsumadin Region (*rajon*) of the Daghestan ASSR. Their language (which they call *ch'amalaldub mits'ts'*) belongs to the Avaro-Andi-Didoi group (Andi sub-group) of the North-East Caucasian languages. It is most closely related to Tindi and Bagulal. It contains many loan-words from Arabic, Persian and Turkish, as well as Avar and Russian; the influence of these last two has been particularly strong in recent years. Chamal is not a written language; Avar serves as the literary language. There is much dialectal variation in Chamal.

The Chamals are Sunni Muslims.

1926 Census figures

Population: 3,438. It was estimated in 1960 (*Narody Kavkaza I*) that there were then about 5,000 Chamals. They are now listed with the Avars.
Urban dwellers: none.
Percentage claiming Chamal as mother tongue: 100 per cent.
Number claiming Russian as their mother tongue: none.
Literacy: 4.9 per cent.

Didois/Tsezes

Own name: *Tsez*: Russian names: *Didoitsy, Tsezy*.

The Didois (also known as Tsezes) live in the Tsuntin Region (*rajon*) of the Daghestan ASSR. Their language belongs to the Avaro-Andi-Didoi group (Didoi or Tsez sub-group) of the North-East Caucasian languages. The Didoi/Tsez language is not a written language, but it has received a considerable amount of attention from scholars of the Caucasian languages; transcriptions of Didoi/Tsez appeared as early as the eighteenth century. It contains a number of loan-words from Arabic, Persian and Turkish, as well as from Avar, Georgian and Russian. Avar is used as the literary language.

The Didois are Sunni Muslims.

1926 Census figures

Population: 3,276. It was estimated in 1960 (*Narody Kavkaza I*) that there were then about 7,000 Didois. They are now listed with the Avars.
Urban dwellers: none.
Percentage claiming Didoi as their mother tongue: 97.6 per cent.
Number claiming Russian as their mother tongue: none.
Literacy: 0.2 per cent.

Godoberins

Own name: according to village; Russian name: *Godoberintsy*.

The Godoberins live in two villages in the Botlikh Region (*rajon*) of the Daghestan ASSR, Godoberi (*Ghid-u*) and Zibirkhali (*Shchal-u*). Their language belongs to the Avaro-Andi-Didoi group (Andi sub-group) of the North-East Caucasian languages. It is closely related to Botlikh. It contains a number of loan-words from Arabic, Persian and Turkish, as well as Avar and Russian; these last two have had a particularly strong influence in recent years. Godoberin is not a written language. Avar is used as the literary language.

The Godoberins are Sunni Muslims.

1926 Census figures

Population: 1,425. It was estimated in 1960 (*Narody Kavkaza I*) that there were then about 2,000 Godoberins.
Urban dwellers: none.
Percentage claiming Godoberin as their mother tongue: 99.3
Number claiming Russian as their mother tongue: none.
Literacy: 6.4 per cent.

Inghiloys

Own names: *Ingiloi, Ingilo*; Russian name: *Ingilojtsy*.

The Inghiloys are Georgians from the eastern province of Kakhetia who adopted Islam in the early seventeenth century, when this area was under the rule of Shah Abbas I of Persia. The name *Ingilo* is a Georgian derivation from Turkic *engilav* ('newly converted'). After the unification of eastern Georgia with Russia in 1801, some of the Inghiloys reverted to Christianity, but the majority remained Muslim.

Their language is basically Georgian, but has some distinctive features of its own, in particular a strong Azerbaidzhani influence on the vocabulary. The Inghiloys' chief occupation used to be agriculture, but today they also work in such industries as silk-making and canning. Most of them now live in the western regions of the Azerbaidzhan SSR. It is not known exactly how many of them there are, since they are not listed separately in the census; however, according to *Narody Kavkaza I*, there were just over 10,000 Inghiloys in 1871 (of whom 7,126 were Muslims, the rest being Orthodox Christians) and 5,183 in 1926. The community was thus diminishing in the early twentieth century, probably due to assimilation by the neighbouring Azerbaidzhanis and Georgians. It is likely that this trend has continued. Whether anything survives of their dialect or other distinguishing features is not clear, but as regards religion, in the vicinity of the Azerbaidzhanis the Inghiloys would almost certainly have remained Muslims, for they, like the majority of Azerbaidzhanis, are Shi'i.

Kaitaks

Own name: *Khaidak*; Russian names: *Kara-Kaitaki, Kaitagtsy, Khaidaki.*

The Kaitaks live in the Kaitak and southern Dakhadajev Regions (*rajony*) of the Daghestan ASSR, between the Darghins and the Tabasarans. They came under Arab rule in the early eighth century and were among the first of the Caucasian peoples to begin to accept Islam. Their conversion was not complete, however, until several centuries later; a fifteenth-century Venetian traveller noted that some of the Kaitaks were then Christian and that Catholic and Armenian missionaries were working amongst them. In the thirteenth century they were conquered by the Mongols; in the late fourteenth century their land was ravaged during the war between Timur and the Golden Horde. During the fifteenth century they succeeded in establishing a more or less independent principality of their own (known as the *Utsmiyat*, under the leadership of a feudal prince entitled the *Utsmi*); this became one of the most important of the Daghestan states, holding sway over a number of other peoples, including the Laks, Darghins and some of the Kumyks. The Utsmi (who claimed descent from the Arab commanders who had first introduced Islam to the Caucasus) pursued a shrewd foreign policy, playing off the Ottomans against the Persians.

The social structure of the Kaitaks was based on a hierarchy of free and non-free classes; in addition to this, they (like many of the other Caucasian paoples) had a system of 'free societies', who owned nominal allegiance to the Utsmi. Arabic was the literary medium of the Caucasus; thus, when the *adat* (customary law) of the Kaitaks was codified in the seventeenth century by the Utsmi Rustam Khan, it was written in this language.

The Utsmiyat remained strong throughout the eighteenth century, but by the turn of the century it was unable to resist Russian pressure: in 1802 it became a Russian protectorate; in 1820 direct Russian administration was introduced in 'Lower Kaitak' (the area bordering the Caspian Sea) and in 1862 in 'Kara-Kaitak' (the mountain regions); the Utsmiyat was abolished in 1844.

The traditional occupation of the Kaitaks was the raising of sheep and goats and this continues to be of importance today. Agriculture was largely restricted to the cultivation of cereals such as wheat and barley. It has now been greatly developed and in addition to these crops, vegetables and fruit (particularly grapes) are widely cultivated.

The Kaitak language is considered to be a dialect of Darghin, which belongs to the North-East Caucasian group of languages (see p. 145). Kaitak is not a written language: in the past, Arabic served as the literary language, while today Darghin fulfils this role.

The Kaitaks are Sunni Muslims of the Shafi'i school.

1926 Census figures

Population: 14,430. The Kaitaks are now listed with the Darghins.
Urban dwellers: 7 people.
Percentage claiming Kaitak as their mother tongue: 100 per cent.
Number claiming Russian as their mother tongue: 3 people.
Literacy: 2.0 per cent.

Kapuchins/Bezhetins

Own name: according to village; Russian names: *Bezhetintsy, Kapuchintsy.*

The Kapuchins take their name from the Georgian form of one of their largest villages, the village Kapucha. The Russian name of this village, Bezh(i)ta, gives rise to the other designation by which they are sometimes known, the Bezhetins. They live in the Tsuntin Region (*rajon*) of the Daghestan ASSR. Their language belongs to the Avaro-Andi-Didoi group (Didoi sub-group) of the North-East Caucasian languages. It is very closely related to Gunzib. As with many of the other languages of this group, it has a large number of Arabic, Persian and Turkish loan-words; Georgian, Avar and, particularly during recent years, Russian have also played an important part in the formation of the Kapuchin vocabulary. There are three main dialects, corresponding to the three Kapuchin settlements in Bezhita, Tljadal and Khochar-Khota. The differences between them are phonetic and morphological. Kapuchin is not a written language. Avar is used as the literary language.

The Kapuchins are Sunni Muslims.

1926 Census figures

Population: 1,448. In 1960 (*Narody Kavkaza I*) it was estimated that there were then some 2,500 Kapuchins. They are now listed with the Avars.
Urban dwellers: none.
Percentage claiming Kapuchin as their mother tongue: 100 per cent.
Number claiming Russian as their mother tongue: none.
Literacy: 7.4 per cent.

Karapapakhs

Own name: *Karapapakh*; Russian name: *Karapapakhi*.

The Karapapakhs are a group of Turkic-speaking tribes, the great majority of whom live outside the Soviet Union. Within the Soviet Union a few thousand are found in the south of the Azerbaidzhan SSR, in the vicinity of the River Araks. Their language is a dialect of Azerbaidzhani, but even in 1926 hardly any of the Soviet Karapapakhs spoke it. Most of them are Sunni Muslims, but a few are Shi'is. In the 1926 Soviet Census the Karapapakhs were listed separately, but later they were included with the Azerbaidzhanis.

1926 Census figures

Population: 6,316; of these, 6,311 (99.9%) lived in Transcaucasia.
Urban dwellers: none.
Number claiming Karapapakh as their mother tongue: 5 people.
Number claiming Russian as their mother tongue: none.
Number claiming a language other than Russian or Karapapakh (presumably Azerbaidzhani) as mother tongue: 6,311 (99.9%).
Literacy: 6.2 per cent.

Karapapakhs outside the Soviet Union

In Iran: approximately 20,000.
In Turkey: approximately 40,000.

Karatais/Karatins

Own name: *K'k'irdi*; Russian names: *Karatai, Karatintsy*; Avar name: *K'j'aralal*.

The Karatais live in the Akhvakh Region (*rajon*) of the Daghestan ASSR. Their principal village, from which they take their name, is Karata. Their language belongs to the Avaro-Andi-Didoi group (Andi sub-group) of the North-East Caucasian languages. It is not written; Avar serves as the literary language. The influence of Avar on Karatai has always been strong; not only are there many Avar loan-words in Karatai, it was also the medium through which Arabic, Persian and Turkish loan-words entered the language. In recent years Russian has provided Karatai with a fund of new terms.
    The Karatais are Sunni Muslims.

1926 Census figures

Population: 5,305. It was estimated in 1960 (*Narody Kavkaza I*) that there were then about 6,000 Karatais. They are now listed with the Avars.
Urban dwellers: none.
Percentage claiming Karatai as their mother tongue: 100 per cent.
Number claiming Russian as their mother tongue: none.
Literacy: 3.9 per cent.

Khemshins/Khemshils

Own name: *Khamshenly*; Russian names: *Khemshiny, Khemshily*.

The Khemshins are Armenian Muslims. The great majority live in Turkey, but there are a few in the Soviet Union. They used to live in the Adzhar ASSR, close to the Lazes, but during the last war they were deported and their present whereabouts are unknown. They were listed separately in the 1926 Soviet Census, but not thereafter.

1926 Census figures

Population: 629.

Urban dwellers: 2 people.

Number claiming Armenian as their mother tongue: 2 people (627 Khemshins claimed a language other than that of their national group, i.e. Armenian, as mother tongue, presumably Turkish).

Number claiming Russian as their mother tongue: none.

Literacy: 3 people; none of these were literate in their own language.

Khinalugs

Own name: *Ketsh khalkh*; Russian name: *Khinalugtsy.*

The Khinalugs are one of the three small tribes that live in the environs of the Shahdag Mountain, in one of the highest and least accessible parts of the Caucasus range. The majority of them live in the village Khinalug (hence their name in Russian; their own name for the village is *Ketsh*), in the Konakhkend Region (*rajon*) of the Azerbaidzhan SSR. Their language belongs to the Lezghi group (Shahdag sub-group) of Caucasian languages. It is not written. The majority of the Khinalug speak Azerbaidzhani, which also serves as the literary language. There are no real dialectal subdivisions, but there are certain marked differences in the speech of the three main clans of the Khinalug village (possibly pointing to differences in ancestry) and also between the generations. Typically, there are far more loan-words from Azerbaidzhani and Russian in the speech of the younger generation than in that of the older; there are also differences in speech tempo, the use of euphemisms and taboo words etc, giving great variety within this small language.

The Khinalugs are Sunni Muslims.

1926 Census figures

Population: 105. In 1967 (*Jazyki narodov SSSR IV*) it was estimated that there were then some 900–1,000 Khinalugs.

Urban dwellers: none.

Percentage claiming Khinalug as their mother tongue: 100 per cent.

Number claiming Russian as their mother tongue: none.

Literacy: not a single person was literate.

Khunzals/Gunzibs

Own name: according to village; Russian names: *Khunzaly, Gunzibtsy*.

The Khunzals live for the most part in the Tsuntin Region (*rajon*) of the Daghestan ASSR. They take their name from their villages, the largest of which is called in Russian Gunzib. Their language belongs to the Avaro-Andi-Didoi group (Didoi sub-group) of North-East Caucasian languages. It is not a written language; Avar is used as the medium of instruction for primary education and also serves as the literary language. The Khunzal (Gunzib) language has a large number of Arabic, Persian, Turkish and Avar loan-words, as well as some Georgian and, particularly in recent years, Russian.

The Khunzals are Sunni Muslims.

1926 Census figures

Population: 106. In 1967 (*Jazyki narodov SSSR IV*) it was estimated that there were then some 600 Khunzals. They are now listed with the Avars.

Urban dwellers: 8 people.

Percentage claiming Khunzal as their mother tongue: 99.1 per cent.

Number claiming Russian as their mother tongue: 1 person.

Literacy: 14.2 per cent.

Khvarshins

Own name: *Kedaes hikwa*; Russian name: *Khvarshiny*.

The majority of the Khvarshins live in the Tsumadin Region (*rajon*) of the Daghestan ASSR. The name given to them in Russian is taken from the Russian form of their largest village, Khvarshi. Their language belongs to the Avaro-Andi-Didoi group (Didoi sub-group) of the North-East Caucasian languages. The vocabulary has been much influenced by Avar, which also served as the medium through which many Arabic, Persian and Turkish loan-words entered the language. Khvarshin is not a written language; Avar is used as the literary language. Each village has its own dialect.

The Khvarshins are Sunni Muslims.

1926 Census figures

Population: 1,019. In 1960 (*Narody Kavkaza I*) it was estimated
that there were then some 800 Khvarshins; They are now listed
with the Avars.
Urban dwellers: none.
Percentage claiming Khvarshin as their mother tongue: 99.9 per
cent.
Number claiming Russian as their mother tongue: none.
Literacy: 7.0 per cent.

Kryzes/Dzheks

Own name: *Kryts'ar* or according to village; Russian names:
Kryztsy, Dzhektsy.

The Kryzes belong to the Shahdag group of tribes, who inhabit the
high mountain valleys of the Kuba Region (*rajon*) in the Azerbaidzhan SSR. They take their name from their villages, one of which
is called Kryz, another Dzhek. They have a number of other villages, but names derived from them have not gained such wide
currency as these two. The term *Dzhek* used to be the most common
(and was used in the 1926 Census), but *Kryz* has now taken over as
the general name for both the people and for their language; however, each village has its own dialect (consisting of many sub-dialects), which are sufficiently different for them to be considered by
some to constitute separate languages. The whole complex belongs
to the Lezghi group (Shahdag sub-group) of Caucasian languages.
None of the dialects are written. Most Kryzes/Dzheks have a good
knowledge of Azerbaidzhani and this language is used as the literary
language. In the Kryz language (or group of languages) there are
already a large number of loans from Azerbaidzhani and this trend
is increasing as contacts between the Kryzes and the Azerbaidzhanis
grow. There is also a substantial proportion of Russian loan-words
in Kryz.
    The Kryzes are Sunni Muslims.

1926 Census figures

Population: 607. In 1967 (*Jazyki narodov SSSR IV*) it was
estimated that there were then about 6,000 Kryz-speakers.

They are no longer listed separately.
Urban dwellers: 2 people.
Percentage claiming Kryz as their mother tongue: 99.7 per cent.
Number claiming Russian as their mother tongue: none.
Literacy: 4.1 per cent.

Kubachis

Own name: *Urbugan*; Russian names: *Kubachi, Kubachintsy*.

The Kubachis' own name for themselves is derived from that of their one village, Arbukanti (known in Russian as 'Kubachi'), which is situated in the Dakhadajev Region (*rajon*) of the Daghestan ASSR. For centuries the Kubachis have been famous for their skill as metal-workers. According to the *Derbend-name* (a late sixteenth-century history of Daghestan), they used to be called *Zerehgaran* (Persian: 'armourers, makers of chain-mail') and later *Kubachi*, a Turkish word of the same meaning. They speak a dialect of Darghin, a language of the North-East Caucasian group of languages. Arabic used to be the literary medium of the area, but its place has now been taken by Darghin, since Kubachi itself is not a written language.

The Kubachis are Sunni Muslims.

1926 Census figures

Population: 2,371. They are now listed with the Darghins.
Urban dwellers: 2.1 per cent.
Percentage claiming Kubachi as their mother tongue: 99.8 per cent.
Number claiming Russian as their mother tongue: 1 person.
Literacy: 4.5 per cent.

Lazes

Own name: *Lazi*; Russian name: *Laztsy*.

The Lazes are a south Caucasian people who inhabit the south-east coast of the Black Sea. The majority are found in Turkey, but a small number live across the border in the adjacent region of the Soviet Union, the Adzhar ASSR (see p. 244). They have been settled in this area since ancient times (Ptolemy and Arrian, amongst others, locate them here). It formed part of the kingdom of Colchis; after the fall of Colchis, the Lazes created a powerful state of their own, known as Lazica. They adopted Christianity in the early sixth century (the Laz king Tsate was baptized in 523). During this period (539–62) Byzantium and Persia were vying for mastery of the southern shores of the Black Sea and Lazica became deeply embroiled in the struggle as it strove to manoeuvre a course between these two great powers. In the tenth century it was incorporated into Georgia. In 1461 it was conquered by Mehmet II and remained under Ottoman control for the next four centuries. During this time the Lazes were converted to Islam. In 1878 Russia gained possession of Batumi (as a result of the Russo-Turkish war of 1877–8) and thus those Lazes who lived in its vicinity came under Russian rule, while the rest (the greater proportion) remained under Turkish rule.

The traditional occupations of the Lazes were farming, fishing and trading. However, many used to leave home to work in the cities; in pre-Revolutionary Russia they were particularly well-known as bakers.

The Laz language belongs to the Kartvelian group of Caucasian languages. It is closely related to Georgian. It is not a written language. It was much influenced by Greek and then, from the eighteenth century, by Turkish. One of the earliest sources for material on the Laz language is provided by the writings of the seventeenth-century Turkish traveller Evliya Chelebi.

The Lazes are Sunni Muslims (Shafi'i school).

1926 Census figures

Population: 643. They are no longer listed separately.
Urban dwellers: 6.8 per cent.
Percentage claiming Laz as their mother tongue: 58.3 per cent.
Number claiming Russian as their mother tongue: none.
Literacy: 11.8 per cent; of these 32.9 per cent were literate in
    their own language.

Lazes outside the Soviet Union

There are about 50,000 Lazes in Turkey.

Meskhetian Turks

Own name: *Turk*; Russian names: *Meskhi, Turki, Azerbajdzhantsy*.

The Meskhetian Turks are of mixed descent: some are descended from Turks, others from Turkicized Georgians. Meskhetia, a part of Georgia, came under Turkish rule in the sixteenth century. Many of the indigenous population became Muslims and adopted Turkish as their language. After the Treaty of Adrianople (1829), the northern region of Meskhetia was incorporated into the Russian Empire (which by then included Georgia) and only the south remained in Turkish possession. Amongst the other Turkic or Turkicized people of Meskhetia were Turkmen (who also called themselves 'Turks'), Karapapakhs, Khemshins (or Khemshils), Armenians and Turkicized Kurds.

Under Soviet rule, schools with Turkish as the medium of instruction were provided until 1935–6, after which they were replaced by Azerbaidzhani-medium schools. In 1944 all the Meskhetian Turks and other Turkic or Turkicized peoples were deported from this region, possibly for reasons of military security, since it borders north-eastern Turkey. In all, they numbered some 200,000. They were exiled to Central Asia and Kazakhstan, mostly to the Hungry Steppe. During and immediately after the deportation, 30,000–50,000 of them died. The survivors were granted the right to return to Meskhetia in 1968, but up till the present few have actually been allowed to return. Since 1970, they have been asking for permission to emigrate to Turkey, if denied the possibility of going back to Meskhetia.

In the 1926 Census the Meskhetian Turks were listed as 'Turks' (as were the Azerbaidzhanis); after 1935 they were known as 'Azerbaidzhanis', but since 1959 have reverted to the designation 'Turk'. Of the 92,689 Turks listed in the 1979 Census, most (if not all) are Meskhetian Turks, but whether this represents the whole of the community it is impossible to say. Of these Turks, the 1979 Census states that 84.7 per cent claim the language of their nationality (i.e. Turkish) as their mother tongue; 46.4 per cent claim a good knowledge of Russian (as second language).

Persians

The Persians of Transcaucasia are not directly connected with the Persian communities in Central Asia. Trade, the close proximity of Persia and the fact that this region was often under Safavid rule accounts for their presence in Armenia, Azerbaidzhan, Daghestan and Georgia. In 1926 there were just over 20,000, nearly half of them in Azerbaidzhan. The Persians in these areas are no longer listed separately in the census and it is possible that they have been more or less completely assimilated by the surrounding population. See p. 357 for more detailed statistics concerning the Persians.

Shahsevens

'Shahseven' (literally 'Shah-lover') is the name by which a group of Turkic tribes of Transcaucasia are known. Some of their traditional grazing lands came under Russian rule in the mid-eighteenth century, but they were still able to migrate backwards and forwards between Russian and Persian territory until 1884. After this date the borders were closed, but it is possible that a certain amount of movement continued to take place. According to Soviet sources (e.g. *Jazyki narodov SSSR I*) there are still some Shahseven in the south of the Azerbaidzhan SSR. They have never been listed separately in the census: they are included with the Azerbaidzhanis, and it is not possible to know the size of the community, but it is likely to be small (a few thousand?).

The Shahseven are Shi'i Muslims.

Shahseven outside the Soviet Union

The majority of Shahseven are in Iran, but no exact figures regarding the size of the population are available; estimates vary between 18,000 and 200,000.

Talysh

Own names: *Tolish*, *Talush*; Russian name: *Talyshi*.

The Talysh are descended from indigenous tribes of the south eastern corner of the present-day Azerbaidzhan SSR and the neigh bouring region of the Iranian province of Azerbaidzhan. They represent an intermingling of Caucasian and Iranian elements. The area which they inhabit has for centuries been fought over by rival empires. It was conquered by the Mongols in the thirteenth century; in the sixteenth century it came under Safavid rule; by the eighteenth century, Turkey, Russia and Persia were all three struggling for possession of Azerbaidzhan and, consequently, the Talysh lands. After the death of Nadir Shah (1747), a number of more or less independent principalities established themselves in this region, e.g. the Khanates of Kuba, Baku, Shemakha, Karabagh and Gandzhej. Amongst them was the Talysh Khanate, under the rule of their *Hakim*. There was no unity amongst the khanates: they fought as much with one another as with foreign powers. By 1805 a number of them had already become Russian protectorates; after the Russo-Persian War (1805–13) several more, including part of the Talysh Khanate, came under Russian rule. This was confirmed by the Treaty of Gulistan (1813), then, after that had been abrogated by Iran in 1826, was reaffirmed by the Treaty of Turkmanchai (1828).

The Talysh are today found in both the Soviet Union and Iran. The Soviet Talysh live in the south of the AzSSR in such regions (*rajony*) as Lenkoran' and Astara. Their principal occupation is agriculture: they cultivate tea, citrus fruits and sub-tropical plants such as bamboos and eucalyptus; rice was one of their most important traditional crops and remains so today. The Talysh are skilled as carpet-weavers; they are particularly well-known for the so-called 'Talysh runners', long, narrow rugs of distinctive geometric ornamentation.

The Talysh language belongs to the North-West group of Iranian languages. During the 1930s a number of publications appeared in Talysh (for which a special writing system was created). Since the war it has ceased to be used as a literary language, though a grammar appeared in 1953 and a Talysh-Russian dictionary in 1976. Most Talysh now speak Azerbaidzhani and this is the medium of instruction in schools. The radio and press also use Azerbaidzhani. There are dialectal differences between the various areas in which Talysh is spoken (e.g. Lenkoran', Astara), but they are fairly small and mostly confined to phonetic variations.

The Talysh are Shi'i Muslims.

1926 Census figures

Population: 77,323. They are now listed with the Azerbaidzhanis;
  however, in 1959 it was noted that there were 10,514 Talysh
  speakers in the AzSSR.
Urban dwellers: 0.4 per cent.
Percentage claiming Talysh as their mother tongue: 97.7 per cent.
Number claiming Russian as their mother tongue: none.
Literacy: 3.0 per cent.

Talysh outside the Soviet Union

No recent figures are available, but in 1949, according to Soviet
sources, there were 84,700 Talysh in Iran (*Jazyki narodov SSSR I*).

Tindis

Own name: according to village; Russian names: *Tindii, Tindaly*.

The Tindis live in five villages in western Daghestan, close to the
Bagulals and Chamals. The term by which they are known in Russian is derived from the Avar name for one of their villages, *T'indi*.
The local name is *Idari* and the language of this group of people is
known as *idarab mits'i*. Like the closely related Bagulal and
Chamal, it belongs to the Avaro-Andi-Didoi group (Andi subgroup) of the North-East Caucasian languages. It has not been
studied in much detail, but there appears to be little dialectal variation. The vocabulary contains a large number of Avar, Arabic and
Turkish loan-words, as well as many recent borrowings from Russian. Tindi is not a written language.
  The Tindis are Sunni Muslims.

1926 Census figures

Population: 3,812. It was estimated in 1960 (Narody Kavkaza I)
  that there were then some 5,000 Tindis. They are now listed
  with the Avars.
Urban dwellers: none.
Percentage claiming Tindi as their mother tongue: 94.9 per cent.
Number claiming Russian as their mother tongue: none.
Literacy: 4.0 per cent.

Truchmen

Own name: *Turkpen*; Russian name: *Truchmeny*.

The Truchmen are a branch of the Turkmen people who moved to the Northern Caucasus in the eighteenth century. The majority belonged to the Chaudor tribe (see p. 313). They live today in the Stavropol' Territory (*kraj*) in the RSFSR; for this reason they are sometimes known as 'Stavropol' Turkmen. Formerly nomadic herdsmen, they now lead a settled existence, their chief occupations being farming and animal husbandry. Their language is basically Turkmen, but with some notable differences, mainly due to contact with the neighbouring Nogais and Kumyks. The Truchmen, like the Turkmen, are Sunni Muslims. They are not listed separately in the census, but in 1926 there were 4,102 Turkmen in the Stavropol' area and in 1970, 8,313; these are all almost certainly Truchmen. In 1970, 8,150 (98.0 per cent) claimed the language of their nationality (presumably Truchmen) as their mother tongue; 67.1 per cent claimed a good knowledge of Russian (as second language).

Miscellaneous

The Turkic- and Persian-speaking tribes of Transcaucasia and northern Persia who now find themselves split between the Soviet Union and Iran are, in the Soviet Union, listed with the Azerbaidzhanis. Very little information is available about them, but their numbers are likely to be very small (cf. the Shahseven, p. 262). The majority are probably Shi'i Muslims, as are some 70 per cent of the Soviet Azerbaidzhanis. Included amongst them are the Padars, Kyzyl-bash, Karabaghs and Qajars. The Qajars were settled in western Azerbaidzhan (Karabagh Khanate) and Merv (modern Mary) in the seventeenth and eighteenth centuries as part of the Safavid campaign to win control of these regions. In 1794 a Qajar leader, Agha Mohammed, overthrew the ruling Zend dynasty of Iran and established the Qajar line, which held sway until in turn ousted by Reza Shah in 1925. There are some 25,000 Qajars today, the great majority of whom live in the Mazanderan province of northern Iran.

5
Central Asia and Kazakhstan

UZBEKS

Own name: *Ozbek*; Russian name: *Uzbeki*.

In pre-Revolutionary times the town-dwelling Uzbeks were generally called 'Sarts', a term which was also applied to other sedentary peoples, e.g. the Tadzhiks. They were often identified by their place of location too, e.g. Tashkent Uzbeks, Nurata Uzbeks, etc.

The majority of Uzbeks live in the Uzbek SSR, but there are also communities of some size in the Tadzhik, Kirghiz, Kazakh and Turkmen SSRs, mostly in the regions adjoining the Uzbek SSR.

1 HISTORICAL BACKGROUND

The territory of present-day Uzbekistan has been inhabited since prehistoric times and has been the site of many different civilizations. In the sixth century BC much of it was ruled by the Persian Achaemenians. Alexander the Great invaded Central Asia in 329 BC and after his death Uzbekistan formed part of the Graeco-Bactrian state. In the first century AD the Kushan Empire reigned supreme; it was finally toppled by an invasion of the Huns (Ephthalites) in 425. By the mid-sixth century the area was under the sway of the Turkish Khaganate. The Arabs conquered Central Asia in the second half of the seventh century, bringing Islam and the Arabic script to its heterogeneous population. The Samanid dynasty of Bukhara achieved pre-eminence when Ismail Samani established himself as the master of Transoxiana and Khwarezmia (corresponding approximately to the territory of the nineteenth-century Khanate of Khiva) in 892. The Samanids were overthrown by the Karakhanids, a predominantly Turkic people, in 999. (Mahmud Kashgari includes such tribes as the Kipchak, Pecheneg, Oghuz, Kirghiz, Uighur and Bashkird amongst the Karakhanids.) Seljuk tribes had begun to settle in Transoxiana in the late tenth century; by the early twelfth century they were in control of most of modern Uzbekistan, but in 1141 they suffered a major defeat at the hands of the Kara Khitai. The Kara Khitai themselves were overthrown by the Khwarezmshahs, whom they had originally helped to power, towards the end of the twelfth century.

The Mongols erupted on to the scene in 1219. Within months they had taken Bukhara, Samarkand and Khwarezmia, not to mention vast new territories to the north, south, east and west. Previous invasions had done little to alter the tenor of life in Central Asia, but the Mongol conquest disrupted the old patterns of trade and agriculture and threw the cultural life of the region into turmoil. The harm it caused took many centuries to undo. In one sense, though, it foreshadowed the future, for it established the first tenuous territorial links between Russia and Central Asia. Uzbekistan came within the Ulus of Chagatai, Genghiz Khan's second son, while the north-western wing of the Mongol Empire fell to the lot of Dzhuchi, his eldest son. Dzhuchi's patrimony was soon divided into two parts, the Golden Horde (centred on the Volga) and the White Horde (based between the Syr Darya and the Irtysh, i.e. much of modern Kazakhstan). There was always friction between the different sections of the Mongol Empire and this was exacerbated as the individual states became more independent of the central control. Towards the end of the fourteenth century Toktamysh, a prince of the White Horde, sought the help of Timur (who had made himself master of the Ulus of Chagatai in 1370) to gain the throne of the Golden Horde. His other ally in this venture was Vitaut, Grand Duke of Lithuania, and for a brief period Toktamysh succeeded in establishing a power base that spanned the future territory of the Soviet Union diagonally from the north-west to the south-east. It took another five and a half centuries for these regions to be united in a single state.

When the White Horde began to weaken, its beneficiaries were two tribal groupings that had previously formed part of the Ulus of Dzhuchi: the Nogais and the Uzbeks. The Uzbeks, who apparently took their name from Khan Uzbek (1282–1342), the ruler responsible for the conversion of the Golden Horde to Islam, were basically a conglomeration of Turkic tribes, though their leaders were Mongols. The foundations of Uzbek power in Central Asia were

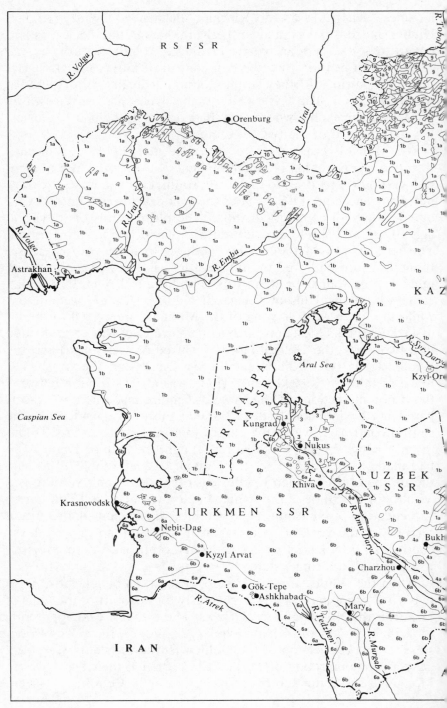

Ethnic Dist

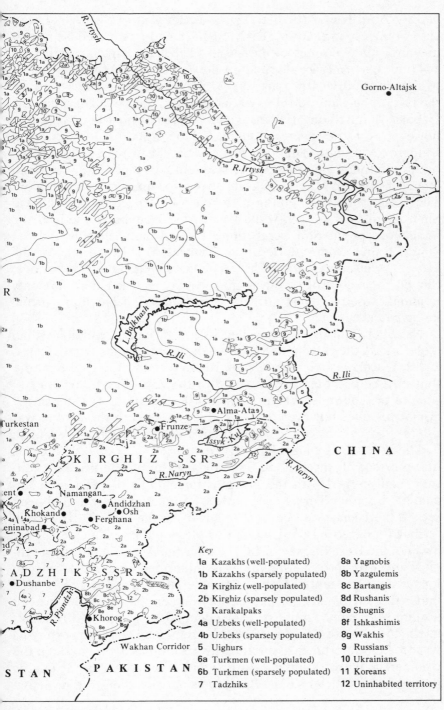

Key
1a Kazakhs (well-populated)
1b Kazakhs (sparsely populated)
2a Kirghiz (well-populated)
2b Kirghiz (sparsely populated)
3 Karakalpaks
4a Uzbeks (well-populated)
4b Uzbeks (sparsely populated)
5 Uighurs
6a Turkmen (well-populated)
6b Turkmen (sparsely populated)
7 Tadzhiks

8a Yagnobis
8b Yazgulemis
8c Bartangis
8d Rushanis
8e Shugnis
8f Ishkashimis
8g Wakhis
9 Russians
10 Ukrainians
11 Koreans
12 Uninhabited territory

laid by Abul Khayr (b. 1412/13), a descendant of Sheiban, Dzhu
chi's youngest son. By 1431 Abul Khayr had conquered Khwarez
mia and subdued much of the Desht-i Kipchak (Kipchak Plain); by
1447 he was firmly established on the Syr Darya. At the beginning
of the sixteenth century his son, Muhammed Sheibani, overthrew
the last of the Timurid rulers of Samarkand, thereby confirming the
Uzbeks' domination of Transoxiana. It was a short-lived triumph
however, for they were soon ousted by Babur (future Moghul
Emperor of India). The lost territory had been regained by 1505
but in the following years power frequently changed hands as Shah
Ismail, Babur and the Uzbeks all strove for mastery of the region
The struggle had something of a religious aspect, as the Safavid
Shah Ismail was a Shi'i, while Babur, the Uzbeks and indeed the
indigenous population were Sunnis (though naturally this did no
hinder Babur from entering into alliances with Ismail against the
Uzbeks when necessary). The Sheibanids were finally victorious
though their control of the region was more often than not only
nominal, petty local rulers frequently achieving virtual
independence.

The Sheibanid dynasty reached its zenith under Abdullah Khan
(ruler of Bukhara from 1557; of all the Uzbek lands from 1583 to
1598). During his reign the Uzbek Khanate held sway over territory
that included Khotan and Kashgar to the east, Balkh and Badak
shan to the south, Tashkent to the north. Abdullah was almost the
last of his line, however, for after his son's death the throne was
offered to a prince of the Astrakhan Khanate (to whom Abdullah
had been related by marriage). By this period the Uzbeks, who had
first imposed themselves on Transoxiana during the fifteenth cen
tury, had merged with the previous inhabitants of the region, in
cluding the other Turkic peoples (e.g. Karakhanids) who had been
settled there since well before the advent of the Uzbeks. The name
'Uzbek' came to be used for the whole population (including, for
a while, the Kazakhs: see p. 287). Under the Astrakhanids the tend
ency towards local autonomy was intensified and there was no
longer a single, united Uzbek Khanate (though, admittedly, even
under the Sheibanids this had not often been the case), but instead
a number of small, more or less independent groupings. Bukhara
itself, the seat of the Astrakhanids, remained very powerful, its
wealth and importance assured by its position as a vital node in the
commercial network linking Europe and Asia (typical of the energy
and initiative with which the Bukharans pursued their trading activi

ties is the group who moved to Siberia in the fifteenth and sixteenth centuries, the better to exploit the opportunities offered by that rich market; see Bukharans of Siberia, p. 98). In Khwarezmia, a region which had always been somewhat apart from Transoxiana, belonging formerly to the Golden Horde rather than the Ulus of Chagatai, an independent state developed, the Khanate of Khiva, which seriously challenged Bukhara's territorial claims. Yet another rival was the Khanate of Khokand in Ferghana, which grew steadily stronger throughout the eighteenth century. The three states were implacable enemies and remained in a constant state of conflict until the time when they were rendered powerless by the Russians.

In 1740 Nadir Shah of Persia briefly gained control of Central Asia. A protégé of his, Muhammad Rahim Bi, assumed the throne of Bukhara in 1753, supplanting the last of the Astrakhanids. Muhammad Rahim, who adopted the title 'Emir' in place of the traditional 'Khan', inaugurated the Manghit dynasty, which ruled Bukhara until it became a People's Republic in 1920. Towards the end of the eighteenth century the Manghits (under the Emir Ma'-sum) subjugated much of the territory to the south, devastating Merv in 1785, raiding Khorasan and all but capturing Khiva. Khiva's power was reasserted by Muhammad Amin, who in 1804 became ruler of the Khanate, founding the Kungrat dynasty which ruled Khiva until it, too, became a People's Republic in 1920.

In the early nineteenth century the Khanate of Khiva controlled the southern shore of the Aral Sea (corresponding approximately to the present-day Karakalpak ASSR), the Bukharan Emirate most of the modern Uzbek and Tadzhik SSRs and the Khokand Khanate the land either side of the Syr Darya, from the Aral Sea to the modern Kirghiz SSR. The first step in the Russian domination of Central Asia had already been taken in the eighteenth century when the Kazakh Hordes came under Russian protection. In the first half of the nineteenth century, sharply increased trade contacts and scientific expeditions paved the way for a further penetration of the area. An abortive Russian assault on Khiva in 1839 did not achieve much, but it signalled only a brief reprieve for the Khanates: Tashkent (part of Khokand) was taken in 1865, Samarkand in 1868; that same year the Emirate of Bukhara became a Russian Protectorate, followed by the Khanate of Khiva in 1873. Russian domination of the area was completed by the annexation of the Khanate of Khokand in 1876. The Province (*gubernija*) of Turkestan (as part of the Russian Empire) was created in 1867, under the jurisdiction of a Governor-General; in 1886 it was transformed into the Turkestan Territory (*kraj*). The development of the railroad system was undertaken almost at once: the Transcaspian line was extended to Samarkand in 1888, to Tashkent in 1898 and to Andidzhan in the Ferghana Valley in 1899; the Orenburg-Tashkent line was completed in 1906. This greatly facilitated contacts between Central Asia and the rest of the Russian Empire and was as useful for trade as for military purposes.

Tashkent, formerly of secondary importance in relation to such cities as Bukhara and Samarkand, became the new administrative, commercial and industrial centre of the area acquiring in the process a large Russian population. (Today, as the capital of the Uzbek SSR, it is still the most important city in Central Asia; it rates as the fourth largest city in the whole of the Soviet Union, coming after Moscow, Leningrad and Kiev in size of population.) Nineteenth-century Russian immigration into Uzbekistan was mostly restricted to urban areas, particularly those served by the railway, unlike the situation in Kazakhstan, where the main influx was directed towards the rural areas. The reason for this difference of emphasis is to be found in local conditions: Kazakhstan afforded opportunities for the types of grain farming to which the Russian settlers were already accustomed, while in Uzbekistan large-scale irrigation was necessary for cultivation and the traditional crop of the region was cotton, of which the Russians had had no previous experience.

Russian had an immediate impact on the indigenous culture. New ideas, and new words to express them, were rapidly assimilated. This was at first particularly evident in the fields of technology and civil and military administration, but as Uzbek intellectuals learned Russian and translated its classics into their own language, Russian culture in general began to permeate the Uzbek environment more deeply. It was by no means the only influence to which the Uzbeks were subject, however, for all the Turkic peoples of the Russian Empire were becoming increasingly aware of a corporate identity and were conscious, too, of their cultural and ethnic links with the Ottoman Turks. The Tatars (see p. 59) were particularly influential in this period of national reawakening and reassessment. *Dzhadidism*, the movement for educational reform (from Arabic *dzhadid*, 'new'), was largely inspired by the work of the Crimean Tatar Ismail Gaspirali (or Gasprinsky: 1851–1914), who was acutely aware of the need to equip the Turkic/Islamic population of the Russian

Empire to play their part in the modern world. His newspaper *Terdzhuman-Perevodchik* ('The Interpreter'), the first Turkic-language newspaper in the Russian Empire, represented a significant step in this process; its impact on the Turkic peoples was reflected in its wide circulation, which reached throughout Central Asia as far as Kashgar in Eastern Turkestan. The growing pan-Turkic awareness, allied to a deep commitment to Islam, emphasized a gulf between the European immigrants and the indigenous Central Asian population which the intellectuals on either side could only bridge at a somewhat superficial level. Even though the attitudes of the Central Asians were not necessarily intrinsically anti-Russian, the relationship between the two peoples was not an easy one and on more than one occasion exploded into overt violence. The most notable uprisings were those in 1898 in Andidzhan, led by the Naqshbandi *ishan* Muhammad Ali (not the only occasion on which this Sufi order was at the centre of civil unrest) and in 1916, when the whole of Central Asia was engulfed by a revolt sparked off by the decree drafting Central Asians, formerly exempt from all forms of military service, into non-combatant army units.

Soviet power was first established in Tashkent in November 1917. The Turkestan ASSR, comprising the former Turkestan Territory, was proclaimed in April 1918 (as part of the RSFSR). By the summer of that year it had been cut off from the rest of the RSFSR by anti-Bolshevik forces and there was fierce opposition, too, within the new republic: from the British (who invaded through Persia), the White Army and the nationalist Basmachi movement (particularly strong in the Ferghana, Samarkand and Syr Darya Districts, as well as in the Khanates). Soviet control of Turkestan was finally re-established in September 1919, through a campaign led by M. Frunze and V. Kujbyshev. The Emir of Bukhara and the Khan of Khiva were deposed in 1920 and their states became the People's Soviet Republics of Bukhara and Khorezm respectively (the Khanate of Khokand had been abolished in 1876). The Basmachi movement retained its hold over these areas for sometime longer, however, particularly in eastern Bukhara (see p. 376), where the Turk Enver Pasha strove to keep aloft the twin banners of Pan-Turkism and Pan-Islamism. He was killed in 1922, and in 1924, following the full incorporation of the former Khanates into the Soviet Union, the National Delimitation of the Central Asian Republics took place. This entailed dividing the region up into separate units along broadly ethnic/linguistic lines and as a result the Uzbek

and Turkmen Republics, the Tadzhik, Kazakh and Kirghiz Autonomous Republics and the Karakalpak Autonomous Province were
created in late 1924–5. The Uzbek SSR came into being on 27
October 1924; it encompassed the Amu Darya, Syr Darya, Samarkand and Ferghana districts of the former Turkestan Territory, part
of Bukhara (including the city of Bukhara) and part of Khiva
(including the city of Khiva). Until 1929 it also included the Tadzhik
ASSR, but this acquired full Union republic status in that year.
The Karakalpak ASSR was united with the Uzbek SSR in 1936 (it
had previously formed part of the RSFSR). There was a minor
territorial adjustment in 1963, when part of the Hungry Steppe
region was transferred from the Kazakh SSR to the Uzbek SSR.

Uzbek SSR (Özbekistan Sovet Sotsialistik Respublikasy), also
known as *Uzbekistan*

Situated mainly between the Amu Darya and Syr Darya, much of
it lies in the desert zone (it includes the south-west part of the Kyzyl
Kum desert), but in the south-east it is mountainous (encompassing
the western outcrop of the Tien Shan range); it is bordered to the
north and north-west by the Kazakh SSR, to the east and north-
east by the Kirghiz and Tadzhik SSRs, to the south-west by the
Turkmen SSR, to the south by the Amu Darya, which constitutes
the state boundary between the USSR and Afghanistan. *Area*:
447,400 sq. km. *Capital*: Tashkent (population in 1979: 1,780,000;
it is the 4th largest city in the USSR). The Republic has 93 towns
and 95 settlements. *Population* (1979): 15,389,307. Average density
of population per sq. km (1979): 34.4.

Chief resources: vast reserves of natural gas; important deposits
of oil, coal, copper, molybdenum, tungsten, uranium, gold, aluminium ore, fluorspar and various building materials (e.g. marble);
rivers provide a major source of hydroelectric power; irrigation has
made possible the large-scale cultivation of cotton.

Industries include: extraction of natural gas and oil, refining of
oil, machine-building (main producer in Central Asia of equipment
for the cultivation of cotton and the textile industry), mining and
processing of minerals, iron and steel, chemical, power and coal
industries; cotton-ginning, textiles, food (the canning and processing of local fruit and vegetables etc.) and other light industries.

Agriculture: cultivation of cotton (this is the chief cotton-growing
area of the USSR); other crops include kenaf, a plant used for

sacking (main source in the USSR), jute, grain (particularly rice), fruits and vegetables, grapes; stockbreeding, especially of sheep for astrakhan pelts (the main producer in the USSR); pigs are also raised (368,000 head in 1979); sericulture (the main producer of silk cocoons in the USSR).

The Uzbek SSR contains within its boundaries one Autonomous Republic, the Karakalpak ASSR. All statistics for the Uzbek SSR automatically include the Karakalpak ASSR, unless otherwise stated. For separate information on the Karakalpak ASSR, see p. 340.

2 NUMBER AND DISTRIBUTION

Number of Uzbeks

1926	1959	1970	1979
3,904,622	6,015,416	9,195,093	12,455,978

Age structure of the Uzbek population in 1970

Age-group	Number	% of total
0–10	3,553,570	38.6
11–15	1,183,250	12.9
16–19	643,961	7.0
20–29	903,717	9.8
30–39	995,826	10.8
40–49	661,752	7.2
50–59	377,047	4.1
60 and over	756,259	8.2
age unknown	119,711	1.3

Percentage of males/females in relation to total Uzbek population

	1926	1970
Men	53.0	50.1
Women	47.0	49.9

Percentage of married Uzbeks in specified age-groups

Age-group	16–19	20–29	30–39	40–49	50–59	60 and over
Men						
In 1959	6.5	62.7	95.6	96.8	95.9	89.8
In 1970	2.7	57.6	94.9	96.2	94.7	88.2
Women						
In 1959	31.8	88.3	90.4	77.9	60.1	27.5
In 1970	21.7	86.3	94.3	87.5	69.2	34.0

Regional distribution of Uzbeks

	1926	1959	1970	1979
UzSSR*	3,299,713 (84.5%)	5,038,306 (83.8%)	7,724,715 (84.0%)	10,569,007 (84.9%)
Kaz.ASSR/SSR	213,498 (5.5%)	135,932 (2.3%)	216,340 (2.4%)	263,295 (2.1%)
Kir.ASSR/SSR	109,776 (2.8%)	218,640 (3.6%)	332,638 (3.6%)	426,194 (3.4%)
TurkSSR	104,971 (2.7%)	125,231 (2.1%)	179,498 (2.0%)	233,730 (1.9%)
Tadzh.ASSR/SSR	175,627 (4.5%)	455,038 (7.6%)	665,662 (7.2%)	873,199 (7.0%)
RSFSR†	942 (0.0%)	29,512 (0.5%)	61,588 (0.7%)	72,385 (0.6%)
Elsewhere in USSR	95 (0.0%)	12,757 (0.2%)	14,652 (0.1%)	18,168 (0.1%)

*Not including the Tadzhik ASSR in 1926, which is listed separately below.
†Not including the Kazakh and Kirghiz ASSRs in 1926, which are listed separately above.

Percentage of Uzbeks in relation to total population of individual republics

	1926	1959	1970	1979
UzSSR	66.0	62.1	65.5	68.7
Kaz.ASSR/SSR	3.3	1.5	1.7	1.8
Kir.ASSR/SSR	11.1	10.6	11.3	12.1
TurkSSR	10.8	8.3	8.3	8.5
Tadzh.ASSR/SSR	21.2	23.0	23.0	22.9

Migration of Uzbeks in 1968–9

Total number of migrants: 127,500.
Percentage who migrated within the UzSSR: 76.0
Percentage who migrated to the TadzhSSR: 14.8
Percentage who migrated to the KirSSR: 3.9
Percentage who migrated to the TurkSSR: 3.3
Percentage who migrated to the KazSSR: 2.0

Urban/rural distribution of Uzbeks (in main areas of habitation)

	1926		1970	
	Urban	*Rural*	*Urban*	*Rural*
UzSSR*	605,019 (18.3%)	2,694,694 (81.7%)	1,776,368 (23.0%)	5,948,347 (77.0%)
Kaz.ASSR/SSR	58,283 (27.3%)	155,215 (72.7%)	87,305 (40.4%)	129,035 (59.6%)
Kir.ASSR/SSR	51,727 (47.1%)	58,049 (52.9%)	119,946 (36.1%)	212,692 (63.9%)
TurkSSR	8,475 (8.1%)	96,496 (91.9%)	98,054 (54.6%)	81,444 (45.4%)
Tadzh.ASSR/SSR	4,040 (2.3%)	171,587 (97.7%)	145,888 (21.9%)	519,774 (78.1%)
RSFSR†	826 (87.7%)	116 (12.3%)	51,957 (84.4%)	9,631 (15.6%)

*Excluding the Tadzhik ASSR in 1926, which is listed separately below.
†Excluding the Kazakh and Kirghiz ASSRs in 1926, which are listed separately above.

Ethnic composition of the UzSSR

	1926	1959	1970	1979
Total population	5,267,658	8,119,103	11,799,429	15,389,307
Uzbeks	3,475,340 (66.0%)	5,038,306 (62.1%)	7,724,715 (65.5%)	10,569,007 (68.7%)
Karakalpaks	26,563 (0.5%)	168,274* (2.1%)	230,258 (2.0%)	297,788 (1.9%)
Tatars	28,401 (0.5%)	445,036† (5.5%)	573,733 (4.9%)	648,764 (4.2%)
Kazakhs	106,980 (2.0%)	342,692 (4.2%)	476,310 (4.0%)	620,136 (4.0%)
Tadzhiks	967,728 (18.4%)	311,366‡ (3.8%)	448,541 (3.8%)	594,627 (3.9%)

	1926	1959	1970	1979
Kirghiz	90,743	92,695	110,726	142,182
	(1.7%)	(1.1%)	(0.9%)	(0.9%)
Koreans	30	138,453	147,538	163,062
	(0.0%)	(1.7%)	(1.3%)	(1.1%)
Jews	37,834¶	94,344	102,855	99,908
	(0.7%)	(1.2%)	(0.9%)	(0.6%)
Russians	246,521	1,092,468	1,473,465	1,665,658
	(4.7%)	(13.5%)	(12.5%)	(10.8%)
Ukrainians	25,804	88,388	111,676	113,826
	(0.5%)	(1.1%)	(0.9%)	(0.7%)
Others	261,714	307,081	399,612	474,349
	(5.0%)	(3.7%)	(3.3%)	(3.1%)

* The enormous increase in the number of Karakalpaks in the period 1926–59 is due to the transfer of the Karakalpak ASSR from the RSFSR to the UzSSR in 1936; the number of Karakalpaks within the Karakalpak ASSR itself remained fairly constant (see p. 341).
† The increase in the number of Tatars is due in large part to the presence of the exiled Crimean Tatars in the UzSSR.
‡ The decrease in the number of Tadzhiks is due to the transformation of the Tadzhik ASSR, which formed part of the UzSSR in 1926, into an independent Union republic in 1929; the number of Tadzhiks within the area remained fairly constant (see p. 307).
¶ This figure includes 19,611 Jews, 18,172 Central Asian Jews, 31 Georgian Jews and 20 Mountain Jews, all of which groups were listed separately at this time, though later listed together.

Percentage of mixed nationality marriages in the UzSSR

	1959	1970
Total	8.2	10.9
In urban areas	14.7	18.4
In rural areas	4.7	5.7

Growth rate of the UzSSR per 1,000 of the population

1940	1965	1970	1979
20.6	28.8	28.1	27.4

Size of family units (living together) in the UzSSR

	1970	1979
Average size of families	5.3	5.5
Average size of families in urban areas	4.5	4.6
Average size of families in rural areas	5.8	6.2

Percentage of family units of different sizes in relation to total number of families in the UzSSR

No. in family	2	3	4	5	6	7	8	9	10 and over
1970	13.1	15.0	15.8	13.7	12.7	10.4	8.4	5.5	5.4
1979	13.4	14.3	16.3	12.6	11.2	9.3	8.1	5.8	9.0

Urban/rural distribution in the UzSSR in 1970

	Urban	Rural
Total	4,321,603	7,477,826
Uzbeks	1,776,368 (41.1%)	5,948,347 (79.5%)
Karakalpaks	68,604 (1.6%)	161,654 (2.2%)
Tatars	421,022 (9.7%)	152,711 (2.0%)
Kazakhs	131,163 (3.0%)	345,147 (4.6%)
Tadzhiks	112,899 (2.6%)	335,642 (4.5%)
Kirghiz	6,950 (0.2%)	103,776 (1.4%)
Russians	1,312,309 (30.4%)	161,156 (2.2%)
Ukrainians	96,744 (2.2%)	14,932 (0.2%)
Others	395,544 (9.2%)	254,461 (3.4%)

3 STATUS

The Uzbeks enjoy full Soviet citizenship. They are found in all occupations and in all income brackets. Their standard of housing

is comparable to that of other national groups in the Soviet Union.
The women go out to work, but probably less than elsewhere in
the Soviet Union.

Literacy

In 1926	In 1970
3.8%	Over 99%

In 1926, 146,757 Uzbeks were literate in their own language (98.0
per cent of the total literate Uzbek population).

**Level of education per 1,000 Uzbeks living in the UzSSR of 10 years of age and
above**

	1959	*1970*
Primary		
Total	187	278
Men	192	272
Women	182	283
Higher and secondary (complete and incomplete)		
Total	318	420
Men	392	476
Women	251	365
Higher only		
Total	9	26
Men	16	39
Women	4	13

Number of schools in the UzSSR in 1979/80 (not including special schools e.g. for
the deaf): 9,400
Number of pupils: 4,000,000*
*Number of higher educational establishments in the UzSSR in
1979/80*: 43
Number of students: 272,900*

*These figures refer to the total number of pupils/students in the UzSSR and
therefore include Uzbeks and non-Uzbeks alike.

4 LANGUAGE

The national language is Uzbek. It belongs to the East Turkic group
(*Fundamenta* classification); it can also be classed as belonging to
the Karluk group, Karluk-Khorezm sub-group (Baskakov). The
language it is most closely related to is (Modern) Uighur.

Uzbek possesses a great variety of dialects. They fall into two main groupings: the central dialects (including those of Tashkent, Samarkand, Bukhara, Andidzhan and Khokand), which have lost synharmonism and have only six vowel phonemes; all the others, which have preserved synharmonism and have a vowel system of ten phonemes. Within this second grouping there are two sub-groups: the north-western (including the southern Khorezmian dialects) and the southern (including those of Kashka Darya and the Samarkand region). The modern literary language is based on the Tashkent-Ferghana group of dialects (i.e. those which have lost synharmonism). Its vocabulary is basically Turkic, but contains an important element of Arabic and Persian loan-words. Russian borrowings have been entering the language since the mid-nineteenth century. At first they were modified to conform with Uzbek pronunciation, e.g. *istorizh* for *storozh* ('watchman'); now they are generally adopted in their original form. In the early years of the Soviet period it seemed as though the Arabic-Persian layer would be made obsolete by the flood of new Russian acquisitions, but recently a balance seems to have been achieved, with a word such as *iktisod* ('economy') holding its own beside *ekonomika*.

Uzbek is used along with Russian for administrative, judicial and other official proceedings.

Percentage of Uzbeks claiming Uzbek as their mother tongue

	1926	1959	1970	1979
Total	99.1	98.4	98.6	98.5
In urban areas	99.2	96.7	96.9	n.a.
In rural areas	99.1	98.9	99.2	n.a.

Percentage of Uzbeks with good knowledge of Russian

	1926	1959	1970	1979
As mother tongue	0.0 (196 people)	0.5	0.5	0.6
As second language	n.a.	n.a.	14.5	49.3

Percentage of speakers claiming Uzbek as their mother tongue in the UzSSR

1926	1970
68.9	65.4 (of these, 99.1 per cent are Uzbeks)

The majority of schools in the Uzbek SSR are Uzbek-medium schools; they provide the full range of schooling (primary, secondary complete and incomplete). In 1958 the following languages were also used as media of instruction in the UzSSR: Russian, Kazakh, Kirghiz, Turkmen, Tadzhik and Karakalpak (this last in the Karakalpak ASSR); outside the UzSSR, in 1958 Uzbek was used as a medium of instruction in the Kazakh, Kirghiz, Turkmen and possibly also Tadzhik SSRs (Lipsett, pp. 185–6). More recent information is not available. There are two universities in the UzSSR: the Central Asian University in Tashkent (founded in 1920, renamed the Tashkent Lenin State University in 1961) and the Samarkand Alisher Navai State University (founded in 1933); there is some tuition in Uzbek in the arts faculties in both these universities. There are also a number of specialized institutes (e.g. of Agriculture, Medicine), where tuition appears to be entirely in Russian, though in the Pedagogical Institutes trainee teachers do receive a certain amount of their education in Uzbek.

In the UzSSR there are radio and television broadcasts in Uzbek, as well as in Russian and Kazakh; there are radio broadcasts only in Tadzhik, Uighur, Karakalpak and Tatar (probably Crimean Tatar only, not Volga Tatar). Since 1975 there have been foreign (i.e. beamed abroad) broadcasts in English, Farsi, Arabic, Hindi, Urdu, Uighur and Uzbek. Outside the UzSSR there are radio and television broadcasts in Uzbek in the Kazakh SSR.

In the UzSSR newspapers are published in Uzbek, as well as in Russian, Greek, Tadzhik and Crimean Tatar. Newspapers in Uzbek are also published in the Kazakh SSR (2 regional papers) and in the Tadzhik SSR. The first Uzbek newspaper appeared in 1870; it was published in Tashkent and was in the form of a supplement to the Russian-language *Turkestanskije vedomosti* ('Turkestan News') from 1870 to 1872; in 1883 it came out as a separate publication under the title *Turkiston vilojatining gazeti* ('Turkestan Province Newspaper'). It was followed by a number of other Uzbek papers in the post-1905 period (e.g. *Aina*, *Khurshid*, *Sada-i Turkestan*, *Turan*, *Ulugh Turkestan*). The first Soviet Uzbek paper was *Ishtirokijun* ('The Communist'), which appeared in 1918. Amongst the main Uzbek newspapers of today are *Sovet Ozbekistoni* ('Soviet Uzbekistan' – first appeared in 1918), *Josh Leninchi* ('Young Leninist' – first appeared in 1925), *Ozbekistan madanijati* ('Culture of Uzbekistan' – first appeared in 1957). There are also a number of Uzbek journals and periodicals, e.g. *Shark julduzi* ('Star of the

East' – first appeared in 1933), *Gulistan* ('Flower Garden' – first appeared in 1925) and *Ozbekiston khotin-kizlari* ('Women and Girls of Uzbekistan' – first appeared in 1950).

Books and pamphlets are published in Uzbek in the UzSSR and in other republics in the Soviet Union (e.g. a total of 677 titles in 1976; of these, 211 were specialized textbooks on technical and scientific subjects). More titles are published in Uzbek than in any other language of the Muslim peoples of the USSR.

Number of newspapers, journals and other periodicals published in the UzSSR in selected years, with annual circulation

	1965	1979
No. of newspapers	172 (404,000,000)	273 (886,000,000)
In Uzbek only	100 (270,000,000)	185 (649,000,000)
No. of journals	119 (37,600,000)	83 (135,300,000)
In Uzbek only	37 (22,000,000)	32 (89,900,000)

Number of books and pamphlets published in Uzbek in selected years throughout the Russian Empire/USSR

	1913	1940	1965	1979
No. of titles	37	687	1,005	1,058
Print run	86,000	9,509,000	18,863,000	26,399,000

Number of books and pamphlets published in the UzSSR in 1979, with print run

Total no. of titles	2,289	(37,500,000)
No. of titles in Uzbek	1,048	(26,300,000)

Scripts and alphabets

Until 1865	Arabic script (originally 29 symbols; by the fifteenth century 31 symbols)
1865–1923	Arabic script, slightly modified alphabet
1923–30	Arabic script, further modified alphabet
1930–4	Latin script, first alphabet
1934–40	Latin script, second alphabet
1940	Cyrillic script (minor modifications in 1956)

The present alphabet is not considered to be wholly satisfactory for the representation of Uzbek and further changes are foreseen.

One of the main problems is that this alphabet was developed to serve the requirements of the dialect group that had lost synharmonism and consequently needed far fewer symbols for vowel phonemes than the other and larger group which has preserved synharmonism. Even within the former group it seems likely there is greater differentiation between vowel phonemes than the present alphabet is able to express. Thus there are a considerable number of words that are now written identically but are etymologically quite different and, for the great majority of Uzbek-speakers, pronounced differently. This has caused confusion both for those learning to read and for older people whose reading ability is limited.

5 RELIGION

The Uzbeks are Sunni Muslims (Hanafi school). The headquarters of the Spiritual Directorate of Central Asia and Kazakhstan are in Tashkent. The Chairman of the Directorate is Mufti Ziauddin Ishan Babakhanov (Ziauddinkhan ibn Ishan Babakhan). Born in Tashkent in 1908, he comes from a long line of Muslim scholars; after studying at the Barak-Khan and Kukal-Tash medresses, he became Kazi of the Uzbek SSR in 1943. In 1947 he graduated from Al-Azhar. He served as Deputy Chairman of the Directorate for nearly fifteen years, then, on the death of his father, the first Chairman of the Directorate, he himself became Chairman in 1957. He has held this office for over twenty years, more than half the time that the Directorate has been in existence. Babakhanov has come to be the Soviet Union's chief spokesman on Muslim affairs and is a familiar figure at Muslim conferences abroad. He is an Islamic scholar of some repute and has a magnificent command of Arabic. His deputies at the Directorate are Sheikh Abdulgani Abdullajev and Yusufkhan Shakirov.

The only two Soviet medresses are in the Uzbek SSR: the Mir-i Arab in Bukhara (founded in 1530, closed after the Revolution, reopened after the Second World War) and the Imam Ismail al-Bukhari in Tashkent (originally known as the Barak-Khan medresse; it was founded in the mid-sixteenth century, closed after the Revolution, reopened in 1958, closed again and once more reopened in 1971; it was renamed in Bukhari's honour in 1974, to commemorate the 1,200th Muslim-year anniversary of his birth). These two train all the *ulema* in the Soviet Union. They operate under the aegis of the Spiritual Directorate of Central Asia and Kazakhstan. Mufti Babakhanov and his deputies personally teach in the Tashkent medresse.

This Spiritual Directorate is also responsible for almost all of the limited amount of Islamic publications that are produced in the Soviet Union. These include the quarterly journal *Muslims of the Soviet East* (published in four editions: Arabic, English, French and Uzbek; the Uzbek edition is in the Arabic script, which was abolished in Uzbekistan in 1930 and is therefore incomprehensible to the vast majority of the population); six editions of the Qur'an (the last produced in conjunction with the three other Directorates) and three editions of the Hadith of al-Bukhari (the whole collection, *al-Jami as-Sahih*, the Hadith concerning personal good conduct, *al-Adab al-Mufrad* and the three-item Hadith, *as-Sulasiyat*). The Hadith of at-Tirmizi are due to appear shortly.

There are mosques open for worship in most of the large cities in the Uzbek SSR, e.g. in Tashkent, Bukhara, Samarkand, Andidzhan, Ferghana and Namangan. According to a recent Soviet publication (Vakhabov, p. 37), these mosques are 'packed with thousands of believers' on festival days; while the men are at prayer, crowds of women and children wait outside.

Sufism has flourished in Uzbekistan since Islam was first introduced into the region. Two of the greatest medieval centres of Sufi learning were situated within its present borders, those of Bukhara and Khiva. Both gave rise to schools of mysticism that were of significance for the whole of the Muslim world: in Khiva, Najm ad-din al-Kubra (AD 1145–1221) formulated the *tariqa* ('way') known as the Kubrawi, and in Bukhara, Baha ad-din an-Naqshbandi (AD 1318–89) the Naqshbandi or *tariqat al-Khwajagan* ('way of the Masters'). The latter became particularly influential, spreading throughout Central Asia, the Caucasus, the Volga region, Anatolia, Kurdistan and India. Today it is the largest of the Sufi schools and is continuing to attract new adherents in the East and the West. Baha ad-din is buried just outside Bukhara; in 1544 the Emir Abdul Aziz Khan erected a mausoleum for him there. Even now, Baha ad-din is held in such reverence that for many, two or three pilgrimages to his tomb are considered to be equivalent in merit to making the Hajj to Mecca (Demidov, *Sufizm . . .*, p. 72).

The Naqshbandi was probably the most widespread *tariqa* in Uzbekistan, but others could also claim a substantial following. These were the Kubrawi (mainly in Khiva), the Yasavi (throughout the region), the Qadiri (mainly in Ferghana) and the Chisti (mainly in Khokand). Sufism, closely connected as it was with trade guilds and neighbourhood communities, was an integral part of urban life and in large cities it was not uncommon to find representatives of several different schools. The nineteenth-century traveller Schuyler recorded that in Tashkent there were three hundred mosques and each one had its own imam and Sufi. It was possible to attend a variety of public *zikr* sessions, some 'loud', some 'silent', on almost every day of the week. The region was studded with the shrines of holy men, both those of world renown, such as Baha ad-din, and others of more local significance, such as Zengi-baba (buried near Tashkent), Chopan-ata (buried in the Ferghana Valley) and Hodzha Akrar (buried near Samarkand). Their anniversaries were the occasion for great celebrations and were important in the social, as well as the religious, life of the community.

No information is available on the state of Sufism in Uzbekistan today, but it is possible to glean indications from sources such as Demidov (op. cit.) that many of the shrines are still visited, especially on festival days. Popular religion, strongly tinged with superstition appears to be surviving, but there is no evidence, positive or negative, of the intellectual reawakening of interest in Sufi philosophy, and indeed religion as a whole, that is manifesting itself elsewhere in the world.

6 OUTSIDE THE SOVIET UNION

According to Soviet sources, there are approximately 1,200,000 Uzbeks in Afghanistan, mostly concentrated in the region directly adjacent to the USSR. (Cf. the higher estimate of 1,649,000 given in *Soviet Asian Ethnic Frontiers*, p. 147.) There are also some 15 – 18,000 Uzbeks in the Xinjiang-Wei-wu-er (Sinkiang-Uighur) Autonomous Region of the People's Republic of China; this region, too, is contiguous with the USSR.

KAZAKHS

Own names: *Kazakh, Kazak*; Russian name: *Kazakhi*.

The Kazakhs were formerly known as *Kirghiz, Kirghiz-Kaisak, Kaisak-Kirghiz* or *Kazakh-Kirghiz* (see p. 327). The confusion between the Kirghiz and the Kazakhs is found in the earliest European sources, with the name 'Kirghiz' being applied to both peoples; the Kazakhs themselves, however, did not use it, but always called themselves 'Kazakh'.

The majority of Kazakhs live in the Kazakh SSR, but groups of them are found in the other Central Asian republics, particularly the Turkmen SSR and in the RSFSR, mostly in western Siberia.

1 HISTORICAL BACKGROUND

The Kazakhs are descended from Turkic and Mongol tribes who settled in the area now known as Kazakhstan from about the end of the first century BC, if not earlier. In the sixth century AD the area formed part of the Turkish Khaganate, a loose confederation of nomadic tribes which survived in one form or another until the eighth century. From the tenth to the twelfth centuries southern Kazakhstan (Semirech'je) was ruled by the Karakhanids. The Karakhanids were overthrown by the Kara Khitais and these in turn were defeated by the Mongols in 1219–21. In the mid-thirteenth century Orda, the eldest son of Dzhuchi (himself the eldest son of Genghiz Khan) formed the White Horde, a semi-independent division of the Golden Horde which established itself in the region between the lower Syr Darya and the Alatau Mountains. The White Horde soon gained control of Semirech'je and most of Eastern Turkestan, but though its rulers were Mongols of the line of Genghiz, the majority of its people were Turkic and it was they who were to play the decisive role in the future of the region. The White Horde was succeeded by two new powers, the Nogais (from the Golden Horde) and the Uzbeks. The latter conquered Khwarezmia in 1430–1 and by 1447 held sway over the lands between the Irtysh and the Syr Darya. The Kazakh inhabitants of the region came to be known as 'Uzbek Kazakhs'. The White Horde was still not completely vanquished, however, and the period was marked by continuous fighting as the power struggle continued. Several of the Kazakh tribes migrated out of the area, to the Khanate of Mogolistan in the south-east. Mogolistan, originally part of the Ulus of Genghiz Khan's second son, Chagatai, was now an independent state ruled by Mongol Khans, but with a predominantly Turkic population that included many of the Kirghiz. In 1465 two of the princes of the White Horde, Dzhanibek and Girey, also

moved to Mogolistan, bringing with them a large retinue of followers (again, mostly Turkic tribes). The Khan of Mogolistan welcomed them and allocated them lands to the west of his own
territory, on the Chu and Talass Rivers. This formed the nucleus
of a state which came to be known as the 'Kazakh Khanate' and
which by the late fifteenth century had grown powerful enough to
extend its dominion over much of the Desht-i Kipchak (the Kipchak
Plain), formerly under Uzbek control.

By the beginning of the sixteenth century the majority of the
Kazakh group of tribes (which included Kipchaks, Naimans, Usuns
and Dulats) were united under a single ruler, Kasim Khan (1511–
18). It was a period of relative tranquillity, to be broken after
Kasim's death by renewed internecine fighting. As the Kazakh state
began to disintegrate, it received an influx of tribes from the neighbouring Nogai Horde, itself in the process of dissolution. During
the seventeenth century there was a decisive division of power, as
a result of which, three independent Kazakh hordes (*dzhuz*) were
formed: the Great (*Ulu*) in Semirech'je, the Little (*Kishi*) between
the Aral and Caspian Seas, the Middle (*Orta*) in the central steppe
region. When the Dzhungarian Oirots (Kalmyks) from Mongolia
began to make incursions into the Kazakh lands in the mid seventeenth century, the Kazakhs were in no position to offer a unified
resistance. The struggle between the Kazakhs and the Oirots continued into the early eighteenth century, when the Kazakhs, briefly
united, scored a number of victories. The Oirot menace was not
completely removed, however, until they were vanquished by the
Manchus in 1758. By this time, most of the Kazakhs had had
recourse to Russian protection: the Little Horde in 1731, the Middle
Horde in 1740 and part of the Great Horde in 1742. Contacts
between the Kazakhs and the Russians, which had started in the
sixteenth century, grew steadily stronger and the Kazakhs found
themselves drawn ever more firmly into the Russian orbit. They
attempted to resist this through a number of uprisings in the second
half of the eighteenth century, but by the mid-nineteenth century
their lands were completely under Russian control (except for the
eastern region, which was part of the Manchu Empire). The power
of the Khans was abolished: the Khan of the Middle Horde was
deposed in 1822, of the Little Horde in 1824 and of the Great
Horde in 1848. A garrison was established at Vernoje (later Vernyj,
today Alma-Ata, the capital of the Kazakh SSR) in 1854. Russian
settlers began to appear in Kazakhstan and gradually the Kazakhs

were dispossessed of their most fertile lands.

A section of the Little Horde split off from the main group to form a new horde, the Bukej or Inner Horde, at the beginning of the nineteenth century. In 1799 Bukej, younger son of Khan Nurali of the Little Horde, petitioned the Russian authorities to be allowed to settle in the lands between the Urals and the Volga, left vacant when the Oirots (Kalmyks) fled to China. He received permission for this in 1801 and proceeded to move westwards, taking about 5,000 tents with him (some 22,770 people); another 1,625 tents joined him later. Bukej was confirmed Khan of the new horde in 1812. At first he and his people came under the jurisdiction of the Orenburg Province, but they frequently migrated long distances and it was only towards the end of the century that they settled more or less permanently in the region of Astrakhan and came under the jurisdiction of that province. By this period the Bukej Horde consisted of 150,000 tents, the Great of 100,000, the Middle of 406,000 and the Little of 800,000.

It was during the nineteenth century that the final conversion of the Kazakhs to Islam took place. Ironically, perhaps, this was due to the Russians. Islam had become established amongst the settled communities of Kazakhstan in the seventh to ninth centuries. The tribal nobility became Muslims during the sixteenth century, largely under the influence of the Nogais who joined forces with the Kazakhs at this period. The bulk of the nomad peoples, however, remained unaffected by the new religion and it was only due to strong pressure from the Russian government and energetic proselytizing on the part of the Tatars that they were eventually converted. The Russians appear to have felt that Islam would act as a civilizing, as well as a unifying force, drawing the tribes together and thereby enabling them to be controlled more effectively. The building of mosques was actively encouraged and each tribal unit was provided with an imam. The Tatar influence grew accordingly and Tatar became the official language of communication between the administration and the indigenous peoples. Then, in the middle of the century, official policy was reversed: mosques could only be built with special permission, the number of imams was severely curtailed and the activities of Christian missionaries much increased. By this time, though, Islam was firmly, albeit rather superficially, established amongst the Kazakhs and they resisted any further changes of religion.

Many of the Kazakh aristocracy received an excellent Russian education and this had a profound effect on their outlook. Unlike, for example, the Uzbeks, who had their own great literary heritage, the Kazakhs' culture was rooted in the nomad way of life, with a strong emphasis on oral traditions. They were particularly receptive to Russian culture and became its sincere advocates. The three greatest Kazakh writers and scholars of this period were typical in their pro-Russian bias: Chokan Valikhanov (1835–65), Ibraj Altynsarin (1841–89) and Abaj Kunanbajev (1845–1904). Kunanbajev holds a special place in Kazakh history, for he is considered to be the father of modern Kazakh literature, but all three played a major part in the development of the literary language, as also in the general cultural and intellectual life of their people. Altynsarin was particularly concerned with educational reform and in addition to writing several textbooks, he invented an alphabet for Kazakh based on the Cyrillic script. This was not generally adopted, however, and the Arabic script remained in use until the Soviet period. The first Russian-Kazakh (called 'Kirghiz' at this time) school was opened in 1841 and was soon followed by many others. Meanwhile, as the Russian influence spread, so the popularity of the Tatars waned. They had formerly dominated the education of the Kazakhs, but the latter became disenchanted with their pan-Turkic ideals and evinced a bitter reaction against them. The Russians, who had originally encouraged the Tatars' activities in the steppes, also sought to limit their role and thereby to curb the spread of Islam. Thus the Tatars were gradually ousted from their position of power as intermediaries between the colonizers and the colonized and found themselves without support from either side.

However, the pro-Russian euphoria did not survive the advent of the Russian settlers, who descended on the Kazakhs at the turn of the century and robbed them of their lands. The deep resentment of the indigenous population paved the way for disaffection and in 1916 there was a major rebellion against Russian rule. It was fiercely repressed, but not before many Russians had been killed and much property damaged. The immediate cause of the uprising was the drafting of Kazakhs into the Russian army for non-combatant duties. The situation had scarcely improved before the outbreak of the 1917 Revolution. As elsewhere in Central Asia, there then began a bitter fight between the foreign Interventionists, the Red Army, the White Army (under Kolchak) and the Nationalists (led by the Alash Orda party). Soviet rule was finally established in 1920. On 26 August 1920 the Kirghiz (i.e. 'Kazakh') ASSR was created within the RSFSR. After the National Delimitation of 1924–5 the Syr Darya and Semirech'je's provinces, which had originally formed part of the Turkestan Republic, were transferred to the Kirghiz (Kazakh) ASSR, since their populations were mainly Kazakh. In 1925 the Kirghiz ASSR was officially renamed the Kazakh ASSR. During this period, the Karakalpak Autonomous Province came within the Kazakh ASSR; in 1932 it became the Karakalpak ASSR and was detached from the Kazakh ASSR, joining the Uzbek SSR in 1936. On 5 December 1936 the Kazakh ASSR was transformed into a full Union republic, the Kazakh SSR.

Kazakh SSR (Kazakh Sovettik Sotsialistik Respublikasy), also known as *Kazakhstan*

Situated between the Caspian Sea and the Tien Shan Range, with an extremely varied relief that includes mountain ranges and deserts; its lowest point is 132 m below sea level, its highest over 5,000 m above; it is bordered to the north and west by the RSFSR, to the south by the Turkmen, Uzbek and Kirghiz SSRs, to the east by the People's Republic of China. *Area*: 2,717,300 sq. km (the second largest republic in the USSR). *Capital*: Alma-Ata, known as Vernyj until 1921 (population in 1979: 910,000). The Republic has 82 towns and 193 settlements. *Population* (1979): 14,684,283. Average density of population per sq. km (1979): 5.4.

Chief resources: Kazakhstan is richly endowed with a variety of resources; its mineral reserves include major deposits of coal, iron ores, lead, zinc, copper and oil; also chromite, nickel, molybdenum, tin, antimony, cadmium, bauxite, gold, silver, several rare metals and phosphates; it has vast stretches of good arable land and fine pastures; its many rivers (which include the Syr Darya, the Irtysh and the Ili) provide a valuable source of hydroelectric power and the basis for important irrigation schemes.

Industries include: It is a highly industrialized republic; its industries include: the extraction and processing of ferrous and nonferrous metals, fuel, power, chemical, machine-building and cement industries; textile, footwear, food (especially meat-canning) and other light industries.

Agriculture: grain farming (one of the chief grain-producing areas of the USSR); fruit, vegetables, grapes, sugar beet, potatoes and cotton are also cultivated; stockbreeding of livestock for meat and dairy produce (one of the chief meat-producing areas of the USSR);

sheep are bred for their wool (fine-fleeced varieties) and astrakhan pelts; pigs are also raised (2,857,000 head in 1979); fishing is highly developed.

2 NUMBER AND DISTRIBUTION

Number of Kazakhs

1926	1959	1970	1979
3,968,289	3,621,610*	5,298,818	6,556,442

*The fall in the number of Kazakhs in the period 1926–59 is attributable to the great losses through starvation (possibly a result of enforced collectivization during the 1920s, when large numbers of livestock perished; bad harvests were also a contributory factor); it is estimated that by 1939 there were nearly 1 million less Kazakhs than would normally have been anticipated (Lorimer, p. 121).

Age structure of the Kazakh population in 1970

Age-group	Number	% of total
0–10	1,939,130	36.6
11–15	661,823	12.5
16–19	379,460	7.2
20–29	609,154	11.5
30–39	528,458	10.0
40–49	378,680	7.1
50–59	250,391	4.7
60 and over	477,447	9.0
age unknown	74,275	1.4

Percentage of males/females in relation to total Kazakh population

	1926	1970
Men	52.7	49.5
Women	47.3	50.5

Percentage of married Kazakhs in specified age-groups

Age-group	16–19	20–29	30–39	40–49	50–59	60 and over
Men						
In 1959	5.6	58.7	95.4	97.4	97.0	90.8
In 1970	1.6	49.8	92.4	95.9	95.3	87.9
Women						
In 1959	28.7	83.2	88.6	72.1	56.8	29.0
In 1970	12.3	75.8	91.6	83.3	62.1	32.6

Regional distribution of Kazakhs

	1926	1959	1970	1979
Kaz.ASSR/SSR	3,713,394 (93.6%)	2,787,309 (77.0%)	4,234,166 (79.9%)	5,289,349 (80.7%)
RSFSR (not incl. Kaz.ASSR)	138,267 (3.5%)	382,659 (10.6%)	477,820 (9.0%)	518,060 (7.9%)
UzSSR	106,980 (2.7%)	342,692 (9.5%)	476,310 (9.0%)	620,136 (9.5%)
TurkSSR	9,471 (0.2%)	69,552 (1.9%)	68,519 (1.3%)	79,539 (1.2%)
Elsewhere in USSR	177 (0.0%)	39,398 (1.0%)	42,003 (0.8%)	49,358 (0.7%)

Percentage of Kazakhs in relation to total population of individual republics

	1926	1959	1970	1979
Kaz.ASSR/SSR	57.1	30.0	32.6	36.0
RSFSR (not incl. Kaz.ASSR)	0.1	0.3	0.4	0.4
UzSSR	2.0	4.2	4.0	4.0
TurkSSR	1.0	4.6	3.2	2.9

Migration of Kazakhs in 1968–9

Total number of migrants: 236,500.
Percentage who migrated within the KazSSR: 82.9 per cent
Percentage who migrated to the RSFSR: 10.4 per cent
Percentage who migrated to the UzSSR: 6.0 per cent
Percentage who migrated to the TurkSSR: 0.7 per cent

Urban/rural distribution of Kazakhs (in main areas of habitation)

	1926		1970	
	Urban	*Rural*	*Urban*	*Rural*
Kaz.ASSR/SSR	77,554	3,635,840	1,115,299	3,118,867
	(2.1%)	(97.9%)	(26.3%)	(73.7%)
RSFSR (not incl.	5,754	132,513	107,413	370,407
Kaz.ASSR)	(4.2%)	(95.8%)	(22.5%)	(77.5%)
TurkSSR	471	9,000	39,875	28,644
	(5.0%)	(95.0%)	(58.2%)	(41.8%)

Ethnic composition of the Kaz.ASSR/SSR

	1926	1959	1970	1979
Total population	6,500,895	9,294,741	13,008,726	14,684,283
Kazakhs	3,713,394	2,787,309	4,234,166	5,289,349
	(57.1%)	(30.0%)	(32.6%)	(36.0%)
Uzbeks	213,498	135,932	216,340	263,295
	(3.3%)	(1.5%)	(1.7%)	(1.8%)
Tatars	80,642	191,680*	287,712	313,460
	(1.2%)	(2.1%)	(2.2%)	(2.1%)
Uighurs	10,510	59,840	120,881	147,943
	(0.2%)	(0.6%)	(0.9%)	(1.0%)
Germans	51,102	658,698	858,077	900,207
	(0.8%)	(7.1%)	(6.6%)	(6.1%)
Koreans	42	74,019	81,598	91,984
	(0.0%)	(0.8%)	(0.6%)	(0.6%)
Russians	1,279,979	3,972,042	5,521,917	5,991,205
	(19.7%)	(42.7%)	(42.4%)	(40.8%)
Ukrainians	860,822	761,432	933,461	897,964
	(13.2%)	(8.2%)	(7.2%)	(6.1%)
Others	290,906	653,789	754,574	788,876
	(4.5%)	(7.0%)	(5.8%)	(5.4%)

Note: The Karakalpak have not been included here, because though their
Autonomous Province was contained within the Kazakh ASSR in 1926, it was

transferred to the Uzbek SSR in 1936 (having already been transformed into an ASSR), so that the sudden disappearance of the Karakalpak from the Kazakh SSR is due to political-administrative changes, not to migrations. For information on the distribution etc. of the Karakaplak, see pp. 341.
*The sharp increase in the Tatar population between 1926 and 1959 is due in large measure to the deportation to Kazakhstan of the Crimean Tatars in 1944. (The same applies to the German population, which was augmented by the deported Volga Germans.)

Percentage of mixed nationality marriages in the KazSSR

	1959	1970
Total	14.4	20.7
In urban areas	17.5	23.8
In rural areas	11.9	17.1

Growth rate of the KazSSR per 1,000 of the population

1940	1965	1970	1979
19.4	21.0	17.4	16.3

Size of family units (living together) in the KazSSR

	1970	1979
Average size of families	4.3	4.1
Average size of families in urban areas	3.9	3.7
Average size of families in rural areas	4.8	4.7

Percentage of family units of different sizes in relation to total number of families in the KazSSR

No. in family	2	3	4	5	6	7	8	9	10 and over
1970	17.8	21.5	22.7	15.2	9.4	5.6	3.7	2.2	1.9
1979	21.1	24.7	23.5	12.1	6.8	4.3	3.0	2.0	2.5

Urban/rural distribution in the KazSSR in 1970

	Urban	*Rural*
Total	6,538,652	6,470,074
Kazakhs	1,115,299 (17.1%)	3,118,867 (48.2%)
Uzbeks	87,305 (1.3%)	129,035 (2.0%)
Tatars	203,110 (3.1%)	84,602 (1.3%)
Uighurs	29,618 (0.5%)	91,263 (1.4%)
Russians	3,818,295 (58.4%)	1,703,622 (26.3%)
Ukrainians	501,337 (7.7%)	432,124 (6.7%)
Others	783,688 (11.9%)	910,561 (14.1%)

3 STATUS

The Kazakhs enjoy full Soviet citizenship. They are found in all occupations and in all income brackets. Their standard of housing is comparable to that of other national groups in the Soviet Union. The women go out to work, but probably less than elsewhere in the Soviet Union.

Literacy

In 1926	In 1970
7.1%	Over 99%

In 1926, 271,097 Kazakhs were literate in their own language (96.5 per cent of the total literate Kazakh population).

Level of education per 1,000 Kazakhs living in the KazSSR of 10 years of age and above

	1959	*1970*
Primary		
Total	221	291
Men	229	294
Women	215	289
Higher and secondary (complete and incomplete)		
Total	282	403
Men	369	464
Women	207	347
Higher only		
Total	12	31
Men	20	44
Women	5	20

Number of schools in the KazSSR in 1979/80 (not including special schools, e.g. for the deaf): 8,800
Number of pupils: 3,300,000*
Number of higher educational establishments in the KazSSR in 1979/80: 53
Number of students: 251,000*
* These figures refer to the total number of pupils/students in the KazSSR and therefore include Kazakhs and non-Kazakhs alike.

4 LANGUAGE

The national language is Kazakh. It belongs to the Central Turkic group (*Fundamenta* classification); it can also be classed as belonging to the Kipchak group, Kipchak-Nogai sub-group (Baskakov). The languages it is most closely related to are Nogai and Karakalpak.

The dialects of Kazakh have not yet been studied in great detail, but it is evident that there is little divergence between them, as a result of which Kazakh is a remarkably unified language. Its vocabulary is basically Turkic, but contains loan-words from a variety of sources, e.g. Arabic, Persian, Mongol and Russian. Many of the Mongol loans date from the twelfth and thirteenth centuries. Russian words entered Kazakh in both the pre- and post-Revolutionary periods. The early borrowings underwent considerable phonetic modification, e.g. *oblys* for *oblast'* ('area, province'); those made during the Soviet period have preserved their original form. Kazakh also has loan-words from neighbouring languages such as Chinese, Tatar and Uzbek. They are particularly common in the dialects, e.g. Chinese loans predominate in the north-east, Uzbek in the south, Tatar in the west.

Kazakh is used along with Russian for administrative, judicial and other official proceedings.

Percentage of Kazakhs claiming Kazakh as their mother tongue

	1926	1959	1970	1979
Total	99.6	98.4	98.0	97.5
In urban areas	98.4	96.7	95.8	n.a.
In rural areas	99.6	98.9	98.8	n.a.

Percentage of Kazakhs with good knowledge of Russian

	1926	1959	1970	1979
As mother tongue	0.1.	1.2	1.6	2.0
As second language	n.a.	n.a.	41.8	52.3

Percentage of speakers claiming Kazakh as their mother tongue in the Kazakh ASSR/SSR

1926	1970
57.2	32.3 (of these, 99.7 per cent are Kazakhs)

In the Kazakh SSR there are schools in which Kazakh is the medium of instruction, but since the Kazakhs form only 36 per cent of the total population of the republic it is unlikely that schools in which their language is the medium of instruction constitute the major proportion. It is probable that they provide the full range of schooling, but precise information is not available. In 1958 in the Kazakh SSR there were also schools in which the following languages were used as media of instruction: Russian, Uzbek, Uighur, Dungan and Tadzhik; outside the Kazakh SSR in 1958 Kazakh was used as a medium of instruction in the Uzbek and Turkmen SSRs and possibly also in the Kirghiz and Tadzhik SSRs (Lipsett, pp. 185–6); in the RSFSR it was used in grades 1–10 (complete secondary) in the Kazakh national schools and this was still the case in 1972, when it was also being taught as an individual, optional subject in Russian-medium schools (Silver, p. 34). More recent information is not available. As the use of languages other than the titular language of a republic and Russian have been much curtailed since the early 1960s, it is probable that in the Kazakh SSR there is little if any tuition now in the minority languages cited above and the same applies to the use of Kazakh as a medium of instruction outside it (with the possible exception of the RSFSR). There is one university, the Kirov Kazakh State University (founded in 1934) in Alma-Ata in which tuition is provided in both Kazakh and Russian. There are also a number of specialized institutes (e.g. of Agriculture, Medicine, Pedagogy, Polytechnic and Industry) and a Conservatoire. The medium of instruction in these institutes is likely to be Russian, except in those of Pedagogy, where there is probably some training in Kazakh.

In the Kazakh SSR there are radio and television broadcasts in Kazakh, as well as in Russian, Uzbek, Uighur, German and Korean. Outside the KazSSR there are radio and television broadcasts in Kazakh in the Uzbek SSR.

In the Kazakh SSR newspapers are published in Kazakh, as well as in Russian, Uzbek, Uighur and German. The first Kazakh periodical publication was *Turkistan vilajatining gazeti* ('Turkish Province Newspaper'), published in Tashkent as a supplement to the Russian-language *Turkestanskije vedomosti* ('Turkestan News') from 1871 to 1883 (this supplement originally appeared in Uzbek in 1870, then alternated with the Kazakh edition on a bi-monthly basis until it became an independent Uzbek-language publication in 1883). It was followed by *Dala vilajeti* ('Steppe Province') published in Omsk from 1888 to 1902, also as a supplement to a Russian journal, *Kirgizskaja stepnaja gazeta* ('Kirghiz Steppe Newspaper'). The first independent Kazakh publication was *Kazakh gazeti* ('Kazakh Newspaper'), which appeared in 1907; it was suspended after its first number, but was soon followed by others, the most influential of which was *Kazakh* ('Kazakh'), published at Orenburg from 1913 to 1918. The first Soviet Kazakh newspaper was *Durystyk dzholy* ('Road to Truth' – first appeared in 1919). The main Kazakh-language newspapers today include *Sotsialistik Kazakhstan* ('Socialist Kazakhstan' – first appeared in 1919, under the title *Enbekshi kazakh*), *Leninshil dzhas* ('Young Leninist' – also first appeared in 1919) and *Kazakh adebijeti* ('Kazakh Literature' – first appeared in 1934). Amongst the main Kazakh-language journals and periodicals are *Kazakhstan kommunisti* ('Kazakh Communist' – first appeared in 1921), *Kazakhstan ajelderi* ('Kazakh Women' – first appeared in 1925), *Kazakhstan mektebi* ('Kazakh School' – first

appeared in 1925), *Dzhuldyz* ('Star' – first appeared in 1928) and
Medeniet dzhene turmys ('Culture and Life' – first appeared in
1958). Since 1976 the periodical *Bizdin otan* ('Our Fatherland') has
been published in Alma-Ata in the Arabic script; there is also an
Uighur edition of this in the Arabic script.

Books and pamphlets in Kazakh are published in the KazSSR,
as well as in other republics of the Soviet Union (e.g. a total of 450
titles in 1976; of these, 109 were specialized textbooks on technical
and scientific subjects).

**Number of newspapers, journals and other periodicals published in the KazSSR
in selected years, with annual circulation**

	1965	1979
No. of newspapers	294 (548,000,000)	429 (1,060,000,000)
In Kazakh only	101 (168,000,000)	159 (318,000,000)
No. of journals and periodicals	76 (16,500,000)	114 (53,300,000)
In Kazakh only	17 (10,100,000)	30 (27,500,000)

**Number of books and pamphlets published in Kazakh in selected years
throughout the Russian Empire/USSR**

	1913	1940	1965	1979
No. of titles	40	387	572	720
Print run	161,000	4,244,000	8,217,000	13,504,000

**Number of books and pamphlets published in the KazSSR in 1979, with total
print run**

Total no. of titles	2,171 (27,000,000)
No. of titles in Kazakh	716 (13,500,000)

Scripts and alphabets

Until 1924	Arabic script, Arabic alphabet
1924–9	Arabic script, modified alphabet
1929–38	Latin script, first alphabet
1938–40	Latin script, second alphabet
1940	Cyrillic script (slightly modified in 1957)

The present alphabet is considered to be perfect for representing
Kazakh.

5 RELIGION

The Kazakhs are Sunni Muslims (Hanafi school). They come under the jurisdiction of the Spiritual Directorate of Central Asia and Kazakhstan. The Directorate's present representative (*Kazi*) in Kazakhstan is Sheikh Yahya Baisenbajev.

The Kazakhs became Muslim relatively late (for the most part in the early nineteenth century) and even after their conversion, pagan practices and beliefs remained strong amongst them. Their knowledge of Islam was very limited and they prayed little. Wandering Tatar mullahs, who travelled from village to village, provided their chief link with the Muslim world. It would be interesting to know if the Kazakhs have now become more orthodox in their religious habits, but unfortunately no information is available on this point. The number of anti-Islamic attacks in the Kazakh press would seem to indicate that, orthodox or not, they are still firmly Muslim. There are mosques open for worship in several of the large towns, but probably few, if any, in the countryside (where the majority of the Kazakhs live).

The Tatar mullahs who spread Islam amongst the Kazakhs in the nineteenth century were most probably Sufis, but this was not the first appearance of Sufism in this region: the most famous of all Turkic Sufis came from Yasy in southern Kazakhstan. He was the twelfth-century mystic Ahmed Yasavi, whose followers carried Islam throughout the Turkic-speaking world; as late as the sixteenth century adherents of his school were still active in Central Asia. Yasavi studied for a while in Bukhara, but most of his life was spent at Yasy, where he was eventually buried. The city became a great centre of Sufism and Yasavi's tomb was revered as one of the most sacred shrines in Central Asia. Timur built a mosque over it in 1397 and pilgrims from as far afield as India and China came to visit it. The Khans of the Middle and Little Kazakh Hordes were buried there (the Kazakh nobility having adopted Islam centuries before the bulk of the ordinary tribesmen) and so, too, was the wife of Abul Khayr, Ulugh Beg's daughter and Timur's great-grand-daughter. In the sixteenth century the name of the city was changed to 'Turkestan' (Babur refers to it as such in his Memoirs). It is still called this today and its mosque, the Hazret Mosque, continues to be a place of pilgrimage.

6 OUTSIDE THE SOVIET UNION

There are approximately the following numbers of Kazakhs in:
Afghanistan   3,000
China   600,000–700,000
Mongolia   40,000
There are also a few hundred Kazakhs (mostly of the Kirei tribe)
in Salihli and Develi (western and central Anatolia). They went
to Turkey from Chinese Turkestan in 1951 (*Kazak Exodus*, G.
Lias, London, 1956).

TADZHIKS

Own name: *Todzhik*; Russian name: *Tadzhiki*.

The term is used both for the Tadzhiks of the plain (the Tadzhiks
'proper') and for the Tadzhiks of the mountains (also known as the
'Pamiri peoples': see p. 374). Most of the former live in the central
and western parts of the Tadzhik SSR, but there are also sizeable
colonies in the Uzbek and Kirghiz SSRs.

1 HISTORICAL BACKGROUND

The Tadzhiks exemplify the complexity of the Central Asian heritage since, unlike the other large ethnic groups that now inhabit
the area, they are Iranian-speakers, not Turkic. They represent the
development of one of the early layers of Central Asian civilisation,
predating the advent of the Turks. The history of Tadzhikistan is
particularly bound up with that of Uzbekistan, for the two areas
are not only contiguous, but have often been governed by the same
rulers and subject to the same invasions, with Tadzhikistan providing access to the plains of Transoxiana for generations of conquerors
from the south and the east. During the sixth century BC it became
part of the empire of the Persian Cyrus I of the Achaemenian
dynasty; in the fourth century BC (334–1) it was conquered by
Alexander the Great; after his death and the subsequent dismem-
berment of his empire it formed part of the Graeco-Bactrian state.
At the turn of the millennium it was overrun by invading Scythian
(Saka-Massagete) tribes. They in turn were driven southwards
(eventually into India) by the Greater Yueh-Chih, a people whom

the Greek geographer Strabo (first century BC) helps us to identify with the Tokharians. They took possession of the area known as Bactria so completely that it was thereafter called Tokharistan. One of the Tokharian clans, led by Kwei-shuang, gained ascendancy over the others and in doing so laid the foundations of the Kushan Empire, for some two centuries the foremost power in Central Asia (*c.* first to third centuries AD).

By the end of the third century AD the Kushans were in decline and in 425 their last ruler was expelled from Bactria by the incoming Huns (Ephthalites). It is possible that these Huns were of Turkic origin, but the first indisputably Turkic irruption into the area was during the sixth to eighth centuries, when the power of the Turkish Khaganate was at its height. The Arabs conquered Central Asia in the mid-seventh century, but there was a new Turkic influx under the Karakhanids in the tenth century and the Seljuks in the eleventh and twelfth centuries. The original inhabitants of most of Central Asia were Iranian-speakers of the eastern group, but the successive waves of Turkic immigrants caused a Turkification of the region which was so pervasive that even the Mongol invaders (thirteenth century) were affected by it. By the fourteenth century, both the Ulus of Dzhuchi (also known as the Golden Horde) and the Ulus of Chagatai were Turkic states and Timur himself, though of Mongol descent, spoke a form of Turkish. The incursions of the Uzbek tribes from the Kipchak steppe (*Desht-i Kipchak*) in the early sixteenth century put the final seal on the Turkification of Transoxiana. The only peoples to escape this process were the Pamiri (Galchah) peoples in the high valleys of the western Pamirs (see p. 375), who remained speakers of East Iranian languages (as the early inhabitants of the area had been) and the forebears of the Tadzhiks, who were speakers of a West Iranian language very close to Persian.

It is possible that the Tadzhiks formed a distinctive ethnic group as early as the eighth century AD, but apart from their language, their main distinguishing feature was that they were sedentary, unlike the nomadic Turks and Mongols. The name by which they have come to be known has undergone several shifts of meaning, indicative, perhaps, of the tenuousness of their national identity in the early stages. It is derived from the Arabic tribal name *Taiy*; the original form was *Tazik/Tezik*, which came to be used simply for 'Arab' in Central Asia; later, by extension, it was used for the Iranian subjects of the Arabs, in contrast to the Turks; a further widening brought it to mean anyone who had accepted Islam, i.e.

'a Muslim'. For Russians in the sixteenth and seventeenth centuries, the implication was wider still: simply 'a trader from Central Asia'. This connection with trade and an essentially urban way of life was so strong that until the early twentieth century the Tadzhiks were often known by the alternative term *Sart*, a word used for the sedentary population of Central Asia (and applied to peoples other than the Tadzhiks, e.g. the Uzbeks).

The Tadzhiks were never a dominant factor in the kaleidoscopic changes of power that constituted Central Asian politics, but under the overlordship of the Uzbeks, small, semi-independent Tadzhik states were formed along the margin of the Uzbek lands to the south-east. In the mid-nineteenth century, as the Russian Empire steadily expanded southwards towards Afghanistan, Tadzhik centres such as Ura-Tjube and Khodzhent (now known as Lenin-abad) were annexed; at the same time the Emirate of Bukhara was also expanding and it gained control of such areas as Karategin and Darwaz in 1877–8. Thus before the end of the century the north of Tadzhikistan was under Russian rule and the south under Bukhara. In 1918 Soviet power was established in most of the former Russian possessions in Central Asia and northern Tadzhikistan was included in the Turkestan ASSR, created in April 1918. Three years later, in 1921, the Red Army entered eastern Bukhara and took Du-shanbe (though in theory the Emirate was still an independent state). There was fierce opposition from nationalist elements (mainly the so-called *Basmachis*), as well as foreign interventionists (including Enver Pasha) and the White Army; they were not finally overcome in the south-east of the Pamir region until 1925 (see p. 376).

When the National Delimitation of the Central Asian Republics took place in 1924, the Tadzhik ASSR was created as part of the Uzbek SSR; on 16 October 1929 it was transformed into the Tad-zhik SSR and acquired, in addition to its existing territory, the Khodzhent District (*okrug*), formerly a part of the Uzbek SSR (see also Uzbeks: Historical background, p. 266).

Tadzhik SSR (Respublikai Sovetii Sotsialistii Todzhikiston), also known as *Tadzhikistan*

Situated in the south-eastern corner of Central Asia, mostly in the Pamir and Tien Shan ranges (93 per cent of its territory lies in the mountains, almost half of it more than 3,000 m above sea level); it is bordered to the north by the Uzbek and Kirghiz SSRs, to the east by the People's Republic of China, to the south by Afghanistan, to the west by the Uzbek SSR. *Area*: 143,100 sq. km. *Capital*: Dushanbe, known as Stalinabad from 1929 to 1961 (population in 1979: 494,000). The Republic has 18 towns and 49 settlements. *Population* (1979): 3,806,220. Average density of population per sq. km (1979): 26.6.

Chief resources: rich deposits of minerals, including iron, tungsten, lead, zinc, copper, tin, mercury, antimony, gold, uranium, salt and fluorspar; coal, oil and natural gas; precious and semiprecious stones; its rivers are such an important source of energy that it is one of the major producers of hydroelectric power in the USSR.

Industries include: power, mining and processing of non-ferrous metals, extraction of oil, gas and coal, machine-building (particularly of equipment for the cotton industry), chemical and aluminium industries; cotton-ginning, textile, knitwear, clothing, footwear, food (particularly the drying and canning of local fruits), wine-making and other light industries; carpet-making.

Agriculture: extensive irrigation is necessary; cotton is the main crop (one of the main producers of long-staple cotton in the USSR); others include grapes, other fruits, vegetables and grain (wheat and barley); stockbreeding (particularly of sheep and cattle); pigs are also raised (123,000 head in 1979); sericulture is widespread.

The Tadzhik SSR contains within its boundaries one Autonomous Province, that of Gorno-Badakhshan. All statistics for the Tadzhik SSR automatically include the Gorno-Badakhshan Autonomous Province unless otherwise stated. For separate information on the Gorno-Badakhshan Autonomous Province see the section on the Pamiri Peoples, p. 376.

2 NUMBER AND DISTRIBUTION

Number of Tadzhiks

1926	1959	1970	1979
978,680	1,396,939	2,135,883	2,897,697

Age structure of the Tadzhik population in 1970

Age-group	Number	% of total
0–10	852,301	39.9
11–15	264,021	12.4
16–19	140,830	6.6
20–29	212,368	9.9
30–39	241,345	11.3
40–49	155,220	7.3
50–59	85,463	4.0
60 and over	156,794	7.3
age unknown	27,541	1.3

Percentage of males/females in relation to total Tadzhik population

	1926	1970
Men	52.8	50.6
Women	47.2	49.4

Percentage of married Tadzhiks in specified age-groups

Age-group	16–19	20–29	30–39	40–49	50–59	60 and over
Men						
In 1959	6.0	61.3	95.1	96.8	96.2	90.4
In 1970	2.5	55.0	94.3	96.2	94.9	89.0
Women						
In 1959	36.6	89.6	90.4	78.4	58.0	25.0
In 1970	24.9	90.0	94.8	87.7	69.2	32.3

Regional distribution of Tadzhiks

	1926	1959	1970	1979
Tadzh.ASSR/SSR	617,125 (63.1%)	1,051,173 (75.2%)	1,629,920 (76.3%)	2,237,048 (77.2%)
UzSSR (not incl. Tadz. ASSR/SSR)	350,603 (35.8%)	311,366 (22.3%)	448,541 (21.0%)	594,627 (20.5%)
Kir.ASSR/SSR	2,667 (0.3%)	15,221 (1.1%)	21,927 (1.0%)	23,209 (0.8%)
Elsewhere in USSR	8,285 (0.8%)	19,179 (1.4%)	35,495 (1.7%)	42,813 (1.5%)

Percentage of Tadzhiks in relation to total population of individual republics

	1926	1959	1970	1979
Tadzh.ASSR/SSR	74.6	53.1	56.2	58.8
UzSSR (not incl. Tadzh.ASSR)	6.7	3.8	3.8	3.9
Kir.ASSR/SSR	0.3	0.7	0.7	0.7

Migration of Tadzhiks in 1968–9

Total number of migrants: 43,900
Percentage who migrated within the TadzhSSR: 89.8
Percentage who migrated to the UzSSR: 10.2

Urban/rural distribution of Tadzhiks (in main areas of habitation)

	1926		1970	
	Urban	Rural	Urban	Rural
Tadzh. ASSR/SSR	29,568 (4.8%)	587,557 (95.2%)	416,001 (25.5%)	1,213,919 (74.5%)
UzSSR (not incl. Tadzh.ASSR)	119,256 (34.0%)	231,347 (66.0%)	112,899 (25.2%)	335,642 (74.8%)
Kir.ASSR/SSR	165 (6.2%)	2,502 (93.8%)	6,200 (28.3%)	15,727 (71.7%)

Ethnic composition of the Tadzh.ASSR/SSR

	1926	1959	1970	1979
Total population	827,083	1,980,547	2,899,602	3,806,220
Tadzhiks	617,125 (74.6%)	1,051,173 (53.1%)	1,629,920 (56.2%)	2,237,048 (58.8%)
Uzbeks	175,627 (21.2%)	455,038 (23.0%)	665,662 (23.0%)	873,199 (22.9%)
Tatars	950 (0.1%)	56,893 (2.9%)	70,803 (2.4%)	79,529 (2.1%)
Kirghiz	11,410 (1.4%)	25,665 (1.3%)	35,485 (1.2%)	48,376 (1.3%)
Kazakhs	1,636 (0.2%)	12,555 (0.6%)	8,306 (0.3%)	n.a.†
Turkmen	4,148 (0.5%)	7,115 (0.4%)	11,043 (0.4%)	13,991 (0.4%)
Russians	5,638 (0.7%)	262,611 (13.3%)	344,109 (11.9%)	395,089 (10.4%)

	1926	*1959*	*1970*	*1979*
Ukrainians	1,090	26,921	31,671	35,826
	(0.1%)	(1.4%)	(1.1%)	(0.9%)
Others	9,459	82,576	102,603	123,162
	(1.1%)	(4.1%)	(3.5%)	(3.2%)

† Specific data not available yet, hence they are included under 'Others'.

Percentage of mixed nationality marriages in the TadzhSSR

	1959	*1970*
Total	9.4	13.2
In urban areas	16.7	22.3
In rural areas	5.5	6.5

Growth rate of the TadzhSSR per 1,000 of the population

1940	*1965*	*1970*	*1979*
16.5	30.2	28.4	30.1

Size of family units (living together) in the TadzhSSR

	1970	*1979*
Average size of families	5.4	5.7
Average size of families in urban areas	4.5	4.5
Average size of families in rural areas	6.0	6.6

Percentage of family units of different sizes in relation to total number of families in the TadzhSSR

No. in family	*2*	*3*	*4*	*5*	*6*	*7*	*8*	*9*	*10 and over*
1970	12.5	14.3	15.4	13.2	12.6	11.2	8.9	5.8	6.1
1979	13.1	14.1	15.1	11.9	10.4	9.4	8.3	6.6	11.1

Urban/rural distribution in the TadzhSSR in 1970

	Urban	Rural
Total	1,076,700	1,822,902
Tadzhiks	416,001 (38.6%)	1,213,919 (66.6%)
Uzbeks	145,888 (13.5%)	519,774 (28.5%)
Tatars	63,536 (5.9%)	7,267 (0.4%)
Kirghiz	5,105 (0.5%)	30,380 (1.7%)
Turkmen	821 (0.1%)	10,222 (0.6%)
Russians	322,674 (30.0%)	21,435 (1.2%)
Ukrainians	29,430 (2.7%)	2,241 (0.1%)
Others	93,245 (8.7%)	17,664 (0.9%)

3 STATUS

The Tadzhiks enjoy full Soviet citizenship. They are found in all occupations and in all income brackets. Their standard of housing is comparable to that of other national groups in the Soviet Union. The women go out to work, but probably less than elsewhere in the Soviet Union.

Literacy

In 1926	In 1970
2.2%	Over 99%

In 1926, 15,401 Tadzhiks were literate in their own language (69.6 per cent of the total literate Tadzhik population).

Level of education per 1,000 Tadzhiks living in the TadzhSSR of 10 years of age and above

	1959	1970
Primary		
Total	210	302
Men	223	293
Women	198	311
Higher and secondary (complete and incomplete)		
Total	298	387
Men	370	452
Women	229	321
Higher only		
Total	8	21
Men	13	35
Women	2	7

Number of schools in the TadzhSSR in 1979/80 (not including special schools, e.g. for the deaf): 3,000
Number of pupils: 1,000,000*
Number of higher educational establishments in the TadzhSSR in 1979/80: 9
Number of students: 55,000*
* These figures refer to the total number of pupils/students in the TadzhSSR and therefore include Tadzhiks and non-Tadzhiks alike.

4 LANGUAGE

The national language is Tadzhik. It belongs to the South-West Iranian group of languages. It is closely related to Persian, with which it shares a common literary and linguistic heritage. Differences between literary Persian and literary Tadzhik are of comparatively recent date: Classical Persian was used until the Soviet period, after which local forms, earlier considered to be colloquialisms, were introduced into the literary language. There are four main dialect groups: the northern (Samarkand-Bukhara, east and west Ferghana, Ura-Tjube, Pendzhikent, etc.), the central (Zeravshan, Rishtan and Sokh), the southern (Badakhshan, north and south Kulab, Karategin, etc.) and the south-eastern (Darwaz group). The differences between them are phonetic. The central dialect of the Zeravshan valley provides the educated norm of present-day pronunciation.

Tadzhik is used along with Russian for administrative, judicial and other official proceedings.

Percentage of Tadzhiks claiming Tadzhik as their mother tongue

	1926	1959	1970	1979
Total	98.3	98.1	98.5	97.8
In urban areas	99.3	96.4	96.7	n.a.
In rural areas	98.1	98.6	99.1	n.a.

Percentage of Tadzhiks with good knowledge of Russian

	1926	1959	1970	1979
As mother tongue	0.0 (18 people)	0.6	0.6	0.8
As second language	n.a.	n.a.	15.4	29.6

Percentage of speakers claiming Tadzhik as their mother tongue in the Tadzh.ASSR/SSR

1926	1970
74.2	56.3 (of these, 99.3% are Tadzhiks)

The majority of schools in the Tadzhik SSR are Tadzhik-medium schools; they provide the full range of schooling (primary, secondary complete and incomplete). In 1958 the following languages were also used as media of instruction in the TadzhSSR: Russian and probably also Kazakh, Kirghiz, Turkmen and Uzbek. Outside the TadzhSSR, in 1958 Tadzhik was used as a medium of instruction in the Kazakh, Kirghiz and Uzbek SSRs (Lipsett, pp. 185–6). More recent information is not available. There is one university in the TadzhSSR, the Lenin Tadzhik State University (founded in 1948) in Dushanbe. It has departments of Tadzhik Philology and Arabic and Persian Language and Literature. Tuition in most subjects is in Tadzhik and Russian. There are also a number of specialized institutes (e.g. of Medicine, Agriculture), where tuition is primarily in Russian.

In the TadzhSSR there are radio and television broadcasts in Tadzhik, as well as in Russian and Uzbek. There are also radio and television broadcasts in Tadzhik in the UzSSR.

In the TadzhSSR newspapers are published in Tadzhik, as well as in Russian and Uzbek. Newspapers in Tadzhik are also published in the UzSSR. From 1912 to 1913 two Persian-Uzbek papers were published in Bukhara, *Bukhara-i sharif* ('Bukhara the Noble') and

Turan ('Turan'). In 1919 a weekly Persian paper appeared in Samarkand. The first Tadzhik newspaper was *Idi Todzhik* ('Tadzhik Festival'), which first appeared in March 1925; it has had its name changed and since 1955 has come out under the title *Todzhikistoni Soveti* ('Soviet Tadzhikistan'). Other Tadzhik papers include: *Komsomoli Todzhikiston* ('Tadzhik Komsomol' – first appeared in 1930), *Pioneri Todzhikiston* ('Tadzhik Pioneer' – first appeared in 1932) and *Maorif wa madanijat* ('Education and Culture' – first appeared in 1932). The first journal in Tadzhik was *Shu'lai inkilob* ('Flame of Revolution'), which was published from April 1919 to December 1921. It was followed by several others, including *Kommunisti Todzhikiston* ('Communist of Tadzhikistan' – first appeared in 1936) *Maktabi Soveti* ('Soviet School' – first appeared in 1926), *Sadoi Shark* ('Voice of the East' – first appeared in 1939) and *Zanoni Todzhikiston* ('Tadzhik Women' – first appeared in 1932).

Books and pamphlets are published in Tadzhik in the TadzhSSR, as well as in other republics in the Soviet Union (e.g. a total of 218 titles in 1976; of these, 49 were specialized textbooks on technical and scientific subjects).

Number of newspapers, journals and other periodicals published in the TadzhSSR in selected years, with annual circulation

	1965	1979
No. of newspapers	48 (119,000,000)	59 (258,000,000)
In Tadzhik only	35 (69,000,000)	51 (165,000,000)
No. of journals and periodicals	37 (3,400,000)	55 (17,000,000)
In Tadzhik only	12 (2,700,000)	17 (10,000,000)

Number of books and pamphlets published in Tadzhik in selected years throughout the Russian Empire/USSR

	1913	1940	1965	1979
No. of titles	43	300	330	306
Print run	——	2,476,000	2,929,000	3,767,000

Number of books and pamphlets published in the TadzhSSR in 1979, with print run

Total no. of titles	705 (5,500,000)
No. of titles in Tadzhik	301 (3,800,000)

Scripts and alphabets

Until 1930   Arabic script
1930–40   Latin script
1940   Cyrillic script

5 RELIGION

Most Tadzhiks are Sunni Muslims (Hanafi school) but there are some Shi'i communities, mainly amongst the Mountain Tadzhiks (see p. 379). The Tadzhiks come under the jurisdiction of the Spiritual Directorate of Central Asia and Kazakhstan. The Directorate's representative (*Kazi*) in the Tadzhik SSR is Haji Abulladzhan Kalonov.

6 OUTSIDE THE SOVIET UNION

There are some 2,000,000 Tadzhiks in Afghanistan, but as the term is used there to include all Persian speakers, this figure does not reflect the size of the community that is ethnically close to the Soviet Tadzhiks. The nearest relations of the latter are those who live in the Maimana-Badakhshan region. There are also some 20,000 Tadzhiks in China and small groups in northern Iran and Pakistan.

TURKMEN/TURCOMANS

Own name: *Türkmen*; Russian name: *Turkmeny*.

Tribal awareness is still strong amongst the Turkmen. The main modern groupings are as follows: *Tekke, Yomut, Ersary, Chaudor, Salyr/Salor, Saryk* and *Göklen*.

The majority live in the Turkmen SSR, but there are also groups of Turkmen in the Uzbek, Tadzhik and Kazakh SSRs, in the Karakalpak ASSR and in the Stavropol' Territory (*kraj*) of the RSFSR (for the last-mentioned see p. 264).

1 HISTORICAL BACKGROUND

Turkmenia has been inhabited since prehistoric times. Its earliest inhabitants were Iranian-speaking tribes such as the Massagetes. It formed part of the Achaemenian Empire from the sixth to the fourth centuries BC, then fell to the Parthians. As the Parthian Empire weakened in the early third century AD, the Sasanids established control over southern Turkmenia. In the fifth century the area was invaded by Huns (Ephthalites), who drove the Sasanids back to the Kopet Dag mountains. In the mid-seventh century the Arabs invaded Khorasan and shortly afterwards established a capital at Merv (modern Mary) in south-east Turkmenia, which served as a base for their subsequent conquest of Transoxiana. The Samanid dynasty of Bukhara held sway over most of Turkmenia from the late ninth century until the rise of the Ghaznavids at the end of the tenth century.

Turkic tribes had been penetrating the south-western region of Central Asia since the fifth and sixth centuries, gradually changing it from an Iranian-speaking into a Turkic-speaking preserve. The decisive influx came somewhat later, however, when Oghuz tribes (originally from Mongolia) migrated into the area between the Urals and the Aral Sea in the tenth century. By the end of the century, those who had taken possession of the right bank of the Syr Darya had accepted Islam. Makdisi, an Arab historian of the same period, refers to these people as 'Turkmen', the earliest use of this term. The etymology of the word is unclear, but it is possible that it was at first intended to distinguish between the Muslim and the non-Muslim Oghuz. Whatever its origin, it eventually ousted the term 'Oghuz' completely, making the latter obsolete by the Mongol period. During the eleventh century there was a great Seljuk-Oghuz expansion to the south-west: by 1048 the Seljuks had swept through Azerbaidzhan, Mesopotamia and Asia Minor; Merv had already been taken in 1036 and the Ghaznavids were expelled from Khorasan in 1059. The Oghuz tribes who moved into this area were the principal forebears of the modern Turkmen; those who continued their migration further to the west gradually lost their ethnic identity, the only significant Oghuz/Turkmen states to be founded outside Central Asia being those of the Kara-koyunlu and Ak-koyunlu dynasties in Azerbaidzhan in the fifteenth century (see p. 106).

By the fourteenth and fifteenth centuries the Oghuz tribes in

Turkmenia had coalesced to the point where it becomes possible to regard them as a single people, though their tribal divisions remained so strong that they were bound together by little more than a common language and common traditions. Each tribe had its own lands, which it defenced against other tribes as fiercely as against any other intruders. Territorial unity was not encouraged by the fact that during the Mongol period Turkmenia was divided between the Ulus of Dzhuchi (i.e. the Golden Horde), of Chagatai and of Hulagu (i.e. the Il-Khans of Persia). The south was always vulnerable to attack from Persia and had frequently formed part of Persian empires since the days of the Achaemenians. In the fifteenth to seventeenth centuries it was again under Persian rule, this time of the Safavids, while the north was under the sway of the Uzbek khans of Khiva and Bukhara. There was constant warfare in the area, however, and no one could truly be said to be master of it for long. In the early seventeenth century Shah Abbas (1585–1626) settled some 15,000 Kurds in the Kopet Dag mountains, in an attempt to protect the north-eastern borders of his empire (see p. 208). Nadir Shah invaded Turkmenia in the early eighteenth century and went on to take possession of Khiva and Bukhara in 1740. In the second half of the eighteenth century Bukhara regained its power and ravaged the neighbouring states. The Emir Ma'sum of Bukhara (who assumed the title Shah Murad) took Merv in 1785; having laid waste the city and destroyed its famous irrigation system, he deported almost the entire population to Bukhara. Amongst the deportees there was a community of Persians, whose descendants are still to be found in Bukhara (see p. 357).

From the sixteenth century water shortages had gradually caused the Turkmen tribes to move to the oases of southern Turkmenia. By the early nineteenth century the Tekke were settled in the region of the Ahal and Tedzhent oases, the Sariks round the Merv oasis, the Salors on the upper reaches of the Tedzhent River, the Yomuts between Khiva and Khorasan, the Ersary on the upper reaches of the Amu Darya and the Göklen between the Atrek and Gurgan Rivers. The Tekke and the Ersary were the largest tribes at this period, numbering some 40,000 tents; the Yomuts and the Sariks were half their size, with 20,000 tents each. The Göklen were next, followed by the Salor, the smallest of the six main groupings. The disposition of the tribes was still far from permanent and raids and reprisals made them move *en masse* to new territory on more than one occasion. They vacillated between submission to the Persian

governor of Khorasan and the Khan of Khiva, but continued to
make forays into the territory of both. The attack on the Persians
in 1861 was particularly successful and as a result of it they flooded
the Khivan and Bukharan markets with Persian slaves (see p. 356).
By this time the Tekke had gained supremacy over the other tribes;
they wrested Merv from the Sariks and the Sariks in turn took over
the territory of the Salors. In 1871 the Salors were incorporated
into the Tekke confederation.

At this juncture Russia had control over the Kazakh steppes and
was rapidly reducing the Khanates to a state of vassaldom. The
Turkmen lands were, inevitably, the next objective. The campaign
against them was commenced in 1877, but it was the battle of Gök
Tepe in 1881 that finally sealed the Russian conquest of Turkmenia.
Merv, Sarakhs and Pende fell soon after, opening the road to
Afghanistan. These new acquisitions aroused great concern in Eng-
land, who saw its own position in the sub-continent threatened.
After a tense period of confrontation in 1885–6, it was agreed that
there should be a demarcation of Afghanistan's northern border.
A joint Anglo-Russian Boundary Commission was appointed and
in 1895 agreement was reached on the division of territory, establishing a limit to Russia's expansion to the south and curbing for
almost a century the spread of its sphere of influence in this direction. As a result of the demarcation, some of the Turkmen tribes,
like the Mountain Tadzhiks, found themselves separated from their
kin by the international boundary (see p. 376).

In 1899 the District (*oblast'*) of Transcaspia was added to the
Turkestan Territory (*kraj*), which had been established in Transoxiana in 1867 (originally as a *general-gubernatorstvo* 'Governor-Ge-
neralate'). In 1916 Turkmenia, like the rest of Central Asia, was
involved in the great revolt prompted by the conscription of the
indigenous peoples (formerly exempt from all forms of military
service) for non-combatant duties in the army. The Bolsheviks
attempted to seize power there in 1917, but were unable to establish
themselves permanently. The Turkestan ASSR, which encompassed Transcaspia, was proclaimed on 30 April 1918 (as part of
the RSFSR), but in July of that year Soviet rule in Ashkhabad was
overthrown by nationalist elements (including Mensheviks and
right-wing Social Revolutionaries), aided by a British mission
from Meshhed. An independent government was set up and at its
invitation, British troops (under General Malleson) were garrisoned
in Ashkhabad. The new state posed a serious threat to Soviet-held

Tashkent, but not for long, however, for it fell soon after the withdrawal of the British force and by early 1920 the region was firmly in the hands of the Red Army (led by Frunze and Kujbyshev). In 1924 the National Delimitation of Central Asian Republics took place, as a result of which the Turkmen and Uzbek SSRs, the Kazakh, Kirghiz and Tadzhik ASSRs and the Karakalpak Autonomous Province were created. The Turkmen SSR came into being on 27 October 1924; its territory included the former Transcaspian District (*oblast'*), the Ashkhabad, Krasnovod, Tedzhend and Merv Districts (*ujezdy*) and the Turkmen regions of the former Khorezmian (Khivan) and Bukharan People's Republics (e.g. the Tashauz and Urgench regions in the former and the Chardzhou and Kerki in the latter).

Turkmen SSR (Turkmenistan Sovet Sotsialistik Respublikasy), also known as *Turkmenia* or *Turkmenistan*

Situated in south-west Central Asia, in the desert zone, bordered to the west by the Caspian Sea; it is bordered to the south by Iran, to the south-east by Afghanistan, to the north-east by the Uzbek SSR, to the north by the Kazakh SSR. *Area*: 488,100 sq. km. *Capital*: Ashkhabad, known as Askhabad until 1919, as Poltoratsk from 1919 to 1927 (population in 1979: 312,000). The Republic has 15 towns and 74 settlements. *Population* (1979): 2,764,748. Average density of population per sq. km (1979): 5.7.

Chief resources: major reserves of oil and natural gas; important sources of iodine and bromine, natural sodium sulphate (the Kara-Bogaz-Gol adjoining the Caspian Sea is one of the world's largest deposits), ozocerite, bentonite, sulphur and potash; there are also deposits of lead, zinc, copper, mercury, common salt and a variety of building materials (sands, clays, limestones, etc.).

Industries include: extraction of oil and natural gas (one of the main producers of oil and gas in the USSR), oil refining, mining of sulphur and sodium sulphate, power and chemical industries; textile, food (mainly directed towards the processing of local produce, particularly meat), wine-making and other light industries; carpet-making (hand and factory) is of major importance.

Agriculture: irrigation is essential for most of the land under cultivation; the main crop is cotton (one of the main cotton-producing areas of the USSR); others include grain (wheat, barley, maize, sorghum and millet), grapes, potatoes and other vegetables and fodder crops (particularly lucerne); stockbreeding is highly developed; sheep are reared for astrakhan pelts and wool for carpet-making; horses, camels and pigs are also raised (148,000 head of pigs in 1979); sericulture is well established and fishing is gaining in importance.

2 NUMBER AND DISTRIBUTION

Number of Turkmen

	1926	1959	1970	1979
	763,940	1,001,585	1,525,284	2,027,913

Age structure of the Turkmen population in 1970

Age–group	Number	% of total
0–10	585,914	38.4
11–15	192,930	12.6
16–19	102,094	6.7
20–29	147,103	9.6
30–39	164,295	10.8
40–49	114,046	7.5
50–59	71,046	4.7
60 and over	101,051	6.6
age unknown	46,805	3.1

Percentage of males/females in relation to total Turkmen population

	1926	1970
Men	52.5	50.1
Women	47.5	49.9

Percentage of married Turkmen in specified age-groups

Age group	16–19	20–29	30–39	40–49	50–59	60 and over
Men						
In 1959	8.4	68.6	94.7	95.0	91.6	80.4
In 1970	4.8	61.3	92.8	94.4	91.8	81.0
Women						
In 1959	32.0	92.3	88.6	70.1	53.4	28.0
In 1970	19.1	86.9	94.5	85.8	62.8	34.2

Regional distribution of Turkmen

	1926	1959	1970	1979
TurkSSR	719,792 (94.2%)	923,724 (92.2%)	1,416,700 (92.9%)	1,891,695 (93.3%)
UzSSR	25,954 (3.4%)	54,804 (5.6%)	71,041 (4.7%)	92,285 (4.5%)
Elsewhere in USSR	18,194 (2.5%)	23,057 (2.3%)	37,543 (2.4%)	43,933 (2.2%)

Percentage of Turkmen in relation to total population of individual republics

	1926	1959	1970	1979
TurkSSR	73.8	60.9	65.6	68.4
UzSSR	0.5	0.7	0.6	0.6

Migration of Turkmen in 1968–9

Total number of migrants: 21,200.
Percentage who migrated within the TurkSSR: 96.4.
Percentage who migrated to the UzSSR: 3.6.

Urban/rural distribution of Turkmen (in main areas of habitation)

	1926		1970	
	Urban	Rural	Urban	Rural
TurkSSR	9,790 (1.4%)	710,002 (98.6%)	448,872 (31.7%)	967,828 (68.3%)
UzSSR	836 (3.2%)	25,118 (96.8%)	8,761 (12.3%)	62,280 (87.7%)

Ethnic composition of the TurkSSR

	1926	1959	1970	1979
Total population	975,599	1,516,375	2,158,880	2,764,748
Turkmen	719,792	923,724	1,416,700	1,891,695
	(73.8%)	(60.9%)	(65.6%)	(68.4%)
Uzbeks	104,971	125,231	179,498	233,730
	(10.8%)	(8.3%)	(8.3%)	(8.5%)
Kazakhs	9,471	69,552	68,519	79,539
	(1.0%)	(4.6%)	(3.2%)	(2.9%)
Tatars	4,769	29,946	36,457	40,432
	(0.5%)	(2.0%)	(1.7%)	(1.5%)
Russians	75,357	262,701	313,079	349,170
	(7.7%)	(17.3%)	(14.5%)	(12.6%)
Ukrainians	6,877	20,955	35,398	37,118
	(0.7%)	(1.4%)	(1.6%)	(1.3%)
Others	54,362	84,266	109,229	133,064
	(5.5%)	(5.5%)	(5.1%)	(4.8%)

Percentage of mixed nationality marriages in the TurkSSR

	1959	1970
Total	8.5	12.1
In urban areas	14.9	20.0
In rural areas	2.5	3.4

Growth rate of the TurkSSR per 1,000 of the population

1940	1965	1970	1979
17.4	30.2	28.6	27.3

Size of family units (living together) in the TurkSSR

	1970	1979
Average size of families	5.2	5.5
Average size of families in urban areas	4.6	4.6
Average size of families in rural areas	6.0	6.5

Percentage of family units of different sizes in relation to total number of families in the TurkSSR

No. in family	2	3	4	5	6	7	8	9	10 and over
1970	14.6	16.2	15.8	12.3	11.4	9.7	8.2	5.7	6.1
1979	13.8	15.3	16.2	12.0	10.3	8.8	7.7	6.1	9.8

Urban/rural distribution in the TurkSSR in 1970

	Urban	Rural
Total	1,034,199	1,124,681
Turkmen	448,872 (43.4%)	967,828 (86.1%)
Uzbeks	98,054 (9.5%)	81,444 (7.2%)
Kazakhs	39,875 (3.9%)	28,644 (2.5%)
Tatars	33,464 (3.2%)	2,993 (0.3%)
Russians	299,471 (29.0%)	13,608 (1.2%)
Ukrainians	29,486 (2.9%)	5,912 (0.5%)
Others	84,977 (8.2%)	24,252 (2.2%)

3 STATUS

The Turkmen enjoy full Soviet citizenship. They are found in all occupations and in all income brackets. Their standard of housing is comparable to that of other national groups in the Soviet Union. The women go out to work, but probably less than elsewhere in the Soviet Union.

Literacy

In 1926	In 1970
2.3%	Over 99%

In 1926, 15,884 Turkmen were literate in their own language (91.1 per cent of the total literate Turkmen population).

Level of education per 1,000 Turkmen living in the TurkSSR of 10 years of age and above

	1959	1970
Primary		
Total	174	279
Men	185	277
Women	165	281
Higher and secondary (complete and incomplete)		
Total	363	433
Men	427	486
Women	302	382
Higher only		
Total	11	25
Men	20	42
Women	3	10

Number of schools in the TurkSSR in 1979/80 (not including special schools, e.g. for the deaf): 1,800
Number of pupils: 700,000*
Number of higher educational establishments in the TurkSSR in 1979/80: 6
Number of students: 34,400*
*These figures refer to the total number of pupils/students in the TurkSSR and therefore include Turkmen and non-Turkmen alike.

4 LANGUAGE

The national language is Turkmen. It belongs to the South Turkic group (*Fundamenta* classification); it can also be classed as belonging to the Oghuz group, Oghuz-Turkmen sub-group (Baskakov).

Turkmen consists of a number of dialects that fall into two main divisions: those of the major tribes, such as the Tekke, Yomut, Salor, Saryk, Ersary and Göklen; those of the tribes bordering Iran and Uzbekistan, such as the Nokhurli, Khasarli, Anauli, etc. Within these main divisions, the individual tribal dialects differ one from the other. The modern literary language is based on an amalgam of the main dialects.

The Truchmen language, spoken by the Turkmen of the North Caucasus, is basically Turkmen, but much influenced by the neighbouring Turkic language, Nogai (see section on the Truchmen).

The Turkmen vocabulary contains loan-words from Arabic, Persian and Russian. The early Russian loans underwent some phonetic modification, e.g. *semavar* for *samovar*, but later Soviet loans are adopted in their original form. Turkmen has also borrowed individual morphemes and affixed them to their own roots, e.g. *kontrurgy*, 'counter-blow'. The modern vocabulary has been enlarged through using the resources of the language itself (semantic widenings, new combinations, calques, etc.), as well as by direct loans from Russian. The dialects have also contributed to the development of the standard language, since a particular tribe often has a rich vocabulary for certain occupations (e.g. the Ahal-Tekke for viticulture, the Yomuts for fishing) and some of their terms have been incorporated into the literary language.

Turkmen is used along with Russian for administrative, judicial and other official proceedings, though apparently to a lesser extent than the languages of the titular peoples in some of the other Union republics (street signs and other public notices, for example, are all in Russian in Ashkhabad, whereas in Tashkent they are in Uzbek or Uzbek and Russian).

Percentage of Turkmen claiming Turkmen as their mother tongue

	1926	*1959*	*1970*	*1979*
Total	97.3	98.9	98.9	98.7
In urban areas	98.8	97.3	97.2	n.a.
In rural areas	97.3	99.4	99.6	n.a.

Percentage of Turkmen with good knowledge of Russian

	1926	*1959*	*1970*	*1979*
As mother tongue	0.0 (72 people)	0.7	0.8	1.0
As second language	n.a.	n.a.	15.4	25.4

Percentage of speakers claiming Turkmen as their mother tongue in the TurkSSR

1926	*1970*
73.4	65.5 (of these, 99.3% are Turkmen)

Turkmen is used as the medium of instruction in most rural schools in the Turkmen SSR; in urban areas there are more

Russian-medium schools, but the overall majority of schools in the TurkSSR are probably Turkmen-medium, providing the full range of schooling (primary, secondary complete and incomplete). In 1958 Russian, Uzbek and Kazakh were also used as media of instruction in the TurkSSR; outside the TurkSSR, Turkmen was used as a medium of instruction in the Uzbek SSR and possibly also in the Tadzhik SSR (Lipsett, pp. 185–6); in the RSFSR, it was used as a medium of instruction in grades 1–4 at this period (Silver, p. 34). More recent information is not available. There is one university, the Gorky Turkmen State University (founded in 1950) in Ashkhabad, where there is a department of Turkmen Philology; apart from that there does not appear to be any tuition in Turkmen. There are also some specialized institutes (e.g. of Pedagogy), where most, if not all, tuition is in Russian.

In the Turkmen SSR there are radio and television broadcasts in Turkmen, as well as in Russian.

Newspapers, journals and other periodicals are published in Turkmen, as well as in Russian. There was no real Turkmen-language press before the Revolution. The first Soviet Turkmen paper was *Turkmenistan* ('Turkmenia'), which began to appear in 1920. Amongst the main Turkmen-language newspapers of today are *Sovet Turkmenistany* ('Soviet Turkmenia' – first appeared in 1920) and *Jash kommunist* ('Young Communist' – first appeared in 1925); the main periodicals include *Sovet Turkmenistanynyn ajallary* ('Soviet Turkmen Women' – first appeared in 1952) and *Sovet edebijaty* ('Soviet Literature' – first appeared in 1928).

Books and pamphlets are published in Turkmen in the Turkmen SSR, as well as in other republics of the Soviet Union (e.g. a total of 93 titles in 1976; of these, 10 were specialized textbooks on technical and scientific subjects).

Number of newspapers, journals and other periodicals published in the TurkSSR in selected years, with annual circulation

	1965	1979
No. of newspapers	37 (81,000,000)	58 (196,000,000)
In Turkmen only	27 (60,000,000)	45 (143,000,000)
No. of journals and periodicals	30 (3,500,000)	31 (9,300,000)
In Turkmen only	11 (2,900,000)	15 (9,000,000)

Number of books and pamphlets published in Turkmen in selected years throughout the Russian Empire/USSR

	1913	1940	1965	1979
No. of titles	——	280	352	282
Print run	——	2,015,000	3,009,000	4,974,000

Number of books and pamphlets published in the TurkSSR in 1979, with print run

Total no. of titles	572 (6,300,000)
No. of titles in Turkmen	278 (5,000,000)

Scripts and alphabets

Until 1922	Arabic script, Arabic alphabet
1923–9	Arabic script, Arabic alphabet, slightly modified (additional modifications introduced in 1925)
1929–40	Latin script (somewhat modified in 1930, 1934 and 1936)
1940	Cyrillic script

The latest alphabet is considered to be reasonably satisfactory for the representing of Turkmen and also Russian loan-words, but there is room for further improvement, as there is no way at present of distinguishing between the long and short vowels of Turkmen.

5 RELIGION

The Turkmen are Sunni Muslims (Hanafi school). They come under the jurisdiction of the Spiritual Directorate for Central Asia and Kazakhstan. There is a representative (*Kazi*) of the Directorate in the Turkmen SSR.

The Turkmen have always had a reputation for fierce, unorthodox piety. The women did not wear the veil, but worked and at times fought alongside their menfolk. They never had many mosques, though the number did increase sharply at the turn of the century when the Russians tried to promote 'orthodox' Islam: in 1890–6 there were 161 mosques, by 1911, 481. The number of mullahs also rose in proportion (Demidov, *Sufizm* . . . p. 103). Now, seventy years later, there are only five mosques open for worship in Turkmenia (op. cit., p. 17). They include the Talhatan-Baba in Jolatan, the Hodzha Yusup-Baba (Hamadani) in Bajram Ali and one in the vicinity of Ashkhabad.

Sufi orders have traditionally had great influence amongst the Turkmen. Some of the earliest and greatest Sufi centres were in Turkmenia (e.g. at Merv, Sarakhs and Nisa). The many famous sheikhs connected with the region include Abul Abbas Seyyari (d. 953/4, buried near Merv), Hodzha Yusuf Hamadani (d. 1140, buried near Merv), Abu Seid Meikheni (a disciple of Junaidi, d. 1049, buried in the village of Meana, Kaakhkinskij Region) and Gözli-Ata (fourteenth century, buried north-east of Krasnovodsk). The tombs of these and of many others besides have been places of pilgrimage for centuries and are still visited daily (op. cit., p. 148). One of the most sacred is that of Kurban-myrat, the Naqshbandi sheikh who was instrumental in rousing the Turkmen to make their historic last stand against the Russians in 1881. He is buried slightly to the north of the ruins of Gök Tepe fortress. Traditionally, a cemetery would develop around the tomb (or even legendary halting place) of a holy man, who, as *gonam-bashy* ('head of the cemetery'), would be able to extend his *baraka* ('benevolence') over the dead. Such cemeteries were often found along distinct routes, radiating across the country in all directions. They were usually tended by a sheikh (*ishan*) and formed links in the network of Sufi centres that embraced the whole region. When the pre-Revolutionary Russian government tried to oppose 'orthodox' (and therefore 'visible') Islam to the nebulous Sufis, the rise in the numbers of mosques and registered mullahs appeared to be accompanied by a corresponding drop in the numbers of sheikhs and *murids* ('disciples'); by 1904, in the Ashkhabad District (*ujezd*), for example, there were only 13 known *ishans* and 626 *murids* for a Turkmen population of 70,000 (op. cit., p. 103). However, Demidov's book makes it quite clear that far from dying away, Sufism is very much alive in Turkmenia today. He puts forward the interesting idea that a map should be made showing the holy places in the region, since pilgrimages to them are still such a common phenomenon and represent a major problem for atheist 'missionaries' to combat (op. cit., p. 161).

6 OUTSIDE THE SOVIET UNION

There are approximately the following numbers of Turkmen in:

Afghanistan	270,000	400,000
Iraq	90,000	500,000
Iran	330,000	500,000
Jordan	2,000	—
Syria	2,000	—
Turkey	70,000	300,000

(The first column gives Soviet estimates, the second those in *Soviet Asian Ethnic Frontiers*, p. 84.)

The main tribal groupings outside the USSR are:

Afghanistan	Tekke, Ersary, Salor, Chaudor, Beshir
Iran	Tekke, Göklen, Yomut

KIRGHIZ

Own name: *Kyrgyz*; Russian name: *Kirgizy*.

The Kirghiz (not to be confused with the Kazakhs, who were also known as 'Kirghiz', 'Kirghiz-Kaisak' or 'Kazakh-Kirghiz': see p. 286) were formerly sometimes called the 'Black Kirghiz' (*Kara Kyrgyz*) or the 'Kirghiz *Dikokamennyje*'. They occasionally referred to themselves as *Burut*, the name by which they were known to the Kalmyks.

The majority live in the Kirghiz SSR; there are also groups of Kirghiz in the Namangan, Andidzhan and Ferghana Districts (*oblasti*) of the Uzbek SSR in the Gorno-Badakhshan, Garm and Pamir regions of the Tadzhik SSR and in the part of the Kazakh SSR that is adjacent to the Kirghiz SSR.

1 HISTORICAL BACKGROUND

A people identifiable with the Kirghiz are first mentioned in ancient Chinese chronicles under the name *Kien-kuen*. The name *Kyrgyz* is first found in the early Turkic Orkhon inscriptions (eighth century AD). The Kirghiz were at that time settled on the Upper Yenisei River and are therefore sometimes referred to as 'Yenisei Kirghiz'; they appear to have been responsible for the Turkic inscriptions dating from the fifth to seventh centuries that have been found on this section of the Yenisei River. In 840 they overthrew the Uighur state in north-west Mongolia and occupied the lands between the Yenisei and the Orkhon Rivers. They in turn were driven out by the Khitai in the early tenth century. The rise of the Mongol Empire (beginning of the thirteenth century) caused some of the Kirghiz to migrate towards the south, whilst others remained in the Minusinsk Basin, where their descendants eventually became part of the Khakass and Tuvinian groups (see p. 400). From long before this, however, Kirghiz tribes had been moving into the Tien Shan range, an area roughly equivalent to present-day Kirghizia. This region came under the rule of successive waves of Turkic peoples, such as the Turgesh, the Karluks and, from the tenth to the twelfth centuries, the Karakhanids. It was conquered by the Mongols in the thirteenth century and formed part of the Ulus of Chagatai, Genghiz Khan's second son; this Ulus also contained Samarkand and Bukhara, cities which had already had trade contacts with Kirghizia for several centuries previously. In the fourteenth century the area came under the Khanate of Mogolistan (which originally fell within the Ulus of Chagatai, but became an independent state in the fifteenth century, though remaining under the domination of Mongol khans). There was a brief alliance between the Kirghiz of the Tien Shan and the Kazakh tribes in the mid-seventeenth century, but in 1683–85 the Kirghiz lands were overrun by the Dzhungarian Oirots (Kalmyks). This prompted the migration of some of the Kirghiz to Eastern Turkestan (e.g. to Yarkand, Kashgar and Khotan); a number of them returned to the Tien Shan after the Oirots had been defeated by the Manchus in 1758.

The Kirghiz began to be converted to Islam in the mid-seventeenth century. In their epics the struggle against the Oirots is portrayed as a religious war, though their attachment to Islam was in fact still very tenuous. After 1758 they were nominally Chinese subjects, but in reality they were virtually independent, governed only by their own *manaps* and *biys*. Their chief occupation was nomadic herding, in the practice of which they migrated considerable distances. During the early nineteenth century they came under attack from the Khanate of Khokand and by the 1830s had become its vassals, paying tribute to the Khan. At this period, under the influence of Khokand, Islam gained a much stronger hold on the Kirghiz. In 1868 the Khanate became a Russian Protectorate and in 1876 it was formally integrated into the Russian Empire as the Ferghana Province (*oblast'*). The Kirghiz living in the area thus also came under Russian rule. A Russian garrison had been established at Pishpek (today known as Frunze, the capital of the Kirghiz SSR) in 1862 and the conquest of the Alay Valley in 1876 completed their occupation of the region. The coming of the Russians caused some of the Kirghiz tribes to migrate to the Pamirs and Afghanistan. In 1916 Central Asia was shaken by a serious outbreak of violence when the Russian government ordered the conscription of the indigenous Turkic peoples for non-combatant duties in the army; it prompted another major migration of the Kirghiz, this time to China.

After a period of great confusion and fierce fighting between the Nationalists, the White Army, the foreign Interventionists and the Red Army, Soviet power was established in Kirghizia by 1919, though the struggle continued in some parts, particularly the south, until 1922. In 1918 the Turkestan ASSR was proclaimed (as part of the RSFSR) and Kirghizia was included within it until the National Delimitation of 1924, when the Kara-Kirghiz Autonomous Province was created (also within the RSFSR). It was renamed the 'Kirghiz' Autonomous Province in May 1925 and transformed into the Kirghiz ASSR on 1 February 1926. On 5 December 1936 it became a full Union republic.

Kirghiz SSR *(Kyrgyz Sovettik Sotsialistik Respublikasy)*, also known as *Kirghizia* or *Kyrghyzstan*

Situated in the Tien Shan and north-eastern Pamir-Alay mountains; it is bordered to the north and north-west by the Kazakh SSR, to the south by the Tadzhik SSR, to the south-west by the Uzbek SSR, to the south-east by the Chinese People's Republic. *Area*: 198,500 sq. km. *Capital*: Frunze, known as Pishpek until 1926 (population in 1979: 533,000). The Republic has 18 towns and 31 settlements. *Population* (1979): 3,522,832. Average density of population per sq. km (1979): 17.8.

Chief resources: major deposits of antimony, mercury, uranium and coal (the USSR's main producer of the first two and amongst its main producers of the second two); also of oil, natural gas, lead, zinc, copper pyrites, fluorspar and other minerals; a variety of building materials, including granite, marble, limestone, marl, gypsum and loess; mountain rivers such as the Naryn, Talass and Chu provide an important source of hydroelectric power and are the basis of large-scale irrigation networks; there is excellent pasturage and some good arable land.

Industries include: power, mining and processing of non-ferrous metals, extraction of coal, gas and oil, machine-building (e.g. of agricultural machinery and precision instruments), prefabricated building units, cement and other building materials; textile, footwear, food (particularly meat and sugar) and other light industries.

Agriculture: cultivation of grain (wheat), sugar beet, tobacco and cotton; stockbreeding, particularly of fine-fleeced sheep; pigs are also raised (298,000 head in 1979).

2 NUMBER AND DISTRIBUTION

Number of Kirghiz

	1926	1959	1970	1979
	762,736	968,659	1,452,222	1,906,271

Age structure of the Kirghiz population in 1970

Age-group	Number	% of total
0–10	565,707	39.0
11–15	186,140	12.8
16–19	97,668	6.7
20–29	131,426	9.0
30–39	159,028	11.0
40–49	110,053	7.6
50–59	51,631	3.6
60 and over	123,118	8.5
age unknown	27,451	1.9

Percentage of males/females in relation to total Kirghiz population

	1926	1970
Men	52.4	49.2
Women	47.6	50.8

Percentage of married Kirghiz in specified age-groups

Age-group	16–19	20–29	30–39	40–49	50–59	60 and over
Men						
In 1959	6.9	68.0	96.4	98.0	97.8	95.0
In 1970	1.9	56.7	94.4	97.0	96.9	93.3
Women						
In 1959	44.2	90.0	89.0	77.4	58.8	28.1
In 1970	20.1	86.3	93.7	85.0	65.5	29.0

Regional distribution of Kirghiz

	1926	1959	1970	1979
Kir.ASSR/SSR	661,171 (86.7%)	836,831 (86.4%)	1,284,773 (88.5%)	1,687,382 (88.5%)
UzSSR (not incl. Tadzh.ASSR)	79,333 (10.4%)	92,695 (9.6%)	110,726 (7.6%)	142,182 (7.5%)
Tadzh.ASSR/SSR	11,410 (1.5%)	25,665 (2.7%)	35,485 (2.4%)	48,376 (2.5%)
Kaz.ASSR/SSR	10,477 (1.4%)	6,810 (0.7%)	9,612 (0.7%)	n.a.†
Elsewhere in USSR	345 (0.0%)	6,658 (0.7%)	11,626 (0.8%)	29,271 (1.5%)

*Population estimates are only available in thousands as yet.
†Since data not available, Kirghiz in the KazSSR are included in 'Elsewhere in USSR'.

Percentage of Kirghiz in relation to total population of individual republics

	1926	1959	1970	1979
Kir.ASSR/SSR	66.8	40.5	43.8	47.9
UzSSR (not incl. Tadzh.ASSR)	1.8	1.1	0.9	0.9
Tadzh.ASSR/SSR	1.4	1.3	1.2	1.3
Kaz.ASSR/SSR	0.2	0.1	0.1	n.a.

Migration of Kirghiz in 1968–9

Total number of migrants: 35,000.
Percentage who migrated within the KirSSR: 95.4.
Percentage who migrated to the UzSSR: 2.4.
Percentage who migrated to the TurkSSR: 2.2.

Urban/rural distribution of Kirghiz (in main areas of habitation)

	1926		1970	
	Urban	*Rural*	*Urban*	*Rural*
Kir.ASSR/SSR	5,556 (0.8%)	655,615 (99.2%)	185,955 (14.5%)	1,098,818 (85.5%)
UzSSR (not incl. Tadzh.ASSR)	1,949 (2.5%)	77,384 (97.5%)	6,950 (6.3%)	103,776 (93.7%)
Tadzh.ASSR/SSR	69 (0.6%)	11,341 (99.4%)	5,105 (14.4%)	30,380 (85.6%)

Ethnic composition of the Kir.ASSR/SSR

	1926	1959	1970	1979
Total population	989,971	2,065,837	2,932,805	3,522,832
Kirghiz	661,171 (66.8%)	836,831 (40.5%)	1,284,773 (43.8%)	1,687,382 (47.9%)
Uzbeks	109,776 (11.1%)	218,640 (10.6%)	332,638 (11.3%)	426,194 (12.1%)
Tatars*	4,902 (0.5%)	56,266 (2.7%)	69,373 (2.4%)	72,018 (2.0%)
Kazakhs	1,766 (0.2%)	20,067 (1.0%)	21,998 (0.8%)	27,442 (0.8%)
Uighurs	73 (0.0%)	13,757 (0.7%)	24,872 (0.8%)	29,817 (0.8%)
Kashgarlyks†	7,467 (0.8%)	—	—	—
Taranchis†	523 (0.1%)	—	—	—
Germans	4,291 (0.4%)	39,915 (1.9%)	89,834 (3.1%)	101,057 (2.9%)
Russians	116,436 (11.8%)	623,562 (30.2%)	855,935 (29.2%)	911,703 (25.9%)
Ukrainians	64,128 (6.5%)	137,031 (6.6%)	120,081 (4.1%)	109,324 (3.1%)
Others	19,438 (2.0%)	119,768 (5.8%)	133,301 (4.5%)	157,895 (4.5%)

*The increase in the Tatar population in the period 1926–59 is due in large part to the influx of the exiled Crimean Tatars; the same applies to the German population, whose numbers were augmented by the exiled Volga Germans.
† In 1959, 1970 and 1979 listed with the Uighurs.

Percentage of mixed nationality marriages in the KirSSR

	1959	*1970*
Total	12.3	14.9
In urban areas	18.1	20.9
In rural areas	9.2	10.6

Growth rate of the KirSSR per 1,000 of the population

1940	*1965*	*1970*	*1979*
16.7	24.9	23.1	21.8

Size of family units (living together) in the KirSSR

	1970	*1979*
Average size of families	4.6	4.6
Average size of families in urban areas	4.0	3.8
Average size of families in rural areas	5.1	5.3

Urban/rural distribution in the KirSSR in 1970

	Urban	*Rural*
Total population	1,097,498	1,835,307
Kirghiz	185,955 (16.9%)	1,098,818 (59.9%)
Uzbeks	119,946 (10.9%)	212,692 (11.6%)
Tatars	55,719 (5.1%)	13,654 (0.7%)
Germans	33,702 (3.1%)	56,132 (3.1%)
Russians	564,239 (51.4%)	291,696 (15.9%)
Ukrainians	61,253 (5.6%)	58,828 (3.2%)
Others	76,684 (7.0%)	103,487 (5.6%)

Percentage of family units of different sizes in relation to total number of families in the KirSSR

No. in family	2	3	4	5	6	7	8	9	10 and over
1970	17.3	19.1	19.8	14.2	10.2	7.4	5.7	3.5	2.8
1979	18.8	20.1	19.6	12.5	8.7	6.7	5.3	3.7	4.6

3 STATUS

The Kirghiz enjoy full Soviet citizenship. They are found in all occupations and in all income brackets. Their standard of housing is comparable to that of other national groups in the Soviet Union. The women go out to work, though possibly less so than elsewhere in the Soviet Union.

Literacy

In 1926	In 1970
4.6%	Over 99%

In 1926, 32,669 Kirghiz were literate in their own language (93.9 per cent of the total literate Kirghiz population).

Level of education per 1,000 Kirghiz living in the KirSSR of 10 years of age and above

	1959	1970
Primary		
Total	188	284
Men	189	282
Women	186	285
Higher and secondary (complete and incomplete)		
Total	309	407
Men	403	469
Women	228	349
Higher only		
Total	10	28
Men	17	41
Women	4	15

Number of schools in the KirSSR in 1979/80 (not including special schools, e.g. for the deaf): 1,700
Number of pupils: 900,000*
Number of higher educational establishments in the KirSSR in 1979/80: 10
Number of students: 55,100*
*These figures refer to the total number of pupils/students in the KirSSR and therefore include Kirghiz and non-Kirghiz alike.

4 LANGUAGE

The national language is Kirghiz. It belongs to the Central Turkic group (*Fundamenta* classification); it can also be classed as belonging to the Kirghiz-Kipchak group (Baskakov). It shares some characteristics with the Altai (formerly known as Oirot) language.

There are three dialect groups: the northern, south-eastern and south-western. Due to the frequent migrations of the Kirghiz their dialects have followed separate lines of development; those of the south-west have been particularly strongly influenced by the Iranian languages. Within each group there are often wide variations. The modern literary language was developed during the Soviet period and while it incorporates features from all the dialects, it is strongly biased towards the northern group. Its vocabulary is characterized by a particularly large Mongol element. It has groups of Iranian loans, relating to agriculture and trade (borrowed from the settled communities with whom the Kirghiz had contacts), Arabic loans (relating mainly to religion and abstract thought) and Russian loans, the majority of which date from the Soviet period.

Kirghiz is used, along with Russian, for administrative, judicial and other official proceedings.

Percentage of Kirghiz claiming Kirghiz as their mother tongue

	1926	*1959*	*1970*	*1979*
Total	99.0	98.7	98.8	97.9
In urban areas	96.1	97.4	97.6	n.a.
In rural areas	99.0	98.9	99.0	n.a.

Percentage of Kirghiz with good knowledge of Russian

	1926	*1959*	*1970*	*1979*
As mother tongue	0.0 (141 people)	0.3	0.3	0.5
As second language	n.a.	n.a.	19.1	29.4

Percentage of speakers claiming Kirghiz as their mother tongue in the Kir.ASSR/ SSR

1926	*1970*
66.6	44.0 (of these, 99.2 per cent are Kirghiz)

In the Kirghiz SSR Kirghiz-medium schools provide the full range of schooling (primary, secondary complete and incomplete). In 1958 in the KirSSR there were also schools in which the following languages were used as media of instruction: Russian, Uzbek, Tadzhik and possibly Kazakh (or Dungan?); outside the KirSSR, Kirghiz was used as a medium of instruction in the Uzbek SSR and possibly also in the Tadzhik SSR (Lipsett, pp. 185–6). More recent information is not available. The Kirghiz State University in Frunze (founded in 1951) provides tuition in most subjects in both Kirghiz and Russian. There are also a number of specialized institutes (e.g. of Agriculture, Medicine) where the tuition appears to be entirely in Russian. In the Pedagogical Institutes (which include one specially for women), there is some training in Kirghiz.

In the KirSSR there are radio and television broadcasts in Kirghiz, as well as in Russian, German and Dungan.

Newspapers are published in Kirghiz, as well as in Russian and Dungan. Before the Revolution there was no Kirghiz-language press. The first Soviet Kirghiz newspaper was *Erkin-Too* ('Free Mountains'), published in Tashkent in 1924. Amongst the main Kirghiz-language newspapers of today are *Sovettik Kyrgyzstan* ('Soviet Kirghizia' – first appeared in 1924), *Leninchil dzhash* ('Leninist Youth' – first appeared in 1926), *Mugalimder gazetasy* ('Teacher's Paper' – first appeared in 1953), *Kyrgyzstan madanijati* ('Kirghiz Culture' – first appeared in 1967); amongst the main Kirghiz journals and periodicals are *Kommunist* ('Communist' – first appeared in 1926), *Den sooluk* ('Health' – first appeared in 1960), *Kyrgyzstan ajaldary* ('Kirghiz Women' – first appeared in 1951) and *Dzhash Leninchi* ('Young Leninist' – first appeared in 1952).

Books and pamphlets are published in Kirghiz in the KirSSR, as well as in other republics in the Soviet Union (e.g. a total of 282 titles in 1976; of these, 37 were specialized textbooks on technical and scientific subjects).

Number of newspapers, journals and other periodicals published in the KirSSR in selected years, with annual circulation

	1965	1979
No. of newspapers	83 (115,000,000)	108 (234,000,000)
In Kirghiz only	45 (64,000,000)	60 (132,000,000)
No. of journals and periodicals	54 (8,000,000)	31 (30,700,000)
In Kirghiz only	18 (2,900,000)	17 (8,600,000)

Number of books and pamphlets published in Kirghiz in selected years throughout the Russian Empire/USSR

	1913	1940	1965	1979
No. of titles	——	177	422	467
Print run	——	1,015,000	2,279,000	3,408,000

Number of books and pamphlets published in the KirSSR in 1979, with print run

Total no. of titles	1,094	(8,600,000)
No. of titles in Kirghiz	463	(3,400,000)

Scripts and alphabets

Until 1923	Arabic script, Arabic alphabet
1924–8	Arabic script, modified alphabet
1928–40	Latin script
1940	Cyrillic script

The present alphabet is considered to be adequate, but certain problems still remain and further improvements are likely to be made.

5 RELIGION

The Kirghiz are Sunni Muslims (Hanafi school). They come under the jurisdiction of the Spiritual Directorate of Central Asia and Kazakhstan. There is a representative (*Kazi*) of the Directorate in the Kirghiz SSR.

The Kirghiz, like the Kazakhs, were converted to Islam relatively late. In the nineteenth century they still subscribed to many pagan customs and beliefs, but they were, nevertheless, devout Muslims and several went on the Hajj to Mecca. Their first *ulema* came from Uzbekistan: then, as the Tatars became more active in Central Asia, from the Volga region. There are Friday mosques open for worship in Frunze and Osh, a large town in western Kirghizia. It is not known how many others are open.

The Sufi movement played an important part in the conversion of the Kirghiz to Islam. The Naqshbandi order used to be particularly powerful in this region. Nothing is known of the strength of Sufism in Kirghizia today.

6 OUTSIDE THE SOVIET UNION

There are approximately the following numbers of Kirghiz in:
Afghanistan   25,000
China   80,000
Turkey   1,000

KARAKALPAKS

Own names: *Karakalpak, Karalpak, Kalpak*; Russian name:
Karakalpaki.

The majority of Karakalpaks live in the Karakalpak ASSR (within
the Uzbek SSR), but there are also communities of Karakalpaks in
the Khorezm and Ferghana Districts (*oblasti*) of the Uzbek SSR,
the Tashauz District of the Turkmen SSR, some parts of the Kazakh
SSR and the Astrakhan District of the RSFSR.

1 HISTORICAL BACKGROUND

The Karakalpaks represent an intermingling of indigenous
Iranian-speaking peoples of the Aral Sea region with immigrant
Turkic-speakers, such as the Oghuz and Pechenegs, who began to
penetrate the western areas of Central Asia in the sixth century
AD. The Pechenegs already contained a certain Ugric element,
having previously assimilated some of the Uralic tribes (cf. the
Bashkirs). According to tradition, some of the Karakalpaks accompanied the Seljuks on their great expansion to the south and west
during the eleventh century, but the majority remained in the vicinity of the Aral Sea. The name *Karakalpak*, literally 'Black Cap',
is first found in Russian chronicles of the twelfth century, where it
is used in the Russian form *Chernyje Klobuki* to refer to a people
with whom the Kievan princes entered into alliance as a protection
against marauding Kipchak (Polovtsian/Cuman) tribes. These
'Black Caps' were given lands on the River Dniepr (in the Ukraine)
as a reward for their services. They are evidently the same people
as the Pecheneg-Oghuz settlers of the Aral region, but how or when
the term came to be applied to the group as a whole is not clear;
there is no record of the actual form *Karakalpak* being used before
the sixteenth century.

Very little is known for certain of the early history of the Karakalpaks. Many centuries of Turkic immigration into the region between the Urals and the Aral Sea had resulted in the creation of a Turkic-speaking population there. In the eleventh and twelfth centuries the Turkic element was further strengthened by an influx of Kipchak tribes. From the early thirteenth century the area was under the sway of the Golden Horde. Linguistic evidence indicates that the Karakalpaks were in close contact with the Nogais at some point and it is very probable that as the Golden Horde began to weaken and new hordes were formed, the Karakalpaks came under the Nogai Horde. By the sixteenth century, when they first begin to be referred to by name, they were settled on the lower reaches of the Syr Darya and virtually independent. They were not united: each tribe was governed by its own *bijs* and *batyrs*. In the seventeenth century they were nominally subject to the Khanate of Bukhara and later to the Little Horde of the Kazakhs. Between 1722 and 1740 they made several appeals to Peter the Great, asking for protection against the depredations of neighbouring peoples, but no practical assistance was forthcoming; meanwhile, the raids of the Kazakhs became more ruthless and this, plus the incursions of the Dzhungarians (see p. 288) caused the Karakalpaks to migrate. Some moved up the Syr Darya to the Ferghana Valley, but the majority moved closer to the Aral Sea, whilst small groups continued further westwards still, towards the Ural and Volga Rivers. Eighteenth-century sources indicate this division of the Karakalpaks by referring to them as 'upper' and 'lower' Karakalpaks. In the second half of the eighteenth century the 'lower' Karakalpaks again migrated, leaving the delta of the Syr Darya and moving south to the delta of the Amu Darya (the area roughly corresponding with the Karakalpak ASSR of today). In 1811 these Karakalpaks came under the rule of the Khanate of Khiva.

The Karakalpaks did not take kindly to Khivan rule. The following years were marked by a succession of uprisings, notably those of 1827, when they succeeded in taking the town of Kungrat, and 1855. In 1873 the part of the Khivan Khanate which lay on the right bank of the Amu Darya was annexed to Russia and the Karakalpaks living on that side of the river came under direct Russian rule; those on the opposite bank remained under the rule of the Khanate, which now became a Russian Protectorate. After the 1917 Revolution the Karakalpaks on the right bank were incorporated into the Turkestan ASSR (which was proclaimed in 1918, though fight-

ing between the various opposing factions continued until 1920).
Meanwhile, the left bank was still part of the Khivan Khanate. The
Khanate was abolished in 1920 and the Khorezm People's Soviet
Republic was established in its stead. This only lasted four years:
in 1924 it became a part of the Soviet Union and as a result of the
National Delimitation, the Karakalpak Autonomous Province (including both banks of the Amu Darya) was created within the
Kirghiz (i.e. Kazakh) ASSR (itself within the RSFSR), on 11 May
1925. On 20 March 1932 the Karakalpak Autonomous Province
was transformed into an autonomous republic, no longer attached
to the Kazakh ASSR but still within the RSFSR; on 5 December
1936 it was transferred to the Uzbek SSR and still forms part of
this Union republic today.

Karakalpak ASSR (Karakalpakstan Avtonomijaly Sovet Sotsialistik
Republikasy) also known as *Karakalpakia* or *Karakalpakstan*

Situated in the north-west of the Uzbek SSR, bordering the southern shores of the Aral Sea; it lies mostly in the desert zone, its
eastern region being taken up by the Kyzyl Kum Desert; it is
bordered to the north, north-east, and west by the Kazakh SSR, to
the south by the Turkmen SSR, to the south-east by the Uzbek
SSR. *Area*: 165,600 sq. km. *Capital*: Nukus (population in 1979:
109,000). The Republic has 9 towns and 13 settlements. *Population*
(1979): 905,500. Average density of population per sq. km (1979):
5.5.
    Chief resources: deposits of common and Glauber's salt, oil,
natural gas, non-ferrous and rare metals, building materials (granite, marble, marl, etc.), asbestos, mica and graphite.
    Industries include: mainly cotton-ginning and the processing of
other local produce; the production of building materials and some
light industry.
    Agriculture: irrigation is essential; the main crop is cotton; others
include grain (particularly rice), lucerne, grapes and other fruits,
vegetables; stockbreeding, especially of sheep for astrakhan pelts;
pigs are also raised (178,000 head in 1979); fishing; hunting; fur-
farming (of musk-rats: one of the largest producers in the USSR);
sericulture.

2 NUMBER AND DISTRIBUTION

Number of Karakalpaks

	1926	*1959*	*1970*	*1979*
	146,317	172,556	236,009	303,324

Regional distribution of Karakalpaks

	1926	*1959*	*1970*	*1979*
Karakalpak Aut. Prov./ASSR*	116,125 (79.4%)	155,999 (90.4%)	217,505 (92.2%)	281,809 (92.9%)
UzSSR (not incl. Karakalpak ASSR)	26,563 (18.2%)	12,275 (7.1%)	12,753 (5.4%)	15,979 (5.3%)
Elsewhere in USSR	3,629 (2.5%)	4,282 (2.5%)	5,751 (2.4%)	5,536 (1.8%)

* In 1926 it was an Autonomous Province within the Kazakh ASSR (itself part of the RSFSR); in 1932 it was transformed into the Karakalpak ASSR (within the RSFSR) and in 1936 transferred to the UzSSR.

Urban/rural distribution of Karakalpaks in the UzSSR and RSFSR

	1926		*1970*	
	Urban	*Rural*	*Urban*	*Rural*
RSFSR	4,082 (3.5%)	114,135 (96.5%)	—	—
UzSSR	79 (0.3%)	26,484 (99.7%)	68,604 (29.8%)	161,654 (70.2%)

Ethnic composition of the Karakalpak Autonomous Province/ASSR

	1926	*1959*	*1970*	*1979*
Total population	304,539	510,101	702,264	905,500
Karakalpaks	116,125 (38.1%)	155,999 (30.6%)	217,505 (31.0%)	281,809 (31.1%)
Uzbeks	84,099 (27.6%)	146,783 (28.8%)	212,597 (30.3%)	285,400 (31.5%)
Kazakhs	85,782 (28.2%)	133,844 (26.2%)	186,038 (26.5%)	243,926 (26.9%)
Turkmen	9,686 (3.2%)	29,225 (5.7%)	37,547 (5.3%)	48,655 (5.4%)
Tatars	884 (0.3%)	6,177 (1.2%)	7,622 (1.1%)	n.a.

	1926	*1959*	*1970*	*1979*
Russians	4,924 (1.6%)	22,966 (4.5%)	25,165 (3.6%)	21,287 (2.4%)
Others	3,039 (1.0%)	15,107 (3.0%)	15,790 (2.2%)	24,423 (2.7%)

Urban/rural distribution in the Karakalpak ASSR in 1970

	Urban	*Rural*
Total population	249,414	452,850
Karakalpaks	65,308 (26.2%)	152,197 (33.6%)
Uzbeks	64,035 (25.7%)	148,562 (32.8%)
Kazakhs	76,920 (30.8%)	109,118 (24.1%)
Turkmen	2,370 (1.0%)	35,177 (7.8%)
Tatars	6,305 (2.5%)	1,317 (0.3%)
Russians	22,144 (8.9%)	3,021 (0.6%)
Others	12,332 (4.9%)	3,458 (0.8%)

3 STATUS

The Karakalpaks enjoy full Soviet citizenship. They are found in all occupations and in all income brackets, but the majority are agricultural workers on collective farms. Their standard of housing is comparable to that of other national groups in the Soviet Union. The women go out to work, though probably less than elsewhere in the Soviet Union.

Literacy

In 1926	In 1970
1.3%	Over 99%

In 1926, 1,307 Karakalpaks were literate in their own language (66.3 per cent of the total literate Karakalpak population).

Level of education per 1,000 Karakalpaks living in the UzSSR of 10 years of age and above

	1959	*1970*
Primary		
Total	196	300
Men	186	279
Women	206	320
Higher and secondary (complete and incomplete)		
Total	252	384
Men	344	459
Women	160	311
Higher only		
Total	10	30
Men	17	49
Women	2	12

4 LANGUAGE

The national language is Karakalpak. It belongs to the Central Turkic group (*Fundamenta* classification); it can also be classed as belonging to the Kipchak group, Kipchak-Nogai sub-group (Baskakov). The languages it is most closely related to are Nogai and Kazakh.

Karakalpak possesses two main dialectal divisions: the north-eastern group and the south-western group. Amongst the differences between the two groups are the use of *y* in the north-eastern group in place of *u* in the south-western (cf. NE *myltyk*, SE *multuk*, 'gun'); also the use of initial *b* in the north-east in place of *p* in the south-east (cf. NE *bakyr-*, SE *pakyr-*, 'to shout'). There are also peripheral sub-dialects that are heavily influenced by the neighbouring peoples, e.g. Kazakhs, Turkmen and Uzbeks. The modern literary language was developed during the Soviet period. It is based on the north-eastern dialects. The vocabulary is basically Kipchak, with a large admixture of Arabic and Persian loan-words.

Percentage of Karakalpaks claiming Karakalpak as their mother tongue

	1926	*1959*	*1970*	*1979*
Total	87.5	95.0	96.6	95.9
In urban areas	99.3	96.8	97.6	n.a.
In rural areas	87.2	94.6	96.2	n.a.

Percentage of Karakalpaks with good knowledge of Russian

	1926	1959	1970	1979
As mother tongue	0.0	0.3	0.4	0.5
	(18 people)			
As second language	n.a.	n.a.	10.4	45.1

There are also a few borrowings from Chinese and, in recent years, a growing influx from Russian.

Russian or Uzbek is used for administration, judicial and other official proceedings, but in theory Karakalpak can be used if necessary.

In 1972 Karakalpak was used as the medium of instruction at all levels in the national schools (Silver, pp. 28–41). Further information is not available, but there are almost certainly Russian- and Uzbek-medium schools in the Karakalpak ASSR, in addition to the Karakalpak-medium schools. There is a Pedagogical Institute and, since 1976, a university in Nukus.

Karakalpak is used in radio and television transmissions in the Karakalpak ASSR; so are Russian, Uzbek and Turkmen.

Newspapers are published in Karakalpak and Russian. Amongst the main Karakalpak newspapers are *Soviet Karakalpakstany* ('Soviet Karakalpakia' – first appeared in 1924), *Dzhetkinshek* ('Shift' – first appeared in 1932) and *Dzhas leninshi* ('Young Leninist' – first appeared in 1931). There are also journals and periodicals such as *Emuder'ja* ('Amu Darya' – first appeared in 1932).

Books and pamphlets are published in Karakalpak (e.g. 53 titles in 1976; of these, 5 were specialized textbooks on technical and scientific subjects).

Scripts and alphabets

Karakalpak first became a written language during the Soviet period, when an alphabet based on the Arabic script was devised for it.

1924–32	Arabic script, modified alphabet
1928	Latin script, first alphabet
1932–8	Latin script, second alphabet
1938–40	Latin script, third alphabet
1940–57	Cyrillic script, first alphabet
1957	Cyrillic script, second alphabet

The differences between the three Latin alphabets were very slight indeed. There were greater differences between the two Cyrillic scripts, but a number of problems still remain to be solved and further changes are likely.

5 RELIGION

The Karakalpaks are Sunni Muslims (Hanafi school). It is not known precisely when they adopted Islam, but it was probably during the tenth to thirteenth centuries, the period when they were emerging as a distinct ethnic group. They gained a reputation for fanatical piety. Dervish orders were numerous and very powerful amongst them. The Sufi 'way' (*tariqa*) most closely associated with the region is the Kubrawi. Its founder was Najm ad-din Kubra (AD 1145–1221). Kubra, who was a native of Khiva, studied in Egypt and Tabriz; he followed the tradition of Junaidi of Baghdad. There is a perceptible Shi'i influence in the Kubrawi school. Kubra's tomb is not far from Khiva. Sufism still appears to be strong in Karakalpakia. Demidov speaks of *zikr* ('recitation of Divine Names') sessions being held there in the 1950s (*Sufizm* . . ., p. 150), but implies that this is no longer the case.

6 OUTSIDE THE SOVIET UNION

There are approximately 2,000 Karakalpaks in Afghanistan.

UIGHURS

Own name: *Uighur*; Russian name: *Uigury*.

The majority of the Soviet Uighurs live in the Uzbek SSR, but there are also groups in the Kazakh and Kirghiz SSRs and a small number in the Turkmen SSR.

1 HISTORICAL BACKGROUND

The first known mention of the term *Uighur* occurs in the early Turkic Orkhon inscriptions (eighth and ninth centuries AD). It is later found in Chinese sources (in the form *wejwur*), but after the fifteenth century was apparently no longer used, until resurrected during the Soviet period for a people who certainly include some elements of the ancient Uighurs, but cannot be considered to be their direct descendants.

The ancient Uighurs were a Turkic people who by AD 745 had formed a powerful state in Eastern Turkestan and the north-west of Mongolia. They were overwhelmed by the Yenisei Kirghiz (see p. 327) in 840 and forced out of the territory between the Orkhon and Yenisei Rivers, but they soon re-established themselves in two new areas, in the north-east of modern Xinjiang (Sinkiang) and in Western Turkestan, where they merged with the Karakhanids (tenth to twelfth centuries). The Uighurs attained a high level of artistic and intellectual sophistication and even when they did not represent an independent power, they continued to play an important part in the history of Central Asia. Their language was for some time the common literary medium of the area and under the Mongols (from the early thirteenth century onwards) they fulfilled an indispensable administrative function.

After the disintegration of the Mongol Empire towards the end of the fourteenth century, the Uighurs gradually lost their pre-eminence and nothing more is heard of them. The area in which there was the greatest concentration of Uighurs was Eastern Turkestan. People of many different origins converged here (e.g. Mongol, Iranian, Turkic) and in time distinct communities emerged around the oases, the product of an intermingling of the various elements. They became known by names derived from their location, e.g. *Kashkalik*, 'from Kashgar', *Turpanlik*, 'from Turfan', *Aksuluk*, 'from Aksu', *Yakanlik*, 'from Yarkand'. Since the Turkic element predominated, these groups were Turkic-speaking, but dialects differed from one area to another. In the mid-eighteenth century the Chinese government resettled some 6,000 families from Kashgaria in the Ili Valley. They were primarily agriculturalists and became known by the Chinese word for 'farmer', *Taranchi*. The Ili Valley was taken by the Russians in 1871 and after they returned it to the Chinese in 1882 nearly all the Taranchis moved further west, into Russian-held territory (see p. 380). The continuing unrest amongst the Muslim peoples of north-west China caused many thousands more of the Turkic population of this area to migrate from the Manchu Empire to the Russian. Often whole villages went together, sometimes seeking refuge, sometimes looking for work and better material conditions. The majority settled in the Ferghana

Valley (part of the Khokand Khanate, annexed by the Russians in 1876) and a smaller contingent in Kazakhstan. The two groups have retained their separate identity to this day, the Ferghana settlers being closer to the Uzbeks in their way of life, those of Kazakhstan closer to their kin across the border in China.

As mentioned above, the name *Uighur* was not used after the fifteenth century. In 1921 it was decided to revive it as a collective term for this particular group of Turkic people from north-west China, thereby replacing the separate locational names by which they had come to be identified. In the 1926 Soviet Census the Taranchis and the Kashgarlyks (see p. 380) were still listed separately, but they are now included with the Uighurs. The term *Uighur* is also used for members of this ethnic group in the People's Republic of China.

2 NUMBER AND DISTRIBUTION

Number of Uighurs

	*1926**	*1959*	*1970*	*1979*
	42,550	95,208	173,276	210,612

*The figures for this year are only approximate estimates.

Regional distribution of Uighurs

	1926	*1959*	*1970*	*1979*
UzSSR	31,941 (75.1%)	19,377 (20.4%)	23,942 (13.8%)	n.a.
Kaz.ASSR/SSR	10,510 (24.7%)	59,840 (62.9%)	120,881 (69.8%)	147,943 (70.3%)
Kir.ASSR/SSR	73 (0.2%)	13,757* (14.4%)	24,872 (14.4%)	29,817 (14.2%)
Elsewhere in USSR	26 (0.0%)	2,234 (2.3%)	3,581 (2.0%)	

*The apparently extraordinary increase in the number of Uighurs in the KirSSR in the period 1926–59 is due to the fact that the Taranchis and Kashgarlyks were included with the Uighurs in 1959 (and later).

Percentage of Uighurs in relation to total population of individual republics

	1926	1959	1970	1979
UzSSR	0.6	0.2	0.2	n.a.
Kaz.ASSR/SSR	0.2	0.6	0.9	1.0
Kir.ASSR/SSR	0.0	0.7	0.8	0.8

Urban/rural distribution of the Uighur (in main areas of habitation)

	1926		1970	
	Urban	Rural	Urban	Rural
UzSSR	2,649	29,292	9,353	14,589
	(8.3%)	(91.7%)	(39.1%)	(60.9%)
Kaz.ASSR/SSR	208	10,302	29,618	91,263
	(2.0%)	(98.0%)	(24.5%)	(75.5%)
Kir.ASSR/SSR	36	37	11,548	13,324
	(49.3%)	(50.7%)	(46.4%)	(53.6%)

3 STATUS

The Uighurs enjoy full Soviet citizenship. They are found in all occupations and in all income brackets, but the majority work on collective farms. Their standard of housing is comparable to that of other national groups in the Soviet Union. The women go out to work, but possibly less than elsewhere in the Soviet Union.

Literacy

In 1926	In 1970
4.6%	Over 99%

In 1926, 1,059 Uighur were literate in their own language (53.7 per cent of the total literate Uighur population).

4 LANGUAGE

The national language is (Modern) Uighur. It belongs to the East Turkic group (*Fundamenta* classification); it can also be classed as belonging to the Karluk group, Karluk-Khorezm sub-group (Baskakov). The language it is most closely related to is Uzbek.

Uighur contains four main dialectal divisions: the southern group (including the dialects of Yarkand, Kashgar, Khotan, Aksu and Yangi Hissar); the northern group (including the dialects of Turfan, Karashar and the Ili); the Lobnor dialect (really a Kirghiz dialect, but much influenced by Uighur); the Hansu group (Salar and Yellow or *Sary* Uighur). The northern group represents the dialects spoken by the Uighurs of the Soviet Union; the other dialects are spoken by the Chinese Uighurs. The literary languages of the Soviet and Chinese Uighurs differ slightly, due to their different dialectical basis. In both Soviet and Chinese modern Uighur there are loan-words from Arabic, Persian, Chinese and Russian (Russian loans began entering the language during the second half of the nineteenth century); in China, however, the Chinese influence is becoming stronger and edging out the Russian influence, while in the Soviet Union the reverse is happening, with Russian ousting the Chinese (as well as Arabic and Persian).

Russian is generally used for administrative, judicial and other official proceedings, but in theory Uighur can be used if necessary. The national languages of the republics in which they live can also be used (e.g. Uzbek, Kazakh).

Percentage of Uighurs claiming Uighur as their mother tongue

	1926	1959	1970	1979
Total	52.7	85.0	88.5	86.1
In urban areas	53.4	n.a.	86.4	n.a.
In rural areas	52.6	n.a.	89.4	n.a.

Percentage of Uighurs with good knowledge of Russian

	1926	1959	1970	1979
As mother tongue	0.0 (3 people)	2.3	2.8	3.6
As second language	n.a.	n.a.	35.6	52.1

Percentage of Uighurs with good knowledge of a language other than Uighur or Russian (presumably Uzbek or Kazakh)

	1926	1970	1979
As mother tongue	47.2	8.8	10.3
As second language	n.a.	9.5	9.0

In 1958 there were some Uighur-medium schools in the Kazakh SSR, but none in the Uzbek or Kirghiz SSRs (Lipsett, pp. 185–6). More recent information is not available.

Uighur is used in radio and television broadcasts in the Kazak and Uzbek SSRs, but not (apparently) in the Kirghiz SSR.

Newspapers are published in Uighur in the Kazakh SSR; the main one is *Kommunizm tugi* ('The Banner of Communism' – first appeared in 1957); since 1970 there has been a supplement in the Arabic script (still used in China), entitled *Jeni khajat* ('New Life'). In 1976 a second paper in the Arabic script appeared, *Bizdin vatan* ('Our Fatherland'); a Kazakh edition of this is also printed in the Arabic script. No newspapers in Uighur are published in the Uzbek and Kirghiz SSRs. No journals or periodicals are published in Uighur.

Books and pamphlets are published in Uighur (e.g. 44 titles in 1976; one of these was a specialized technical textbook).

Scripts and alphabets

The Old Uighur script, used by the Uighurs before their conversion to Islam and subsequent adoption of the Arabic script, was based on the New Sogdian. It was adopted by the Mongols and used for a time by the Golden Horde (before they, too, became Muslims and began to use the Arabic script). The Yellow Uighurs used it until the early nineteenth century and it is still used today, in a slightly modified form, in Inner Mongolia. The majority of Uighurs, however, used the Arabic script with no changes or additions from the time of their conversion up till the Soviet period.

Until 1925   Arabic script, Arabic alphabet
1925–30   Arabic script, modified alphabet
1930–47   Latin script
1947   Cyrillic script

The present alphabet is still considered to be in need of improvement, although, being the last Turkic language of the Soviet Union to adopt the Cyrillic script, it appears to have profited from the experience of the others and there are far fewer problems to be solved. The main difficulty, as for most of the other Turkic languages, is the question of whether to use a single symbol for the combinations $i+a$, $i+e$, $i+o$, $i+u$ or two separate symbols. The former course would be more in keeping with Russian orthography, making the spelling of Russian loan-words easier, but would have the disadvantage of blurring the morphemic boundaries. As the influence of Russian on the Uighur vocabulary is now too great to be ignored, a solution must be found that takes account of both Uighur and Russian requirements.

5 RELIGION

The modern Uighurs are Sunni Muslims (Hanafi school). The ancient Uighurs were Buddhists, but their descendants and the other forebears of the modern Uighurs were no doubt converted to Islam by the fourteenth or fifteenth centuries if not earlier. The Ili (Uighur) Muslims were very lax in their observance of Islamic precepts before their move to Kazakhstan, but once there they became noted for their piety. In the town of Dzharkent there were twenty-five mosques before the Revolution, including a late nineteenth-century copy of the great Kuldzha mosque, built in an amalgam of Chinese and Muslim styles of architecture. This replica of the Kuldzha mosque was commissioned by Vali Akhun Yuldash, one of the leading representatives of the Uighur community in Russia.

6 OUTSIDE THE SOVIET UNION

According to Soviet estimates, there are approximately 4,200,000 Uighurs in the People's Republic of China (95 per cent of the total Uighur population). *Soviet Asian Ethnic Frontiers* (p. 195) suggests a much higher figure, about 5,000,000. The majority of the Chinese Uighurs live in the Xinjiang-Wei-wur (Sinkiang-Uighur) Autonomous Region, which is adjacent to the Soviet Union. There are also some 2,000 Khotons, a people closely related to the Uighurs, in the People's Republic of Mongolia.

DUNGANS

Own names: *Lao hui hui, Donggan ren*; Russian name: *Dungane*.

Most of the Soviet Dungans live in the Kirghiz and Kazakh SSRs, particularly in the valley of the River Chu.

1 HISTORICAL BACKGROUND

The Dungans are Chinese Muslims who migrated to Russian-held territory after the anti-Manchu Muslim Uprising of 1862–77. They came from the Chinese provinces of Shaanxi (Shensi), where the Uprising began, Gansu (Kansu) and Xinjiang (Sinkiang). The main exodus was led by Boyan Akhun (also known as Muhammad Ayyub) from Gansu to Semirech'je in 1877–8, but other groups came somewhat later, between 1881–4.

Little is known of the ethnic origins of the Dungans. There are two basic theories: (a) that they are Chinese who were converted to Islam through prolonged contact with Arab, Persian and Turkic Muslims; (b) that they are Arab, Persian and Turkic Muslims who were brought to China as prisoners by the Mongol emperors and were assimilated by the indigenous population in all but religion. Soviet scholars favour the former theory, Chinese the latter. The matter is further complicated by the history of the term 'Dungan', which is as obscure as that of the people to whom it is applied. It first appeared in north-west China in the eighteenth century with reference to immigrants from central China (mostly soldiers and their camp-followers). It was apparently a term of abuse used by the local Turkic Muslims (e.g. Uighurs) for the newcomers of non-Turkic stock, whom they took to be relatively recent converts. The Dungans, on the other hand, referred to themselves simply as *Hui zu ren* ('Muslim-race person'). The Russians adopted the term 'Dungan' in the early nineteenth century, but it did not become firmly established until the Soviet period, when 'Dungan' was made the official ethnic designation of the Chinese Muslims in the Soviet Union. When the term is now used in Soviet and western European sources with reference to China, it is not clear whether it is being used with a particular ethnic connotation, or whether it is merely a collective name for all the non-Turkic Chinese Muslims.

The Dungans who first settled in Semirech'je were mostly farmers and artisans. They introduced the cultivation of rice, opium poppies and new varieties of vegetables into the area. Agriculture remains their principal occupation today. In their food, clothing and general way of life they have retained Chinese customs (there were even cases of feet-binding as late as the 1940s), but this is gradually changing as the younger generation are more exposed to extraneous influences (e.g. Russian, Kazakh and Kirghiz).

2 NUMBER AND DISTRIBUTION

Number of Dungans

	1926	1959	1970	1979
	14,600	21,928	38,644	51,694

Regional distribution of Dungans

	1926	1959	1970	1979
Kir.ASSR/SSR	6,004 (41.1%)	11,088 (50.6%)	19,837 (51.3%)	26,661 (51.6%)
Kaz.ASSR/SSR	8,455 (57.9%)	9,980 (45.5%)	17,284 (44.7%)	22,491 (43.5%)
Elsewhere in USSR	141 (1.0%)	860 (3.9%)	1,523 (3.9%)	2,542 (4.9%)

Urban/rural distribution of Dungans

	1926	1970
Urban	4,694 (32.2%)	8,727 (22.6%)
Rural	9,906 (67.8%)	29,917 (77.4%)

3 STATUS

The Dungans enjoy full Soviet citizenship. They are found in all occupations and in all income brackets; the majority work on collective farms, but some work in industry. Their standard of housing is comparable to that of other national groups in the Soviet Union. The women go out to work, as elsewhere in the Soviet Union.

Literacy

In 1926	In 1970
8.6%	Over 99%

In 1926, 505 Dungans were literate in their own language (40.1 per cent of the total literate Dungan population).

4 LANGUAGE

The national language is Dungan. It belongs to the North Chinese group of languages. There are two main dialects: the three-tone dialect of Gansu (Kansu), and the four-tone dialect of Shaanxi (Shensi). The three-tone dialect provides the basis for the modern standard language. The number of loan-words in Dungan is less than in many of the other Central Asian languages, amounting to about 10 per cent of the total vocabulary. There are a number of Arabic loan-words (mainly relating to religion) which appear to date from the fourteenth century; a much smaller group of Turkic loans (relating to everyday life) was apparently acquired during the eighteenth century, after the Dungans had settled in Xinjiang (Sinkiang); Russian loans began to be acquired during the nineteenth century and now constitute the largest group of loan-words.

The first scholar to study the Dungan language in detail was V. I. Tsibuzgin. Towards the end of the nineteenth century he carried out research on the language of the Dungans who had settled in the Russian Empire. Amongst Soviet scholars working on Dungan today, the foremost is Ja. Shivaza, himself a Dungan and a writer of distinction. Outside the USSR, S. Rimsky-Korsakoff Dyer has in recent years specialized in the language of the Soviet Dungans; following a field trip in 1977, she has also written about their present way of life.

Russian is generally used for administrative, judicial and other official proceedings, but in theory Dungan can be used if necessary. The national languages of the republics in which the Dungans are found (e.g. Kirghiz and Kazakh) can also be used.

Percentage of Dungans claiming Dungan as their mother tongue

	1926	1959	1970	1979
Total	99.2	95.1	94.3	94.8
In urban areas	98.3	89.6	88.4	n.a.
In rural areas	99.6	96.4	96.0	n.a.

Percentage of Dungans with good knowledge of Russian

	1926	1959	1970	1979
As mother tongue	0.1	1.6	2.3	2.4
As second language	n.a.	n.a.	48.0	62.8

The use of Dungan as a medium of instruction was introduced in 1929; there is no information available on its use at present. Primary and incomplete secondary education was available (medium of instruction not known) in all areas with a compact population of some size in the 1960s; boarding schools provided education for those who lived in remote areas. More recent information is not available, but the situation is probably still much the same. Even if there is little or no instruction in Dungan, it is probably taught as an individual, optional subject in Russian, Kazakh or Kirghiz-medium schools in Dungan settlements. There is a Dungan Pedagogical Institute in Frunze (KirSSR) and a Dungan section in the Kirghiz Academy of Sciences. There were problems in persuading girls to complete their education at first; the situation is likely to have improved somewhat by now, but as elsewhere in Central Asia, there is probably still an element of resistance to women's education.

There are some radio and television broadcasts in Dungan in the Kirghiz SSR. The first newspaper to appear in Dungan was *Dong Huoshi* ('Spark of the East'), which was published in the KirSSR in 1932–9; since 1957 a second paper has come out, *Shiyue di qi* ('Banner of October'), also published in the KirSSR.

A few books and pamphlets are published in Dungan (e.g. 3 titles in 1976; none of these were specialized textbooks on scientific or technical subjects).

Scripts and alphabets

The Chinese script was never widely known amongst the Dungans who moved to Russian Central Asia. Literacy was still very low when the Latin script was introduced in 1928.

1928–53   Latin script
1953   Cyrillic script

5 RELIGION

The Dungans are Sunni Muslims (Hanafi school). They are known for their strict observance of Islamic precepts. Before 1917, in the Karakunduz settlement alone there were forty-seven mosques and houses of prayer. It is not known how many of these are still open for worship, but there was apparently at least one still functioning in Przhevalsk, in eastern Kirghizia, in the 1960s (*Narody Srednej Azii i Kazakhstana II*) and there is another in Dzhambul, in Southern Kazakhstan. The Dungan mosques are built in the Chinese style, with no nails, bolts or other metallic elements.

6 OUTSIDE THE SOVIET UNION

There are Dungans and Muslims of other ethnic origins in China, but their number is unknown: estimates vary from 3 million to over 80 million. One recent calculation (*Journal of the Institute of Muslim Minority Affairs*, vol. 2) shows that it could be as high as 115 million.

PERSIANS/IRANIS

Own names: *Irani*, *Farsi*; Russian names: *Irantsy*, *Persy*.

The majority live in the Turkmen and Uzbek SSRs. There are also some Persians in the Daghestan ASSR.

1 HISTORICAL BACKGROUND

There are two distinct groups of Persians in Central Asia: those who call themselves *Irani* and others, far more numerous, who call themselves *Farsi*. The 1926 Soviet Census was careful to differentiate between them, referring to the former as *Irani*, the latter as *Persy*; in 1970 they were listed together under the heading *Irantsy (Persy)*, in 1979 simply as *Persy*. (They are not, of course, to be confused with Iranian nationals, who, as foreign subjects, are always listed separately.)

There have been Persians in Central Asia for centuries: apart from the various Safavid incursions into the area and the attraction of the great centres of Islamic learning, Persians went there to trade; many were also brought as captives of the Turkmen to be sold in the slave markets (mid-nineteenth-century travellers put the numbers of Persian slaves in Bukhara at 200,000 and in Khiva at over 700,000; sometimes there was such a glut after a particularly successful raid that their price fell to almost nothing). There is clearly a difference in origin between the *Farsi* and the *Irani* groups, but insufficient historical and linguistic evidence is available to distinguish between them. It appears that the Irani formed a compact community in the Samarkand district, while the Persians were fairly evenly divided between Merv and Ashkhabad in Turkmenia and Bukhara and Samarkand in Uzbekistan. Some of the Bukhara Persians are certainly descendants of the 40,000 families sent there from Merv by Shah Murad in 1785 (see p. 315).

2 NUMBER AND DISTRIBUTION

Number of Persians/Iranis

	1926		1959	1970	1979
	Persians	*Iranis*			
	43,971	9,188	20,766	27,501	31,313

Regional distribution of Persians/Iranis

	1926		1959	1970	1979
	Persians	*Iranis*			
UzSSR	9,830 (22.4%)	9,182 (99.9%)	n.a.	15,457 (56.2%)	n.a.
TurkSSR	7,153 (16.3%)	3 (0.0%)	n.a.	5,068 (18.4%)	n.a.
AzSSR	9,446 (21.5%)	——	n.a.	——	n.a.
ArmSSR	5,043 (11.5%)	——	n.a.	——	n.a.
GeorgSSR	2,220 (5.0%)	——	n.a.	——	n.a.
DaghASSR	3,448 (7.8%)	——	n.a.	——	n.a.
Elsewhere in USSR	6,831 (15.5%)	3 (0.0%)		6,976 (25.4%)	

Urban/rural distribution of Persians/Iranis

	1926		1970
	Persians	*Iranis*	
Urban	28,137 (64.1%)	2,500 (27.2%)	14,472 (52.6%)
Rural	15,834 (36.0%)	6,688 (72.8%)	13,029 (47.4%)

3 STATUS

The Persians enjoy full Soviet citizenship. They are found in all occupations and in all income brackets. Their standard of housing is comparable to that of other national groups in the Soviet Union. The women go out to work, as elsewhere in the Soviet Union.

Literacy

	In 1926	In 1970
Persians	*Iranis*	
14.1%	7.9%	Both over 99%

In 1926, 2,884 Persians and 70 Irani were literate in their own language (46.4 per cent and 9.6 per cent respectively of the total Persian/Irani literate population).

4 LANGUAGE

The national language is Persian. It belongs to the South-West group of Iranian languages; it is closely related to Tadzhik. As early as 1926 a great many Persians and Irani no longer claimed it as their mother tongue and those who still do consider it as such are now very much in the minority. The others, though they identify themselves as Persian/Irani, have been assimilated to the extent that they have adopted the language of the surrounding majority (Uzbek or Turkmen).

Russian is used along with the language of the titular people in the Union republics (e.g. Turkmen, Uzbek, etc.) for administrative, judicial and other official proceedings, but in theory Persian can be used if necessary.

Percentage of Persians/Iranis claiming Persian as their mother tongue

	1926		1959	1970	1979
	Persians	*Iranis*			
Total	67.8	16.3	44.7	36.9	30.7
In urban areas	79.5	45.3	36.0	33.0	n.a.
In rural areas	46.9	5.5	59.4	41.4	

Percentage of Persians/Iranis with good knowledge of Russian

	1926		1959	1970	1979
	Persians	*Iranis*			
As mother tongue	2.5	0.0 (3 people)	12.4	10.3	9.8
As second language	n.a.	n.a.	n.a.	33.9	57.1

Percentage of Persians/Iranis with good knowledge of a language other than Russian or Persian (presumably Uzbek, Turkmen, etc.)

	1926		1970	1979
	Persians	*Iranis*		
As mother tongue	28.9	83.6	52.8	59.5
As second language	n.a.	n.a.	12.7	10.6

There is apparently no tuition in schools in Persian.

There are no internal broadcasts in Persian, though since 1975 there have been external (beamed abroad) broadcasts in Persian from the Uzbek SSR. There are no publications in Persian for internal distribution (with the exception, of course, of some scholarly editions of Persian classics).

5 RELIGION

The Persians and Iranis are Shi'is, unlike the majority of other Central Asian Muslims, who are Sunni.

6 OUTSIDE THE SOVIET UNION

The overwhelming majority of Persians are found in Iran.

BALUCHIS

Own names: *Baluch, Baloch, Baludzh*; Russian name: *Beludzhi*.

Almost without exception the Soviet Baluchis live in the Turkmen SSR in the region of Mary (formerly known as Merv).

1 HISTORICAL BACKGROUND

The Baluchis are an Iranian people. They are first mentioned in historical records by Arab writers of the ninth and tenth centuries. Their original homeland was in the Kerman region, but under pressure from invasions such as those of the Seljuks and Mongols, they gradually migrated to the south, then to the east, to settle in the area which came to be known as 'Baluchistan'. This area is today divided between Pakistan and Iran. During the late nineteenth to early twentieth centuries, Baluchis began to move into Central Asia, but the main migration was in the period 1923–8. They were nomads until recent times, moving with their flocks of sheep and goats two or three times a year. Their tents were made of goat-hair, quite unlike the felt yurts of the indigenous Central Asian peoples. Some of the older people still use their traditional-style tents in the summer months.

The Soviet census estimates include with the Baluchis a small group of Brahuis, an Indian people of Dravidian origin, who have long been settled amongst the Baluchis and apparently migrated to Central Asia with them.

2 NUMBERS AND DISTRIBUTION

Number of Baluchis

1926	1959	1970	1979
9,974	*7,842	12,582	18,997

* The drop in the population in the period 1926–59 is due in large part to the fact that there was a tendency for Baluchis to identify themselves as 'Turkmen'. This process seems to have been halted after 1959. There were also serious losses during the process of collectivization in the early Soviet period and a further depletion due to migrations back to Afghanistan at this time.

Regional distribution of Baluchis

	1926	1959	1970	1979
TurkSSR	9,974 (100%)	7,626 (97.2%)	12,374 (98.3%)	18,584 (97.8%)
Elsewhere in USSR	——	216 (2.8%)	208 (1.7%)	413 (2.2%)

Urban/rural distribution of Baluchis

	1926	1970
Urban	22 (0.2%)	1,249 (9.9%)
Rural	9,952 (99.8%)	11,333 (90.1%)

3 STATUS

The Baluchis enjoy full Soviet citizenship. They are found in all occupations and in all income brackets, but the great majority work on collective farms. Their standard of housing is comparable to that of other national groups in the Soviet Union. The women go out to work, as elsewhere in the Soviet Union.

Literacy

In 1926	In 1970
0.3%	Over 99%

In 1926, 20 Baluchis were literate in their own language (58.8 per cent of the total literate population).

4 LANGUAGE

The national language is Baluchi. It belongs to the North-West group of Iranian languages. It has two main dialect groups, a north-eastern and a south-western. The Baluchi spoken in the Soviet Union belongs to the latter group; it closely resembles the Baluchi of Khorasan. There are no dialectal divisions amongst the Soviet Baluchis. In recent years they have acquired a number of Russian loan-words, which tend to undergo phonetic modification. In the Soviet Union, Baluchi is not a written language. In the 1930s an attempt was made to introduce an alphabet based on the Latin script and a newspaper and a few books were published in it. It was soon abandoned, however, and Baluchis now use Turkmen as their literary language.

In Pakistan the Arabic script is used for Baluchi and there have been a number of publications there in Baluchi over the last 25–30 years.

Russian is generally used for administrative, judicial and other official proceedings; Turkmen can also be used and in theory, Baluchi can be used if necessary.

Percentage of Baluchis claiming Baluchi as their mother tongue

	1926	1959	1970	1979
Total	99.9	94.9	98.1	98.1
In urban areas	0.0	74.1	92.6	n.a.
In rural areas	99.9	96.7	98.7	n.a.

Percentage of Baluchis with good knowledge of Russian

	1926	1959	1970	1979
As mother tongue	0.0	1.5	0.6	0.7
As second language	n.a.	n.a.	2.9	4.9

Percentage of Baluchis with good knowledge of a language other than Baluchi or Russian (presumably Turkmen)

	1970	1979
As mother tongue	1.3	1.3
As second language	40.4	53.0

Baluchi is not used as a medium of instruction. Most Baluchis attend Turkmen-medium schools, which provide the full range of educational facilities.

There is no information on the use of Baluchi in broadcasting; it is probably not used. There are no publications in Baluchi now, although a Baluchi reader was published in Ashkhabad in 1935.

5 RELIGION

The Baluchis are Sunni Muslims (Hanafi school).

6 WORLD DISTRIBUTION OF BALUCHIS

There are no reliable figures available for the total world population of Baluchis, but the following approximate estimates were given in Soviet sources of the 1960s:

Afghanistan	200,000	(11.0%)
Arab countries	10,000	(0.5%)
India	50,000	(3.0%)
Iran	600,000	(32.0%)
Pakistan	1,000,000	(53.0%)
USSR*	7,800	(0.5%)

* Based on the 1959 Soviet Census estimate

The estimates in *Soviet Asian Ethnic Frontiers* (p. 84) tally with the above, except in the case of Afghanistan where the much lower figure of 40,000 is suggested.

AFGHANS

Own names: *Pukhtu, Pushtu*; Russian name: *Afgantsy*.

The majority of the Soviet Afghans live in the Turkmen SSR, smaller groups are found in the Uzbek and Tadzhik SSRs.

1 HISTORICAL BACKGROUND

A small group of Afghans have been settled in Central Asia for many years. Nothing definite is known of their origin, but it is probable that they, like the Baluchis and Dzhamshids, migrated from northern Afghanistan into Turkmenia (particularly to the Merv oasis, where the majority of them settled), Uzbekistan and Tadzhikistan towards the end of the nineteenth century.

2 NUMBER AND DISTRIBUTION

Number of Afghans

1926	1959	1970	1979
5,348	1,855	4,184	n.a.

Regional distribution of Afghans in 1926*

TurkSSR	3,947
	(73.8%)
UzSSR (incl. Tadzh.ASSR)	1,294
	(24.2%)
Tadzh.ASSR only	666
	(12.5%)
Elsewhere in USSR	107
	(2.0%)

*Not listed subsequently.

Urban/rural distribution of Afghans

	1926	*1970*
Urban	519	2,180
	(9.7%)	(52.1%)
Rural	4,829	2,004
	(90.3%)	(47.9%)

3 STATUS

The Afghans enjoy full Soviet citizenship. They are found in all occupations and in all income brackets. Their standard of housing is comparable to that of other national groups in the Soviet Union. The women go out to work, as elsewhere in the Soviet Union.

Literacy

In 1926	In 1970
2.1%	Over 99%

In 1926, 47 Afghans were literate in their own language (41.6 per cent of the total literate Afghan population).

4 LANGUAGE

The national languages of the Afghans are Pushtu (an East Iranian language) and Dari (a West Iranian language). It is not known which of the two is spoken by the Afghans in the Soviet Union. In 1926 only about a quarter of the Afghans who were then Soviet citizens claimed the 'language of their nationality' (Pushtu perhaps?) as their mother tongue. By 1959 the situation had changed remarkably, with nearly three-quarters of them claiming the 'language of their nationality' as mother tongue. It may be supposed that this increase was due to an influx of Afghans from Afghanistan, yet the Afghan population in the Soviet Union does not appear to have increased unduly during this period.

Russian is generally used for administrative, judicial and other official proceedings, but in theory Pushtu (or Dari) can be used if necessary. The language of the republic in which the Afghans live can also be used (e.g. Turkmen, Uzbek or Tadzhik).

Percentage of Afghans claiming their own language (Pushtu or Dari) as mother tongue

	1926	*1959*	*1970*	*1979*
Total	24.0	71.8	70.7	n.a.
In urban areas	83.8	72.8	62.8	n.a.
In rural areas	17.6	71.1	79.2	n.a.

Percentage of Afghans with good knowledge of Russian

	1926	*1959*	*1970*	*1979*
As mother tongue	0.2 (10 people)	4.0	4.3	n.a.
As second language	n.a.	n.a.	26.7	n.a.

Percentage of Afghans with good knowledge of a language other than their own or Russian (presumably Turkmen, Uzbek or Tadzhik)

	1926	*1970*	*1979*
As mother tongue	75.8	25.1	n.a.
As second language	n.a.	31.9	n.a.

No information is available on the use of Pushtu or Dari as media of instruction; they are probably not used at all.

No information is available on the use of Pushtu or Dari in internal broadcasts; they are probably not used at all.

No newspapers or periodicals are published in Pushtu or Dari. Some books and pamphlets are published in Pushtu and Dari (6 each in 1978, mostly political; the lists of titles in the two languages were almost identical); they are probably not intended for internal distribution.

5 RELIGION

The great majority of Afghans in Afghanistan are Sunni Muslims (Hanafi school), but those of Persian origin are Shi'is. It is not known whether the Afghans in the Soviet Union are Sunni or Shi'i, but it is probable that they are the former.

6 OUTSIDE THE SOVIET UNION

The overwhelming majority of Afghans live in Afghanistan.

Arabs

Own name: *Arab*; Russian name: *Araby*.

The majority live in the UzSSR, along the middle and lower reaches of the Zeravshan River and the lower reaches of the Kashka-Darya. There used to be a substantial community (nearly 6,000) in Bukhara and a smaller group in Samarkand. There is still a small group of Arabs in the Tadzhik SSR.

1 HISTORICAL BACKGROUND

There are many theories and legends regarding the origins of the Central Asian Arabs. The main possibilities are: (a) that they are descended from the Arab invaders of the seventh and eighth centuries; (b) that they were with Timur on his expedition to Arabia; he wished to punish them for some reason and condemned them to exile in China, but relented and allowed them to settle in Karshi and Hissar, from whence they eventually migrated to their present location; (c) that they were part of a body of migratory Arabs who found their way to Central Asia through northern Afghanistan in the mid-sixteenth century and settled in Bukhara, Samarkand and along the Kashka-Darya. The Timur story is the least reliable, for popular belief ascribes most significant historical events to his time, but the variety of explanations is interesting, since there is evidence (partly linguistic) to indicate that these Arabs may well have come to Central Asia at different times and from different places. During the nineteenth century the Central Asian Arabs were still nomadic. They formed a sizeable community (30,000 or more) within the Bukharan state, where they were particularly famed for the sheep they reared. During the Soviet period they were obliged to settle and this prompted many to migrate to Afghanistan. Their clan system, which used to be very strong, has almost disappeared in recent times, though tribal names such as 'Kureish', 'Shaiboni', 'Sanoni' etc. are still remembered. Their sense of communal identity appears to have undergone a similar weakening. When they adopted a settled existence, they at first lived together in a particular quarter of a town or in separate villages. Now they are usually dispersed amongst the overwhelmingly more numerous Uzbeks or Tadzhiks and many today tend to refer to themselves (at least to outsiders) as belonging to one or other of these two groups. Where they have remained in fairly compact communities, however, they have preserved some of the distinctive features of their way of life. In such areas they also generally marry within their own family group, marriages between cousins still being very common.

2 NUMBER AND DISTRIBUTION

Number of Arabs*

1926	1959
28,978	7,987

* Not listed in 1970 and subsequently.

Regional distribution of Arabs in 1926*

UzSSR (not incl.) Tadzh.ASSR)	24,717 (85.3%)
Tadzh.ASSR/SSR	3,260 (11.2%)
Elsewhere in USSR	1,001 (3.5%)

* Not listed subsequently.

Urban/rural distribution of Arabs in 1926

Urban	1,261
	(4.4%)
Rural	27,717
	(95.6%)

3 STATUS

The Arabs enjoy full Soviet citizenship. They are almost entirely agricultural workers (though those who have become assimilated to the majority ethnic group are probably found in a variety of occupations and income brackets). Their standard of housing is comparable to that of other national groups in the Soviet Union. The women go out to work, as elsewhere in the Soviet Union.

Literacy

In 1926	In 1970
1.2%	Over 99%

In 1926, 38 Arabs were literate in their own language (10.8 per cent of the total literate Arab population).

4 LANGUAGE

Arabic is a Semitic language. The Arabic spoken in the Soviet Union has some Central Arabian features; it also shows affinities with Iraqi Arabic and in particular, with the language of Iraqi folklore. In the Soviet Union there are two main dialect groups: the Bukhara and the Kashka-Darya. They are virtually mutually incomprehensible and speakers of the two communicate with each other through Uzbek or Tadzhik. The differences between them are morphological, phonetic and lexical. The Bukhara dialect has been much influenced by Tadzhik, the Kashka-Darya by Uzbek and other Turkic languages. The chief Soviet authority on the language of the Central Asian Arabs is G. V. Tsereteli, who collected a considerable corpus of material in the years 1935–40.

Russian is used alongside Uzbek or Tadzhik (depending on the republic) for administrative, judicial and other official proceedings, but in theory Arabic can be used if necessary.

Percentage of Arabs claiming Arabic as their mother tongue

1926	1959
15.9	34.1

The rise in the percentage of Arabs claiming Arabic as their mother tongue is due to the overall decrease in the number of Arabs identifying themselves as Arabs: only those who are most conscious of their 'Arab-ness' now categorize themselves in this way.

Percentage of Arabs claiming Russian as mother tongue

1926	1959
0.1	1.8

Percentage of Arabs claiming a language other than Russian or Arabic as mother tongue (Uzbek or Tadzhik)

1926	1959
83.8	64.1

Arabic is not used as a medium of instruction in schools (except, possibly, in special 'foreign language' schools).

No information is available on the use of Arabic in broadcasting within the Soviet Union; it is almost certainly not used at all (but Arabic broadcasts have been beamed abroad from the UzSSR since 1975).

Arabic (in the Soviet Union) is not a written language, hence there are no publications in Arabic for internal consumption (though books in Arabic are published for the foreign market and there are, of course, some scholarly editions of works in Classical Arabic).

5 RELIGION

The Arabs are Sunni Muslims.

6 OUTSIDE THE SOVIET UNION

The overwhelming majority of Arabs live in the Arab countries.

There is a small community of Central Asian Arabs (related to the Soviet Arabs) in Afghanistan.

Chalas

Some of the Jews of Bukhara adopted Islam and were known as *chala* ('imperfect'). Those who became true Muslims were gradually assimilated by the main body of the Muslim community, but those who remained 'crypto-Jews' married within their own group and kept secret contact with the Jewish community.

The term *chala* was also used in a non-religious sense to refer to the offspring of mixed marriages, e.g. *chala-kazakh*, *chala-kalmyk*, if the father were a Kazakh or Kalmyk respectively and the mother of some other ethnic origin.

Dzhamshids (Jamshids)

The Dzhamshids are one of the *Chahar Aymak* ('Four tribes') group of semi-nomadic peoples of western Afghanistan. The majority of Dzhamshids are centred around Koshk, just north of Herat, but a small number are found across the border in the adjoining Turkmen SSR. They were settled in this region in the reign of Nadir Shah (mid-eighteenth century) to act as a defence against the incursions of the Turkmen tribes. In their way of life they were close to the Turkmen, Vámbéry noted, but their language was a dialect of Persian. In the 1926 Soviet Census they were listed separately, but thereafter were included with the Tadzhiks. By religion the Dzhamshids are Sunni Muslims.

1926 Census figures

Population: 932.
Urban dwellers: 1 person.
Percentage claiming own language as their mother tongue: 87.2.
Number claiming Russian as their mother tongue: none.
Literacy: 1.2 per cent (11 people: all were literate in their own language).

Gypsies of Central Asia

Own name: *Mughat* (Arabic plural from Tadzhik *mug/mag* 'fire-worshipper'); this is sometimes qualified by place-names indicating location, e.g. *Mughat Samarkandi, Mughat Bukhori* 'Gypsies of Samarkand', 'of Bukhara' etc.; Tadzhik name: *Dzhugi, Mazang*; Uzbek name: *Luli*; Russian name: *Sredneaziatskije tsygany*.

The early history of the Gypsies of Central Asia is a mystery. According to their own legends, they were already living there at the time of Timur. This is supported by evidence from various historical sources. It is believed that they originally came from India, but they have no traditions concerning this and have even lost the ethnonym *Rom*. They have also lost their own language, adopting instead Tadzhik or Uzbek, though they still have a jargon of their own, *lavzi mughat*, akin to the medieval beggars' cant. They have absorbed many of the indigenous customs and, like the surrounding population, are devout Muslims. In most things they follow orthodox Sunni practice, but traces of non-Islamic superstitions do survive.

Until the 1930s the Gypsies of Central Asia were nomadic, although it was customary for them to make long winter stops on the outskirts of cities and this eventually led to the development of distinct Gypsy quarters. They are now settled, but in summer some of them still prefer to live in tents alongside their houses. Their chief occupations used to be those traditionally associated with Gypsies: peddling, tinkering, fortune-telling, begging, singing and dancing. The women specialized in making hair-netting for the veils of other Muslim women, though they themselves did not wear the veil. One group, the Mazang, always kept apart from the others, never intermarrying with them and even following a different trade, that of woodworking. Now that the Gypsies are settled, they are becoming urbanized and many of the younger generation find work on building sites or in factories. Some of them have higher education and have become teachers.

The Gypsies are scattered all over Central Asia, though the majority are now settled in the UzSSR. The Central Asian Gypsies are not listed separately from other Gypsies (i.e. those of the European USSR), but most of those living in the Central Asian republics may be assumed to belong to the particular group under discussion here. In 1926 this amounted to approximately 5,000, though as the Gypsies were nomadic it was impossible to estimate their number with any accuracy. In 1959 there were 7,860 Gypsies in the UzSSR and 1,556 in the TadzhSSR; in 1970 there were 11,362 in the UzSSR, but none were listed in the TadzhSSR. Just under 50 per cent of those in the UzSSR were urban dwellers. One rather confusing point is that some 50 per cent (5,586) of the present Uzbek Gypsies are said to claim the 'language of their nationality' as mother tongue. If this refers to Romany (as would normally be expected), it would mean that in all probability these Gypsies do not belong to the ancient Central Asian community, since the latter have for centuries only known Uzbek or Tadzhik; consequently, only half of the 11,000-odd Uzbek Gypsies would be Muslims.

Hazaras and Barbaris

The Hazaras are a people of northern Afghanistan, thought to be descendants of the Mongols of Genghiz Khan's army who invaded the region *c.* 1218. The name *Hazara* is taken from the Persian word for 'thousand', an early loan in Mongol. There are several groups of Hazaras, one of which is the Barbari. According to Vámbéry, they take their name from the city Shehri-Berber, which was situated between Kabul and Herat. Until recent times the Hazaras spoke a language of their own that was quite unlike that of the Persian or Turkic languages of their neighbours; this language has now been lost, however, and they speak a dialect of Persian. They were virtually independent of outside rule until 1884, when the Amir Abdur Rahman succeeded in subjugating Badakhshan and bringing it under the control of Kabul. The Hazaras had become Shi'i Muslims during the reign of Shah Abbas I, but in the time of Nadir Shah (mid-eighteenth century), the Barbari group, which was settled along the upper Murghab, became Sunni. The majority of Hazaras are found in Afghanistan, but a small number of Barbaris are still found in the Turkmen SSR in the Murghab Valley. They were listed separately in the 1926 Soviet Census, but not thereafter. They are probably now included with the Turkmen and may well have been completely assimilated by them, or by the Persians (*Irani*: see p. 356) with whom they have traditionally intermarried. In 1926 there were also 12 'Hazaras' (*Khazara, Khazarejtsy*), as distinct from the Barbari Hazaras, who were included with the Persians.

1926 Census figures

Population: 146.
Urban dwellers: 63.0 per cent.
Percentage claiming own language as their mother tongue: 50.0.
Number claiming Russian as their mother tongue: none.
Literacy: 2.1 per cent (3 people; of these, 1 was literate in his own language).

Kashgarlyks

Own names: *Kashgarlyk, Kashkilik*; Russian name: *Kashgartsy*.

The Kashgarlyks are a group of 'modern' Uighurs (see p. 347) from the Kashgar oasis in Eastern Turkestan. They moved to the Ferghana Valley in the mid-nineteenth century. In the 1926 Census they were listed separately, but are now included with the Uighurs. Their language is a southern dialect of (Modern) Uighur.

1926 Census figures

Population: 13,010, of whom 7,467 (57.4 per cent) lived in the Kirghiz ASSR, 4,421 (34.0 per cent) in the Uzbek SSR.
Urban dwellers: 44.6 per cent.
Percentage claiming own language as their mother tongue: 85.9.
Number claiming Russian as their mother tongue: 8 people.
Literacy: 717 (5.5 per cent); of these, 270 were literate in their own language (37.7 per cent of the total literate population).

Kipchaks

Own name: *Kipchak*; Russian name: *Kipchaki (ferganskije)*.

The Kipchaks are a non-Uzbek people of the Ferghana Valley. They are possibly directly descended from the Kipchak (Cuman/ Polovtsian) tribes who invaded Central Asia in the thirteenth and fourteenth centuries. Their language shows affinities with Kirghiz and Kazakh. In the 1926 Census they were listed separately, but are now included with the Uzbeks.

1926 Census figures

Population: 33,502.
Urban dwellers: 1.5 per cent.
Percentage claiming own language as their mother tongue: 99.7.
Number claiming Russian as their mother tongue: 1 person.
Literacy: 477 (1.4 per cent); of these, 452 were literate in their own
   language (94.8 per cent of the total literate population).

Kuramas

Own name: *Kurama*; Russian name: *Kuramintsy*.

The Kuramas are a Turkic people whose precise origin is unclear.
They are probably descended from a variety of Turkic peoples, e.g.
Uzbeks, Kazakhs and Karakalpaks. By the beginning of the nineteenth century, if not earlier, they were leading a settled existence
in the Ferghana Valley. Soviet ethnographers classify them as Uzbeks and although they were listed separately in the 1926 Census,
they are now included with the Uzbeks.

1926 Census figures

Population: 50,079.
Urban dwellers: 0.2 per cent.
Percentage claiming own language as their mother tongue: 16.4.
Number claiming Russian as their mother tongue: none.
Literacy: 1,196 (2.4 per cent); of these, 158 were literate in their
   own language (13.2 per cent of the total literate population).

Pamiris/Galchahs/Mountain Tadzhiks

The Pamiris (also known as Galchahs or Mountain Tadzhiks) are
small communities who, though living in close geographic proximity, nevertheless represent quite distinct ethnic groups; even their
languages, while belonging to the same linguistic family, are virtually mutually incomprehensible. The following Pamiri peoples are
found in the Soviet Union (see top of p. 375).
   They are known collectively as Tadzhiks (Russian *Tadzhiki*).
They live in the south-west of the Gorno-Badakhshan ('Mountain

Own name	Russian name	English name
Badzhuwedzh	Badzhujtsy	Badzhuis
Bartangidzh	Bartangtsy	Bartangis
Khik	Vakhantsy	Wakhis, Wakhanis
Khufidzh	Khuftsy	Khufis
Khugnon	Shugnantsy	Shugnis
Rykhen	Rushantsy	Rushanis
Shikomshi	Ishkashimtsy	Ishkash(i)mis
Zgamig	Jazgulemtsy/Jazgulamtsy	Yazgulemis

Badakhshan') Autonomous Province in the Tadzhik SSR. To the south runs the River Pjandzh (Panj), which forms the international frontier with Afghanistan; to the west lies the Afghan province of Badakhshan, to the south, across the narrow Wakhan corridor, is Pakistan. The area is one of the most remote in the whole of the Soviet Union. It used to be almost inaccessible from the outside world, but it is now linked by road with Dushanbe (in the Tadzhik SSR) and Osh (in the Kirghiz SSR).

1 HISTORICAL BACKGROUND

Invading armies have crossed and re-crossed the Pamirs from the beginning of recorded history and no doubt earlier, each succeeding wave leaving its mark. Local tradition holds that the leaders of some of the mountain states were descended from the Greek commanders of Alexander the Great's army and this is in all probability true. The earliest written references to the states of Shugnan, Rushan and Wakhan are found in Chinese chronicles of the second century AD. They are known to have been under Tibetan rule during the eighth and ninth centuries; in the tenth century they achieved a measure of independence, but in later periods were almost always under the overlordship of one of the stronger neighbouring states, e.g. Badakhshan, Darwaz or Kunduz. Far from being united amongst themselves, they were in constant conflict with one another and with the Kirghiz of the eastern Pamirs.

In the mid-eighteenth century an independent Afghan state was formed under Ahmad Shah Durrani (1747–72). This included in its territory the principalities of Balkh, Kunduz and Badakhshan and, consequently, their vassal states. It took more than a century for Afghan power to be firmly established in this region, however, and in the meanwhile it was controlled by Uzbek and Tadzhik chieftains. The Uzbek Khan of Kunduz, Murad Beg (1815–40) was particularly powerful and succeeded in subjugating many of the surrounding lands, including Badakhshan. It was not until the reign of Abdur Rahman (1880–1901), that Shugnan, Rushan and Badakhshan were brought firmly under the rule of Kabul. Meanwhile, the Emir of Bukhara was also seeking to expand his possessions to the south; Balkh had been taken as early as 1793 and in the mid-nineteenth century new gains were made. In 1878 Bukhara, by now a Russian Protectorate, took Darwaz. Britain was at this time rapidly advancing through India towards the Hindu Kush and in order to limit each other's 'spheres of influence' Britain and Russia agreed on a demarcation of Afghanistan's northern frontier in 1895. The River Pjandzh provided a natural geographical division. The left (southern) bank of the river was given to Afghanistan, while most of the right (northern) bank fell to the lot of the Emir of Bukhara, in exchange for his possessions on the opposite side of the river. His acquisitions included parts of Shugnan, Rushan and Wakhan. Since the River Pjandzh had never been an ethnic frontier, its use as an international boundary meant the indiscriminate division of the traditional lands of the mountain peoples. Many tribesmen suddenly found themselves cut off from their kin and in several cases separate communities of the same group developed on either side of the border.

In 1904 Russia annexed the Pamiri possessions of the Emir of Bukhara. In 1917, after the Revolution (the area is so remote that it took several months for news of the Revolution to reach there), the White Army gained control; later the Emir sought to re-establish his rule, but by 1920 the Red Army had succeeded in wiping out the main pockets of resistance. On 2 January 1925 the *Osobaja Pripamirskaja oblast'* ('Special Pamir Province'), renamed after a few months the 'Gorno-Badakhshan ('Mountain Badakhshan') Autonomous Province', was created within the Tadzhik ASSR (later transformed into the Tadzhik SSR).

Gorno-Badakhshan Autonomous Province

Situated in the western Pamir range, in the south-eastern corner of the Tadzhik SSR; it is bordered to the east by the People's Republic of China, to the south and west by Afghanistan. *Area*: 63,700 sq.

km (comprising 44.5 per cent of the total territory of the Tadzhik SSR). *Capital*: Khorog (population in 1971: 13,000). The Province has 1 town and no settlements. *Population* (1979): 127,709. Average density of population per sq. km (1979): 2.0.

Chief resources: deposits of common salt, gold, rock crystal, mica, semi-precious stones and asbestos; thermal springs; mountain rivers and waterfalls; pasture lands.

Marco Polo (1274) recounts that silver, lapis lazuli and rubies were mined in this area. Today, however, most of these deposits have been exhausted. The chief occupation is rearing animals (sheep, goats, cattle and, in the east, yaks); there is also some cultivation of cereals, potatoes and tobacco.

2 NUMBER AND DISTRIBUTION

The Pamiri peoples have always been listed together with the Tadzhiks in the Soviet census reports. An approximate estimation of the size of the various groups (*c.* 1960) is given in *Jazyki narodov SSSR I*:

Shugnis   20,000
Rushanis   7–8,000
Wakhanis   6–7,000
Bartangis   3–4,000
Yazgulemis   1,500–2,000
Khufis   1,000–1,500
Ishkashimis   500

They live in compact groups in the Gorno-Badakhshan Autonomous Province of the Tadzhik SSR, in the valleys of rivers such as the Pjandzh and Bartang.

Ethnic composition of the Gorno-Badakhshan Autonomous Province in 1970

Total population	97,796
Tadzhiks (incl. Pamiri peoples)	89,314 (91.3%)
Kirghiz	6,930 (7.1%)
Russians	764 (0.8%)
Others	788 (0.8%)

Urban/rural distribution in the Gorno-Badakhshan Autonomous Province in 1970

	Urban	Rural
Total population	12,295	85,501
Tadzhiks (incl. Pamiri peoples)	11,441	77,873
	(93.1%)	(91.1%)
Kirghiz	40	6,890
	(0.3%)	(8.1%)
Russians	408	356
	(3.3%)	(0.4%)
Others	406	382
	(3.3%)	(0.4%)

3 STATUS

The Pamiri peoples enjoy full Soviet citizenship. Almost all of them work on collective farms. Their standard of housing is comparable to that of other national groups in the Soviet Union. The women go out to work, as elsewhere in the Soviet Union.

4 LANGUAGE

Each tribal grouping has its own language. They are sometimes referred to as the 'Galchah languages' or the 'Pamiri dialects'. They belong to the East Iranian group of languages. Despite the fact that the areas in which they are spoken are in such comparatively close proximity, these languages are almost entirely mutually incomprehensible. Tadzhik has for centuries served as the medium of intertribal communication. However, some of the languages do have enough points of similarity for it to be possible to link them together in a single category. These are Shugni, Badzhui, Rushani and the closely-related Khufi, Bartangi and Sarikol (this last spoken only in the Chinese region of the Pamirs), which together form the Shugnano-Rushani sub-group. The other Pamiri languages represented in the Soviet Union are Wakhi, Yazgulemi and Ishkashimi. This last has three distinct dialects, of which only Yazgulemi 'proper' is known in the USSR; the other two, Zebaki and Sanglechi, are spoken in Afghanistan.

None of the Pamiri languages have a written tradition. An attempt was made to provide a special alphabet for Shugni in the

1930s and a children's primer was published in it in Stalinabad/ Dushanbe in 1931, but the project was soon abandoned. Grammars and texts of Wakhi and Bartangi appeared in 1974 and 1976 respectively, which may indicate some revival of interest. Meanwhile, Tadzhik serves as the literary language of the region and is also the medium of instruction in schools.

5 RELIGION

Most of the Pamiri peoples have been Isma'ili Muslims since the eleventh century; the exceptions are the Bartangis and some of the Yazgulemis, who are Sunni Muslims (Hanafi school).

6 OUTSIDE THE SOVIET UNION

There are Pamiri peoples in Afghanistan, India, Pakistan and China:

Shugnis ⎱
Rushanis ⎰ approx. ⎱ 20,000 ⎰ in the Afghan province of
Ishkashimis ⎰ ⎰ 8,000 ⎰ Badakhshan
⎰ 2,000 ⎰

Wakhis probably less than 6,000 settled in the area where the borders of China, India, Pakistan and the USSR converge

Sarikols approximately 5,000 in China, Xinjiang-Wei-wu-er (Sinkiang-Uighur) Autonomous Region

Sart Kalmyks

Own name: *Oirot*; Russian name: *Kalmyki*.

The Kalmyks are a western Mongolian people. The majority lived in the Kalmyk ASSR until 1943, when they were deported to Siberia and Central Asia. They were 'rehabilitated' and allowed to return home to their reinstated autonomous republic in 1957-8. In the late nineteenth century, however, a small group of Kalmyks had already moved to Central Asia and settled in the Tien Shan range in Kirghizia, in the vicinity of Lake Issyk-kul'. In the 1926 Soviet Census they were listed as 'Sart Kalmyks', as distinct from the Kalmyks of the Kalmyk ASSR on the lower Volga. They are no longer listed separately, but it is not known whether they are now included with the Kalmyks or with the Kirghiz.

The Sart Kalmyks are Sunni Muslims; the other Kalmyks are Lamaist Buddhists.

1926 Census figures

Population: 2,793; of these, 2,539 (90.9 per cent) lived in the Kirghiz ASSR.
Urban dwellers: 6.2 per cent.
Percentage claiming own language as their mother tongue: 88.3.
Number claiming Russian as their mother tongue: 8 people.
Literacy: 14.3 per cent; none of these were literate in their mother tongue.

Taranchis

Own name: *Taranchi*? – today probably *Uighur*; Russian name: *Taranchi*.

The Taranchis (term derived from the Chinese word for 'farmer') were a group of some 6,000 'modern' Uighur families who were transported by the Chinese government from Kashgaria to the Ili Valley in the mid-eighteenth century; 4,100 families were settled on the right bank, 1,900 on the left bank. They cultivated the region and eventually formed their own semi-independent principality. In 1871 the Ili Valley was occupied by the Russians; it was returned to the Chinese in 1882, but 45,373 of the Taranchis (who by then numbered over 51,000) moved to Russian territory, where they were settled in the Semirech'je district. In the 1926 Soviet Census the Taranchis were listed separately, but are now included with the Uighurs. In the early twentieth century there were still about 8,200 Taranchis in China, but it is not known how many, if any, there are today.

The Taranchis speak a dialect of (Modern) Uighur. Like the other 'modern' Uighur groups, they are Sunni Muslims (Hanafi school). See p. 345.

1926 Census figures

Population: 53,010; of these, 51,803 (97.7%) lived in the Kazakh ASSR.

Urban dwellers: 20.2 per cent.
Percentage claiming own language as their mother tongue: 99.5.
Number claiming Russian as their mother tongue: 7 people.
Literacy: 4,481 (8.5 per cent); of these, 4,095 were literate in their own language (91.4 per cent of the total literate population).

Turks of Ferghana and Samarkand

Own name: *Turk*; Russian name: *Turki ferganskije i samarkandskije*.

The Turks of Ferghana and Samarkand are a non-Uzbek people of Uzbekistan. They live, as their name suggests, in the Ferghana Valley. Although much influenced by the neighbouring Uzbeks, they have preserved up till the present a sense of their separate identity. Little work has been done on their historical background, but they are most probably the descendants of Turkic tribes who settled in the Ferghana region before the advent of the Uzbeks *c*. AD 1400. They were listed separately in the 1926 Census, but are now included with the Uzbeks. ('Turks' are listed separately in the 1979 Census, but these are almost certainly Meskhetian Turks; see p. 261.)

1926 Census figures

Population: 537.
Urban dwellers: 0.6 per cent.
Percentage claiming own language as their mother tongue: 6.5.
Number claiming Russian as their mother tongue: none.
Literacy: 6 people (1.1 per cent); of these one was literate in his own language.

Ottoman Turks

Own name: *Osmanli*; Russian name: *Tjurki osmanskije*.

In 1926 there were a number of 'Ottoman Turks' living in Central Asia. They are no longer listed separately in the census, so they have presumably either left the Soviet Union or been assimilated by the indigenous population.

1926 Census figures

Population: 8,570.
Urban dwellers: 30.8 per cent.
Percentage claiming own language as their mother tongue: 86.3.
Percentage claiming Russian as their mother tongue: 5.6.
Literacy: 1,693 (19.8 per cent); of these, 977 were literate in their
   own language (57.7 per cent of the total literate population).

Yagnobis

Own name: *Yagnobi*; Russian name: *Jagnobtsy*.

They live in the Tadzhik SSR in an outcrop of the Pamir mountains.
The majority are concentrated in the valley of the River Yagnob
(hence their name), but there are a few settlements further to the
south, along the River Varzob (immediately to the north of
Dushanbe).

The Yagnobis are an Iranian people. The territory they inhabit
formed part of the Sogdian empire and their language, which belongs to the East Iranian group, traces its development from the
Sogdian group of dialects. It is possible that the Yagnobis were
considerably more numerous in the past than they are now and that
they controlled a larger area, for Yagnobi place-names are found
well outside the present Yagnobi lands. A curious feature of the
Yagnobis' language is their so-called 'secret language', in which
cryptic equivalents are substituted for the normal terms. This form
of linguistic defence is used against outsiders, such as the Tadzhiks
of the plains, but also between the sexes and between peer groups.

The first transcriptions of Yagnobi were made in 1870 by A. L.
Kun and Mirza Abdurrahman. Since then it has been the subject
of a number of studies; it is of special interest to philologists due
to its links with Sogdian. It is an extremely limited language, its
vocabulary consisting of only about 2,500 words (more than half of
which are Tadzhik loans). However, it contains two dialects, an
eastern and a western; the differences between them are phonetic.
As Yagnobi has no alphabet of its own, Tadzhik is used as the
literary language and as the medium of instruction in schools. All
Yagnobis are now said to be bi-lingual in Tadzhik and Yagnobi.

The Yagnobis are Muslims. Most are Sunnis, but a few are
Isma'ilis.

In the 1926 Soviet Census the Yagnobis were listed separately; thereafter they were included with the Tadzhiks.

1926 Census figures

Population: 1,829. It was estimated in 1966 (*Jazyki narodov SSSR I*) that there were then 2,000 or more Yagnobis.
Urban dwellers: none.
Percentage claiming Yagnobi as their mother tongue: 99.9.
Number claiming Russian (or any other language) as mother tongue: none.
Literacy: 0.0 per cent (not a single person).

NOTE
Ratbek Nisanbai has recently been elected Kazi of Kazakhstan replacing Yahya Baisenbayev mentioned on pages 34 and 301.

Appendix:
Non-Muslim Turkic peoples of the Soviet Union

No exact figures are available for the total world population of the Turkic peoples, but Baskakov (*Vvedenije . . .* p. 6) gives a detailed regional survey of the subject, based on data for 1962, and estimates that in that year there were 58,638,000 Turkic speakers. If the world population of Turkic speakers has increased at the same rate as that of the Turkic speakers within the Soviet Union, they should now number almost 100 million. About 40 per cent of this total population lives within the Soviet Union. The Turks of Turkey constitute the largest single group (some 40 million), the Uzbeks (12.5 million) the next largest. All the other Turkic groups are considerably smaller, some of them (e.g. the Tofas) consisting of no more than a few hundred.

The earliest stages in the emergence of the Turkic peoples are still matters of speculation, but it is generally accepted that their original homeland was in the region of Mongolia, from where they fanned out in ever-widening arcs across Asia and eventually into Europe. It is almost impossible to identify them with any certainty until about the sixth century AD, since before this period their history is inextricably interwoven with that of the other nomadic peoples of the steppe, such as the Mongolian and Tungusic groups. It is conceivable that the Huns (Ephthalites), who irrupted into Central Asia in the early fifth century, were Turkic, but this has not been proved conclusively.

The Turkic penetration of the territory that now constitutes the Soviet Union took place in three main waves, each one carrying them further to the west: into Central Asia and Siberia *c.* AD 500, into Transcaucasia *c.* 1050, into the Volga region and beyond *c.* 1230. In addition to these major movements, there was an almost constant undercurrent of outward migration, which in effect paved the way for the larger expansions and made it easier for the Turkic

384

peoples to settle in new areas and to adapt to new conditions. They had a remarkable propensity for assimilating other ethnic groups and as a result, although they themselves were to some extent affected by the indigenous peoples, the territories which they conquered generally became Turkic-speaking. In some cases, several layers of Turkic migration into a particular region can be distinguished and the present population represents a fusion of a variety of Turkic as well as non-Turkic elements.

The Turkic presence in Central Asia becomes perceptible from about the beginning of the sixth century. By the middle of that century the nomadic tribes of Semirech'je had united to form the first Turkic (Göktürk) empire or 'khaganate'. It soon split into two halves, a western and an eastern, but both survived in one form or another until the mid-eighth century, when a new Turkic power emerged, the Uighurs. The Uighurs were overthrown by the Kirghiz and they, in turn, were conquered by yet other Turkic peoples. Some of the Kirghiz moved into Siberia, possibly preceded by other Turkic groups (e.g. the Tuba tribes). Turkic inscriptions dating from the fifth to seventh centuries have been found on the Yenisei and near Lake Baikal; they closely resemble the famous Orkhon inscriptions of the same period found in Mongolia. These early settlers in Siberia were the forebears of such peoples as the Khakass, Altais and Tuvinians of today.

Meanwhile, in Central Asia (using the term in its widest sense) Turkic domination of the region continued to be reinforced by wave upon wave of invading hordes, until it culminated in another great surge of expansion. This occurred during the eleventh century, when the Seljuk-Oghuz tribes (forebears of the modern Turkmen) embarked on a series of campaigns that soon won them an empire that stretched from the Oxus (Amu-Darya) to the Euphrates. Transcaucasia formed part of the Seljuk conquests and as a result was inundated with Turkic speakers. It was not, however, the first Turkic empire in the region; the Khazars had held sway there for some three centuries previously and when their state disintegrated some of them took refuge in the Caucasus mountains. Their descendants are thought to include such groups as the Karachais and Balkars. The Karaims, who migrated to the Crimea and later to the Grand Duchy of Lithuania, are probably also descended from them.

The final stage in the Turkic penetration of what was later to become the Russian Empire was brought about by the Mongol invasion. The term 'Mongol' is something of a misnomer here, since

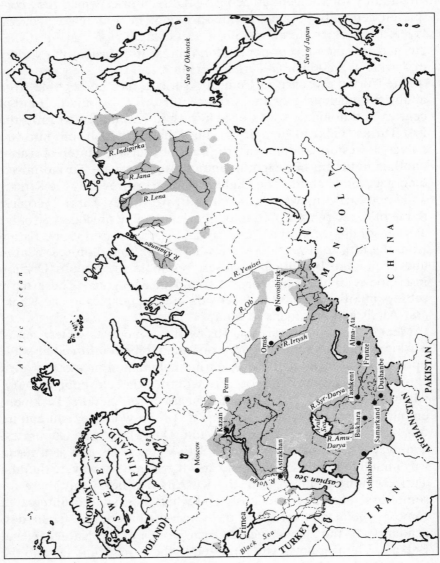

Regional Distribution of the Turkic Peoples of the Soviet Union

though its leaders were Mongols, the great mass of its fighting force was composed of Turkic tribes. The influence of the latter was so great that the two wings of the Mongol Empire that had control of this region, the Ulus of Dzhuchi (i.e. the Golden Horde) and the Ulus of Chagatai, had both become completely Turkified by the fourteenth century. Central Asia, which formed the basis of Chagatai's state, was already virtually a Turkic preserve, but even beyond the Urals there was a well-established Turkic element. The Bolgars (not to be confused with the Slav Bulgars) had settled along the Volga and Kama by the seventh century AD, the Pechenegs dominated the lands between the Danube and the Don from the eighth to the eleventh centuries, while the Kipchaks (also known as Cumans or Polovtsians) were in control of the steppes of southern Russia and central Kazakhstan as far as the Irtysh, the so-called *Desht-i Kipchak*, from the mid-eleventh century until the advent of the Mongols in the early thirteenth century. These earlier Turkic arrivals all came under the rule of the latest wave of immigrants and to a large extent were absorbed by them.

There do not appear to have been any rigid ethnic distinctions between the various branches of the Mongol Empire and as the central power waned there was considerable movement of tribal groups. This was particularly the case between the states of Chagatai and Dzhuchi; there were no insurmountable physical obstacles in their way and until well into the fifteenth century the situation remained extremely fluid, with individual leaders suddenly gathering up their followers and migrating vast distances. The need for alliances against immediate neighbours also encouraged contacts with more remote forces. In the late fourteenth century, for example, Toktamysh, a Khan of the White Horde, travelled from Troki (Trakai in the present-day Lithuanian SSR) to Samarkand to seek assistance from Timur against rivals on the Volga, a distance of nearly 4,000 km. Gradually, though, more settled patterns emerged. There were still a few instances of whole groups of people moving, as when Bukharans went to Siberia in the fifteenth and sixteenth centuries, or Kazakhs from the Little Horde migrated to the Orenburg district at the beginning of the nineteenth century, but these were the exceptions rather than the rule. (The Kazakhs and Kirghiz, however, appear to have retained their mobility into the twentieth century: in the first decade of the Soviet period some of the Kirghiz moved to Afghanistan and a large number of Kazakhs are thought to have moved to China.)

Some of the Turkic peoples of the Soviet Union were converted to Islam as early as the eighth century, others (the nomadic Kirghiz and Kazakhs) as late as the nineteenth century, but the majority had become Muslim by the fifteenth century. The tiny number who did not adopt Islam were those on the very fringes of the Turkic world, such as the isolated tribes of Siberia and the Gagauz in Bessarabia. The Karaims are exceptional in that for centuries they were surrounded by closely related Muslim Turkic peoples, yet they remained faithful throughout to their own form of Judaism.

Turkic peoples of the USSR as listed in the 1970 and 1979 censuses

'Turkic' is used here both for speakers of Turkic languages and for those of Turkic origin who no longer speak a Turkic language; the non-Muslim Turkic peoples are indicated by†:

	1970	1979	% growth
Uzbeks	9,195,093	12,455,978	35.5
Tatars	5,930,670	6,317,468	6.5
Kazakhs	5,298,818	6,556,442	23.7
Azerbaidzhanis	4,379,937	5,477,330	25.1
Chuvash	1,694,351	1,751,366	3.4
Turkmen	1,525,284	2,027,913	33.0
Kirghiz	1,452,222	1,906,271	31.3
Bashkirs	1,239,681	1,371,452	10.6
Yakuts†	296,244	328,018	10.7
Karakalpaks	236,009	303,324	28.5
Kumyks	188,792	228,418	21.0
Uighurs	173,276	210,612	21.6
Gagauz†	156,606	173,179	10.6
Tuvinians†	139,388	166,082	19.2
Karachais	112,741	131,074	16.3
Turks	(79,000)*	92,689	17.3
Khakass†	66,725	70,776	6.1
Balkars	59,501	66,334	11.5
Altais†	55,812	60,015	7.5
Nogais	51,784	59,546	15.0
Shors†	16,494	16,033	− 2.8
Dolgans†	4,877	5,053	3.6

	1970	1979	% growth
Karaims†	4,571	3,341	−26.9
Tofas†	620	763	23.1
Total	32,358,496	39,779,477	22.9
% of total Soviet population	13.4	15.2	

*Approximate estimate; not listed separately in the 1970 census.

Only just over 2 per cent of the Turkic peoples of the USSR are non-Muslims. All the non-Muslims are Christians, except for the Karaims and Krymchaks (the latter not listed separately) who are Jews. All the Christian Turkic peoples live in Siberia, except for the Gagauz, who live in the Moldavian SSR. The Karaims are rather dispersed, but their main centres are the Crimea, the Lithuanian SSR, Moscow and Leningrad.

Approximate regional distribution of the Turkic peoples of the USSR in 1979

Central Asia and Kazakhstan (Uzbeks, Kazakhs, Turkmen, Kirghiz, Karakalpaks, Uighurs, Turks)	60.0%
European USSR and Siberia (Tatars, Chuvash, Bashkirs, Yakuts, Gagauz, Tuvinians, Khakass, Altais, Shors, Dolgans, Karaims, Tofas)	25.0%
Transcaucasia and Northern Caucasus (Azerbaidzhanis, Kumyks, Karachais, Balkars, Nogais)	15.0%

Republics and Autonomous Provinces in which the titular population is Turkic

	Titular People	% of total population in 1979
Union Republics		
Uzbek SSR	Uzbeks	68.7
Kazakh SSR	Kazakhs	36.0
Azerbaidzhan SSR	Azerbaidzhanis	78.1
Kirghiz SSR	Kirghiz	47.9
Turkmen SSR	Turkmen	68.4

	Titular People	% of total population in 1979
Autonomous Republics		
Bashkir ASSR (RSFSR)	Bashkirs	24.3
Chuvash ASSR (RSFSR)	Chuvash	68.4
Kabardino-Balkar ASSR (RSFSR)	Balkars	9.0
Karakalpak ASSR (Uzbek SSR)	Karakalpaks	31.1
Nakhichevan ASSR (Azerbaidzhan SSR)	Azerbaidzhanis	95.6
Tatar ASSR (RSFSR)	Tatars	47.6
Tuvinian ASSR (RSFSR)	Tuvinians	60.5
Yakut ASSR (RSFSR)	Yakuts	36.9
Autonomous Provinces		
Gorno-Altai Aut. Prov. (RSFSR)	Altais	29.2
Karachai-Cherkess Aut. Prov. (RSFSR)	Karachais	29.7
Khakass Aut. Prov. (RSFSR)	Khakass	11.5

YAKUTS

Own names: *Sakha, Saka*; Russian name: *Jakuty*.

The great majority live in the Yakut ASSR (within the RSFSR), but there are also small groups of Yakuts in other areas of Siberia, e.g. in the Tajmyr and Evenk National Regions of the Krasnojar Territory (*kraj*) and the Magadan, Sakhalin and Amur Districts (*oblasti*) of the RSFSR.

1 HISTORICAL BACKGROUND

The origins of the Yakuts are unclear. Anthropological evidence suggests the presence of two main Mongoloid strains, the Central Asian and the Baikal (Siberian). Soviet scholars are of the opinion that the Yakuts are the product of an intermingling between the indigenous tribes of the Lena and Turkic-speaking immigrants from the south. It is suggested that the last such wave of immigrants reached the Lena in the fourteenth and fifteenth centuries. It is possible that they were driven northwards from Lake Baikal by the arrival of Mongol Buryats, themselves displaced by Genghiz Khan's Mongols at the beginning of the thirteenth century. In the early twentieth century there was still a small Turkic tribe in the Minusinsk area called *Sekha*; this would support the theory that the Turkic-speaking *Sakhalar* (i.e. Yakuts) migrated northwards from an original habitat further to the south.

The Russian name for the Yakuts is derived from the Tungusic term *Jeko, Jekot*. The Russians came in contact with them in the first half of the seventeenth century. By this time the Yakuts were settled on both banks of the Middle Lena, its tributary the Viljuj and the upper reaches of the Jana. They were divided into clans and tribes; the head of a clan or tribe was a *tojon*. The Yakuts' chief occupations were hunting, fishing and animal husbandry (especially horse-breeding, for which they were famous). They were also skilful metal-workers. The Russians began by bartering with the Yakuts; then in 1632 they founded Yakutsk (the present capital of the Yakut ASSR) on the right bank of the River Lena. This marked the beginning of Russian rule in Yakutia; all local resistance (e.g. the uprisings of 1634 and 1642) was firmly crushed and in 1638 the area acquired the status of a Province (*vojevodstvo*) within the Russian Empire.

The Yakuts were required to pay the Russians tribute (*jasak*), first in pelts, later (in part at least) in money. The *tojons* were eventually entrusted with the collection of the tribute and were also invested with certain judicial powers, thereby achieving, though still under Russian rule, a degree of autonomy. Gold was discovered in Yakutia in 1846, adding a new source of wealth to the already rich trade in sable, fox and other furs. As a result Russian commercial interests in Yakutia greatly increased. The region also acquired another type of notoriety as it became a favourite place of exile for politically undesirable elements.

In the early twentieth century a growing sense of national self-awareness became apparent amongst the Yakuts, who began to demand more civil rights and the return of their land. Over the next few years there was much unrest in Yakutia, culminating in the bitter struggles of the Civil War. The Yakut ASSR was created on 27 April 1922, but fighting between the White Army and the Soviets continued in Yakutia until 1923.

Originally Shamanists, the majority of Yakuts were converted to

Christianity during the eighteenth century. Shamanist traditions, however, persisted into the twentieth century.

Yakut ASSR, also known as *Yakutia*

Situated in the RSFSR; it is bordered to the north by the Laptev and East Siberian Seas. *Area*: 3,103,200 sq. km (it is larger than any of the Union republics except the RSFSR; cf. the area of Kazakhstan, second largest Union republic: 2,717,300 sq. km). *Capital*: Yakutsk (population in 1979: 152,000). The Republic has 10 towns and 61 settlements. *Population* (1979): 851,840. Average density of population per sq. km (1979): 0.3.

   Chief resources: industrial diamonds, mica (USSR's main producer of both), gold, tin, coal and natural gas; it has important resources of hydroelectric power and timber.

   Industries include: mining of minerals, power, timber and production of building materials; processing of furs; other light industries.

   Agriculture: stockbreeding (particularly of horses and reindeer); cultivation of grain (wheat, barley and rye), potatoes and fodder crops; trapping of fur-bearing animals; fishing.

2 NUMBER AND DISTRIBUTION

Number of Yakuts

	1926	1959	1970	1979
	240,709	233,344	296,244	328,018

Regional distribution of Yakuts

	1926	1959	1970	1979
RSFSR	240,687	232,814	295,223	326,531
	(100%)	(99.8%)	(99.7%)	(99.5%)
Yakut ASSR only	235,926	226,053	285,749	313,917
	(98.0%)	(96.9%)	(96.5%)	(95.7%)
Elsewhere in USSR	22	530	1,021	1,487
	(0.0%)	(0.2%)	(0.3%)	(0.5%)

Urban/rural distribution of Yakuts in the RSFSR

	1926	*1970*
Urban	5,273 (2.2%)	61,543 (20.9%)
Rural	235,414 (97.8%)	233,680 (79.1%)

Ethnic composition of the Yakut ASSR

	1926	*1959*	*1970*	*1979*
Total population	285,471	487,343	664,123	851,840
Yakuts	235,926 (82.6%)	226,053 (46.4%)	285,749 (43.0%)	313,917 (36.9%)
Tatars	1,671 (0.6%)	5,172 (1.1%)	7,679 (1.2%)	10,980 (1.3%)
Russians	30,156 (10.6%)	215,328 (44.2%)	314,308 (47.3%)	429,588 (50.4%)
Ukrainians	138 (0.0%)	12,182 (2.5%)	20,253 (3.0%)	46,326 (5.4%)
Others	17,580 (6.2%)	28,608 (5.8%)	36,134 (5.4%)	51,029 (6.0%)

Urban/rural distribution in the Yakut ASSR in 1970

	Urban	*Rural*
Total population	374,533	289,590
Yakuts	55,710 (14.9%)	230,048 (79.4%)
Tatars	6,515 (1.7%)	1,164 (0.4%)
Russians	274,688 (73.3%)	39,620 (13.7%)
Ukrainians	18,264 (4.9%)	1,989 (0.7%)
Others	19,365 (5.2%)	16,769 (5.8%)

3 STATUS

The Yakuts enjoy full Soviet citizenship. They are found in all occupations and in all income brackets, though the majority still follow such traditional occupations as hunting, trapping, fishing and farming; many also work in the timber industry. Their standard of housing is comparable to that of other national groups in the Soviet Union. The women go out to work, as elsewhere in the Soviet Union.

Literacy

In 1926	In 1970
5.8%	Over 99%

In 1926, 12,029 Yakuts were literate in their own language (85.7 per cent of the total literate Yakut population).

Level of education per 1,000 Yakuts living in the Yakut ASSR of 10 years of age and above

	1959	*1970*
Primary		
Total	246	320
Men	258	340
Women	235	302
Higher and secondary (complete and incomplete)		
Total	239	374
Men	281	395
Women	199	356
Higher only		
Total	12	33
Men	16	41
Women	7	25

4 LANGUAGE

The national language is Yakut. It belongs to the North Turkic group (*Fundamenta* classification); it can also be classed as belonging to the Uighur-Oghuz group, Yakut sub-group (Baskakov).

It is one of the most isolated of the Turkic languages. It has some features that are characteristic of Oghuz and Old Uighur; of the modern languages, it is closest to Tuvinian, Khakass and Bashkir. It contains many Mongol and Tungusic loan-words and a large number of words of unknown origin. There is also an important group of Russian loans. The oldest of these, which entered Yakut

long before the Soviet period, have undergone considerable phonetic modifications, e.g. *sylabaar* for *samovar*. More recent borrowings have usually been less drastically altered. The modern Yakut
vocabulary makes use of many Russian terms, but it has also been
enlarged by the ingenious expansion of existing words, whereby
concrete terms have often acquired a figurative meaning (e.g. the
word for 'sweat' has yielded a derivative meaning 'exploitation').

The first serious work on the Yakut language was published in
1851 in St Petersburg; this was O. N. Böhtlingk's *Über die Sprache
der Jakuten*. The first dictionary (apart from the one contained in
Böhtlingk's work) began to appear in 1907. Since then, much research has been done on the language, particularly on the standard
literary form. There are two main dialect groups, the '*o*-group' of
the north-west and the '*a*-group' of the north-east (cf. NW *khotun*,
NE *khatyn*, 'woman'). Dolgan (see p. 422) is also a dialect of
Yakut, but it has been isolated from the main language so long that
it has preserved many archaic forms and mutual comprehensibility
is now low.

Russian is generally used for all administrative and other official
purposes, but Yakut can in theory be used if necessary.

Percentage of Yakuts claiming Yakut as their mother tongue

	1926	1959	1970	1979
Total	99.7	97.6	96.3	95.3
In urban areas	96.8	90.8	87.1	n.a.
in rural areas	99.8	99.0	98.7	n.a.

Percentage of Yakuts with good knowledge of Russian

	1926	1959	1970	1979
As mother tongue	0.1	2.4	3.7	4.6
As second language	n.a.	n.a.	41.7	55.6

In 1958 Yakut was the medium of instruction in grades 1–7 in
the national schools; in 1972, in grades 1–8; in 1972 it was also
taught as an optional, individual subject in Russian-medium
schools, grades 1–10 (Silver, p. 33). There is a university (opened
in 1956) and a number of higher educational establishments (e.g.
of Medicine, Pedagogy and River Studies) in the Republic.

In the Yakut ASSR there are radio and television broadcasts in Yakut and Russian.

Newspapers and periodicals are published in both languages; the main Yakut-language paper is *Kyym* ('Spark' – first appeared in 1923).

Books and pamphlets are published in Yakut (e.g. 61 titles in 1976; of these, 5 were specialized textbooks on technical and scientific subjects).

Number of books and pamphlets published in Yakut in selected years

	1913	1940	1965	1979
No. of titles	1	143	100	79
Print run	2,000	1,111,000	610,000	742,000

Scripts and alphabets

The first Yakut texts were transcribed in the late seventeenth century. The first Yakut alphabet, based on the Cyrillic script, appeared in 1819, together with a Yakut translation of the 'Shortened Catechism'. Another, far superior Yakut alphabet (Cyrillic script) was created by Prof. O. N. Böhtlingk in 1851. Several other Yakut alphabets (Cyrillic script) followed within the next few years, the efforts of a number of other scholars, but they made no advance on Böhtlingk's version, which remained the best. A variety of works in Yakut were published, using his alphabet. The Church, however, preferred the alphabet invented by D. V. Khitrov in 1858 and several religious works, as well as the first Yakut grammar, were published using this alphabet. In 1917 a new alphabet was created by S. A. Novgorodov on the basis of the International Phonetic Alphabet. This was the first alphabet to be used on a wide scale for educational purposes.

The scripts and alphabets used during the Soviet period are as follows:

1917–27 Latin script, first alphabet (based on the IPA)
1924–9   Latin script, second alphabet (capital letters introduced)
1929–39 Latin script, third alphabet
1931   Cyrillic script

This last alphabet is still considered to have a number of shortcomings.

5 RELIGION

Most of the Yakut are (or were) nominally Christian.

GAGAUZ

Own name: *Gagauz*; Russian name: *Gagauzy*.

The majority live in the southern regions of the Moldavian SSR and in the contiguous Odessa District (*oblast'*) of the Ukrainian SSR (the area which formerly constituted Bessarabia). Scattered small communities are also found in Central Asia and Kazakhstan (they date from 1908 to 1914, when some of the Gagauz moved there in response to Stolypin's Agrarian Reform of 1906).

1 HISTORICAL BACKGROUND

Very little is known about the origins of the Gagauz. There are two theories concerning them: (a) that they are descended from such Turkic tribes as the Oghuz and the Cumans (Polovtsians), who migrated from the Black Sea region to the Dobrudzha region of eastern Bulgaria sometime during the Middle Ages and there accepted Orthodox Christianity; (b) that they are descended from Bulgarians, who were forcibly Turkified from the fourteenth century onwards, but succeeded in retaining their Orthodox faith. In either case, they are very close to the Bulgarians in their traditions and customs.

During the Russo-Turkish wars of the nineteenth century many of the Gagauz migrated to the Russian Empire, the majority settling in Bessarabia, which had become a part of the Empire in 1812. Bessarabia was under Romanian rule from 1918–1940 (which is why there are so few Gagauz listed in the 1926 Soviet Census), after which it was united with the Soviet Union, forming the Moldavian SSR.

The traditional occupations of the Gagauz were farming, viticulture and animal husbandry. In 1949, soon after the incorporation of Bessarabia into the Soviet Union, a programme of collectivization was introduced amongst the Gagauz. The majority still work on the land.

2 NUMBER AND DISTRIBUTION

Number of Gagauz

	1926	1959	1970	1979
	844	123,821	156,606	173,179

Regional distribution of Gagauz

	1926	1959	1970	1979
RSFSR (Semipalatinsk Province)	830 (98.3%)	——	——	——
Moldavian SSR	——	95,856 (77.4%)	124,902 (79.8%)	138,000 (79.7%)
Ukrainian SSR	——	23,530 (19.0%)	26,464 (16.9%)	n.a.
Elsewhere in USSR	14 (1.7%)	4,435 (3.6%)	5,240 (3.3%)	

Percentage of Gagauz in relation to total population of individual republics

	1959	1970	1979
Moldavian SSR	3.3	3.5	3.5
Ukrainian SSR	0.0	0.1	n.a.

Urban/rural distribution of Gagauz in 1970

	Urban	Rural
Moldavian SSR	43,528 (34.8%)	81,374 (65.2%)
Ukrainian SSR	4,784 (18.1%)	21,680 (81.9%)

3 STATUS

The Gagauz enjoy full Soviet citizenship. They are found in all occupations and in all income brackets, but the great majority work on collective farms. Their standard of housing is comparable to that of other national groups in the Soviet Union. The women go out to work as elsewhere in the Soviet Union.

Literacy

In 1926, 44 Gagauz (5.2 per cent of the total Soviet population of Gagauz) were literate, none in their own language. By 1970, there was over 99 per cent literacy amongst both men and women.

4 LANGUAGE

The national language is Gagauz. It belongs to the South Turkic group (*Fundamenta* classification); it can also be classed as belonging to the Oghuz group, Oghuz-Bulgar sub-group (Baskakov).

There are two main dialect groups in Gagauz, the central and the southern. The former is the more widespread and has been taken as the basis for the modern literary language, though certain phonetic features from the southern have also been incorporated. The first scholar to work on the Gagauz language and folklore was V. A. Moshkov, a Russian ethnographer who collected his material amongst the Bessarabian Gagauz at the beginning of the nineteenth century. In the twentieth century N. K. Dmitriev and his students have done valuable work on the language. Gagauz is closest to the Turkish dialects of north-east Bulgaria. It is of particular interest amongst the Turkic languages due to its large number of Slavonic (Bulgarian, Russian and Ukrainian) and Romance (Moldavian and Romanian) loan-words. It also has a number of Arabic and Persian loans, e.g. *dzhan* ('soul'), *khadzhi* ('pilgrim to Jerusalem', not Mecca, since the Gagauz were Christian), *tefter* ('note-book') and some from Greek, which are almost exclusively connected with Church ritual.

Russian is generally used for all official proceedings, but in theory Gagauz can be used if necessary.

Percentage of Gagauz claiming Gagauz as their mother tongue

	1926	1959	1970	1979
Total	98.2	94.0	93.6	89.3

Percentage of Gagauz with good knowledge of Russian

	1926	1959	1970	1979
As mother tongue	0.8	4.0	4.9	8.6
As second language	n.a.	n.a.	68.3	68.0

No information is available on the use of Gagauz in schools; it is probably not used at all.

No information is available on its use in broadcasting.

No newspapers are published in Gagauz and very few books (e.g. none in 1976, one in 1977 and two in 1978, one of which was a philological study on the language).

Scripts and alphabets

Very little was written in Gagauz up till the Soviet period (and there is little evidence to suggest that much has been written since). The earliest alphabets were created by missionaries and used mainly for translations of religious texts.

1895–1909 Cyrillic script, first alphabet
1909–32   Cyrillic script, second alphabet
1932–57   Latin script
1957   Cyrillic script, third alphabet

5 RELIGION

The Gagauz are Orthodox Christians.

6 OUTSIDE THE SOVIET UNION

There are approximately 5,000 Gagauz in Bulgaria. There are also a few in Romania, but no accurate information is available on the number there.

TUVINIANS

Own names: *Tuba, Tuwa, Tyva (-kizhi)*; Russian name: *Tuvintsy.*

They were formerly also known as Soyons, Soyots and Uriankhais. Almost all the Tuvinians live in south Siberia, in the Tuvinian ASSR (RSFSR).

1 HISTORICAL BACKGROUND

The Tuvinians, like many of the other Turkic-speaking peoples of south Siberia (e.g. the Altais, Khakass, Shors and Tofas), are descended from Turkic and Turkified Kettic, Samoyedic and Mongol tribes. The designation *Tuba/Tuwa* is widespread in this area (cf. the *Tubalar* sub-group of the Altais: see p. 411) and there is a close interrelationship between the different ethnic groups.

The territory of the present-day Tuvinian ASSR came under the rule of the Turkish Khaganate in the sixth century AD. It was conquered by the Chinese in the mid-seventh century, by the Uighurs in the mid-eighth century and the Yenisei Kirghiz in the mid-ninth century (see p. 328). In 1207 the Mongols made their first incursions into the region; it remained under their sway until 1368 (from 1280 under the Yuan dynasty founded by Kubilai Khan in China). Eastern Mongolian states next dominated the area; in the sixteenth century it was ruled by the Altyn Khans, from the second half of the seventeenth century by the Dzhungarians (Oirots/Kalmyks). The Manchus overthrew the Dzhungarians in 1757–8 and the whole region was incorporated into the Chinese Empire. Long before this, however, Russia had already begun to take an interest in the area. Ambassadors were sent there in 1615, but it was only in the nineteenth century that trade contacts were fully developed. They were facilitated by the 1860 Pekin Treaty between Russia and China. Settlers soon appeared in the wake of commerce and by the early twentieth century there was a sizeable Russian colony in what was known as the Urjankhaj Territory (*kraj*). In the aftermath of the Chinese Revolution of 1911 this region was in turmoil and in 1914 the Russians were able to take advantage of the situation to establish a Protectorate there. In 1921 it acquired independent status under the name of the Tannu-Tuva People's Republic. This was incorporated into the Soviet Union in 1944 as the Tuvinian Autonomous Province (forming part of the RSFSR); it was transformed into the Tuvinian ASSR on 10 October 1961 (still within the RSFSR).

Originally Shamanists, the Tuvinians became Lamaist Buddhists in the eighteenth century. They used to be nomadic, their chief occupations being hunting and trapping. These activities have retained their importance, though the Tuvinians now lead a settled existence. In recent years other forms of employment have become available due to the development of farming, stockbreeding and local industry.

Tuvinian ASSR (Tyva Avtonomnung Sovet Sotsialisticheskaja Respublika)

Situated in the RSFSR, bordered to the east by the Buryat ASSR, to the south-east and south by the Mongol People's Republic. *Area*: 170,500 sq. km. *Capital*: Kyzyl (population in 1979: 66,000). The Republic has 5 towns and 3 settlements. *Population* (1979): 267,599. Average density of population per sq. km (1979): 1.6.

Chief resources: deposits of iron ore, asbestos (the largest in the USSR), cobaltite, gold, salt and other minerals; rich forests, which cover about half its territory.

Industries include: mining, timber, production of building materials, food and other light industries based on local produce.

Agriculture: mainly stockbreeding, particularly of sheep and goats; cultivation of grain (particularly wheat), potatoes and other vegetables; trapping of fur-bearing animals; hunting.

2 NUMBER AND DISTRIBUTION

Number of Tuvinians

	1926*	1959	1970	1979
	——	100,145	139,388	166,082

* In 1926 the Tuvinians were not part of the USSR, but there were 229 Soyots/Soyons in the USSR at this time.

Regional distribution of Tuvinians

	1926	1959	1970	1979
RSFSR	229*	99,864 (99.7%)	139,013 (99.7%)	165,426 (99.6%)
Tuvinian Aut.Prov./ASSR only	——	97,996 (97.9%)	135,306 (97.1%)	161,888 (97.5%)
Elsewhere in USSR	——	281 (0.3%)	375 (0.3%)	656 (0.4%)

* 169 Soyons/Soyots were in the Buryat-Mongol ASSR.

Urban/rural distribution of the Tuvinians in the RSFSR in 1970

Urban	23,560 (17.0%)
Rural	115,453 (83.0%)

Ethnic composition of the Tuvinian Autonomous Province/ASSR

	1959	*1970*	*1979*
Total	171,928	230,864	267,599
Tuvinians	97,996 (57.0%)	135,306 (58.6%)	161,888 (60.5%)
Russians	68,924 (40.1%)	88,385 (38.3%)	96,793 (36.2%)
Others	5,008 (2.9%)	7,173 (3.1%)	8,918 (3.3%)

Urban/rural distribution in the Tuvinian ASSR in 1970

	Urban	*Rural*
Total population	86,991	143,873
Tuvinians	21,458 (24.7%)	113,848 (79.1%)
Russians	60,555 (69.6%)	27,830 (19.3%)
Others	4,978 (5.7%)	2,195 (1.5%)

3 STATUS

Level of education per 1,000 Tuvinians living in the Tuvinian ASSR of 10 years of age and above

	1959	*1970*
Primary		
Total	274	359
Men	288	375
Women	259	344
Higher and secondary (complete and incomplete)		
Total	147	336
Men	164	335
Women	126	336
Higher only		
Total	2	20
Men	3	22
Women	1	18

The Tuvinians enjoy full Soviet citizenship. They are found in all occupations and in all income brackets, but the majority work on collective farms. Their standard of housing is comparable to that of other national groups in the Soviet Union. The women go out to work, as elsewhere in the Soviet Union.

Literacy

In 1970	Over 99 per cent.

4 LANGUAGE

The national language is Tuvinian. It belongs to the North Turkic group (*Fundamenta* classification). It can also be classed as belonging to the Uighur-Oghuz group, Uighur-Tukju sub-group (Baskakov). It is related to Tofa (formerly known as 'Karagas'). It contains many archaic features, including Oghuz and Old Uighur elements, and a large number of Mongol loans. The dialects have as yet been very little studied.

Russian is generally used for administrative, judicial and other official proceedings, but in theory Tuvinian can be used if necessary.

Percentage of Tuvinians claiming Tuvinian as their mother tongue

	1959	1970	1979
Total	99.1	98.7	98.8
In urban areas	95.2	94.5	n.a.
In rural areas	99.5	99.6	n.a.

Percentage of Tuvinians with good knowledge of Russian

	1959	1970	1979
As mother tongue	0.8	1.2	1.2
As second language	n.a.	38.9	59.2

In 1958 Tuvinian was the medium of instruction in grades 1–7 in the national schools; in 1972, in grades 1–7 and pre-school; in 1972 it was also taught as an individual, optional subject in Russian-medium schools in grades 1–10 (Silver, p. 33). There is a Pedagogical Institute and a branch of the Krasnojar Polytechnical Institute in the Republic.

In the Tuvinian ASSR there are radio and television broadcasts in Tuvinian, as well as Russian.

Newspapers and periodicals are published in Tuvinian and Russian; the Tuvinian-language papers are *Shyn* ('Truth' – first appeared in 1925) and *Tyvanyng anyjaktary* ('Tuvinian Youth' – first appeared in 1933); there is also a Tuvinian edition of 'Agitator's Note-book' (since 1975).

Books and pamphlets are published in Tuvinian (e.g. 31 titles in 1976; of these, 1 was a specialized textbook on a technical subject).

Numbers of books and pamphlets published in Tuvinian in selected years

	1965	*1979*
No. of titles	53	47
Print run	265,000	239,000

Scripts and alphabets

Tuvinian was written in the Mongol-Tibetan script until the adoption of the Latin script in 1930.

1930–43   Latin script
1943   Cyrillic script

This last alphabet is considered to be fundamentally satisfactory for the representation of Tuvinian, but minor corrections and improvements are still necessary.

5 RELIGION

The Tuvinians are Lamaist Buddhists.

6 OUTSIDE THE SOVIET UNION

There are approximately 18,000 Tuvinians in Mongolia.

KHAKASS

Own name: *Khaas*; Russian name: *Khakasy* (derived from Chinese *Khagias*).

Almost all the Khakass live in Siberia, in the south of the Krasnojar Territory (*kraj*) of the RSFSR, in such areas as the Askiz, Ust'-

Abakan and Shira Regions (*rajony*) of the Khakass Autonomous Province. They are scattered in small groups amongst the vastly larger Russian population.

1 HISTORICAL BACKGROUND

The Khakass are a conglomeration of small, Turkic-speaking tribes. They are descended partly from the Yenisei Kirghiz (who formed the ruling class) and partly from Kettic, Samoyedic and Turkic tribal groups. They also intermingled with the Mongols, who conquered their territory in 1209. Very little else is known of the history of the Khakass until the seventeenth century. They were then settled in the Minusinsk Basin and the Sayan Mountains, where the great majority of them still live today. Their main occupations were cattle-breeding and hunting.

During the seventeenth century they came under Russian rule. Originally animists, many were now converted (nominally at least) to Christianity. Their former semi-nomadic way of life gradually gave way to a more settled existence and they began to build Russian-style houses and to use more advanced methods of farming. In the nineteenth century the gold-mining industry was developed.

In 1917 Soviet power was established in the Minusinsk District (*ujezd*); the White Army gained control of the area in June 1918 and Soviet power was not re-established until September 1919. Fighting continued, however, until 1923. In that year the Khakass National District was formed; in 1925 this was transformed into the Khakass Region and on 20 October 1930 into the Khakass Autonomous Province.

Until the formation of the Khakass District in 1923, the Khakass were called the Minusinsk or Abakan Tatars (or Turks). They were also known by their tribal names: Beltir, Kachin, Koibal, Kyzyl and Sagai. The Beltirs were agriculturalists and cattle-breeders who lived on the Abakan Steppe; the Kachin, semi-nomadic cattle-breeders, lived on the east side of the Abakan River; they were of mixed origin and famous for a particularly rich tradition of epic poetry. The Kyzyl were close neighbours of the Kachin and like them, of mixed origin; the Koibals came from the Sayan Mountains and settled on the Upper Yenisei in the Abakan Steppe, territory abandoned by the Kirghiz early in the nineteenth century; they too were cattle-breeders, mainly of reindeer. As early as the 1926 Census the majority of these people did not use their tribal names, but referred to themselves as 'Khakass'. Some did, however, register themselves according to their tribal affiliation. The estimates for the group as a whole in this first Soviet census are not entirely reliable, due to this confusion in determining the appropriate designation of 'nationality'.

Khakass Autonomous Province, also known as *Khakasia*

Situated in south Siberia, in the Krasnojarsk Territory (*kraj*) of the RSFSR; it is bordered to the south and south-west by the Gorno-Altai Autonomous Province, to the south-east by the Tuvinian ASSR. *Area*: 61,900 sq. km. *Capital*: Abakan (population in 1979: 128,000). The Province has 5 towns and 17 settlements. *Population* (1979): 498,384. Average density of population per sq. km (1979): 8.1.

Chief resources: deposits of coal, iron, copper, gold and various other non-ferrous and rare metals; thick forests cover over half its territory.

Industries include: mining (particularly of coal and gold), timber and food (based on the processing of local produce).

Agriculture: stockbreeding, mainly of sheep, but cattle and horses are also raised; grain farming (particularly of wheat) and the cultivation of fruit and vegetables; apiculture.

2 NUMBER AND DISTRIBUTION

Number of Khakass

	1926	1959	1970	1979
	45,608	56,584	66,725	70,776

Regional distribution of Khakass

	1926	1959	1970	1979
RSFSR	45,608 (100%)	56,032 (99.0%)	65,368 (98.0%)	69,247 (97.8%)
Khakass Nat. Reg./Aut. Prov. only	44,219 (97.0%)	48,512 (85.7%)	54,750 (82.1%)	57,281 (80.9%)
Elsewhere in USSR	——	552 (1.0%)	1,357 (2.0%)	1,529 (2.2%)

Urban/rural distribution of Khakass in the RSFSR

	1926	1979
Urban	492 (1.1%)	16,174 (24.7%)
Rural	45,116 (98.9%)	49,194 (75.3%)

Ethnic composition of the Khakass National Region/Autonomous Province

	1926	1959	1970	1979
Total population	88,850	411,047	445,824	498,384
Khakass	44,219 (49.8%)	48,512 (11.8%)	54,750 (12.3%)	57,281 (11.5%)
Russians	41,390 (46.6%)	314,455 (76.5%)	349,362 (78.4%)	395,953 (79.4%)
Others	3,241 (3.6%)	48,080 (11.7%)	41,712 (9.3%)	45,150 (9.1%)

Urban/rural distribution in the Khakass Autonomous Province in 1970

	Urban	Rural
Total population	266,130	179,694
Khakass	9,637 (3.6%)	45,113 (25.1%)
Russians	234,387 (88.1%)	114,975 (64.0%)
Others	22,106 (8.3%)	19,606 (10.6%)

3 STATUS

The Khakass enjoy full Soviet citizenship. They are found in all occupations and in all income brackets, though the majority work on collective farms raising sheep and cattle. Their standard of housing is comparable to that of other national groups in the Soviet Union. The women go out to work, as elsewhere in the Soviet Union.

Literacy

In 1926	In 1979
12.9%	Over 99%

In 1926, 174 Khakass were literate in their own language (3.0 per cent of the total literate Khakass population).

Level of education per 1,000 Khakass living in the Khakass Autonomous Province of 10 years of age and above

	1959	1970
Primary		
Total	312	366
Men	378	418
Women	263	323
Higher and secondary (complete and incomplete)		
Total	195	301
Men	232	326
Women	167	280
Higher only		
Total	9	22
Men	12	25
Women	6	20

4 LANGUAGE

The national language is Khakass. It belongs to the North Turkic group (*Fundamenta* classification); it can also be classed as belonging to the Khakass sub-group of the Uighur-Oghuz group (Baskakov).

It consists of a number of dialects which fall into two main divisions: the 'hushing' dialects such as Kachin, Koibal, Kyzyl and Shor; the 'hissing', such as Beltir and Sagai (cf. 'hushing' *tash* 'stone', *ach-* 'to open', *chach* 'hair'; 'hissing' *tas, as-, sas*; Turkish *tash, ach-, sach*). The modern literary language has been formed on the basis of the Sagai and Kachin dialects. There are many Mongol and Russian loan-words in Khakass (the latter began to enter the language in the seventeenth century), but almost no Arabic or Persian borrowings. The modern literary language has been enlarged by using the resources of Khakass itself (semantic widenings, calques based on Russian, etc.) as well as by direct loans from Russian.

Russian is used for administrative, judicial and other official proceedings, but in theory Khakass can be used if necessary.

Percentage of Khakass claiming Khakass as their mother tongue

	1926	1959	1970	1979
Total	89.9	86.0	83.7	80.9
In urban areas	62.3	68.4	67.4	n.a.
In rural areas	90.1	90.1	89.3	n.a.

Percentage of Khakass with good knowledge of Russian

	1926	1959	1970	1979
As mother tongue	9.4	13.9	16.3	19.0
As second language	n.a.	n.a.	65.5	68.3

In 1958 Khakass was the medium of instruction in grades 1–4 (primary+1) in national schools; in 1972, only in grades 1–3 and pre-school; in 1972 it was also taught as an individual, optional subject in Russian-medium schools in grades 1–8 (Silver, p. 33). There is a Pedagogical Institute and a branch of the Krasnojar Polytechnical Institute in Abakan.

In the Khakass Autonomous Province there are radio and television broadcasts in Khakass and Russian.

Newspapers and periodicals are published in both languages. The Khakass-language paper is *Khakass* (first appeared in 1927); there is also an annual literary almanac, *Akh-taskhyl* ('The White Mountain').

Books and pamphlets are published in Khakass (e.g. 5 titles in 1976; none of these were specialized textbooks on technical and scientific subjects).

Scripts and alphabets

Khakass was first given a script in 1924.

1924–9   Cyrillic script, first alphabet
1929–39 Latin script
1939–47 Cyrillic script, second alphabet (slightly different from first)

1947–53   Cyrillic script, third alphabet
1953   Cyrillic script, fourth alphabet

This last alphabet is said to be capable of conveying a perfect phonetic representation of the language. It should be noted that the Cyrillic alphabets listed above are not actually very different from one another, but for this very reason have caused considerable confusion in orthographic usage.

5 RELIGION

The Khakass are (or were) Christians, but still retain many animistic traditions.

ALTAIS/OIROTS

Own name: *Altaj-kizhi*; Russian name: *Altajtsy*. Also tribal names (see below).

Almost all the Altais live in Siberia, in the Altai and Kuznetski Alatau mountains. They are settled along such rivers as the Bija, Chulishman, Chuja, Katun' and Lebed', mostly still in their former tribal areas.

1 HISTORICAL BACKGROUND

'Altais' is the collective name given to a number of Turkic-speaking tribes who inhabit the Altai and Kuznetski Alatau Mountains. Historically, they formed two groups: the Northern Altais, consisting of the Tubas (who lived on the left bank of the River Bija and the south-west bank of Lake Teletskoje), the Chelkans (also called *Lebedintsy*, 'Swan People', since they lived in the basin of the River Lebed'), the Kumandins (central and middle reaches of the River Bija) and the Shors (the basins of the Rivers Kondoma and Mras-Su and the upper reaches of the Tom'); the Southern Altais, consisting of the Altais (who lived along the River Katun'), the Telengits (the basin of the Chulyshman and other rivers in the vicinity) and the Teleuts (in the steppe region of the Kemerovo Province and along the Rivers Cherga and Majma).
    The Altais have been known by several different names. They

used to be called *Chernevyje* Tatars (with the exception of the Shors, who were generally called by their own name). The Southern Altais were also known as Altaic, Bijski, Border, Mountain or White Kalmyks, all misnomers, since the Kalmyks are Mongols, whereas the Altais are Turkic. In Tsarist times they were commonly designated 'Altais', although this was originally the name of one particular tribe, but under Soviet rule they were re-named 'Oirots' (not to be confused with the modern 'Oirats', who are Mongols). The Altai tribes had been using this term for themselves since the eighteenth century, when they formed part of the Oirot-Dzhungarian (Kalmyk) Empire.

Contacts between the Oirot/Altais and the Russians began when the latter invaded Dzhungaria in the mid-eighteenth century and gained possession of the Altai region. Soon afterwards Russian colonization of the area began in earnest. The tribes were pushed out of their traditional pasture and hunting lands and became steadily more impoverished, many of them sinking to the level of bonded labourers. Russian exploitation of the region continued throughout the nineteenth century and after the Emancipation of the Serfs (1861) Russian peasants were encouraged to come to the Altai Mountains to settle.

Under Russian rule some of the Altais had been converted to Christianity; before this they had been Mongolian-type Lamaists. Poverty, discontent and resentment of the Russian colonists led to a revival of Lamaism in the early twentieth century, an expression both of nationalism and anti-Russian sentiment. After the Revolution power changed hands several times in the Altai region, but by 1919 it was firmly under Soviet rule; on 1 June 1922, the Oirot Autonomous Province was formed within the RSFSR; its indigenous population, the former Altais, were now called 'Oirots'. In 1948 the name of the Province was changed to Gorno-Altai ('Mountain Altai') and that of its people back to 'Altais'.

In the 1926 Soviet Census there was great confusion over designation: some used the term 'Altai', others tribal names (Kumandin, Telengit, Teleut, Tuba) and only a few the new official term 'Oirot'. In the 1959 and later census returns the whole group is listed as 'Altai'.

Gorno-Altai Autonomous Province

Situated in the Altai Territory (*kraj*) in the RSFSR; it is bordered to the east and north-east by the Khakass Autonomous Province and the Tuvinian ASSR (also in the RSFSR), to the south by the Mongol People's Republic and the Chinese People's Republic, to the south-west by the Kazakh SSR. *Area*: 92,600 sq. km. *Capital*: Gorno-Altajsk, known as Ulala till 1932, as Oirot-Tura from 1932 to 1948 (population in 1971: 35,000). The Province has 1 town and 3 settlements. *Population* (1979): 172,040. Average density of population per sq. km (1979): 1.9.

Chief resources: deposits of some rare and precious metals, also of non-metallic minerals e.g. coal, asbestos and graphite; rich forests, 91 per cent of which are coniferous.

Industries include: mining and processing of minerals, food (based on local produce) and other light industries.

Agriculture: mainly stockbreeding.

2 NUMBER AND DISTRIBUTION

Number of Altais

	1926*	1959	1970	1979
	39,062	45,270	55,812	60,015

* See individual sections for statistics on Kumandins, Oirots, Telengits, Teleuts and Tubas, all of which groups were listed separately in 1926.

Regional distribution of Altais

	1926	1959	1970	1979
RSFSR	39,062 (100%)	44,654 (98.6%)	54,614 (97.9%)	58,879 (98.1%)
Oirot/Gorno-Altai Aut. Prov. only	35,601 (91.1%)	38,019 (84.0%)	46,750 (83.8%)	50,203 (83.7%)
Elsewhere in USSR	——	616 (1.4%)	1,198 (2.1%)	1,136 (1.9%)

Urban/rural distribution of Altais in the RSFSR

	1926	1970
Urban	118 (0.3%)	7,361 (13.5%)
Rural	38,944 (99.7%)	47,253 (86.5%)

The tribes (e.g. Telengits, Teleuts, etc.) not included with the Altais in 1926 were virtually 100 per cent rural dwellers.

Ethnic composition of the Oirot/Gorno-Altai Autonomous Province

	1926	*1959*	*1970*	*1979*
Total population	99,632	157,161	168,261	172,040
Altais	35,601 (35.7%)	38,019 (24.2%)	46,750 (27.8%)	50,203 (29.2%)
Kazakhs	2,326 (2.3%)	4,745 (3.0%)	7,170 (4.3%)	8,677 (5.0%)
Russians	51,812 (52.0%)	109,661 (69.8%)	110,442 (65.6%)	108,795 (63.2%)
Others	9,893 (9.9%)	4,736 (3.0%)	3,899 (2.3%)	4,365 (2.5%)

Urban/rural distribution in the Gorno-Altai Autonomous Province in 1970

	Urban	*Rural*
Total population	39,717	128,544
Altais	3,610 (9.1%)	43,140 (33.6%)
Kazakhs	349 (0.9%)	6,821 (5.3%)
Russians	34,467 (86.8%)	75,975 (59.1%)
Others	1,291 (3.2%)	2,608 (2.0%)

3 STATUS

The Altais enjoy full Soviet citizenship. They are found in all occupations and in all income brackets; the majority are agricultural workers, but some are engaged in the mining industry. Their standard of housing is comparable to that of other national groups in the Soviet Union. The women go out to work, as elsewhere in the Soviet Union.

Literacy

In 1926	In 1970
11.4%	Over 99%

In 1926, 1,276 Altais were literate in their own language (28.6 per cent of the total literate Altai population).

Level of education per 1,000 Altais living in the Gorno-Altai Autonomous Province of 10 years of age and above

	1959	*1970*
Primary		
Total	340	395
Men	418	455
Women	291	351
Higher and secondary (complete and incomplete)		
Total	187	283
Men	236	303
Women	156	268
Higher only		
Total	5	18
Men	6	21
Women	4	15

4 LANGUAGE

The national language is Altai. It belongs to the North Turkic group (*Fundamenta* classification); it can also be classed as belonging to the Kirghiz-Kipchak group (Baskakov).

There are two main groups of dialects: the northern group, consisting of Tuba, Kumandin and Chelkan; the southern group, consisting of Altai, Telengit and Teleut. There are still several thousand speakers of the northern dialects (Baskakov, *Vvedenije* . . ., p. 344). The Altai dialect forms the basis of the modern literary language. The vocabulary is characterized by a large number of Mongol and Russian loan-words, but few Arabic or Persian. There are some ancient borrowings from Sanskrit and Chinese. An interesting feature of the language is the use of euphemisms for taboo words in such fields as personal and animal names. Some of these are for use by men (in particular hunters), others by women.

Russian is generally used for administration, judicial and other official proceedings, but in theory Altai can be used if necessary.

In 1958 Altai was the medium of instruction in grades 1–4 (primary +1) in national schools; in 1972, in grades 1–3; in 1972 it was also taught as an individual, optional subject in Russian-medium

Percentage of Altais claiming Altai as their mother tongue

	1926*	1959	1970	1979
Total	79.4	88.5	87.2	86.4
In urban areas	42.9	58.4	64.6	n.a.
In rural areas	79.5	92.1	91.1	n.a.

Percentage of Altais with good knowledge of Russian

	1926*	1959	1970	1979
As mother tongue	19.8	11.2	12.6	13.5
As second language	n.a.	n.a.	54.9	68.7

* The figures for this year do not include all the other peoples (e.g. Teleuts, Telengits, Kumandins) who were later included with the Altais. In 1926, nearly all the Telengits (99.5 per cent) claimed their own language as mother tongue, but only about half of the Kumandins and Teleuts (45.7 per cent and 57.9 per cent respectively). Half the Kumandins (50.9 per cent) had already adopted Russian, as had a fair proportion of the Teleuts (14.9 per cent).

schools in grades 1–8 (incomplete secondary) (Silver, p. 33). There is a Pedagogical Institute and a Research Institute of History, Language and Literature in Gorno-Altajsk.

In the Gorno-Altai Autonomous Province there are radio and television broadcasts in Altai and Russian.

Newspapers and periodicals are published in both languages. The Altai-language paper is *Altajdyn cholmony* ('Star of Altai' – first appeared in 1923). There is also a periodical, *Agitatordyng bloknody* ('Agitator's Note-book' – first appeared in 1948) and a literary almanac, *Altyn-köl* ('Golden Lake' – first appeared in 1974).

Books and pamphlets are published in Altai (e.g. 21 titles in 1976; none of these were specialized textbooks on technical and scientific subjects).

Scripts and alphabets

1845–1922	Cyrillic script, first alphabet (invented by missionaries)
1922–8	Cyrillic script, second alphabet
1928–38	Latin script
1938–44	Cyrillic script, third alphabet
1944	Cyrillic script, fourth alphabet (similar to second)

5 RELIGION

Most of the Altais are (or were) Christians or Lamaist Buddhists. A few (mainly the Teleuts) are Sunni Muslims.

SHORS

Own names: *Shor-kizhi, Aba(-kizhi), Chysh-kizhi* ('Taiga people'); Russian names: *Shory, Shortsy*. They also used to be known as Tatars (e.g. Kondoma, Kuznetski or Mrass Tatars) or *Abintsy*.

Almost all the Shors live in the region known as *Shorija* in south Siberia, in the RSFSR, Kemerovo District (*oblast'*). Traditionally they lived in the Kuznetski Alatau mountains, on the Rivers Kondoma and Mras-su and Tom', but today about half live in the industrial centres of the Kuznetsk Basin.

1 HISTORICAL BACKGROUND

The Shors are a group of Turkic-speaking tribes, descended from the Kettic, Samoyedic, Turkic and Ugrian peoples of the taiga. The ultimate Turkification of the region was due primarily to the influence of the Yenisei Kirghiz (see p. 327). The Shors came under Russian rule in the early seventeenth century (cf. the Yakuts). Originally Shamanists, they were converted to Christianity under Russian rule. Their chief occupations were trapping, hunting, primitive farming and gathering (berries etc.); they were also highly skilled in mining and working iron, hence *Kuznetsy* or *Kuznetskije Tatary* ('Blacksmiths', 'Blacksmith Tatars'), two of the names by which they used to be known.

Today many of them live on collective farms and are engaged in agriculture and stockbreeding. A large number work in the Kuznetsk Basin coal-fields. A few still trap fur-bearing animals.

The Shor National Region was formed in 1929, but disbanded in 1939. It is now a part of the Kemerovo District in the Northern Altai Mountains, south Siberia, in the RSFSR. To the west lies the Khakass Autonomous Province in the Krasnojar Territory (*kraj*) of the RSFSR.

2 NUMBER AND DISTRIBUTION

Number of Shors

	1926	1959	1970	1979
	12,601	15,274	16,494	16,033

Regional distribution of Shors

	1926	1959	1970	1979
RSFSR	12,586 (99.9%)	14,938 (97.8%)	15,950 (96.7%)	15,182 (94.7%)
Elsewhere in USSR	15 (0.1%)	336 (2.2%)	544 (3.3%)	851 (5.3%)

Urban/rural distribution of Shors

	1926	1970
Urban	83 (0.7%)	8,430 (51.1%)
Rural	12,518 (99.3%)	8,064 (48.9%)

3 STATUS

The Shors enjoy full Soviet citizenship. They are found in all occupations and in all income brackets, but the majority of them work
in industry or on collective farms. Their standard of housing is
comparable to that of all other national groups in the Soviet Union.
The women go out to work, as elsewhere in the Soviet Union.

Literacy

In 1926	In 1970
11.5%	Over 99% (both men and women)

In 1926, 643 Shors were literate in their own language (44.4 per
cent of the total literate population).

4 LANGUAGE

The national language is Shor. It belongs to the North Turkic group (*Fundamenta* classification); it can also be classed as belonging to the Khakass sub-group of the Uighur-Oghuz group (Baskakov).

There are two main dialect groupings: the *z/s*-group (Mrass and Tomsk regions) and the *i*-group (Kondoma and Lower Tom' regions); cf. the former *kes-*, the latter *kij-* for 'dress'.

Russian is used for administrative, judicial and other official proceedings, but in theory Shor can be used if necessary; Khakass is also used.

Percentage of Shors claiming Shor as their mother tongue

	1926	1959	1970	1979
Total	93.8	83.7	73.5	61.2
In urban areas	42.9	74.3	60.8	n.a.
In rural areas	94.1	90.6	86.8	n.a.

Percentage of Shors with good knowledge of Russian

	1926	1959	1970	1979
As mother tongue	4.9	16.0	26.2	38.4
As second language	n.a.	n.a.	59.8	52.6

No information is available on the teaching of Shor in schools (though the *Great Soviet Encyclopedia*, 2nd edn, stated that in 1957 there were national schools in Shorija, i.e. schools using Shor as the medium of instruction).

No information is available on the use of Shor in broadcasting; it is probably not used.

No newspapers or periodicals are published in Shor.

The first book to be published in Shor was a primer: *Shor kizhileri balalaryn michike ügretche* (Kazan, 1885). A few books were published in the 1930s (e.g. 4 books in 1935), but apparently nothing since the war.

Scripts and alphabets

1885–1927	Cyrillic script, first alphabet (invented by missionaries)
1927–9	Cyrillic script, second alphabet

1930–8   Latin script
1938   Cyrillic script

5 RELIGION

The Shors are (or were) nominally Christians.

DOLGANS

Own name: *Dulgaan*; Russian name: *Dolgany*.

Almost all the Dolgans live in northern Siberia, within the Arctic Circle.

1 HISTORICAL BACKGROUND

The Dolgans are a Turkicized Tungusic people. There are four tribes or groups of clans: the Dolgans, Edzhens, Karyntuous and Dongots. In the seventeenth century they lived in the basins of the Rivers Olenek and Lena; they moved to the Tajmyr, their present habitat, in the eighteenth century. In the nineteenth century the name 'Dolgan' began to be used for the whole group of tribes.

Their chief occupations used to be reindeer breeding, hunting and fishing. They still pursue these activities but now, instead of their former nomadic existence, they are settled and live on collective farms. There has been very little migration out of the area; the majority of Dolgans still live in the Tajmyr (Dolgano-Nenetski) National Region in the Krasnojarsk Territory (*kraj*) in the RSFSR.

2 NUMBER AND DISTRIBUTION

Number of Dolgans

1926	1959	1970	1979
656*	3,932	4,877	5,053

*The *Great Soviet Encyclopaedia* (2nd edn) gives the figure, 1,385 for the Dolgan population in 1926, but this is not corroborated by the census.

Regional distribution of Dolgans

	1926	*1959*	*1970*	*1979*
RSFSR	656 (100%)	n.a.	4,718 (96.7%)	n.a.
Elsewhere in USSR	——		159 (3.3%)	

Urban/rural distribution of Dolgans in the RSFSR

	1926	*1970*
Urban	——	524 (11.1%)
Rural	656 (100%)	4,194 (88.9%)

Ethnic composition of the Tajmyr (Dolgano-Nenetski) National Region in 1970

Total population	38,060
Dolgans	4,344 (11.4%)
Nenets	2,247 (5.9%)
Russians	25,465 (66.9%)
Others	6,004 (11.8%)

Urban/rural distribution in the Tajmyr (Dolgano-Nenetski) National Region in 1970

	Urban	*Rural*
Total population	23,590	14,470
Dolgans	261 (1.1%)	4,083 (28.2%)
Nenets	77 (0.3%)	2,170 (15.0%)
Russians	19,702 (83.5%)	5,763 (39.8%)
Others	3,550 (15.0%)	2,454 (17.0%)

3 STATUS

The Dolgans enjoy full Soviet citizenship. They are found in all occupations, though the majority are peasants and collective farm workers. Their standard of housing is comparable to that of other national groups in the Soviet Union. The women go out to work, as elsewhere in the Soviet Union.

Literacy

In 1926	In 1970
1.2% (8 people)	Over 99%

Level of education per 1,000 Dolgans living in the Tajmyr (Dolgano-Nenets) National Region in 1970 of 10 years of age and above

Primary	
Total	375
Men	405
Women	347
Higher and secondary (complete and incomplete)	
Total	198
Men	182
Women	213
Higher only	
Total	11
Men	11
Women	11

4 LANGUAGE

The national language is Dolgan; it is a dialect of Yakut and contains many Yakut and Evenk words. Until recently it was not used as a literary language.

Russian is used for all administrative, judicial and other official proceedings, but in theory Dolgan can be used if necessary.

No information is available on the use of Dolgan in schools; it is almost certainly not used at all as a medium of instruction.

No information is available on its use in broadcasting.

No newspapers, books or pamphlets were published in Dolgan until 1977, when a book of Dolgan poetry appeared.

Percentage of Dolgans claiming Dolgan as their mother tongue

	1926	1959	1970	1979
Total	99.5	93.9	89.8	90.0
In urban areas	—	58.8	72.1	n.a.
In rural areas	99.5	96.1	92.4	n.a.

Percentage of Dolgans with good knowledge of Russian

	1926	1970	1979
As mother tongue	0.0 (none)	9.9	9.8
As second language	n.a.	61.9	72.9

Scripts and alphabets

Dolgan has no special alphabet of its own. The literary language is Yakut (see p. 394).

5 RELIGION

The Dolgans are (or were) Shamanists with a veneer of Christianity.

KARAIMS/KARAITS

Own name: *Karaj*; Russian name: *Karaimy*.

The majority of the Karaims live in the Crimea (now part of the Ukrainian SSR), but there are also communities of ancient origin in Lithuania (Trakai and Vilnius) and the Ukraine (Halych).

1 HISTORICAL BACKGROUND

The history of the Karaims is complicated by the fact that the term is used both for adherents of a religious sect and for a specific ethnic group. The history of the religious sect is, briefly, as follows: 'Karaism' is a non-Talmudic form of Judaism which arose during the eighth century. Its adherents originally called themselves 'Ananites', after their first legislator, Anan ben Dawud of Basra. Later they became known as 'Karaims', probably from Hebrew *kara* 'to read', since they acknowledged no authority except that of the Holy Scriptures and neither commentaries nor 'traditions' were allowed. At an early date the centre of Kara-ism moved to Jerusalem, where its first temple was built (now no longer extant). Missionaries set out from here to proselytize and it is they who appear to have converted the Khazars to the Karaim form of Judaism.

The early history of the ethnic group known as the Karaims is not so clear. All that is certain is that they are of Turkic origin and that they settled in the Crimea at some point before the fourteenth century. It is probable that they are descendants of the Khazars, for nothing more is heard of the latter after the fall of their empire during the tenth century. It is generally assumed that they were submerged by insurgent Kipchak (also known as Cuman or Polovtsian) hordes, who overran the former Khazar lands prior to the Mongol invasion of the early thirteenth century.

Linguistic evidence does indicate a close link between the modern Karaims and the Kipchaks/Cumans/Polovtsians and religious evidence supports a Khazar connection, but as yet there is no more substantial proof of this hypothesis. Their presence in the Crimea in the fourteenth century is the first indisputable fact concerning the history of the Karaim Turks. The next is that during that century a group of 483 families (according to Karaim tradition) moved from the Crimea to the Grand Duchy of Lithuania and in the reign of Grand Duke Vitaut (Witold) settled in such cities as Troki and Vilna (today Trakai and Vilnius in the Lithuanian SSR) and Lutsk and Halych (today part of the Ukrainian SSR).

The Karaims in the Crimea and the Grand Duchy formed exclusive, tightly-knit communities, marrying within their own group and preserving their language, religion and customs until the present day (cf. the Tatars of Byelorussia and Lithuania, who were assimilated by the indigenous population: see p. 85). By the twentieth century some dispersion of the Karaims had taken place, several of them migrating to cities such as Moscow, St Petersburg and Warsaw. A steady decline in their number was accompanied by a decline in the position of their language, as Karaims increasingly adopted Russian, Polish or even the related Turkic language Crimean Tatar as mother tongue. However, unlike the Krymchaks (see p. 433), they succeeded in surviving the German occupation of the Crimea (1941–4), with relatively few losses, due to the fact that the head of the Karaim Religious Board in Lithuania, *Khokhan* Haji Serai

Szapszal, was able to convince the Nazi authorities that the Karaims' connection with Judaism was purely religious and in no way ethnic (Nekrich, p. 16). In the post-war period they were also fortunate, for while the Crimean Tatars were all deported to Central Asia and Kazakhstan (see p. 89), the Karaims once more escaped unscathed and continued to live in the Crimea, Moscow, Leningrad and other areas where they had previously settled.

2 NUMBER AND DISTRIBUTION

Number of Karaims

	1926	1959	1970	1979
	8,324	5,727	4,571	3,341

Regional distribution of Karaims

	1926	1959	1970	1979
Crimean ASSR*	4,213	3,301	2,596	n.a.
(later Ukrainian SSR)	(50.6%)	(57.6%)	(56.8%)	
Elsewhere in USSR	4,111	2,426	1,975	
	(49.4%)	(42.4%)	(43.2%)	

*Disbanded in 1946; the area now forms part of the Ukrainian SSR.

Urban/rural distribution of Karaims

	1926	1970
Urban	7,867	4,420
	(94.5%)	(96.7%)
Rural	457	151
	(5.5%)	(3.3%)

3 STATUS

The Karaims enjoy full Soviet citizenship. They are found in all occupations and income brackets. Their standard of housing is comparable to that of other national groups in the Soviet Union. The women go out to work, as elsewhere in the Soviet Union.

Literacy

In 1926	In 1970
84.9%	Over 99%

In 1926, 771 Karaims were literate in their own language (10.9 per cent of the total literate Karaim population).

4 LANGUAGE

The national language is Karaim. It belongs to the West Turkic group (*Fundamenta* classification); it can also be classed as belonging to the Kipchak group, Kipchak-Polovtsian sub-group (Baskakov).

Karaim took form in the pre-Mongol (pre-thirteenth century) period; it shows considerable affinities with the language of the *Codex Cumanicus* (a Latin-Persian-Cuman dictionary compiled in the late thirteenth century). The liturgical language of the Karaims is Hebrew, but a translation of the Holy Scriptures into Karaim was made at an early period (possibly as early as the tenth century). Many of the religious terms are of Islamic (Arabic/Persian) origin, pointing to Muslim influence at a formative period (cf. *dzhimat*, 'congregation', *kudrat*, 'power', *din*, 'religion'). There is also a considerable Hebrew element.

There is a body of literature (mostly religious) in Karaim, but it does not really survive as a literary language today. There were three dialects, corresponding to the three geographical foci of the Karaims, those of Vilnius-Trakai, Lutsk-Halych and the Crimea. Only the first two can still be said to be alive. The differences between them are mainly phonetic, but there are some lexical divergences too. Slavonic languages (particularly Byelorussian and Ukrainian) have had a marked impact on both dialects.

Russian is used for all administrative, judicial and other official proceedings, but in theory Karaim can be used if necessary.

No information is available on the use of Karaim as a medium of instruction; it is almost certainly not used at all.

No information is available on its use in broadcasting; it is almost certainly not used at all.

It is no longer a literary language in the Soviet Union, hence there are no publications in it.

Percentage of Karaims claiming Karaim as their mother tongue

	1926	1959	1970	1979
Total	36.4	13.9	12.8	16.0
In urban areas	35.4	13.5	12.3	n.a.
In rural areas	53.6	20.6	26.5 (40 people)	n.a.

Percentage of Karaims with good knowledge of Russian

	1926	1959	1970	1979
As mother tongue	60.5	81.3	81.2	81.2
As second language	n.a.	n.a.	11.3	13.3

Scripts and alphabets

Karaim was originally written in the Hebrew script, but from the beginning of the twentieth century Latin and Cyrillic have also been used. There were two versions of the Latin script: the Lithuanian (used in Panivizh/Panevezhysh) and the Polish (used in Lutsk, Halych and Vilna/Vilnius). Allworth reconstructs a pre- and a post-1927 Latin alphabet (*Nationalities of the Soviet East*). A number of publications in Karaim appeared in Lutsk (in the Latin script) during the 1930s, but since then there has been nothing. However, works on the language (e.g. a grammar and a dictionary) have been published in recent years. In these Soviet publications a transcription system based on the Cyrillic script is used. In Poland a Latin transcription is still used.

5 RELIGION

The Karaims are non-Talmudic Jews. They used to have two Religious Boards (cf. the Spiritual Directorates of the Muslims). The one in Jevpatoria (formerly known as Gözleve) in the Crimea was founded in 1837, the other, in Troki/Trakai in the present Lithuanian SSR, was founded in 1857. They were in existence until the Second World War, but it is not known if they are still functioning. Another Karaim Religious Board was founded outside the Soviet Union, in Warsaw, in 1945.

6 OUTSIDE THE SOVIET UNION

There are some 'Karaim Turks' in Poland, but no information is available on their number; it probably amounts to a few thousand.

There are adherents of the Karaim faith (not necessarily of Turkic origin) in Egypt, Turkey and the USA. The Karaim community as a whole (of all ethnic origins) amounts to some 20,000 (Zając-czkowski, p. 9).

TOFAS/KARAGAS

Own name: *Tofa*; Russian name: *Tofalary*.

The Tofas were formerly known as 'Karagas', actually the name of one particular tribe. They live in south Siberia, in the Nizhneuda Region (*rajon*) of the Irkutsk District (*oblast'*). Their traditional lands are along the upper reaches of rivers such as the Birjusa, Uda and Ija.

1 HISTORICAL BACKGROUND

The Tofas are a small group of Turkic-speaking tribes, closely related to the Tuvinians (see p. 400). They represent an intermingling of Turkic, Kettic, Samoyedic and Mongol elements. Like the Kamasins (see p. 431), some of them continued to speak Samoyedic dialects until recent times, in particular the Karagas and Kangat tribal groups. Their original habitat was on the slopes of the Sayan mountains; they moved to their present territory during the seventeenth century. Formerly nomads, their chief occupations were hunting, trapping and the raising of reindeer. They are now settled and the majority live on collective farms.

2 NUMBER AND DISTRIBUTION

Number of Tofas (listed as Karagas in 1926)

	1926	1959	1970	1979
	2,829*	586	620	763

*This figure clearly includes other peoples who at that time chose to identify themselves as 'Karagas'; the *Great Soviet Encyclopaedia* (2nd edn) states that there were 417 Karagas/Tofas in 1926.

Regional distribution of Tofas in 1926

RSFSR	2,829
	(100%)

In 1959 and subsequently, not listed.

Urban/rural distribution of Tofas

	1926	1970
Urban	7	90
	(0.2%)	(14.5%)
Rural	2,822	530
	(99.8%)	(85.5%)

3 STATUS

The Tofas enjoy full Soviet citizenship. They are mostly collective farm workers; their chief occupations are still hunting and cattle-rearing.

They live in modern, timber houses, but they still use the traditional conical, skin or birch-bark covered tents as additional structures for storage etc. The women go out to work, as elsewhere in the Soviet Union.

Literacy

In 1926	In 1970
10.5%	Over 99%

4 LANGUAGE

The national language is Tofa/Karagas. It is a North Turkic language (*Fundamenta* classification); it can also be classed as belonging to the Uighur-Oghuz group, Uighur-Tukju sub-group (Baskakov). It is closely related to Tuvinian.

Russian is used for administrative, judicial and other official proceedings, but in theory Tofa can be used if necessary.

Percentages of Tofas claiming Tofa/Karagas as their mother tongue

	1926	1959	1970	1979
Total	29.1	89.1	56.3	62.1
In urban areas	—	42.1	7.1	n.a.
In rural areas	29.1	90.7	49.2	n.a.

The remarkable rise in the percentage of those claiming Tofa/Karagas as their mother tongue in the period 1926–59 is largely to be explained by the change in application of 'Tofa/Karagas': in 1926 the term was used with much wider ethnic implications than in the subsequent censuses.

Percentage of Tofas with good knowledge of Russian

	1926	1959	1970	1979
As mother tongue	70.8	9.2	42.6	37.1
As second language	n.a.	n.a.	48.7	51.9

No information is available on the use of Tofa/Karagas in schools.

No information is available on its use in broadcasting; it is most probably not used at all.

It is not a literary language, hence there are no publications in Tofa/Karagas.

Scripts and alphabets

It does not have a particular script or alphabet of its own. If it is written, the Cyrillic script is used.

5 RELIGION

The Tofas are (or were) Shamanists.

Kamasins

Own names: *Kanmadzhi, Kalmadzhi*; Russian name: *Kamasintsy*.

The Kamasins are a very small group of Turkic-speakers (about 200 in 1970). Their origins are not clear, but they appear to be the descendants of Turkicized Nenets tribes. By the seventeenth century they had established themselves in their present habitat on the upper reaches of the Rivers Kan and Mana (tributaries of the Yenisei) in southern Siberia. From 1882 they were divided into two groups, those of the taiga (belonging to the Abalakov *ulus*) and those of the steppe (belonging to the Ugamakov *ulus*). The former were hunters and reindeer-herders, the latter shepherds and farmers. The taiga Kamasins continued to speak a Samoyedic dialect up till the beginning of the twentieth century, but the steppe Kamasins spoke a language close to the Kachin dialect of Khakass and this is what is now referred to as the 'Kamasin language'. It is still in active use, but as it has no written form Russian serves as the literary medium. Tuition in the local schools is also in Russian. All the Kamasins now live on collective farms and have been greatly influenced by their Slav neighbours' way of life. In the census returns the Kamasins are not grouped separately, but are listed as 'Russians'.

Krjashens

Own name: *Chokngan*; Russian name: *Krjasheny*.

The *Krjasheny* (Russian for 'baptized') are, as their name suggests, the Volga Tatars who were converted to Christianity. The first wave of converts were baptized by Guryj, Archbishop of Kazan and Bishop Varsonafyj soon after the conquest of the Khanates of Kazan and Astrakhan (1552–6). They came to be known as *starokreshchennyje* ('old converts'); the majority of them quickly reverted to Islam, for after the death of the missionaries who had been responsible for their conversion they were left with no spiritual guidance, no common language with other Christians, no religious writings and very few churches. The new faith was unable to take root in such unpropitious circumstances and it was not until the eighteenth century that significant numbers of Tatars again began to adopt Christianity. The second generation of Christians (known as the *novokreshchennyje*, 'new converts') were better provided for than their predecessors and, moreover, were granted such privileges as exemption from taxes. At the same time the Muslims were being much oppressed and their mosques destroyed (in 1744 alone 418 mosques were demolished). Many became Christians out of necessity, rather than conviction. Despite the efforts to give them a Christian education (the first school for converts was opened in 1863, a seminary in 1872), the Tatars' faith remained very superficial and towards the end of the nineteenth century several thousand again returned to Islam. Nevertheless, in 1926 there were still over 100,000 'Convert Tatars' (about 3 per cent of the total Tatar population). They spoke the same language as the Muslims and apart from their Russianized names and surnames were indistinguishable from them.

The first works for the Krjashens were written in the Arabic script, but in 1862 the Russian scholar and pedagogue N. I. Il'minskij created an alphabet for them that was based on the Cyrillic script. By the turn of the century some 100 books had been published in it. The Krjashen literature was originally entirely religious in content, but just before the Revolution (1915–16) there was some attempt to develop a secular press. In 1922 the modified Arabic script used for Tatar was also introduced for the Krjashens, but the Cyrillic remained in use until 1928, when both were replaced by the Latin script (cf. Tatar, which also adopted the Latin script at this time). The distinction between the Tatars and the Krjashens, based as it was on religious difference, became superfluous during the Soviet period and there do not appear to have been any special publications for the latter in the 1930s. They were listed separately in the 1926 Census, but thereafter were included with the Tatars.

1926 Census figures

Population: 101,447; of these, 99,041 (97.6 per cent) lived in the Tatar ASSR.
Urban dwellers: 1.4 per cent.
Percentage claiming own language (Tatar) as their mother tongue: 99.1.

Percentage claiming Russian as their mother tongue: 0.7.
Literacy: 29.2 per cent (cf. the Tatar literacy rate of 33.6 per
cent).

Krymchaks/Krimchaks

The Krymchaks were a Turkic-speaking, Jewish people who lived
in the Crimea until the Second World War. Nothing is known of
their origins or when they first settled in the Crimea, but they are
thought to have been descended from the Khazars (cf. the Karaims:
p. 423). The Krymchaks professed orthodox, Talmudic Judaism
(unlike the Karaims, who reject the Talmud). They used a special
form of ritual, evolved in the Crimea during the sixteenth century.
Their language, which was written in the Hebrew script, was different from either Crimean Tatar or Karaim. In dress, customs and
occupations (farming, viticulture and various crafts) the Krymchaks
were almost indistinguishable from these other two Turkic groups,
but they practised strict endogamy, never marrying outside their
own community.

The number of Krymchaks had been steadily declining since the
late nineteenth century. In 1926, there were 6,383 'Crimean Jews'
(i.e. Krymchaks; the Karaims were listed separately). Of these,
4,728 (74.1 per cent) claimed their own language as mother tongue.
When the Germans occupied the Crimea in 1941 they were at first
perplexed by these Turkic Jews and could not decide how to treat
them. A query was sent to Berlin: the reply was an order to shoot
them. Between 19 November 1941 and 9 January 1942, 2,504 Krymchaks were liquidated. The survivors are now scattered throughout
the Soviet Union and abroad and are rapidly being assimilated by
larger groups, in particular by the Crimean Tatars (e.g. in 1959
there were 5 Krymchaks in the TadzhSSR, 36 in the UzSSR and 2
in the KazSSR, all claiming Crimean Tatar as their mother tongue);
in 1942 there were about 100 families in New York, but they, too,
were intermarrying with other ethnic groups and losing their
identity.

The Krymchak literature consisted of translations of prayers and
sacred texts. There was a project to write the language in the Latin
script *c.* 1928, but it is not known if anything was actually produced
in this alphabet. There may be a few individuals who still speak
Krymchak, but to all intents and purposes the language is now dead
and the ethnic group no longer survives as a viable unit.

Kumandins

Own names: *Kuvandy, Kuvandyg, Kuvandykh, Kuvanty, Kumandy*; Russian name: *Kumandintsy*.

The Kumandins live on the Rivers Bija, Isha and Kozha. They are divided into the Upper Kumandin (*örö kumandy*) and Lower Kumandin (*altyna kumandy*). They represent an intermingling of Turkic and indigenous southern Siberian tribes. During the last century they have intermarried with the Shors and Russians. They used to have a strong clan system and traces of this still survive. Their traditional occupations were hunting and farming. They now live on collective farms, where they continue to be engaged in agricultural work. The Kumandin language is a dialect of Altai. It belongs to the northern group, along with Tuba and Chelkan, and has strong affinities with Shor and Khakass. It is still a living language, but as it has no written form, Russian and Altai serve as the literary media. Some of the Kumandins are Muslims (Sunni), but the majority are (or were) Christians.

1926 Census figures

Population: 6,335. They are now listed with the Altais.
Urban dwellers: 0.1 per cent.
Percentage claiming own language as their mother tongue: 45.7.
Percentage claiming Russian as their mother tongue: 50.9.
Literacy: 14.3 per cent; of these, 26 people claimed to be literate in their own language, although it was not (and is not) written.

Telengits

Own names: *Telengit, Tölös, Chui-kizhi*; Russian names: *Telengity, Telesy, Chui*.

The Telengits belong to the group of nomadic, Turkic-speaking tribes who were known by the general term 'Tele' (cf. the Teleuts). They were already present in southern Siberia during the time of the Turkish Khaganate (sixth to eighth centuries AD). They are now settled and the majority live on collective farms in the Gorno-Altai Autonomous Province. They are concentrated along the Rivers Chulyshman, Chuja and Argut. Most live in wooden houses, but during the summer some still prefer the traditional felt tents. Their main occupation is animal husbandry, but a few work in the local mining industry. The Telengits' language is one of the southern dialects of Altai and is related to Kirghiz. It is still spoken, but as it has no written form, Russian and Altai serve as the literary languages. Most of the Telengits are (or were) Christians.

1926 Census figures

Population: 3,415; without exception, they lived in the Oirot
   (now the Gorno-Altai) Autonomous Province. They are now
   listed with the Altais.
Urban dwellers: none.
Percentage claiming own language as their mother tongue: 99.5.
Number claiming Russian as their mother tongue: 3 people.
Literacy: 8.8 per cent; of these, 5 people claimed to be literate in
   their own language, although Telengit was not (and is not) a
   written language,

Teleuts

Own name: *Telengut*; Russian name: *Teleuty*.

The Teleuts, like the Telengits, formed part of the group of no-madic, Turkic-speaking tribes known by the general term 'Tele'. They came under the rule of the Turkish Khaganate in the sixth to eighth centuries AD. Towards the end of the sixteenth century they were roaming the steppe between the Irtysh and the Ob' and nom-inally vassals of the Dzhungarians (Kalmyks/Oirots). At this period they had 4,000 tents. In 1609 the Russians gained control of the region and the Teleuts became their subjects. Russian documents of that time refer to them as 'White Kalmyks', although the Kal-myks are Mongols and the Teleuts are not (though, like most of the other peoples of southern Siberia, they have assimilated some Mongol elements). Today the majority of the Teleuts live along the Great and Little Bachat Rivers in the Kemerovo District (*oblast'*) of the RSFSR; a much smaller number live in the Gorno-Altai Autonomous Province. Some of them work on collective farms, others in the mining industry. They have become very Russified in their way of life. Their language is one of the southern dialects of Altai (cf. Telengit) and is therefore related to Kirghiz. It is still spoken, but as it has no written form, Russian and Altai serve as the literary languages. Most of the Teleuts are Sunni Muslims.

1926 Census figures

Population: 1,898. They are now listed with the Altais.
Urban dwellers: 0.4 per cent.
Percentage claiming own language as their mother tongue: 57.8.
Percentage claiming Russian as their mother tongue: 14.9.
Literacy: 19.1 per cent.

Tubas

Own names: *Tuba, Tuwa, Tuma (-kizhi), Jysh-, Tysh-, Dysh-kizhi*;
Russian name: *Tubalary*; formerly also *Chernevyje tatary*.

The name *Tuba* is very common amongst the Turkic tribes of south Siberia (cf. Tuvinians and Tofas; there are also sub-groups of the Khakass and Shors who call themselves *Tuba*). This group of Tubas, however, who are now included with the Altais, consider themselves to be quite separate from other tribes of the same name; according to one of their proverbs, *Tuba tuvganyn tanybas* 'the Tubas know no other Tubas'. They have kept their clan divisions and although one of these shares the same name as the Telengits (*Tölös*), the two are apparently not related. The Altai Tubas speak a northern (Uighur) dialect of Altai. Their traditional lands were on the north-west bank of Lake Teletskoje, between the rivers Bija and Katun'. According to the census, in 1926 there were only 12 Chernevyje Tatars (Tubas), but nearly forty years later, Baskakov estimated that there were some 7,000 of this group who still spoke their own language (*Dialekt chernevykh tatar*, Moscow, Nauka, 1965, p. 8) and therefore linguistically at least preserved a sense of their own identity.

Urums

Own name: *Urum*; Russian name: *Urumy*.

The Urums are Turkish-speaking Greeks (cf. the Greek-speaking Greeks of the Soviet Union, who refer to themselves as *Greki*,

Elliny or *Romei*). The majority live either in the Abkhazian ASSR (within the Georgian SSR) or in the Armenian SSR. The first wave of Urums emigrated from Turkey to Georgia in the second half of the eighteenth century, with the intention of working in the mining industry. The second wave arrived a century later; they settled in Abkhazia and the Kuban' region, taking the place of the Muslim Circassians who moved to the Ottoman Empire. The Urums in this region were mostly farmers and tobacco-growers. Today the majority live on collective farms, where they are still involved in the cultivation of tobacco. They are not listed separately in any of the census reports and there is no information available on the present size of the community. By religion the Urums are (or were) Orthodox Christians.

Chronological table

BC

559 – 330	Achaemenian Empire in Iran, Central Asia and Transcaucasia
330 – 327	Alexander the Great overthrows the Achaemenians, conquers Iran, Central Asia and Transcaucasia
327 – 250	After Alexander's death the Seleucids rule Central Asia; Atropates founds independent state in southern Azerbaidzhan
256 – c. 120	Graeco-Bactrian Empire in Central Asia
c. 170 – AD 226	Parthian Empire in Central Asia and Transcaucasia

AD

1st – early 4th cent.	Kushan Empire in Central Asia
226 – 651	Sasanian Empire in Iran, Central Asia and Transcaucasia
425 – 557	Ephthalites (Huns) dominate Central Asia
552 – 774	Turkish Khaganates (eastern and western) in Central Asia
622	Year of the Hijra (Muhammed's Flight from Mecca to Medina): beginning of the Muslim era
c. 650 – 800	Arabs overthrow the Sasanians and conquer Iran, Central Asia and Transcaucasia
c. 650 – late 10th cent.	Khazar Empire in Transcaucasia and southern Russia
875 – 999	Samanid Empire in Transoxiana and Khwarezm
c. 930 – 1165	Karakhanid Empire in Central Asia
980 – 1015	Reign of Prince Vladimir of Kiev
988 – 90	Conversion of Vladimir and his subjects to Christianity
11th – 13th cent.	Seljuk Empire in Iran, Mesopotamia, Anatolia and Transcaucasia
1137 – 1216	Kara Khitai Empire in Central Asia

438

c. 1147	Founding of Moscow
c. 1150 – 1220	Khwarezmshahs rule Khwarezm
1155/1162/1167 – 1227	Genghiz Khan (exact date of birth unknown)
1219 – 21	Mongol conquest of Central Asia
1221 – 31	Mongol conquest of Transcaucasia
1223	Battle of River Kalka: first Mongol incursion into Russia
1237 – 41	Mongol conquest of Russia; establishment of state of Golden Horde (Ulus of Dzhuchi) in Russia, most of Transcaucasia and Khwarezm; Il-Khans (Ulus of Hulagu) in Iran; Ulus of Chagatai in Central Asia; Yuan dynasty (founded by Kubilai Khan) in China
1252 – 63	Reign of Alexander Nevsky, Grand Prince of Muscovy; beginning of Muscovite power
1370 – 1405	Reign of Timur, conqueror of Transoxiana, Khwarezm, Khorasan, Transcaucasia and northern India; founder of Timurid dynasty in Central Asia
1380	Battle of Kulikovo, first major Russian victory over Golden Horde; Toktamysh becomes supreme ruler of Golden Horde
1382 – 1500	Shirvanshah dynasty rules northern Azerbaidzhan
1386	Timur conquers southern Azerbaidzhan
1395	Toktamysh routed by Timur; power of the Golden Horde begins to wane
c. 1400	Formation of Nogai Horde
1402	Battle of Ankara: Timur defeats Ottoman Sultan Bayezit I
1408 – 68	Kara-koyunlu dynasty rules southern Azerbaidzhan
1438	Formation of Kazan Khanate
1443	Formation of Crimean Khanate
c. 1450	Formation of Uzbek Khanate; formation of Astrakhan Khanate
1451 – 1506	Reign of Sultan Mehmet II (the Conqueror)
1453	Ottomans take Constantinople
1462 – 1505	Reign of Ivan III (the Great), Grand Prince of Muscovy, who marries niece of last Byzantine Emperor; growth of Muscovite power
1469 – 1502	Ak-koyunlu dynasty rules southern Azerbaidzhan
1475	Crimean Khanate becomes vassal of Ottomans
c. 1480	Formation of Siberian Khanate

1483 – 1530	Babur, Prince of Ferghana, later 1st Mogul Emperor of India
c. 1500	Formation of Kazakh Khanate
1502	Shah Ismail takes Tabriz; foundation of Safavid Empire
1505 – 33	Reign of Basil III, Grand Prince of Muscovy; formulation of theory that Moscow is the 'Third Rome'
16th – 17th cent.	Ottomans and Safavids dispute possession of Transcaucasia
1514	Battle of Chaldiran: Ottomans defeat Safavids
1520 – 66	Reign of Sultan Suleyman I (the Magnificent)
1526	Battle of Panipat: Babur defeats Lodi Emperor of Delhi; foundation of Moghul Empire
1533 – 84	Reign of Ivan IV (the Terrible), Grand Prince of Muscovy until 1546, then assumes title of 'Tsar'
1552	Ivan IV conquers Kazan
1555	Treaty of Amasya establishes boundary between Ottomans and Safavids in Georgia and Armenia
1556	Ivan IV conquers Astrakhan; Volga Tatars, Bashkirs and Chuvash come under Russian rule
1584 – 98	Reign of Tsar Fedor, last ruler of Riurik dynasty
1587 – 1628	Reign of Shah Abbas I (the Great)
1590	Ottomans gain possession of Georgia (Tbilisi taken in 1578), Shirvan, Daghestan, Yerevan (1583), Gandzha and Karabagh
1598	Siberian Khanate comes under Russian rule
1599 – 1753	Astrakhanid dynasty rules in Bukhara
c. 1600	Formation of three Kazakh Hordes
1604 – 13	'Time of Troubles' in Russia
1612	Safavids regain Azerbaidzhan and parts of the Caucasus from the Ottomans
1613 – 45	Reign of Mikhail I, first Romanov Tsar
1639	Treaty of Kasr-i Shirin between Ottomans and Safavids confirming Safavid rule in parts of Armenia and the Caucasus
1643 – 63	Abul-Ghazi Khan rules in Khiva
1676 – 81	Russo-Turkish War
1682 – 1725	Reign of Peter I (the Great), Tsar until 1721, then assumes title of 'Emperor'
1696	Russians take Azov; beginning of Russian, in place of Ottoman, domination of Black Sea

1703	Founding of St Petersburg; in 1712 it becomes capital of the Russian Empire
1711 – 13	Russo-Turkish War
1722 – 23	Peter the Great's Persian campaign; Derbent taken in 1722
1724	Treaty of Istanbul between Russians and Ottomans divides Azerbaidzhan between these two powers and gives the Ottomans control of Georgia and Shirvan
1731	Little Kazakh Horde comes under Russian rule
1732	River Araks established as northern boundary between Safavids and Ottomans: the Caucasus comes under Ottoman rule, Azerbaidzhan under Safavid
1734	Russian possessions in Azerbaidzhan relinquished to Iran
1735	Nadir Khan reconquers Daghestan, Shirvan, Georgia and Armenia from the Ottomans
1735 – 39	Russo-Turkish War
1736	Death of Shah Abbas III, last of the Safavid dynasty; Nadir Khan becomes Shah of Iran
1740	Nadir Shah invades Central Asia; Middle Kazakh Horde comes under Russian rule
1747	Nadir Shah assassinated; independent khanates form in Azerbaidzhan, e.g. Baku, Gandzha, Karabagh, Kuba, Nakhichevan, Talysh and Shemakha
1753 – 1920	Manghit dynasty rules in Bukhara
1757	Battle of Plassey: Clive defeats Siraj-ud-Daulah; foundation of British rule in India
1762 – 96	Reign of Catherine II (the Great)
1768 – 74	Russo-Turkish War
1774	Treaty of Küchük Kainarji between Russians and Ottomans
1783	Crimean Khanate comes under Russian rule
1787 – 91	Russo-Turkish War
1791	Treaty of Jassy between Russians and Ottomans
1794	Agha Mohammed establishes Qajar dynasty in Iran; invades the Caucasus
1800 – 09	Alim Khan rules in Khokand
1801	Union of eastern Georgia with Russia
1801 – 25	Reign of Alexander I
1804 – 1920	Kungrat dynasty rules in Khiva
1805 – 13	Russo-Iranian War

1806 – 12	Russo-Turkish War
1812	Treaty of Bucharest between Ottomans and Russians, Russians gain possession of Bessarabia; Napoleon invades Russia
1813	Treaty of Gulistan between Iran and Russia; Daghestan and the khanates of northern Azerbaidzhan come under Russian rule
1817	Caucasian War, resulting in the central Caucasus (e.g. Chechnia) coming under Russian rule
1825 – 55	Reign of Nicholas I
1826	Convention of Akkerman; Ottomans recognize Russian domination of the Caucasus
1826 – 28	Russo-Iranian War
1827	Battle of Navarino: Ottoman fleet destroyed by Allies
1828	Treaty of Turkmanchai between Iran and Russia; Armenia and Nakhichevan come under Russian rule
1828 – 29	Russo-Turkish War
1829	Treaty of Adrianople (Edirne) between Ottomans and Russians
1833	Treaty of Hünkar Iskelesi between Ottomans and Russians
1834 – 59	Imamate of Shamyl in Daghestan and Chechnia
1838 – 42	First Afghan War between British and Afghans
1839	General Perovskij's Khiva campaign
1846	Great Kazakh Horde comes under Russian rule
1853	General Perovskij's Khokand campaign; taking of Ak Mechet
1853 – 56	Crimean War
1855 – 81	Reign of Alexander II
c. 1855 – 85	Main period of migration of Muslim peoples from the Russian to the Ottoman Empire
1856	Pekin Treaty between China and Russia
1857	Indian Mutiny
1865	Russians take Tashkent
1867	Establishment of Governor-Generalship of Turkestan
1868	Russians take Samarkand; Emirate of Bukhara becomes a Russian Protectorate
1873	Khanate of Khiva becomes a Russian Protectorate; Anglo-Russian Agreement on spheres of influence in Central Asia

1876	Khanate of Khokand annexed: Khanate abolished, territory comes under direct Russian rule
1876 – 1909	Reign of Sultan Abdul Hamid II
1877 – 78	Russo-Turkish War
1878 – 80	Second Afghan War with British
c. 1880	Young Turk Movement emerges
1881	St Petersburg Treaty between China and Russia concerning Ili region
1885 – 99	Construction of Trans-Caspian railroad (from Krasnovodsk to the Ferghana Valley via Samarkand and Tashkent)
1891 – 1903	Construction of Trans-Siberian railroad
1894 – 1917	Reign of Nicholas II
1895	Anglo-Russian Boundary Commission establishes frontier between Afghanistan and Russia
1898	Social Democratic Party founded
1900	Boxer Rebellion
1901	Russo-Iranian Treaty
1903	Menshevik-Bolshevik split in Social Democratic Party
1905 – 07	First Russian Revolution
1906	Completion of Orenburg-Tashkent railroad
1907	Anglo-Russian Agreement on spheres of influence in Iran
1908 – 09	Iranian Revolution
1911	British and Russian troops occupy Iran
1914	Outbreak of First World War
1916	Uprising in Central Asia and Kazakhstan; Russia invades eastern Anatolia
1917	February Revolution; abdication of Nicholas II; Provisional Government under Kerensky; Bolshevik October Revolution; Soviet Armistice with the Central Powers
1918	Treaty of Brest-Litovsk; Romania occupies Bessarabia; first Soviet Constitution
1918 – 20	Civil War; Allied Intervention; independent national states formed in Azerbaidzhan, Georgia, Armenia, Northern Caucasus and Trans-Caspia
1918	Formation of Turkestan ASSR
1919	Formation of Bashkir ASSR

1919 – 23	Basmachi Movement strong in Central Asia; Enver Pasha active in it from 1921 until his death in 1922
1920	People's Soviet Republics proclaimed in Bukhara and Khiva (Khorezm); formation of Armenian and Azerbaidzhan SSRs, Tatar and Kirghiz (i.e. Kazakh) ASSRs and Chuvash Autonomous Province
1921	Formation of Georgian SSR, Abkhazian, Adzhar, Crimean, Daghestan and Gorskaja ASSRs (the Gorskaja ASSR incorporated the Balkars, Chechen, Ingush, Kabardians, Karachais and Ossetians); formation of the Kabardian Autonomous Province (1 September); friendship treaties concluded between the Soviet government and Afghanistan, Iran and Turkey
1922	Formation of the Transcaucasian Soviet Federal Socialist Republic (comprising Azerbaidzhan, Armenia and Georgia), the Yakut ASSR and the Chechen, Cherkess, Kabardian-Balkar, Karachai-Cherkess and Oirot Autonomous Provinces; creation of the USSR (30 December); Stalin becomes General Secretary of the Central Committee of the Communist Party
1923	Formation of the Nagorno-Karabakh Autonomous Province (within the Azerbaidzhan SSR); Turkish Republic created
1924	Final dissolution of the Gorskaja ASSR and formation of the Ingush and North Ossetian Autonomous Provinces (the Chechen, Kabardians and Balkars etc. had already been hived off); dissolution of the People's Soviet Republics of Bukhara and Khorezm; National Delimitation in Central Asia, leading to the creation of new national states: Turkmen and Uzbek SSRs, the Tadzhik ASSR (within the Uzbek SSR) and the Kara-Kirghiz (i.e. Kirghiz) Autonomous Province (within the RSFSR); formation of the Nakhichevan ASSR (within the Azerbaidzhan SSR); death of Lenin (21 January); abolition of the Caliphate in Turkey
1925	Formation of Gorno-Badakhshan and Karakalpak Autonomous Provinces; Chuvash, Kazakh and Kirghiz Autonomous Provinces transformed into ASSRs; neutrality treaty concluded with Turkey; Reza Shah establishes Pahlavi dynasty in Iran
1926	Neutrality treaty with Afghanistan; first Soviet census
1927	Neutrality treaty with Iran
1928	Formation of Cherkess Autonomous Province
1930	Completion of Turk-Sib railroad
1932	Karakalpak Autonomous Province transformed into ASSR
1936	New Soviet Constitution; Kazakh ASSR transformed

	into SSR, Chechen, Kabardino-Balkar and North Ossetian Autonomous Provinces into ASSRs; Karakalpak ASSR transferred to the Uzbek SSR
1939	Soviet non-aggression treaty with Germany; outbreak of Second World War
1940	Bessarabia, northern Bukovina and the Baltic republics incorporated into the Soviet Union
1941	German invasion of the Soviet Union; Soviet and British troops occupy Iran; Stalin becomes Premier of USSR
1941 – 44	Crimea occupied by German troops
1942 – 43	Battle for the Caucasus; parts of the Caucasus occupied by German troops
1943	Tehran Conference
1944	Crimea liberated by Soviet troops; Crimean Tatars, Balkars, Chechen, Ingush, Karachais and Kalmyks, amongst others, deported to Central Asia and Siberia for alleged collaboration with Germans; the titular republics and autonomous provinces of these peoples liquidated; the Tuva People's Republic incorporated into the Soviet Union
1945	Yalta Conference; fall of Berlin; Potsdam Conference; end of Second World War
1947	British leave India: creation of independent republics of India and Pakistan
1949	Chinese Communists defeat Nationalists; USSR recognizes People's Republic of China
1953	Death of Stalin; Malenkov becomes Premier; Khrushchev becomes First Party Secretary
1956	Launching of de-Stalinization campaign
1957	Rehabilitation of deported peoples; the majority are repatriated, but the Crimean Tatars and some other peoples still remain in exile; the Chechen-Ingush and Kabardino-Balkar ASSRs and Karachai-Cherkess and Kalmyk Autonomous Provinces are reinstated
1958	Khrushchev becomes Premier
1964	Khrushchev ousted; Kosygin becomes Premier, Brezhnev First Party Secretary
1982	Death of Brezhnev; Andropov becomes First Party Secretary

Selected bibliography

The following works provide a basic general introduction to the questions touched upon in this book; most of them give detailed bibliographies on more specific aspects of these topics.

History, Ethnography and Political Background

Allworth, E., *Uzbek Literary Politics*, Publications in Near and Middle East Studies, Columbia University, The Hague, Mouton, 1964.

Allworth, E., *Central Asian Publishing and the Rise of Nationalism*, New York, New York Public Library, 1965.

Allworth, E. (ed.), *Central Asia: A Century of Russian Rule*, London-New York, Columbia University Press, 1967.

Allworth, E., (ed.), *The Nationality Question in Soviet Central Asia*, London-New York-Washington, Praeger, 1973.

Bacon, E., *Central Asians Under Russian Rule: A Study in Culture Change*, Ithaca, Cornell University Press, 1966.

Bartol'd, V. V., *Four Studies on the History of Central Asia*, 3 vols, (trans. V. and T. Minorsky), Leiden, E. J. Brill, 1956–63.

Bartol'd, V. V., *Istorija kul'turnoj zhizni Turkestana* ('History of the Cultural Life of Turkestan'), Leningrad, AN SSSR, 1927.

Bartol'd, V. V., *Turkestan Down to the Mongol Invasion* (trans. and rev. H. A. R. Gibb), E. J. W. Gibb Memorial Series, London, Luzac, 1928; 2nd edn, 1958.

Bennigsen, A., and Lemercier-Quelquejay, Ch., *La Presse et le mouvement national chez les musulmans de Russie avant 1920*, Paris-The Hague, Mouton, 1964.

Caroe, O., *Soviet Empire: The Turks of Central Asia and Stalinism*, London, Macmillan, 1953.

Carrère d'Encausse, H., *Réforme et révolution chez les musulmans de l'Empire russe: Bukhara 1867–1924*, Paris, Armand Colin, 1966.

Carrère d'Encausse, H., *L'Empire éclaté: la révolte des nations en U.R.S.S.*, Paris, Flammarion, 1978.

Castagné, J., *Le Bolchevisme et l'Islam: Revue du Monde Musulman*, Paris, vol. 51, 1922.

Castagné, J., *Russie Slave et Russie Turque: Revue du Monde Musulman*, Paris, vol. 56, 1923.

Churchward, L. G., *Contemporary Soviet Government*, London, Routledge & Kegan Paul, 1968.

446

Conquest, R., *The Nation-Killers: The Soviet Deportation of Nationalities*, London, Macmillan, 1970.

Conquest, R. (ed.), *Soviet Nationalities Policy in Practice*, London, Bodley Head, 1967.

Czaplicka, M., *The Turks of Central Asia*, Amsterdam, Philo Press, 1918.

Demko, G. J., *The Russian Colonization of Kazakhstan 1896–1916*, Uralic and Altaic Series, Bloomington, Indiana University, vol. 99, The Hague, Mouton, 1960.

Denisov, A., and Kirichenko, M., *Soviet State Law* (trans. S. Belsky and M. Saifulin, ed. by D. Ogden and M. Perelman), Moscow, Foreign Language Publishing House, 1960.

Dyer, S. Rimsky-Korsakoff, *Soviet Dungan Kolkhozes in the Kirghiz SSR and the Kazakh SSR*, Canberra, Australian National University Press, 1979.

Gibb, H. A. R., *The Arab Conquests in Central Asia*, London, Royal Asiatic Society, 1923.

Goldhagen, E. (ed.), *Ethnic Minorities in the Soviet Union*, London-New York-Washington, Praeger, 1968.

Hambly, G., *et al*, *Central Asia*, London, Weidenfeld & Nicolson, 1969.

Hayit, B., *Turkestan im Herzen Eurasiens*, Cologne, Studien Verlag, 1980.

Hostler, C., *Turkism and the Soviets: The Turks of the World and their Political Objectives*, London, Allen & Unwin, 1957.

Katz, Z. (ed.), *Handbook of Major Soviet Nationalities*, London, Collier Macmillan, New York, Free Press, 1975.

Kazemzadeh, F., *The Struggle for Transcaucasia, 1917–1921*, New York, George Ronald, Oxford Philosophical Library, 1951.

Kolarz, W., *Peoples of the Soviet Far East*, London, George Philip, 1954.

Krader, L., *Peoples of Central Asia*, Uralic and Altaic Series, vol. 26, Bloomington, Indiana University Press, 1966.

Lane, D., *Politics and Society in the USSR*, revised and updated edn, London, Martin Robertson, 1978.

Lang, D., *A Modern History of Georgia*, London, Weidenfeld & Nicolson, 1962.

Levin, M. G., and Potapov, L. P., *Peoples of Siberia* (trans. S. Dunn), Chicago-London, Chicago University Press, 1964.

Lewis, R. A., and Rowland, R. H., *Population Redistribution in the USSR: Its Impact on Society 1897–1977*, New York, Praeger, 1979.

Lewis, R. A., Rowland, R. H., and Clem, R. S., *Nationality and Population Changes in Russia and the Soviet Union: An Evaluation of Census Data, 1897–1970*, London-New York-Washington, Praeger, 1976.

Loewenthal, R., 'The Extinction of the Krimchaks in World War II', *Slavic Review*, vol. 10, 1951, pp. 130–6.

Lorimer, F., *The Population of the Soviet Union: History and Prospects*, Geneva, The League of Nations, 1946.

McCagg Jr., W. A., and Silver, B. D. (eds), *Soviet Asian Ethnic Frontiers*, New York-Oxford, Pergamon Policy Studies, 1979.

Manual on the Turanians and Pan-Turanianism, Naval Staff, The Admiralty, London, (1918).

Minority Rights Group, Report no. 6 (new edn), *The Crimean Tatars, Volga Germans and Meskhetians: Soviet Treatment of Some Minorities*, London, 1980.

Narody Kavkaza; *Narody Sibiri*; *Narody Srednej* . . ., see under Tolstov.

Nekrich, A., *The Punished Peoples: The Deportation and Tragic Fate of Soviet Minorities at the end of the Second World War* (trans. G. Saunders), New York, W. W. Norton, 1978.

Nove, A., and Newth, J. A., *The Soviet Middle East: A Model for Development?*, London, Allen & Unwin, 1967.

Park, A. G., *Bolshevism in Turkestan 1917–1927*, New York, Columbia University Press, 1957.

Pierce, R. A., *Russian Central Asia 1867–1917: A Study in Colonial Rule*, Berkeley, University of California Press, 1960.

Pipes, R., *The Formation of the Soviet Union – Communism and Nationalism, 1917–1923*, Cambridge, Mass., Harvard University Press, revised :dn, 1964.

Rakowska-Harmstone, T., *Russia and Nationalism in Central Asia: The Case of Tadzhikistan*, Baltimore-London, Johns Hopkins Press, 1970.

Schapiro, L., *The Government and Politics of the Soviet Union*, London, Hutchinson, 1965.

Schuyler, E., *Turkistan: Notes of a Journey in Russian Turkistan . . .*, London, Sampson Low, Marston, Searle & Rivington, 1876.

Seydamet, Dzh., *Krym* ('The Crimea'), Warsaw, Wydawnictwo instytutu wschodniego, 1930.

Sharlet, R., *The New Soviet Constitution of 1977: Analysis and Text*, Brunswick, Ohio, King's Court Communications, 1978.

Skrine, F. H., and Ross, E. D., *The Heart of Asia: A History of Russian Turkestan and the Central Asian Khanates from the Earliest Times*, London, Methuen, 1899.

Soviet Asian Ethnic Frontiers. See above under McCagg and Silver.

Tokarev, S., *Etnografija narodov SSSR – Istoricheskije osnovy byta i kul'tury* ('The Ethnography of the Peoples of the USSR – The Historical Foundations of Their Way of Life and Culture'), Moscow, Moscow University Press, 1958.

Tolstov, S. P. (main ed.), *Narody jevropejskoj chasti SSSR II, Narody Kavkaza*, 2 vols, *Narody Sibiri, Narody Srednej Azii i Kazakhstana*, 2 vols ('Peoples of the European Part of the USSR II', '. . . of the Caucasus', '. . . of Siberia', '. . . of Central Asia and Kazakhstan'), Moscow, AN SSSR, 1956–63.

Vaidyanath, R., *The Formation of the Soviet Central Asian Republics: A Study in Soviet Nationalities Policy, 1917–1936*, New Delhi, People's Publishing House, 1967.

Vámbéry, A., *Travels in Central Asia . . . performed in . . . 1863*, London, John Murray, 1864.

Wheeler, G., *Racial Problems in Soviet Muslim Asia*, London, Oxford University Press, 1960.

Wheeler, G., *The Modern History of Soviet Central Asia*, London-New York, Weidenfeld & Nicolson, 1964.

Wheeler, G., *The Peoples of Soviet Central Asia*, London, Bodley Head, 1966.

Wimbush, S. Enders, and Wixman, R., 'The Meskhetian Turks: A New Voice in Soviet Central Asia', *Canadian Slavonic Papers*, Toronto, vol. 17, 1975, pp. 320–39.

Zajączkowski, A., *Karaims in Poland: History, Language, Folklore, Science*, The Hague-Paris-Warsaw, Mouton, 1961.

Economics and Geography

Conolly, V., *Beyond the Urals: Economic Developments in Soviet Asia*, London, Oxford University Press, 1967.

Khan, A. R., and Ghai, D., *Collective Agriculture and Rural Development in Soviet Central Asia*, London, Macmillan, 1979.

Lydolph, P., *Geography of the USSR*, New York, John Wiley, 1964.

McAuley, A., *Economic Welfare in the Soviet Union: Poverty, Living Standards, and Inequality*, Madison, University of Wisconsin Press; London, Allen & Unwin, 1979.

Shabad, T., *Basic Industrial Resources of the USSR*, London-New York, Columbia University Press, 1969.

Language

Allworth, E., *Nationalities of the Soviet East: Publications and Writing Systems. A Bibliographical Directory and Transliteration Tables*, London-New York, Columbia University Press, 1971.

Baskakov, N. A., *The Turkic Languages of Central Asia: Problems of Planned Culture Contact* (English trans. annotated S. Wurm), Central Asian Research Centre in Association with St Antony's College (Oxford) Soviet Affairs Study Group, London, 1960.

Baskakov, N. A., *Vvedenije v izuchenije tjurkskikh jazykov* ('Introduction to the Study of the Turkic Languages'), Moscow, Vysshaja shkola, 1969.

Baskakov, N. A., *Voprosy sovershenstvovanija alfavitov tjurkskikh jazykov SSSR* ('Questions Concerning the Perfecting of the Alphabets of the Turkic Languages of the USSR'), Moscow, Nauka, 1972.

Bennigsen, A., and Quelquejay, Ch., *The Evolution of the Muslim Nationalities of the USSR and their Linguistic Problems* (trans. G. Wheeler), Central Asian Research Centre in Association with St Antony's College (Oxford) Soviet Affairs Study Group, London, 1961.

Deny, J., *et al.* (eds), *Philologiae Turcicae Fundamenta*, 2 vols, Wiesbaden, Franz Steiner Verlag, 1959–65.

Desherijev, Yu., *Razvitije mladopismennikh jazykov narodov SSSR* ('Development of the Young Literary Languages of the Peoples of the USSR'), Moscow, Gosudarstvennoje uchebno-ped. izdatel'stvo min. prosveshchenija RSFSR, 1958.

Desherijev, Yu., *Razvitije obshchestvennykh funktsij literaturnykh jazykov* ('The Development of the Social Functions of the Literary Languages'), Moscow, Nauka, 1976.

Dirr, A., *Einführung in das Studium der kaukasischen Sprachen*, Leipzig, Verlag der Asia Major, 1928.

Geiger, B., *et al.*, *People and Languages of the Caucasus*, Janua Linguarum, no. 6, The Hague, Mouton, 1959.

Geiger, W., and Kuhn, E., *Grundriss der iranischen Philologie*, 2 vols, Strassburg, Verlag von Karl J. Trübner, 1896–1904.

Isayev, M. I., *National Languages in the USSR: Problems and Solutions*, Moscow, Progress, 1977.

Jazyki narodov SSSR, see under Vinogradov.

Jünger, H. (ed.), *The Literatures of the Soviet Peoples: A Historical and Biographical Survey*, New York, F. Ungar, 1970.

Klimov, G. A., *Kavkazskije jazyki*, ('Caucasian Languages'), Moscow, Nauka, 1965.

Lewis, E. G., *Multilingualism in the Soviet Union: Aspects of Language Policy and Its Implementation*, Paris-The Hague, Mouton, 1972.

Musajev, K. M., *Alfavity jazykov narodov SSSR* ('Alphabets of the Languages of the People of the USSR'), Moscow, Nauka, 1965.

Philologiae Turcicae Fundamenta. See above under Deny.

Radlov, V. V., *Proben der Volkslitteratur der türkischen Stämme Süd-Sibiriens*, 10 vols, St Petersburg, Imperial Academy of Sciences, 1866–1907.

Vinogradov, V. V. (main ed.), *Jazyki narodov SSSR* ('Languages of the USSR'), particularly vols 1, 2, 4, 5, Moscow, AN SSSR, 1966–8.

Education

Bilinsky, Y., 'Education of the Non-Russian Peoples in the USSR, 1917–1967: An Essay', *Slavic Review*, University of Illinois, Urbana-Champaign, vol. 27, no. 3, 1968, pp. 411–37.
De Witt, N., *Education and Professional Employment in the U.S.S.R.*, Washington, National Science Foundation, 1961.
Lipsett, H., 'The Status of National Minority Languages in Soviet Education', *Soviet Studies*, Glasgow, vol. 19, no. 2, 1967–68, pp. 181–9.
Medlin, W. K., Carpenter, F., and Cave, W. M., *Education and Development in Central Asia: A Case Study on Social Change in Uzbekistan*, Leiden, E. J. Brill, 1971.
Prokof'jev, M. A. (main ed.), *Narodnoje obrazovanije v SSSR: 1917–1967* ('National Education in the USSR: 1917–1967'), Moscow, Prosveshchenije, 1967.
Silver, B., 'The Status of National Minority Languages in Soviet Education: An Assessment of Recent Changes', *Soviet Studies*, Glasgow, vol. 26, no. I, 1974, pp. 28–41.
Tomiak, J. J., *The Soviet Union*, World Education Series, Newton Abbot, 1972.

Religion

Archimandrite Augustin (Lecturer at Leningrad Theological Academy), 'Islam in Russia', *Research Papers*, no. 8, 1980, Centre for the Study of Islam and Christian-Muslim Relations, Selly Oak Colleges, Birmingham.
Arsharuni, A., and Gabidullin, Kh., *Ocherki panislamizma i pantjurkizma v Rossii*, ('Essays on Panislamism and Panturkism in Russia'), Moscow, Ateist, 1931.
Babakhanov, Mufti Ziyauddin Khan, *Islam and the Muslims in the Land of the Soviets*, Moscow, Progress, 1980.
Bartol'd, V. V. (ed.), *Mir islama* ('World of Islam'), St Petersburg, 1912–13.
Bennigsen, A., and Lemercier-Quelquejay, Ch., *Islam in the Soviet Union*, London, Pall Mall; New York, Praeger, 1967; French edn, Paris, Payot, 1968.
Bennigsen, A., 'Muslim Religious Conservatism and Dissent in the USSR', *Religion in Communist Lands*, Keston College, Keston, vol. 6, no. 3, 1978, pp. 153–61.
Bennigsen, A., ' "Official" Islam in the Soviet Union', *Religion in Communist Lands*, Keston College, Keston, vol. 7, no. 3, 1979, pp. 148–59.
Bobrovnikoff, S., 'Moslems in Russia', *The Moslem World*, London, vol. I, no. I, 1911, pp. 5–31.
Demidov, S. M., *Sufizm v Turkmenii (Evolutsija i perezhitki)* ('Sufism in Turkmenia (Evolution and Survivals)'), Ashkhabad, Ylym, 1978.
Klimovich, L., *Islam v tsarskoj Rossii* ('Islam in Tsarist Russia'), Moscow, Gosudarstvennoje antireligioznoje izdatel'stvo ('State antireligious publishing house'), 1936.
Klimovich, L., *Islam*, Moscow, Izdatel'stvo politicheskoj literatury ('publishing house of political literature'), 1961.
Muslims of the Soviet East, quarterly journal published by the Spiritual Directorate of Central Asia and Kazakhstan, Tashkent; it appears in Arabic, English, French and Uzbek (the Uzbek edition is printed in the Arabic script).

Rahman, F., 'Evolution of Soviet Policy Towards Muslims in Russia: 1917–1965', *Journal*, Institute of Muslim Minority Affairs, King Abdulaziz University, Jeddah, vol. I, no. 2, 1980, pp. 28–46.
Religion in Communist Lands: for vol. 6, no. 3 and vol. 7, no. 3, see above under Bennigsen and Lemercier-Quelquejay; for vol. 7, no. 4, see below under Soper.
Smirnov, N. A., *Sovremennyj Islam* ('Contemporary Islam'), Moscow, Bezbozhnik ('Atheist' publishing house), 1930.
Smirnov, N. A., *Ocherki istorii izuchenija Islama v Rossii* ('Essays on the History of the Study of Islam in Russia'), Moscow, AN SSSR, 1954.
Smirnov, N. A., *Mjuridizm na Kavkaze* ('Muridism in the Caucasus'), Moscow, AN SSSR, 1963.
Soper, J., ' "Unofficial" Islam: A Muslim Minority in the USSR', *Religion in Communist Lands*, Keston College, Keston, vol. 7, no. 4, 1979, pp. 226–31.
Vakhabov, A., *Muslims in the USSR*, Moscow, Novosti, 1980.
Zenkovsky, S., *Pan-Turkism and Islam in Russia*, Cambridge, Mass., Harvard University Press, 1960.

Encyclopaedias, Census Returns and other Reference Works

Bol'shaja sovetskaja entsiklopedija ('Great Soviet Encyclopaedia'), Moscow, (Bol'shaja) Sovetskaja entsiklopedija, 1st edn 1926–31, 2nd edn 1949–58, 3rd edn 1970–78; also annual supplements 1975–80.
Cambridge History of Islam, eds P. M. Holt, A. K. S. Lambton and B. Lewis, vol. I, Cambridge University Press, Cambridge, 1970.
Encyclopaedia of Islam, 1st edn eds M. Th. Houtsma, T. W. Arnold, R. Basset and R. Hartmann, 4 vols, Leiden, E. J. Brill, 1913–34; new edn eds H. A. R. Gibb *et al.*, 4 vols (A-Kha), Leiden-London, E. J. Brill and Luzac, 1960–78.
Gazeti SSSR 1917–1960: Bibliograficheskij spravochnik ('Newspapers of the USSR: A Bibliographical Handbook'), eds G. L. Jepiskoposov *et al.*, 3 vols, Moscow, Kniga, 1970.
Itogi vsesojuznaja perepisi naselenija 1959 goda ('Results of the All-Union Census of the Population of 1959'), 16 vols, Moscow, TsSU, Gosstatizdat, 1962–63.
Itogi vsesojuznaja perepisi naselenija 1970 goda ('Results of the All-Union Census of the Population of 1970'), 7 vols, Moscow, TsSU, Statistika, 1972–74.
Jezhegodnik knigi ('Yearbook of the Book': catalogue of all the books published in the USSR within a specific year), Moscow, Kniga, annual publication; here, particularly years 1976–78.
Kul'turnoje stroitel'stvo SSSR. Statisticheskij sbornik ('Cultural Construction in the USSR. A Statistical Compilation'), Moscow, TsSU, 1956.
Letopis' periodicheskikh izdanij SSSR ('Chronicle of Periodical Publications in the USSR': catalogue of all the periodical publications in the USSR), Moscow, Kniga, five-yearly publication with annual supplements; here, particularly 1971–75 (Moscow, 1977).
Narodnoje khozjajstvo SSSR ('The National Economy of the USSR': statistical yearbook), Moscow, TsSU, annual publication; here, particularly for 1978, 1979.
The Soviet Union: 50 Years (statistical returns), Moscow, TsSU, Progress, 1969.
Vestnik statistiki ('Journal of Statistics'), Moscow, Statistika, 1980; nos 2, 6, 7, 12 contain relevant material from the 1979 census.
Vsesojuznaja perepis' naselenija 17 dekabrja 1926 goda ('All-Union Census of the

Population of 17 December 1926'), 17 vols, Moscow, TsSU Sojuza, 1929.
Vsesojuznaja perepis' naselenija 1970 goda: Sbornik statej ('All-Union Census of
the Population of 1970: Collected Articles'), ed. G. M. Maksimov, Moscow,
Statistika, 1976.

Index